TRAVELER

CUBA

NATIONAL GEOGRAPHIC
TRAVELER

CUBA

by Christopher P. Baker
photography by Pablo Corral Vega
and Cristobal Corral Vega

National Geographic
Washington, D.C.

CONTENTS

■ Pages 2–3: A turret at San Carlos de la Cabaña fortress overlooks Havana.
■ Opposite: Caribbean winds sway the palm trees of Cayo Coco. Sun, sand, and reef-fringed waters are some of Cuba's many allures.

TRAVELING WITH EYES OPEN

Alert travelers go with a purpose and leave with a benefit. If you travel responsibly, you can help support wildlife conservation, historic preservation, and cultural enrichment in the places you visit. You can enrich your own travel experience as well.

To be a geo-savvy traveler:

- Recognize that your presence has an impact on the places you visit.

- Spend your time and money in ways that sustain local character. (Besides, it's more interesting that way.)

- Value the destination's natural and cultural heritage.

- Respect the local customs and traditions.

- Express appreciation to local people about things you find interesting and unique to the place: its nature and scenery, music and food, historic villages and buildings.

- Vote with your wallet: Support the people who support the place, patronizing businesses that make an effort to celebrate and protect what's special there. Seek out local shops, restaurants, and inns. Use tour operators who love their home—who love taking care of it and showing it off. Avoid businesses that detract from the character of the place.

- Enrich yourself, taking home memories and stories to tell, knowing that you have contributed to the preservation and enhancement of the destination.

That is the type of travel now called geotourism, defined as "tourism that sustains or enhances the geographical character of a place—its environment, culture, aesthetics, heritage, and the well-being of its residents." To learn more, visit National Geographic's Center for Sustainable Destinations at *nationalgeographic.com/maps/geotourism.*

ABOUT THE AUTHORS & PHOTOGRAPHERS

After earning degrees in geography in London and Latin American studies in Liverpool, **Christopher P. Baker** *(christopherpbaker.com)* settled in California and established a career as a travel writer, photographer, lecturer, and tour leader. He has authored guidebooks to Colombia, Costa Rica, the Dominican Republic, and Panama in the National Geographic Traveler series. His other books on Cuba include *Mi Moto Fidel: Motorcycling Through Castro's Cuba* (National Geographic Adventure Press) plus *Cuba Classics: A Celebration of Vintage American Automobiles.* He has spoken on Cuba on the National Geographic Channel, ABC, CBC, Fox, CNN and NPR. He escorts National Geographic Expeditions' ten-day "Cuba: Discover Its People and Culture" tours.

Pablo Corral Vega is an Ecuadorian photojournalist, artist, and lawyer, and the author of four photographic books: *Bare Earth; Silent Landscapes: The Andes of Ecuador; Ecuador: De la Magia al Espanto;* and National Geographic's *Andes.* He is the founder and director of *nuestramirada.org,* a network of Latin American photojournalists, and is the co-director of "Pictures of the Year Latin America," the largest contest of its kind in the region. He photographs for *National Geographic* and other magazines and lives in Quito, Ecuador.

Cristobal Corral Vega has worked on various film documentaries in his native Ecuador, and contributed as photographer to many publications. His subjects have included bullfighting, religious art, residential design, and tourism. He is author of the book *Ecuador: Espacios de Luz* and co-author of *Ecuador: De la Magia al Espanto.*

CHARTING YOUR TRIP

Visitors to Cuba discover a sensual, often surreal island nation that packs in all that is best about both the Caribbean and Latin America. Its prime quality is its *temps perdu* setting—visitors are engulfed in a 1950s redux.

Along with the vibrancy of Havana, Cuba's colorful and enthralling capital city, you'll discover the charm of Trinidad, Remedios, and other colonial cities. You'll also travel through the timeless beauty of a rural landscape where oxen still plow the fields. And the beaches are simply astounding. Above all, you'll thrill to the music and dance and a lively arts scene—delightful aspects of a communist nation that surprises at every turn.

How to Get Around

Cuba is the largest Caribbean island—about 800 miles (1,300 km) end to end—and has a well-developed (but decayed) road network. Getting around, however, is difficult. Its internal air network connects major cities, but some aircraft are aged and uncomfortable, and its safety record is sobering. Two state-run companies—Aerogaviota *(tel 7/203-0668, aerogaviota.com)* and Cubana *(tel 7/834-4446, cubana.cu)*—offer domestic flights.

Comfortable tourist buses operated by Viazul *(tel 7/883-6092, viazul.com)* run frequent service between most towns and tourist sites. A separate service operated by Ómnibus Nacionales *(tel 7/870-9401)* serves Cubans only, who for short journeys between and within towns are relegated to basic trucks converted to carry passengers. Passenger trains also link Havana to major cities, as far afield as Santiago de Cuba, approximately 566 miles (911 km) southeast of the capital. Bookings can be made through FerroCuba *(tel 7/860-0700)*. In cities, an extensive taxi system makes getting around easy, but taxis are usually in bad repair. Cubataxi *(tel 7/855-5555)* operates radio-dispatched taxis. Tourist taxis are also available

The statue of Che Guevara carrying the Child of the Revolution in Santa Clara

outside major hotels; rates vary between CUC 0.50 and 0.90 per kilometer.

For the intrepid traveler, renting a car is a flexible way to see more of Cuba. Most roads are paved, but the hazards include potholes, stray animals, wayward oxcarts, and other slow-moving vehicles, even on the *autopista*, Cuba's freeway. This runs from Pinar del Río in the west, eastward to Sancti Spíritus, a distance of about 328 miles (527 km). Car rental contracts include several usurious clauses: For example, the renter is liable for maintenance of the vehicle.

Compulsory insurance won't protect you in the event of every accident. Reserve well in advance, as demand always exceeds the number of cars available. The state-run rental agencies include Cubacar *(tel 7/835-0000, email: cubacar@transtur.cu)*, Havanautos *(tel 7/273-2277, email: havanautos@transtur.cu)*, and Rex *(tel 7/835-6830, www.rex.cu)*, all operated by Transtur *(transtur.com)*; and Vía Rent-a-Car *(tel 7/206-9935, gaviota-grupo.com)*.

How to Visit: If You Have One Week

The long distances involved make it hard to see many different parts of Cuba on a short trip, and a minimum of ten days is ideal. Logistically, it makes sense to plan a one-week itinerary around either Havana in the northwest, or Santiago de Cuba in the southeast. Both are served by direct flights from North America and Europe.

For a Havana-based trip, **Day 1** could be spent exploring the four major plazas of Habana Vieja (Old Havana), just east of central Havana. On **Day 2** you'll want to stroll the western fringe of Habana Vieja, taking in the historic buildings around Parque Central, the Capitolio (Cuba's chamber of Congress), the tree-lined boulevard of the Prado, and museums such as the Museo de la Revolución and the Museo Nacional de Bellas Artes. **Day 3** can include a tour of the residential Vedado district, beginning at the Hotel Nacional, continuing up La Rampa to the Habana Libre and the Coppelia ice cream shop and on to the Plaza de la Revolución, the neoclassical Universidad de La Habana, the 1950s-era modernist Hotel Riviera,

Visitor Information

Cuba's **Ministerio de Turismo** *(Ave. 3ra & F, Vedado, Havana, tel 7/836-3245, cubatravel.cu)* has information bureaus in Canada *(1200 Bay St. #305, Toronto, ON, M5R 2A5, tel 416/362-0700)* and the U.K. *(167 High Holborn, London WC1V 6PA, tel 020/7240-6655, travel2cuba.co.uk)*. The ministry will mail brochures and answer questions, but tour companies that specialize in travel to Cuba (see Travelwise p. 233) are more reliable sources. In Cuba, **Infotur** *(Calle 28 #303 e/ 3ra y 5ta, Miramar, tel 7/204-7036, infotur.cu)* has six information booths in Havana, including one at José Martí International Airport, and in most cities and tourist sites. Every hotel has a *buró de turismo*. (See also Travelwise p. 236.)

When to Visit

Cuba's subtropical climate is hot and moist, with semiarid pockets. The island has two seasons: dry (Dec.–April) and wet (May–Nov.). The wet season, during the hottest months, can be stiflingly humid. Temperatures increase eastward, and Santiago de Cuba is best avoided in midyear. July to November is Cuba's hurricane season, when hotel rates drop. Although winter is usually sunny and warm, cold fronts can sweep south, so pack a jacket if visiting December to March. The best time is February to April, when the climate is balmy and the air crystal clear.

U.S. visitors must also consider the political climate: In 2015, U.S. government restrictions on travel to Cuba thawed, although travel for tourism is still prohibited. The regulations are administered by the U.S. Treasury Department's Office of Foreign Assets Control (*1500 Pennsylvania Ave. N.W., Washington, D.C. 20220, tel 202/622-2480, 1.usa.gov/1fzd8n1*). (See also Travelwise pp. 232, 260.)

and the Cementerio de Colón, with its remarkable mausoleums. Your evenings should include dinner at La Guarida (Havana's best private restaurant), plus a not-to-be-missed night at the Tropicana cabaret.

Rent a car (or take an excursion) to spend **Day 4** at Las Terrazas, a sustainable community in the Sierra del Rosario mountains about 50 miles (80 km) west of Havana. Overnight here, then continue on **Day 5** to Viñales, approximately 80 miles (130 km) farther west, for its tobacco farms and remarkable landscapes. Head back to stay overnight in Havana to shorten your drive on **Day 6** to Trinidad, Cuba's colonial gem and a UNESCO World Heritage site. Trinidad lies about 196 miles (315 km) southeast of the capital. Spend **Day 7** walking the cobbled streets and plazas, steeping in the city's aspic quality, before returning to Havana.

If you choose Santiago de Cuba as your base, begin **Day 1** with a horse-drawn coach ride around the old city. Then explore on foot for the rest of **Days 1** and **2**, taking in the main squares and museums. Build in time for a guided excursion to the Spanish colonial fortress of El Morro Castle, and the pilgrimage site of Basilica del Cobre. On **Day 3**, take a trip to the nearby village of Siboney or the Parque Baconao in the eastern suburbs. For **Day 4**, rent a car and head east to Baracoa via Guantánamo and the Zoológico de Piedra, a trip of about 108 miles (174 km). At Baracoa, savor the ancient airs of Cuba's oldest city. Spend the morning of **Day 5** exploring the town, then head east again for several miles to the Río Yumurí for a boat ride. On **Day 6**, hike to the summit of El Yunque—the trip can be arranged through tour agencies in Baracoa. Next day, return to Santiago de Cuba for your homebound flight.

Money Matters

Cuba has a dual monetary system for nationals and tourists. All tourist transactions use Cuban *pesos convertibles* (CUC) or convertible pesos. Euros are accepted in some Havana locations, and in Varadero, Cayo Coco, and Cayo Largo. Otherwise, foreigners must exchange foreign currency for CUC, which is on a par with the dollar (0.95 €). A 10 percent surcharge applies for U.S. dollar conversions. Carry small bills, as outlets won't have change. (See also Travelwise pp. 235–236.)

If You Have More Time

A second week allows you to combine the two itineraries above. For a third week, focus on the

Typical *rejas*, turned wooden spindles, decorate the windows of colonial-style houses in Trinidad.

north-central region east from Havana, where you can savor the beach of Varadero, 88 miles (141 km) from the capital; follow the revolutionary trail in Santa Clara, a farther 135 miles (217 km) east, with its museum and mausoleum of Che Guevara; and take a walk back in time around the colonial town of Remedios, another 32 miles (51 km) to the east. With more time, you can explore as far afield as Camagüey—the "city of plazas," 333 miles (537 km) east of Havana.

If based in Santiago de Cuba, visit colonial Holguín, 89 miles (143 km) to the north, and nearby Birán, birthplace of Fidel and Raúl Castro. Adventurers can hike to the Castros' former guerrilla headquarters at La Comandancia de la Plata. Beach time is best savored at the resort of Guardalavaca, 111 miles (179 km) north, with its hotels, catamaran excursions, steam-train rides, and dolphin shows.

Staying Safe in Cuba

Cuba is a safe country to visit. Violent crimes against tourists are rare and are virtually unheard of in rural areas. But muggings do occur—Havana's Centro and Cerro districts and other impoverished barrios are problem areas. Most tourist areas have a large police presence. Nonetheless, petty crime has increased with tourism. Pickpockets and purse snatchers work crowded areas. Theft by chambermaids occurs (lock your luggage).

To minimize risk, avoid walking alone at night outside tourist zones. Make photocopies of your passport and documents, and leave these in your hotel safe. Never leave items unattended.

Scams to watch out for:
• You change money at a Cadeca (an official exchange bureau) or hotel and receive no receipt showing the exchange rate. Expect to be shortchanged.
• Items that you didn't consume are charged to your restaurant bill.
• You pay for a hotel room, excursion, or tour and are downgraded to a cheaper room or outing, but no refunds are paid.
Beware of pickpockets in all cities:
• Wear a money belt inside the waistband of your trousers or skirt, or around your neck and inside your shirt.
• Carry only as much money as you need.
• Leave jewelry at home or in a hotel safe.
(See also Travelwise pp. 236–237.)

HISTORY & CULTURE

◼ The Cuban flag emulates the elements of the U.S. flag.

◼ The Ballet Nacional de Cuba, based in Havana, performs throughout the world.

CUBA TODAY

Cuba, island of royal palm trees and Day-Glo sugarcane fields. A land of revolution, haunting music, and bedeviling charm. Ethereal and romantic, this chimerical isle of mystery and contradictions is a place where communism takes on tropical layers. Visitors thrill to Cuba's complexities, to its lilting serenity, to its delicious rums, and to the vivacity of its people.

So close and yet so far, Cuba is only 90 miles (145 km) from the neon-lit malls and fast-food franchises of Florida—yet separated by a cultural and political gulf ten times that distance. Despite six frustrating decades of animosity between the U.S. and Cuban governments, Cuba—one of the most engaging and exhilarating

Havana by night: The Hotel Nacional, built in 1930, rises above the waterfront Malecón.

destinations in the Western Hemisphere—has lost none of its romantic appeal. Tourism is booming, with travelers from Canada, Europe, and, increasingly, the U.S., drawn by an open-arms welcome from the island's citizens and the exotic appeals of an unexpectedly haunting realm ripe with eccentricity and eroticism.

Visitors are awed by the time warp that is Cuba. Havana, erstwhile sultry seductress of the Caribbean, is today a stage set. Once glamorous, now patinated by age, Havana recalls the 1950s, when the city was, in Somerset Maugham's piquant phrase, "a sunny place for shady people." Cuba's old sauciness lingers on, beloved by Cubans and found in even the most remote urban backwater. Everywhere, classics from the heyday of Detroit—corpulent Chryslers, chrome-laden Cadillacs, and Studebakers with broad, grinning grilles—rumble down the road on underinflated tires, evoking nostalgia like Elvis Presley tunes of the same era.

> **Havana recalls the 1950s, when the city was, in Somerset Maugham's piquant phrase, "a sunny place for shady people."**

They are a metaphor, this four-wheeled flotsam, for the state of the island, notably the urban landscapes, many of which resemble classical ruins.

The fact that Cuba's cities ache with pathos and penury is part of the enigmatic allure. Cuba's remarkable colonial cities—Camagüey, Remedios, Santiago de Cuba, and Trinidad—are repositories of architectural gems dating back centuries and boasting a spectacular amalgam of styles. Eighteenth-century Spanish cathedrals fuse into 19th-century French rococo mansions, while Art Deco theaters from the 1920s blend into the cool, columned arcades of old palaces in a style called Mudejar. Fortunately, much of Havana's colonial architecture, at least, is being restored.

Beyond the townships, you'll encounter an altogether different montage of timeless vignettes. Silver-sheathed royal palms rise over tobacco fields lovingly tended by *guajiros* (peasant farmers) in straw hats. Oxen plow the cinnamon-colored soil into furrows or lumber down country roads, pulling rickety carts piled high with sugarcane. Cuba is synonymous with sugar: Virtually everywhere you travel you are within sight of cane fields rippling in the breeze. Cuba's exotic, tropical beauty owes much to such calming landscapes. There are beaches, too, dazzlingly white, shelving into waters unbelievably blue, as in an ad for Havana Club rum. And mountains, perfect for birding and hiking. It is easy to understand why Cubans call their isle *"Mi Cubita bella"* (my beautiful little Cuba). Cuba, however, is far removed from the cliché of picture-postcard perfection.

Car washing in the Río de Miel near Baracoa: Cubans are fastidious about their 1950s *cacharros*.

What most enchants visitors is the island's potential for adventure. It's the way the Cubans are full of spontaneity and impromptu fun. The way they wring pleasure from poverty, draw you into their lives, and crank up the music, filling the air with salsa and sensuality. Travelers who restrict themselves to sightseeing without engaging the people will leave without having experienced—and shared—the real magic of Cuba.

You could easily fill your time in Havana—a gritty, seductive city full of museums, theaters, and nightclubs—with sweet rum and the world's finest cigars to be enjoyed fresh from factories that are open to view. But there's also traditional music and dance to be experienced in Santiago de Cuba. You can scuba dive off the Jardines de la Reina, fish to your heart's content in the lagoons of the Ciénaga de Zapata, go birding in the rain forests of the Cuchillas del Toa, or hike in the Sierra del Escambray. Such a highlights-of-Cuba itinerary barely scratches the surface, however. For these reasons and more, most visitors vow to return again soon.

Cubans

Cubans have a uniquely profound culture steeped in Spanish and African traditions. The population of about 11.2 million is fiercely appreciative of its heritage. Strongly nationalistic, *los cubanos* combine a love of tradition with a progressive attitude. They are proud of their distinct identity, their *cubanía,* much of it forged during the years of socialist experiment under Fidel—and then Raúl—Castro.

Cuba's original inhabitants may have numbered as many as 300,000 indigenous peoples. Predominant in the areas where the Spanish first explored were the Taino, members of the Arawak Indian tribe from South America. Most of these aborigines succumbed to disease and the ruthlessness of 16th-century Spanish conquistadores.

As the early Spanish colonists cleared the forests and planted sugarcane, African slaves were imported to Cuba; in time, as many as 600,000 arrived. They were joined by numerous merchants, seafarers, and entrepreneurs who came from England and Europe throughout the 18th and 19th centuries. These groups were quickly assimilated into the mainstream Spanish-speaking culture. In the 1790s, a large infusion of French immigrants added Gallic ways to the culture. They were followed during the next century by a wave of Chinese indentured laborers, who coalesced in Central Havana. Thousands of North Americans settled during the 19th century, which also saw a vast emigration of Cubans to the United States. This was a decisive time in the formation of Cuban nationality. North American ways and values were increasingly absorbed into the Cuban lifestyle and were used as standards for change when Spanish colonialism came to an end in 1898.

The early 1900s saw the arrival of Jamaicans in Santiago and Guantánamo Provinces, where English can still be heard. North Americans continued to flood the island; throughout the first half of the 20th century, U.S. businesses controlled much of the Cuban economy and added to the vigor of Havana's lifestyle. Following the revolution in 1959, most foreign-born residents left Cuba—along with tens of thousands of Cubans—and were gradually replaced by Soviets and other Eastern Europeans. Shunned by the host population, the Soviets kept to themselves; they departed Cuba in the 1990s, leaving few lasting reminders of their presence. Today Cuba is accumulating a resident population of foreign businesspeople—mostly Canadian and European.

In affinities, Cubans look north, not east to Spain. A U.S. embargo on Cuba remains in effect at the time of publication, despite a thaw in 2015, yet Cubans hold no animosity toward Americans—those U.S. travelers who arrive are feted as long-lost friends.

The Cuban Character

The Cubans' distinct identity owes much to six decades of socialism focused on reshaping the human character to form the "New Man"—a person who puts what's best for society before personal ambition. (In Cuba, the term "revolution" is used to refer to the building of a more equal society.) An intensely moral people, Cubans are highly considerate of others. They are gracious and generous to a fault, willing to share what little they may have. They are confident and unreserved, and display resounding gaiety in the face of adversity. Cubans also take pride in personal cleanliness and are unafraid of physical contact. (One reason the Soviets were disliked is that they didn't use deodorant.) They are great jokers, known for a sharp and creative wit and risqué innuendo; most *chistes* are aimed at themselves and the absurdities of life in Cuba. The population is highly literate and displays a voracious intellectual appetite—the product of the government's emphasis on education. This is apparent when you observe well-behaved Cuban schoolchildren in their prim uniforms displaying impressive levels of knowledge. Part of their education—and an essential aspect of becoming

Local Phrases to Know

- **Compañero** and **compañera.** Roughly meaning "companion" (male and female), it has replaced **señor** (sir) and **señora** (madam) since the revolution.
- **Está en candela.** Literally "is aflame," it can signify anything alarming or in excess, such as "He's promiscuous" or "I'm broke."
- **No es fácil.** "It's not easy," referring to daily life.
- **¡Ojalá!** Roughly translates as "I wish!" yet it is tainted with pessimism, as in "Some hope!"
- **Patria o muerte.** "Fatherland or death." This is the Cuban exhortation to defend the revolution at all cost.

a New Man—is to also perform manual labor. Urban youths were until recent years sent to work in the fields and develop a sound work ethic.

Cubans are intensely patriotic and proud of the independence that the revolution has brought. However, most Cubans love American culture. Youths dress in the latest fashions, as much as their meager budgets allow. Cubans also share a northern work ethic. They are entrepreneurial and wizards of invention—a requirement in a society where nothing gets thrown away, and new or replacement parts are almost impossible to come by. *Resolver*—to resolve, to overcome obstacles with ingenuity—is a common concept. The economic crisis of recent decades, however, has seriously challenged Cuba's value system. Youths are especially frustrated.

> **Cubans are intensely patriotic and proud of the independence that the revolution has brought.**

About 50 percent of the population claims to be atheist, reflecting decades of state suppression of religion. In 1991, however, the Communist Party ceased denying membership to those who subscribed to a religion, and a year later the constitution was amended to characterize the nation as secular rather than atheist. Roman Catholicism, introduced by the Spanish, is resurgent, and Protestant evangelism has made inroads. Santería (spirit worship), introduced by slaves, and which blends native African beliefs and Roman Catholicism, is the widely practiced religion in Cuba.

Erasing Color & Class

About 64 percent of Cuba's inhabitants are of Spanish-African ancestry. Throughout the colonial epoch, the white, Spanish-born population looked down on the blacks and the *criollos* (island born), regardless of color. Colonial Cuba was a hierarchical society, with whites at the top of the scale and blacks at the bottom, though relations were notably more relaxed than in the U.S.

On the eve of the revolution, Cuba was a relatively developed yet divided society with a huge, predominantly white middle class spread throughout the island's cities. It shared its economic power with multinational corporations from the U.S. A large, predominantly black underclass lived in marginal conditions, often without basic amenities. The majority of the rural population—white and black alike—was mired in poverty.

Castro's revolution outlawed institutionalized racism and dramatically improved the lot of most blacks and those who lived in rural areas. Malnutrition and common diseases were eradicated. Although blacks still make up a large proportion

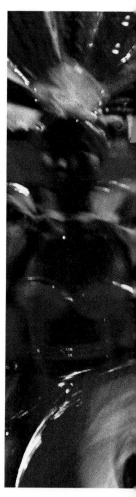

of the impoverished, Cuba is today marked by a harmonious intermingling of ethnicities and multiethnic families.

The social leveling of the revolution also destroyed the middle classes, separating many families and reducing them to a level of paucity that all but the most privileged Cubans share today; almost every Cuban family has at least one family member who has left Cuba to seek a better life. This quest for a classless society has diminished class consciousness. Cubans call each other *compañero* (companion) and greet each other,

■ Cuba's inherent *joie de vivre* explodes during Carnaval in Santiago de Cuba. The colorful celebration dates back to the 18th century, when once a year, after the harvest, slaves were permitted to frolic.

even as strangers, with a *beso* (kiss) and/or *abrazo* (hug). Doctors, lawyers, and other highly trained specialists are no longer regarded as a "separate class."

Today's privileged class is made up of senior Communist Party officials and military figures, who enjoy benefits denied to most Cubans; and of leading artists, musicians, and sports figures, who, uniquely in Cuba, are permitted to earn unrestricted royalties. Recently, new laws have favored the formation of a new class of *cuentas propistas* (small private entrepreneurs) and nouveau riche—*macetas*—with access to *pesos convertibles* (hard-currency CUCs).

Living Conditions

Cuba's annual per capita income in 2015 was estimated at an equivalent of $7,560, although few of the country's citizens receive anywhere near that amount. Its standards of free universal education and primary health care are high: Both life expectancy and infant mortality are on a par with those of most developed nations. Housing and many staples are subsidized, albeit in short supply, and the state provides exemplary care for the elderly and indigent. Thanks to foreign investment, many improvements have been made to the telecommunications system in recent years, but access to computers and the Internet is the lowest of any nation in the Americas.

The revolution eradicated urban homelessness by erecting prefabricated apartment dwellings and by reallocating homes seized from families who fled Cuba. The government then neglected the cities, however. Many urbanites now live in overcrowded housing, much of it crumbling; many inhabit *solares* (slum dwellings), often hidden from view behind more substantial houses. Rural dwellers typically live in traditional rustic *bohios* (thatched huts of wood or adobe) or modern bungalows; the majority have electricity, though many more remote homes still lack running water. Rural folk follow a simple life, tending their tobacco fields, coffee plants, and cows, or laboring for low pay in the sugarcane fields.

> "Things have improved dramatically since 2011, when Raúl Castro initiated free-market reforms intended to spark private enterprise—previously banned."

Material shortages are a fact of daily life. The average urbanite spends long hours struggling to get by. Following the revolution, restaurants, private businesses, and farms were seized by the state, while communist bureaucrats established a dysfunctional distribution system—the *acopio*. Many staples vanished long ago, and *puestos* (grocery stores) are largely without food. Despite broad accomplishments in preventive medicine, the health-care system suffers debilitating shortages while Cuba's biotech industry exports state-of-the-art medicines. City dwellers rely on the government *libreta* (ration book), which meets only a fraction of Cubans' needs. A thriving black market attempts to make up for shortfalls, which the government blames on the six-decades-long *bloqueo* (U.S. embargo). Nothing is thrown away; thus the mummified yet still functional 1950s jalopies that litter the streets. Outside Havana, a common means of transportation is the horse-drawn cart.

The state employs almost all workers, who are paid in near-worthless pesos: The average monthly wage is about 550 pesos, or just over $20. Although Cubans are industrious, workplace ennui is rampant. Cash sent from relatives in Miami brightens

Improvised goalposts and a well-worn ball characterize Cuban street soccer.

many Cubans' lives. Those without access to dollars scrape by. The scramble for pesos convertibles has eroded an ostensibly egalitarian society and given rise to *jineteros* (hustlers) and *jineteras* (prostitutes). Things have improved dramatically since 2011, when Raúl Castro initiated free-market reforms intended to spark private enterprise—previously banned. Combined with an end, in 2015, to restrictions on money that can be sent by U.S. citizens to support private enterprise in Cuba, the result has been a blossoming of *cuentas propistas* and a noticeable uptick in wealth.

Simple Pleasures

On weekends, families pile into their '50s DeSotos and Chevys and head to the beach to play volleyball while couples flirt under the *palapas* (thatched shade umbrellas) and palms. Women pull their *sillones* (rockers) onto sidewalks to share gossip while men, shirtless in the heat, slap dominoes on tables strategically placed in puddles of shade. They smoke cigars, swig cheap *aguardiente* (white rum), and come together for impromptu *cumbanchas*—the local word for a street party, when radios are cranked up and couples dance groin to groin, delighting in overtly sexual rumbas. Flirting is a national pastime; the population is sexually liberal and has elevated casual sex to a defining element of their national culture.

Machismo—part of Cuba's Spanish heritage—remains. Unsolicited compliments are freely offered to female passersby. Nonetheless, the phenomenon of femicide, for example, does not exist.

Ten Things Not to Do in Cuba

• Do not get into private taxis that do not display a valid license.

• Do not sunbathe or spend time in the sun without adequate protection. Cuba's tropical sun can be lethal. Wear a hat with a protective brim and/or sunscreen.

• In hotels as well as in *casas particulares*, always ask to see the room before you rent it.

• Remember that artwork and antiques are subject to customs fees. If you are importing objects of moderate value, you can speak directly to the export office at the airport (but at the risk of not receiving authorization). For valuable artwork and antiques, you must have a certificate signed by the Registro Nacional de Bienes Culturales *(Calle 12 bet. 17, Vedado, Habana)*.

• Prostitution is illegal so if you have anything to do with the *jineteros* or *jineteras* (street jockeys) you will most likely run into some kind of trouble that is often organized by the enticers themselves.

• Do not buy Cuban cigars on the street. They are stolen or often made with low quality tobacco.

• Generally speaking, do not expect rapid service. Dealing with some institutions in particular often involves long waits.

• If you have an appointment with a Cuban, do not expect perfect punctuality: Being half an hour late is not considered a serious offense.

• Don't expect prompt service. Low wages and inefficiencies of the state combine to thwart any notion of speedy service. Expect long lines and lengthy waits.

• Don't attempt to bring GPS devices or walkie-talkies into Cuba. Such items are banned and will be confiscated.

Government & Politics

The 2002 constitution defines Cuba as a socialist state. Cuba is governed by Miguel Díaz-Canel, President of the Council of State. He was elected by the National Assembly in 2018 to take the place of Raúl Castro who continues to head the Communist Party. Raúl had inherited power in April 2006 from his elder brother Fidel, when the latter's life was threatened by illness. Power resides with the Communist Party, which greatly influences decisions made by each government body.

The Council of Ministers runs the country, drafts bills for submission to the National Assembly, which meets twice a year to ratify legislation and government appointments. Members are elected by national ballot; elections are held every five years. The Council of State functions as the executive committee of the National Assembly. The People's Supreme Court, whose members have traditionally been chosen by Fidel or Raúl, is the highest judicial body. The Castros' presidential office, the Council of State, Council of Ministers, and headquarters of the Communist Party are housed in the Presidential Palace, on the east side of the Plaza de la Revolución, in Havana.

The country is divided into 15 provinces: Pinar del Río, Artemisa, Mayabeque, Matanzas, Villa Clara, Cienfuegos, Sancti Spíritus, Ciego de Ávila, Camagüey, Las Tunas, Holguín, Granma, Santiago de Cuba, and Guantánamo, plus the city of Havana. Isla de la Juventud (Isle of Youth) is a "special municipality." Each province is run by an elected Provincial Assembly, while municipal councils run the day-to-day affairs of *municipios*.

The Communist Party of Cuba (PCC) is the sole political party. No other political entities are permitted. The PCC is led by a Politburo and Central Committee, whose members are elected by party members. The party occupies a central role in all state institutions, including mass organizations such as the Union of Communist Youth and the Federation of Cuban Women. The government controls all communications and media. The military, which since the revolution has been headed by Raúl Castro, is a major economic entity, especially active in the promotion of tourism. In recent years Raúl has named military figures to head many corporations—all state-owned—and most ministries.

Fidel used the full force of his personality to bolster mass support. Raúl Castro prefers a different style. Though he may not have his brother's magnetic charm, he is a highly efficient, pragmatic manager who tended toward gradual liberalization from the beginning. At the end of 2014, after arduous mediation on the part of the Vatican, U.S. President Barack Obama and Cuba's Head of State, Raúl Castro, simultaneously issued statements reinstating diplomatic relations between the two countries. The agreement approved the path to lifting the embargo imposed by the U.S. and resuming trade relations after a block that had lasted almost 60 years, but the situation changed when Donald Trump became president of the United States. Direct flights to the island (that had resumed and included numerous commercial flights) and trade relations were blocked. Political relations were suspended, the embargo was reinstated, and American citizens were, once again, prohibited from visiting Cuba.

Cubans & the Revolution

Cubans are split between those who support *fidelismo* and those who crave more personal control of their own lives. Loyalists point to Cuba's impressive welfare programs and generous subsidies, to its enviable achievements in education and health, to the way the revolution has eradicated the worst destitution; they compare the country with Haiti and other nations still beset by true poverty. Communism's base of support is in the countryside, where many of the promises of the revolution have been realized.

EXPERIENCE: Stay With a Cuban Family

As a foreign visitor, you cannot stay as the guest of a Cuban national without the written authorization of the Cuban government. But you can stay at a licensed *casa particular* (room rental), which usually offers a chance to eat, drink, and learn how a Cuban family lives. The following are recommended:

• **Casa Colonial Muñoz**
(Calle Martí #401, Trinidad, tel 41/99-3673, casa.trinidadphoto.com)

• **Casa de Florinda** (Calle I #58, Reparto Sueño, Santiago de Cuba, tel 22/66-3660)

• **Casa de Jorge Coalla Potts**
(Calle I #456, bet. 23 & 21, Vedado, Havana, tel 7/832-9032, havanaroomrental.com)

• **Villa Liba** (Calle Maceo #46, Holguín, tel 24/42-3823, villaliba@nauta.cu)

In the cities, support for the revolution has eroded along with many of the benefits once supported by Soviet largesse. In general, urbanites are weary of sacrifice and paternalism that shoehorn them into conformity and weigh down on daily life. They seek the reality of material progress and roll their eyes at the Castros' "socialism or death!" Raúl's reforms have inspired cautious optimism for the future. The state's greatest adherents are the PCC members invested in a system that rewards them. ■

CUBAN FOOD & DRINK

Cuban fare is simple, but it can be delicious. Havana is experiencing a culinary revival and boasts many fine restaurants, while farther afield dining is no longer a bland affair.

Agricultural produce for sale at a *mercado agropecuario,* or farmers market

Comida criolla, the native cuisine, is country food—the fare of *el campo*—relying on lowly ingredients. Fried or roast chicken *(pollo frito* or *pollo asado)* and roast pork *(cerdo asado)* are ubiquitous—usually served with sides of white rice *(arroz)* and black beans; rice cooked with black beans *(moros y cristianos);* or rice with red kidney beans *(congrí)*—and often enlivened by *sofrito,* a paste of garlic *(ajo),* chopped onion *(cebolla),* peppers *(pimientos),* and lime sizzled with vegetable oil in a hot skillet.

Plantains *(plátanos)* or root vegetables such as cassava *(yuca)* or sweet potato *(boniato)* play supporting roles. The plantain—a relative of the banana—is served fried in strips when ripe, or as fried chips *(mariquitas* or *chicharritas)* or thick fried rounds called *tostones* before it has ripened. Boiled and mashed, plantains make *fufú.* The accompanying salad rarely extends beyond lettuce, cucumber, and tomato; be prepared for the staples of string beans or shredded cabbage.

Seafood, once scarce beyond Havana or coastal communities, is now widely available and lobster *(langosta)* is usually a bargain. Many tourist venues, however, charge top dollar for lobster and shrimp *(camarones).* The fish of choice is red snapper *(pargo),* and in the eastern provinces sea bass *(corvina)* is often served; less common is grouper *(cherna),* swordfish *(emperador, serrucho),* and marlin *(aguja).* Beef and steaks *(bistec)* can be found only at better state restaurants but rarely live up to U.S. standards. Private restaurants substitute lamb *(cordero).* A popular menu item is *bistec uruguayo,* fried beef or pork steak stuffed with ham and cheese. Occasionally you find rabbit *(conejo),* or *ajiaco,* a classic stew of pork and root vegetables.

In most hotels, breakfasts are a simple buffet—*mesa sueca*—with cold cuts, cheese, boiled eggs, pancakes, fruits, and sponge cake the ubiquitous items. Cuban households might serve a plain tortilla and bread and butter *(pan con mantequilla).* Beyond home, urban Cubans rely on peso street stalls selling bland but filling pizzas, and snacks such as small turnovers *(empanadas)* filled with meat, washed down with *refrescos*—chilled fruit drinks.

Fruits are also in short supply (most fruits are pulped to make juice), except at farmers markets *(mercados agropecuarios)*, which the state has permitted since 1993. Here you'll find oranges *(naranjas)*, grapefruit *(toronjas)*, mangoes *(mangos)*, pineapple *(piña)*, guava *(guayaba)*, bananas *(plátanos)*, and papaya *(fruta bomba)*, and favorites such as *mamey colorado*, *guanábana*, and *marañón*. Coconuts are less common since they are not traditionally used in cooking, except around Baracoa.

Despite so much sugar, Cuba's dessert scene rarely extends beyond cookies and sponge cakes, deep-fried donut rings *(rosquitas)*, puff pastries *(pasteles)* filled with cheese, meringue or guava paste, and caramel custard *(flan)*. Cubans, however, are ice-cream fanatics and favor the excellent Coppelia brand, best followed by espresso coffee, drunk thick and sugared *(café cubano)*. *Café americano* is coffee diluted with water. A *cortado* is espresso served with milk, and a *café con leche* is more milk than coffee. Milk, though, is hard to find, except in tasty

How to Make *Ropa Vieja*

Heat a tablespoon of vegetable oil in a large skillet over medium-high heat. Brown 2 pounds (0.9 kg) of marinated flank steak on each side, then shred into thin strips and transfer to a slow cooker. Pour in one cup of beef broth and add an 8-ounce can of tomato sauce. Next add a sliced onion and a green bell pepper sliced into strips, then two chopped garlic cloves, then a teaspoon each of ground cumin and fresh cilantro. Now add a tablespoon each of olive oil and white vinegar, and a 6-ounce (170 g) can of tomato paste. Stir together, then cover and simmer on high for 4 hours, or on low for 10 hours. Serve with white rice and black beans. ¡Delicioso!

batidos—milkshakes often made with fruit.

Sugarcane is the source of Cuba's fine rums. In the countryside, working men drink *aguardiente*, a cheap, clear, white spirit; and *guarapo*, fresh-squeezed sugarcane juice, sold at roadside *guaraperías*. Cubans are also beer drinkers. The *clara* brew is best avoided, as is most wine, except in better restaurants.

EXPERIENCE: Dine Like a Local

When in Cuba, broaden your experience and save money by dining like a local. Here's how:

• Buy a *cajita*, a simple boxed lunch sold streetside. This usually consists of rice and beans with fried chicken and a starch vegetable.

• Eat at *paladares*, private restaurants that typically serve massive portions of *criollo* meals at fair prices.

• Treat yourself to delicious ice cream at **Coppelia** (Calle 23 corner L, Vedado, Havana, closed Sun.–Mon.). Find a local to bring you into the locals-pesos section. Otherwise you'll end up in the pricey tourist section charging in CUC.

If you have access to a kitchen, try your hand at some Cuban recipes, such as *ropa vieja*, a popular dish that means "old clothes" (see recipe in the sidebar above). Places to buy processed foods and fresh produce include:

• **Mercados Agropecuarios.** Every town has at least one farmers market selling Cuban produce such as carrots, beets, and starch vegetables. One of the best is on Calle 19 *(bet. Calles A & B, Vedado)* in Havana.

• **Supermercado 70** *(Ave. 3ta corner Calle 70, Miramar, Havana)* is Cuba's largest supermarket, selling an impressive array of imported foodstuffs.

CUBAN HISTORY

On October 27, 1492, Christopher Columbus sighted a land he believed to be Japan. In fact it was Cuba, a tropical idyll the explorer proclaimed the "fairest on Earth." Within a year, Spain asserted sovereignty, beginning a long, bitter history of conflict. Fidel Castro's revolution, launched in 1956, extends Cuba's centuries-long continuum of struggle against colonial powers.

First Peoples

Although archaeological excavations in Cuba have unearthed carved and polished stone dating back about 10,000 years, the first significant pre-Ceramic culture was that of nomadic hunters and gatherers who settled the archipelago about 8000 B.C. By about 2500 B.C., a second migratory group had settled the coasts, where they made their living by farming and fishing. Eventually both of these groups were displaced by one more advanced—the Taino, a tribe related to the Arawak of South America, who began to settle Cuba between A.D. 1000 and 1100.

The peaceable Taino were skilled agriculturalists whose flourishing civilization was based on the cultivation of corn and yucca. They lived communally in thatched rectangular huts called *bohíos*; circular huts called *caneyes*; and huts called *barbacoas* that were built on stilts in lagoons or other marshy areas. The huts were typically arranged around an open space called a *batey*, with as many as 20 families forming a village under the leadership of a *cacique*, or chief. They painted their bodies and wore only the briefest of garments—loincloths for men and *naguas*, a type of cotton apron, for women—and considered flattened foreheads such a desirable mark of beauty that infants' heads were pressed between boards to restrict their development.

The Taino had no written language or metals and used neither wheels nor beasts of burden. However, they were accomplished potters and were so adept at weaving wild cotton and *henequen* (hemp) into ropes and hammocks that, ultimately, Spanish conquistadores forced them to weave sailcloth for Spanish vessels. The Taino traded with neighboring islands, taking to sea in large *canoas* (canoes) hewn from tree trunks.

Religion was central in their lives. The tribe worshipped a pantheon of gods who were thought to control nature's whims and who displayed their wrath when hurricanes bore down on the isle. During religious ceremonies, which were attended by all in the village, the *behíque*, or priest, would initiate conversations with the gods. First, he purified himself through self-induced vomiting, then he inhaled a powder concocted from the dried leaves of different hallucinogenic plants through a hollow wooden object shaped

Treasure Routes

Although the Spanish found little gold in Cuba, Havana's position at the head of the Gulf Stream—which propelled treasure-filled galleons back to Spain—made it the natural gathering point for twice-annual treasure fleets. Gold, silver, jewels, pearls, and precious spices were carried overland to Cartagena (Colombia), Portobelo (Panama), and Veracruz (Mexico) for shipment to Havana. *Las flotas* then sailed in heavily armed convoys to guard against piracy. So much treasure arrived in Havana that much had to be left behind, contributing to the city's vast wealth.

■ In this 1794 engraving by F. Bartolozzi, a Taino chief greets Columbus on the explorer's landfall in Cuba.

like a Y. Once the *behíque* achieved the desired state, he conversed with the gods about events—past or future—that affected the village.

About 300,000 indigenous people inhabited Cuba when the first Europeans arrived, including descendants of the earliest inhabitants in the far west of the isle. What remains of their cultures is limited to pottery shards, petroglyphs, cult objects—called *cemíes*—carved in stone, and words such as "canoe," "hammock," "hurricane," and "tobacco."

First Europeans

On August 3, 1492, the Genoese explorer Christopher Columbus (1451–1506) set out from Spain on his first voyage to find a western passage to the East Indies.

Sailing aboard the *Santa Maria* and accompanied by the caravels *Niña* and *Pinta* and a crew of 87, Columbus made first landfall in the Bahamas. There he took on indigenous guides, who told him of a large island called Cuba that lay to the southwest. After threading through coral-laced shallows, the expedition sighted the island on October 27. The next day, Columbus first dropped anchor in today's Bahía de Bariay, in the northeast province of Holguín. He scouted along the north coast for a month, arriving at a site that he called Puerto Santo, identified by a large, flat-topped mountain, today believed to be the Silla of Gibara. He then continued on to the Punta de Maisí and east to another island, which the indigenous peoples called Haiti and Columbus named Hispaniola, before returning to Spain. Columbus believed that he had found Japan by the western route, and he named the islands the West Indies, christening their inhabitants "Indians."

> On October 28, 1492, Columbus first dropped anchor in today's Bahía de Bariay, in the northeast province of Holguín.

Columbus returned three more times to the Americas, convinced that beyond Cuba, on the continent, lay the palaces of the Great Khan of Cathay, with their gold, precious stones, and the spices of which Marco Polo had written. In 1508, Columbus's son, Diego, was named governor of the Indies and was commissioned to lead an expedition to colonize Cuba. He set sail for Cuba in 1510, accompanied by Diego Velázquez (1465–1524), Hernán Cortés (1485–1547), and some 300 men. In 1511 they established the first settlement, today's Baracoa, at the island's far eastern end. Six other crude *villas* followed by 1515: today's Bayamo, Camagüey, Sancti Spíritus, Santiago de Cuba, Trinidad, and Havana.

The Taino were viewed as heathen and quickly put to work by the conquistadores, who received land grants and were allotted a specific number of Indian laborers under the *encomienda* system (a modified form of feudalism). The gentle Indians were no more suited, or inclined, to harsh labor than were the Spaniards, and the once noble indigenous peoples began to decline. The Taino were briefly rallied to resistance in 1510 by Hatuey, a heroic chieftain who had fled neighboring Hispaniola after his own people were crushed. Hatuey's insurrection failed, and he was burned at the stake.

Suffering from malnutrition, disease, and spiritual malady, the Indians found a friend in Bartolomé de las Casas (1474–1566), a Dominican friar who arrived with Velázquez. Las Casas's job included identifying sites for washing gold and also winning the commitment and loyalty to the crown of all the tribes. Las Casas witnessed the massacre of Indians and devoted his energies to helping

them. He succeeded: In 1542 the *encomienda* system, ostensibly established with the purpose of converting the heathen to Christianity, was abolished.

But by then it was too late. European diseases such as smallpox, measles, and tuberculosis had combined with sword and musket to swiftly fell the Indians. In less than a century, Cuba's indigenous population was all but extinguished.

Colonial Heyday

Lust for gold filled the minds of the conquistadores who descended on the New World. The Spanish found traces of the precious metal in Cuba but soon exhausted the early mines. The island then became the supply base for expeditions bound for Mexico and other destinations. On one such foray, in 1519, Hernán Cortés and his army sailed to Mexico, where they confronted Aztec emperor Montezuma in his capital and defeated him. Cortés retreated, to return in 1521 to complete his conquest and to plunder the empire's wealth. Indeed, Cuba's importance to Spain lay in its strategic location. The island commanded the sea routes to the Gulf of Mexico, and Havana's sheltered harbor fronted the fast-flowing Gulf Stream, which carried treasure-laden galleons to Spain. Havana was poised for a gilded future, evidenced in

Santiago de Cuba became a bustling port by the 19th century.

1532, when Francisco Pizarro (1476–1541) conquered the Andean empire of the Inca. Gold, silver, and jewels poured into Havana as treasure fleets—*flotas*—assembled for the twice-yearly journey, under naval escort, to Spain.

The island's own wealth lay in its rich soil. Native forests were felled and hardwoods shipped to Spain, and tobacco—along with sugar and other crops—was planted to feed the new smoking craze sweeping Europe. Cattle ranching also became widespread, and Cuban leather grew to be highly prized throughout Europe. The Spanish monarchy, however, made little effort to develop the colony. It enforced a crown monopoly; only the ports of Havana and Santiago de Cuba were entitled to trade (and only with the mother country), and exports were heavily taxed. Colonists were forbidden to manufacture; even the most mundane item had to be imported from Spain.

Unjust laws promoted lawlessness, and many colonists resorted to smuggling. Havana prospered on two-way trade as English, Dutch, and French seamen took advantage of the restrictions to smuggle in goods and much needed slaves. By the mid-16th century, sugarcane plantations were developing rapidly, and with them the slave trade from Africa. English sea captains such as John Hawkins (1532–1595) and Sir Francis Drake (1540–1596) began their illustrious seafaring careers by bringing in slaves for Spanish planters and slipping away with gold, jewels, sugar, and hides. This was easily done under the noses of usually corrupt Spanish officials. When the Spanish armada that was sent to invade England was defeated in 1588, breaking Spanish sea power, the flow of ships packed with African slaves crossed the ocean unchecked.

The Irish Influence in Cuba

Walking the streets of Habana Vieja (see pp. 70–72), visitors may ponder the origin of Calle O'Reilly. This was named for Gen. Alejandro O'Reilly (1722–1794), the second Spanish governor of Louisiana, who earned the nickname "Bloody O'Reilly" by ordering the exile, imprisonment, and execution of rebel Frenchmen in that Spanish colony. His family had been among the "Wild Geese" who fled their Protestant-ruled homeland of Ireland to fight for Catholic powers such as Spain. When England relinquished Cuba in 1763, the Spanish king Charles III sent O'Reilly to reoccupy Havana.

Another Irish name that loomed large in Cuban history was that of O'Farrill. The patriarch of this clan (with roots in Longford) was Ricardo O'Farrill (born ca. 1677), a native of Montserrat. Through sugar production, slave trading, and importing, the O'Farrills rose to prominence in the administration, economy, and culture of Cuba, and became part of Spanish-Cuban aristocracy. By the time Don Ricardo died in 1730, the O'Farrills owned two sugar plantations through which some 25,000 slaves would pass. Ricardo's grandson Rafael built his home in Old Havana at O'Farrill's Corner. The mansion is now the Hotel Palacio O'Farrill. (See Travelwise p. 241.)

In the 20th century, mystery shrouded the identity (Cuban or Spanish?) of the sugar trader Juan Vivión de Valera Acosta (1854–1885), when his son, Éamon de Valera, became *Taoiseach* (Prime Minister) and later President of Ireland. Another notable political link between the two islands is evident in the revolutionary DNA of Ernesto "Che" Guevara (see pp. 126–127), whose Lynch forefathers came from Galway, and of whom his father remarked, "The first thing to note is that in my son's veins flowed the blood of the Irish rebels."

▪ **Cutting and loading the sugarcanes on the Plantation of Las Canas.**

The Age of Pirates

The increased slave trade in the West Indies and the constant warring among Spain and England, France, and Holland during the 16th and 17th centuries brought new enemies to Cuba and its neighboring islands—pirates and *corsarios,* or corsairs. While most pirates acted independently in their harassment of Spanish vessels, *corsarios* were licensed by Spain's rivals and acted with permission and protection as they plundered ships, cities, and plantations.

Havana was a choice target of such privateering. It first fell in 1547, to French pirate Jacques de Sores, who razed the town before sailing off with its treasures. In May 1586, Francis Drake arrived off the coast of Havana with 23 ships. The terror-filled citizens waited for the privateers to attack. What they didn't know was that the plague had broken out among the fleet. After four long days, Drake sailed away. The beleaguered city was ransacked numerous times thereafter, notably in 1662, when notorious English buccaneer Henry Morgan made off with even the church bells.

In 1697 the Treaty of Ryswick put an end to privateering, and England agreed to suppress acts of piracy. But those were fickle times. To safeguard Spanish treasures, King Philip II ordered the construction of a system of fortresses. Havana was protected by El Morro castle, dating from the late 16th to early 17th century and situated on a cliff at the entrance to the bay and harbor. The city prospered, every year growing more elegant and sophisticated, with its gleaming architecture of wrought-iron balconies and carved mahogany doors. Then, in June 1762, the British army stormed El Morro, turned its guns on Havana, and captured the western part of the island, from the Bahía del Mariel to Matanzas. The English immediately opened Havana to unrestricted trade. The flag of St. George flew over Cuba for a mere 11 months before the territory was returned to Spain in exchange for Florida. But a new vitality had gripped the land. Cuba was about to enter its golden age.

Sugar & Slavery

Once the doors to trade had been opened, Spain found it impossible to close them again. Free trade, including with the burgeoning North American colonies, boosted the island's rural economy, based on tobacco, cattle, and sugar. Unparalleled expansion in Cuba's sugar industry created unprecedented demand for slaves to clear forests and work the fields. British slave traders were a permanent fixture in Havana. By the end of the 19th century, the total number of slaves imported to the island since its colonization was more than 600,000. In addition, almost 100,000 immigrants from North America, Spain, and elsewhere in Europe came as laborers or merchants.

The successful slave revolt of 1791 in Santo Domingo (today's Haiti) destroyed that nation's sugar industry. Thousands of refugee planters resettled in Cuba, bringing their expertise with them. Sugar prices soared. Cuba—by 1827 the world's largest producer of sugar—prospered as never before. Provincial cities such as Camagüey, Cienfuegos, and Trinidad flourished as Creole merchants and planters established cultural institutions and

■ The 1898 explosion of the *U.S.S. Maine* in Havana harbor served as a pretext for war.

erected the magnificent stone palaces and mansions that still grace these cities today.

The introduction in the early 19th century of a new type of sugarcane that produced juice with a higher sugar content and more flavor, as well as the advent of steam power and railroads midway through the century, further strengthened the sugar-based economy. For those who toiled daily in the fields, however, life was brutal; with good reason, Spanish officials feared a rebellion. The majority of slaves were *criollos* (born in Cuba) and lived in cities as domestics or laborers. Although many bought their freedom over time and prospered on their own, others remained under the thumbs of their masters. After 300 years of slavery on the island, African blood, beliefs, and traditions mingled with those of the Spanish, and a distinct criollo culture emerged.

Wars of Independence

Most criollos identified with their homeland, considering themselves Cuban instead of Spanish. Heavily taxed and harshly ruled by Spanish-born *peninsulares,* the island-born population had independence fever. By 1835, only Cuba, Puerto Rico, and the Philippines still belonged to Spain, which responded to the criollos' nationalist sentiments with brutality. Spain fought hard to keep its last and most valued possession. When sugar prices crashed in 1857, however, Cuba was ripe for revolt.

First War of Independence: Ten Years' War (1868–1878): On October 10, 1868, Carlos M. de Céspedes, a plantation owner in eastern Cuba, freed his slaves and declared war against Spain. His declaration took the form of an oration known as the "Grito de Yara" ("Cry of Yara"). Fellow planters joined him, and soon an army of poorly armed black and white insurgents had formed, calling themselves *mambísi,* after a freedom fighter named Juan Mambí who had battled for independence in Santo Domingo (Haiti). The *mambísi* were pitted against 100,000 Spanish troops who had rushed to the island. Cuba was ravaged as the patriots, led by Dominican-born Gen. Máximo Gómez and Col. Antonio Maceo, fought a guerrilla war that divided the nation. After a long, hard decade of fighting, the nationalist campaign fizzled. The war had claimed 250,000 lives and left a trail of destruction. Although Spain subsequently ended slavery in two stages (final abolition came in 1886), it clutched the island even more tightly in its iron fist.

Second War of Independence (1895–1898): The independence spirit was kept alive by poet and journalist José Martí (1853–1895), living in exile in the United States. In 1895, with Gómez, Martí returned to Cuba as leader of nationalist forces newly organized under Maceo. Though Martí was killed in the first skirmish of the new war, the *mambísi* swept across Cuba, defeating Spanish forces and torching the sugarcane fields and plantations. Desperate to hold on to their island jewel, Spanish forces seemingly stopped at nothing—including herding 200,000 people from Cuba's rural areas into concentration camps, where thousands died.

Spanish-American War (1898)

Stories of the cruel treatment meted out to the rebels stirred strong support in the U.S. for the *mambísi* movement, and the country eagerly followed news of the war. Americans already were heavily invested in Cuba's sugar industry, and the U.S. government, which had long coveted Cuba, was under pressure to intervene. Then, on February 15, 1898, a U.S. warship—the U.S.S. *Maine*—exploded in Havana harbor. Whether it was by accident or intent may never be known, but that act of aggression spurred the U.S. Congress to declare war on Spain on April 21, 1898.

In swift order the Spanish were routed—notably at a pivotal engagement on July 1 in Santiago de Cuba, where Theodore Roosevelt led a charge up San Juan Hill. Spain ceded control of Cuba to the United States in December 1898, under the terms of the Treaty of Paris. Thus began a new epoch in Cuba's long history of colonial rule.

A Government in Flux

On January 1, 1899, the U.S. military occupied Cuba, where it ruled until May 20, 1902. During that period, the United States wrote the Cuban constitution. This included the Platt Amendment, which granted America use of the Guantánamo naval base and the right to intervene in Cuban affairs to preserve the country's independence and stability. The U.S. sent troops to Cuba off and on over the next two decades to maintain or place friendly governments in power and to protect its business interests. The amendment was repealed in 1934, although the two countries reaffirmed the agreement to lease the Guantánamo naval base to the U.S.

Years of war had devastated Cuba, making the country ripe for American investors. The billions of dollars that flowed into Cuba reinvigorated the economy, notably in sugar, which enjoyed boom years from 1915 to 1920. The influx of money also funded grand civic constructions, plus hotels, casinos, and nightclubs. Although poverty riddled the countryside, the Cuba of the 1920s evolved to become the world's wealthiest tropical country—and gracious, salacious Havana was the jewel of the Caribbean. Tourists flocked for the good and the bad, taking all the more pleasure in their carousing because of the enactment of Prohibition in the United States.

> " Hand in hand with Batista came the Mafia, who flocked to Havana throughout the 1950s, following FBI crackdowns in the U.S. "

In 1924, Gen. Gerardo Machado (1871–1939) won the presidential election, initiating a period of unbridled corruption. Popular discontent was expressed on the streets and met with brutal repression. When the Great Depression hit, Cuba's one-crop economy crashed, and the country descended into violent chaos. In 1933 a general strike toppled Machado. Within six months, a 32-year-old army sergeant named Fulgencio Batista (1901–1973) seized power. Supportive of U.S. business interests and ultimately no less venal than his predecessors, Batista also proved himself a capable, enlightened reformer; notable social and political advances were made in the country. He won the 1940 presidential race, but he was voted out of office in 1944 and retired to Florida, leaving Cuba in the hands of a series of corrupt and mostly inept politicians. The country was plagued by waves of street gangsterism and political assassinations.

In 1952, Batista returned to run for president once more. Fearful of losing his bid for office, however, he staged a bloodless *golpe de estado* (coup d'état) before the balloting could be held and reinstated himself as president. Hand in hand with Batista came the Mafia, who flocked to Havana throughout the 1950s, following FBI crackdowns

■ Cuban armed forces reenact the 1956 landing of Fidel Castro and his rebels in Los Coloradas as part of celebrations marking the 50th anniversary of the 1959 ouster of Batista's regime.

in the U.S. The city entered its frivolous heyday as Americans gravitated to the international playground to indulge in sun, sand, and sin.

One of Cuba's congressional hopefuls whose political ambitions had been thwarted by Batista's coup was a 25-year-old lawyer named Fidel Castro (1926–2016). Castro devoted himself to ousting Batista. On July 26, 1953, his revolutionary group—later to be called the 26th of July Movement—struck at the Moncada barracks in Santiago de Cuba. The armed assault failed, but the torture and assassination of 59 captured revolutionaries angered many Cubans and ignited popular support for the rebels. Castro was sentenced to 15 years' imprisonment but served only 22 months. Immediately upon his release, he launched an anti-Batista crusade. On July 7, 1955, he departed for Mexico to prepare a guerrilla force that would return to overthrow Batista, whose increasingly ruthless and corrupt regime was despised by the public.

The Fight to Topple Batista

On November 25, 1956, Castro and 81 other revolutionaries set sail from Tuxpán, Mexico, in a 38-foot-long (11.5 m), barely seaworthy, overloaded cruiser called the *Granma*. (The boat was named for the previous owner's grandmother.) Seven days later the rebels landed in Los Coloradas, on the south coast of what is now Granma Province. Batista's forces attacked the landing party, killing 8 men in combat and assassinating 18 in the days that followed. Remarkably, survivors of the battle included the rebels' leaders: Fidel Castro, his younger brother Raúl (1931–), Camilo Cienfuegos (1923–1959), and a young Argentinian doctor named Ernesto "Che" Guevara (1928–1967). The beleaguered band took sanctuary in the Sierra Maestra.

Fidel Castro fought a war of attrition in the mountains while urban guerrillas attacked police stations and mounted a terror campaign in the cities. Batista's armed forces and police fought back with increasing brutality, which only further alienated Cuban citizens. By spring 1958, the rebel army controlled the mountain regions of Oriente. Expanding into the province of Las Villas, Castro opened new fronts under the command of Raúl Castro and Juan Almeida Bosque (1927–2009)—and, later that summer, under Camilo Cienfuegos and Che Guevara, who had proved himself Castro's most capable and trusted commander.

After a series of victories, on December 30 Che's troops derailed an enemy troop train and captured the key city of Santa Clara. The following morning at 2:00 a.m., Batista fled Cuba for self-imposed exile. Castro led a triumphant parade to Havana, arriving on January 8, 1959, to a tumultuous welcome.

During his crusade to depose Batista, Castro claimed to have forsaken all allegiance to communism, and in July 1957 he issued the Sierra Maestra Manifesto, committing himself to "free and democratic eléctions." With Batista out of the picture, however, things changed quickly. A provisional government was established in Cuba with backing from the United States, led by respected judge Manuel Urrutia Lleó (1901–1981). Castro simultaneously set up a secret parallel government that worked to subvert Urrutia and promote a far-reaching revolution. This was announced in May 1959, when Castro, who controlled the armed forces, enacted an agrarian reform law that confiscated large landholdings without compensation. Meanwhile Che presided over summary trials that sent thousands of Batista supporters and counterrevolutionaries to the firing squads. Fearing for their lives, professionals and property owners—including architects, doctors, and engineers—fled Cuba (approximately two million Cubans have departed since the revolution). In July, Castro manipulated Urrutia's resignation and took power, to the acclaim of the peasantry and working classes. On May 1, 1960, he suspended the constitution and announced that "the people" had declared elections unnecessary.

The Cuban Missile Crisis

Despite his victory at the Bay of Pigs in 1961, Castro feared a U.S. invasion. History is unclear as to who initiated the visit, but in the summer of 1962 a Soviet delegation arrived in Cuba to propose the installation of medium-range nuclear missiles. On October 14, U.S. intelligence detected the missiles. President John F. Kennedy (1917–1963) ordered them removed and placed U.S. forces on combat alert. The resulting standoff took the world to the brink of nuclear war. After 13 tense days, the Soviets backed down in exchange for a promise that the U.S. would not invade Cuba. The 2000 Hollywood movie *Thirteen Days* dramatized these events.

The previous year, the Soviet Union had officially recognized Castro's revolutionary government. Trade and defense agreements followed. Between August and October 1959, Cuba sold 500,000 tons (453,600 tonnes) of sugar to the U.S.S.R., with another million tons (907,200 tonnes) to follow six months later. The Soviet Union also began to lend financial, technical, and economic support to the island, with the goal of developing industrial, energy, mining, and farming operations. Experts came to the country to train Cubans in science, industry, and defense. When Soviet oil began arriving in Cuba in 1960, President Dwight D. Eisenhower (1890–1969) instructed U.S.–owned refineries not to process it. Castro reacted by nationalizing the refineries. By January 1961, Castro had nationalized all U.S. property in Cuba, and the United States reacted by breaking off diplomatic ties. A trade ban was imposed in March 1961.

Castro made his first speech in Santiago de Cuba in 1959 after toppling Batista's regime.

Bay of Pigs Invasion

While popular with less well-to-do Cubans, Castro's increasingly radical measures generated intense opposition—including among his former commanders, many of whom were later imprisoned or forced into exile. By 1960 counterrevolutionary bands had established a guerrilla front in the Sierra del Escambray; the Lucha Contra Bandidos—Fight Against Bandits—would take Castro six years to quell. Meanwhile, in Miami seething exiles, trained and equipped by the CIA, plotted their return. On April 15, 1961, they bombarded Cuban airfields as a prelude to landing ground forces. On April 17, an invasion force 1,400 strong arrived at Playa Girón, located on the Bahía de Cochinos—the Bay of Pigs. Their intent was to link up with the anti-Castroites and incite a counterrevolution. The exile force was swiftly defeated, however, and the debacle served only to strengthen Castro's hold over Cuba.

The Revolution

Castro was now free to pursue his socialist revolution. Literacy brigades fanned out into the countryside to teach peasants to read and write. Money flowed into health care, and prices of rents, utilities, and transportation were dramatically lowered. The cities, however, were neglected as energies were focused on raising rural living standards. The state also eroded personal liberties and worked to destroy

■ **President Obama is welcomed to Cuba by President Raúl Castro in 2016.**

the middle class in an effort to create the "New Man"—an individual motivated not by personal ambition but by egalitarianism and the desire to contribute to the collective welfare. Che Guevara, as minister of finance and industry, supervised economic reforms that culminated in 1968, when the government seized all private businesses. Socialist planning replaced "market anarchy." Chaos ensued. By 1962, the economy was in ruin and rationing was introduced. Attempts to diversify the sugar-based economy failed, prompting a disastrous effort, in 1970, to produce a bumper crop of sugar—10 million tons (9.07 m tonnes). Most of Cuba's resources were dedicated to that goal, and the economy stalled. In the end, Castro sacrificed ideals of self-sufficiency and supplied sugar to the Soviets in exchange for oil, rice, and grains.

While the Soviets had adopted a policy of coexistence with the U.S., Cuba's iconoclastic leader was intent on exporting his revolution and baiting his nemesis. In 1966, Castro launched his Fifth International, with the goal of creating "as many Vietnams as possible." International revolutionaries took military training in Cuba, and Cuban troops fanned out to aid leftist movements in Africa and elsewhere. In 1965, Che Guevara departed to lead revolutionary movements abroad; he was killed in Bolivia in 1967. Cuban doctors and technical specialists provided aid throughout the Third World, while at home campaigns targeted intellectuals, homosexuals, Roman Catholics, and other "social deviants."

A Glimmer of Hope

Castro's adventurism added frost to the icy relations between Havana and Washington. In 1977, however, in an effort at rapprochement, President Jimmy Carter eased the trade embargo and lifted travel restrictions. The two nations established Interests Sections as a prelude to restoring full diplomatic relations. But tensions flared again in 1980, in part because of Cuba's continuing aid to Marxist regimes in Africa and the Middle East and in part due to the pressure that Miami's anti-Castro movement was exerting on the U.S. government. When 12 Cubans sought refuge in the Peruvian Embassy in Havana that year, Carter announced that he would welcome political refugees from Cuba. Castro promptly sent off disaffected citizens, prisoners, and other "antisocial elements." More than 120,000 refugees boarded boats for Florida. The incident sealed Cuban–U.S. hostility, with the U.S. dealing Cuba a blow in 1983 when American forces ousted a Cuban-backed regime in Grenada.

A brief dalliance with free-market experiments in the mid-1980s bolstered Cuba's faltering economy, but Castro ended the flirtation in 1986 and swung back toward communist orthodoxy. He rejected Mikhail Gorbachev's policy of *perestroika* (restructuring), which was meant to revive the Soviet Union's ailing economy by introducing some elements of capitalist competition. After *perestroika* failed, the Soviet bloc began to unravel in 1989, precipitating a crisis in Cuba as oil, foodstuffs, and other goods upon which the island relied ceased to arrive. Warlike austerity measures were imposed in Cuba during the *Periodo especial* (Special Period), as it is called, and the economy slipped into a coma. Cuba's population faced terrible hardships, riots broke out, and a grim slogan from the 1970s reappeared: ¡*Socialismo o Muerte!*—Socialism or Death!

Modern Times

The Cuban government enacted urgent reforms. A ban on U.S. dollars was ended, self-employment for certain occupations was legalized, and foreign corporations were invited to partner with Cuban state companies. Meanwhile, an exodus of Cubans became a flood after deadly riots in Havana in August 1994. More than 30,000 *balseros* (boat people) washed up in Florida before Washington and Havana negotiated an accord to stem the tide.

A new crisis arose in February 1996, and as a result, President Bill Clinton imposed new sanctions. Tourism from Europe, Canada, and Latin America grew, providing revenue needed for Cuba's recovery. Cuba received a further boost in January 1998, when Pope John Paul II visited, initiating a loosening of restrictions on religion. His successor, Pope Benedict XVI visited the island in 2012. In

■ **The tomb of Fidel Castro in the Santa Ifigenia Cemetery in Santiago de Cuba.**

May 2002, the visiting former President Jimmy Carter called for greater political freedoms. The state, however, enacted a harsh political crackdown and reined in self-employment as it reasserted control of an economy now boosted by cheap oil from Venezuela.

In July 2006 Fidel transferred power to Raúl, who in 2010 began to expand opportunities for self-employment, to divest state involvement in agriculture and food distribution, and to permit greater freedom of expression. Other liberalizations followed, such as term limits for elected government officials (including his own). In April 2015, Raúl and President Barack Obama met at the Summit of the Americas—a prelude to the reestablishment of diplomatic relations after two years of secret negotiations hosted by Pope Francis. President Obama also eased restrictions on travel and trade, and in March 2016 became the first U.S. president in 88 years to visit Cuba.

On November 25, 2016, the former Cuban president and leader, Fidel Castro, died at the age of 90. ■

LAND & LANDSCAPE

Cuba is a tropical Eden of 42,830 square miles (110,922 sq km), caressed by warm trade winds. The name means "land of abundance" in the language of the Taino. South of the Tropic of Cancer, and separated from the U.S. by the 90-mile-wide (145 km) Straits of Florida, Cuba is washed by the Atlantic to the north and the Caribbean to the south. Haiti lies 48 miles (77 km) east across the Windward Passage. This 780-mile-long (1,255 km) island stretches from Cabo San Antonio in the west to Punta Maisí in the far east.

Cuba's vast plains are a gently undulating sea of chartreuse—sugarcane fields, dusted in summer with delicate white blossoms. Semidesert merges into mountain rain forest, and white-hot beaches dissolve into seas that gleam an impossible peacock blue. Offshore, scores of coral cays dot the hazy horizon. Throughout the isle, the scenery unfolds dramatically—palm-tufted, and framed in the distance by mauve-colored *mogotes* (see pp. 106–107), rounded limestone hillocks that are Cuba's signature landforms. Between the mogotes are valleys filled with red loamy soil. Oxen till the fields, and tropical scents rise from the fragrant earth.

Some 14 percent of Cuba's landmass is protected in 80 national and 195 local reserves. These include 14 national parks, 22 ecological reserves, 8 nature reserves, 11 wildlife reserves, 2 protected natural landscapes, and 11 flora reserves. Seven protected areas are designated as UNESCO biosphere reserves: the Península de Guanahacabibes and Sierra del Rosario, in Pinar del Río; Baconao and Cuchillas del Toa in Santiago de Cuba; Parque Nacional Alexander Von Humboldt in Guantánamo; Ciénaga de Zapata in Matanzas; and Buenavista and Parque Nacional Caguanes-Santa Maria in Ciégo de Ávila.

> **Some 14 percent of Cuba's landmass is protected in 80 national and 195 local reserves.**

One-fifth of the population lives in Havana, the sprawling capital in the northwest. A majority of the rest live in provincial capitals and dusty agricultural towns scattered throughout the country.

Far West

Cuba's far west is made up of mountains and plains. West of Havana, the Cordillera de Guaniguanico fringes the narrow north coast, where offshore isles float in a warm, fecund sea. Divided into four ranges—Sierra del Rosario, Sierra de los Órganos, Alturas de Pizarra del Norte, and the Alturas y Montañas de Pizarra del Sur—and dramatically sculpted with plump mogotes, these mountains are cut through with deep valleys.

They culminate in the broad Valle de Viñales, whose rich red soils are perfect for growing tobacco. The pine-clad Sierra del Rosario offers good hiking and birding, especially at Soroa and Las Terrazas. Caves provide opportunities for exploration. East of Havana, rolling uplands—*alturas*—enfold the port city of Matanzas. Broad plains extend inland from the southern shore, flat as a pool table and just as green from the sugarcane that swathes much of the land. The rivers that flow south from the mountains eventually lose themselves amid swampy marshlands. These are drained by watery sloughs that transform the coastal lowlands into a patchwork of rice fields and lagoons, and tan carpets of sedge. Profuse coral reefs and warm waters draw scuba divers to Bahía de Corrientes, sheltered by the slender, scrub-covered Península de Guanahacabibes, a rugged refuge for wildlife.

The Valle de Viñales is among the most beautiful of Cuba's landscapes.

■ Farming in the Valle de Viñales: Ox-drawn plows cast a time-warp beauty over Cuba.

Western Plains

Swampland extends across much of the vast *llanuras* (flatlands) of southern Matanzas like a soggy carpet. The *ciénaga* (swamp) that smothers the shoe-shaped Península de Zapata forms a 1,745-square-mile (4,520 sq km) wetland teeming with game fish, crocodiles, and birds that can be viewed by boat or from blinds. Manatees inhabit more remote regions of the reserve. From the north, citrus groves push up against the swamps. The richest soils are tilled for potatoes, legumes, and sugarcane, extending into Villa Clara and Cienfuegos Provinces across plains as flat as a carpenter's level. The region is traversed east to west by the Autopista Nacional (the nation's only freeway) and, to the north, by the Carretera Central, connecting time-weary towns like pointillistic dots on an emerald canvas. The Península de Hicacos, jutting from the north shore, is the setting for Cuba's major resort, Varadero. The southern shore boasts Playa Girón, a white-sand beach that was a landing site during the 1961 Bay of Pigs invasion. Tucked into a deep bay is Cienfuegos, an industrial port that wears its history on its sleeve.

Central Uplands

Dominating the midpoint of Cuba, a rolling massif rises gradually from the north coastal plain. The uplands stairstep southward in ridges enfolding exquisite valleys studded with mogotes; the fertile vales of Vuelta Abajo are a regional center of tobacco production. Farther south, the ragged Sierra del Escambray rises abruptly over a narrow coastal plain, attaining 3,762 feet (1,147 m) atop Pico San Juan. Upper slopes wear a lush green shawl of eucalyptus and pine. Birds such as the Cuban trogon *(tocororo)* and the *zunzún,* or Cuban emerald hummingbird, brighten the woodlands, which are easily explored at Topes de Collantes. From there trails lead to cascading waterfalls. The old city of Trinidad sits on the southeast flank of the mountains; Playa Ancón—the region's only white-sand beach—unfolds nearby and is being developed for tourism. Eastward lies the Valle de los Ingenios, historically important as a center of sugar production. The waters of Presa Zaza teem with bass, providing another angle on adventure. The regional capitals of Santa Clara and Sancti Spíritus, straddling the Carretera Central, serve as gateways to the region.

Eastern Plains

Spanning five provinces, the plains of east-central Cuba put the island's scale in perspective. To the west, pancake-flat Ciego de Ávila Province is farmed in sugarcane fields, which sprawl across the *llanuras* inland of the Atlantic and Caribbean shores. A narrow upland spine—the Periplano de Florida, Camagüey, Las Tunas—runs east-west through the center of Camagüey and Las Tunas Provinces. Growing in scale as it swings north through Holguín, this ridge culminates in the Grupo Montañoso Maniabón, dramatically adorned with mogotes. These rolling uplands are dominated by *ganaderías* (cattle ranches) and *vaqueros* (cowboys), who add an intriguing element to the terrain. North of the Periplano, the verdant landscapes wither to a lowland savannah carpeted by scrub and wild grassland munched by floppy-eared, humped cattle. Arching east, the Río Cauto cascades down from the Sierra Maestra, snakes across a great green wash of plain, and pours into the Golfo de Guacanayabo. Swampland extends along the sparsely populated southern shore. The north coast is incised with deep bays and dabbed with the white-sand beaches of Guardalavaca, Pesquero, and Santa Lucía—all of which are prime tourist resorts.

Eastern Sierra

Sawtooth mountains define eastern Cuba. The Sierra Maestra, the dominant chain, extends along an east-west axis from Cabo Cruz to the city of Santiago de Cuba.

EXPERIENCE: Hop in the Saddle

Rural Cuba is true cowboy country, and the *campesino* (peasant) culture depends heavily on the horse for mobility. Regardless of where you find yourself in Cuba, horses are sure to be available for rent. A handful of ranches offer trail rides, while newly relaxed self-employment laws now permit individuals to offer guided excursions for traveling city slickers longing to play the Marlboro Man. Here are three options:

• **Centro Ecuestre**, in Havana's Parque Lenin *(Calzada de Bejucal, tel 7/844-1058)*, offers one-hour trips as well as horse-riding lessons.

• **"Horse whisperer" Julio Muñoz** offers horseback riding at a rustic farmstead near Trinidad *(Calle Martí #401, Trinidad, tel 41/99-3673, trinidadphoto.com)*.

• **Rancho La Guabina** is a horse-breeding center that offers rides to visitors *(Carretera de Luis Lazo Km 9.5, Pinar del Río, tel 48/79-6120, email: ecoturpr@enet.cu, $$)*.

These are Cuba's highest peaks, rising to 6,476 feet (1,974 m) atop Pico Turquino—high enough that the dwarf forest is ribboned with wispy cloud tendrils. Much of the forest is protected within Parque Nacional Pico Turquino.

The mountains plummet to a narrow, ruler-straight coast that lies in a rain shadow; in places the coastline is so dry that cacti push up within yards of the sea. Gray-sand beaches have attracted a bevy of resorts whose emergence in recent years attempts to bring a new cachet to the region. The culturally rich city of Santiago de Cuba and dowdy Guantánamo city are surrounded by mountains at the head of long, narrow bays. The cities simmer in intense heat, and the cool, pine-clad mountains that lie north and east are deluged by rain. Moisture-laden clouds race in from the east to dump their cargo, and bruised clouds swirl ominously about the windswept summits of the Sierra del Purial, Sierra del Cristal, and Cuchillas del Toa. Dense, humid forests teem with birds, today protected within a series of national parks being promoted for outdoor adventures.

Offshore Isles

Scores of low-lying cays, large and small, are separated from the mainland by warm, shallow seas. The majority span a 300-mile (480 km) arc stretching

■ **Royal palms rise over the Sierra del Cristal.**

EXPERIENCE: Humanitarian Tourism

Key organizations you can volunteer to work for in Cuba include:
• **Animal Experience International** (30 Owen St., Barrie, Ontario, Canada L4M 3G7, tel (001) 705/726-7070, animalexperience international.com). You can volunteer as a field assistant in scientific studies of Cuban bats at Varadero and elsewhere in Matanzas province.
• **First-Hand Aid** (P.O Box 150171 Grand Rapids, MI 49515-0171, tel 49/515-0171, firsthandaid.org). Help distribute humanitarian aid to Cuba's needy by supplying hospitals and feeding and providing hygiene products to the indigent elderly in Havana and the town of Güines.
• **GlobeAware** (6500 E. Mockingbird Ln. #104, Dallas, TX 75214-2497, tel 877-588-4562, globeaware.org). You can lend a helping hand teaching English, repairing playgrounds and schools, and assisting with rehabilitation for the elderly.

east-west in a long line at an average distance of 15 miles (24 km) off the north coast; they are known collectively as the Archipiélago de Sabana-Camagüey. One cay, Cayo Sabinal, is connected to the mainland by an isthmus measuring a hairbreadth; three more (Cayo Coco, Santa María, and Rosario) by *pedraplénes*—causeways—that shoot across the limpid lagoons where flamingos wade. The seaward shores are edged by frost white sands and coral reefs and turquoise ocean. The Cuban government is wise to the untainted allure of the cays—hotels are going up thick and fast.

The Archipiélago de los Canarreos (south of Havana Province) and Jardines de la Reina (south of Ciego de Ávila and Camagüey Provinces) are similar jewels in a sapphire sea. Cayo Largo, part of the Canarreos grouping, offers perhaps the finest beaches in all of Cuba and is filled with tourist hotels. Its largest island, Isla de la Juventud, although undeveloped for tourism, offers a chance to see crocodiles lumber around in the Lanier swamp; it is also a good destination for birding. Stunning beaches are swept by warm currents that bring ashore marine turtles, and scuba divers are awed by the wrecks and coral reefs off Cabo Francés.

Flora & Fauna

Over the course of four centuries, two-thirds of Cuba's forest cover has been felled to make room for sugarcane fields, yet remnants of almost every native ecosystem remain. More than half of the island's 6,700 plant species are endemics, for example, lending even the cities a quintessentially Cuban persona.

The undisputed symbol of Cuba (it graces the national coat of arms) is the ubiquitous royal palm, rising over the lyrical landscapes like silver-sheathed Corinthian columns. Cuba has some 90 species of palms, including the endangered antediluvian cork palm, found only in Pinar del Río. Among the most striking of other tree species are giant kapoks, with roots flanged like missiles; towering ceibas (silk cotton trees), revered in the Santería religion; and the *jagüey*, dropping its roots from its branches.

Flowering species speckle the forests of the cays in impressionist colors: yellow *corteza amarilla*, scarlet *poró*, and bright orange *Spathodea*, locally called the Jesús Cristo tree because it blooms blood-red at Easter. Frangipani, hibiscus, and bougainvillea brighten colonial townscapes; bromeliads, orchids, and other epiphytes also thrive in the hot, humid climate. The national flower is the *mariposa blanca,* or white butterfly, whose pendulous white blossoms emit a nocturnal scent.

Wide variety also characterizes the wildlife that populates Cuba's varied landscapes. Mammals include deer, wild boars, and the *Solenodon cubanus* or *almiquí,* an endangered insectivore found only in the Sierra del Cristal. The *jutía*—a cat-size rodent living in uplands and offshore cays—is more common. It looks like a fat, tailless squirrel with thin legs and has the tiptoeing gait of a deer. At night, bats command the sky. Cuba has 27 species, from the diminutive butterfly bat—160 together would weigh only 1 pound (0.5 kg)—to the Jamaican fruit bat, with a wingspan of 20 inches (50 cm).

Of Cuba's 46 lizard species, the most colorful is the blue anole, in its debonair cloak of blue and green. When threatened, the male unfolds an orange dewlap below its throat to signal a territorial warning. Lizards are harmless. So, too, are the several species of nonvenomous snakes, the iguanas in their headdresses of leathery spines, and dozens of amphibian species, including the world's smallest frog—*Eleutherodactylus iberia,* which measures $^3/_4$ of an inch (18–19 mm). Cuba also has six species of painted land snails (see sidebar left). About 200 species of Cuba's plant and animal species are listed as endangered or threatened, including hawksbill, green, and loggerhead turtles, which nest on the beaches of Isla de la Juventud and the southern cays.

The Legend of the Shells

The Cuchillas del Toa mountains in the eastern Oriente region are known for *Polymita pictas*—a tiny species of land snail, unique to the region, known for its colorful shell. Each snail has its own color scheme. Some are bright yellow, others orange or white or black. The majority are whorled in delicate, multicolored stripes. The snail shells were initially colorless, according to local legend. The story goes that one particular snail grew jealous of the local beauty and asked to borrow some green from the mountains, blue from the sky, yellow from the sands, and so on. Seeing these colors, the other snails followed suit. Alas, collectors have now decimated their numbers.

Making a comeback is *Crocodylus rhombifer,* the indigenous Cuban crocodile once hunted to near extinction. Now protected in the Zapata and Lanier swamps, this saurian giant is more pugnacious than the American crocodile.

Zapata's waters also shelter the endangered manatee and vast populations of avian fauna—from the purple gallinules and jacanas to scarlet and white ibises with their long, curving beaks. The sandhill crane is found only in the Lanier swamp, populated also by the emerald green Cuban parrot *(cotorra)* and by the roseate spoonbill, named for its spatulate bill. Flocks of greater flamingos wade the lagoons of Zapata and Cayerías del Norte and skim the water as they fly.

The Cuban green woodpeckers and red-billed woodpeckers are common, as are turkey vultures and cattle egrets, white as snow against the cane fields. Pelicans call the shorelines home, while frigate birds hang in the sky like kites tethered on invisible strings. Of the 368 species of birds recorded in Cuba, 25 are endemics, including the charming bee hummingbird, or *zunzuncito,* the world's smallest bird, which barely tips the scales at 0.07 ounce (2 g). The elegant Cuban trogon or *tocororo,* plumed in the colors of the Cuban flag, is beloved as the national bird. ■

EXPERIENCE: Birding at Its Best

Cuba is a birders' nirvana, with 368 recorded species. The list runs the gamut from migratory waterfowl to Cuba's 25 endemic species found nowhere else. The Holy Grail is surely the ivory-billed woodpecker. Once common throughout the southern U.S. and Cuba, this bird was considered extinct in the 1940s. In the mid-1980s, it was sighted in the Cuchillas de Toa mountains, prompting creation of a biosphere reserve. Alas, it hasn't been seen since.

Bird-watchers are virtually guaranteed better luck with the *zunzuncito*—the bee hummingbird—the world's smallest bird. Cubans call it *pajaro mosca*—fly bird—for its tiny size. To spot it, head to the Reserva de la Biosfera Ciénaga de Zapata. Zapata is also one of several environments where you might see the endemic and endangered Cuban parrot, which also frequents the forests of the Isla de la Juventud. Another quintessential endemic is the *tocororo*, or Cuban trogon. The national bird, it inhabits woods countrywide with its telltale *có-co-có-co-có-co* call.

The bee hummingbird: the world's smallest bird

Although Cuba has numerous nature reserves teeming with birds, facilities for birding are relatively meager. There are few eco-lodges and trained natural guides. You'll need to bring your own binoculars and/or spotting scopes—they can't be purchased or borrowed—plus a copy of *Birds of Cuba* by Orlando H. Garrido.

Top Birding Sites

• **Las Terrazas** (*Reserva Sierra del Rosario, Havana Province, tel 048/57-8700, lasterrazas.cu*). This eco-resort has naturalist guides who can help identify species such as the Cuban solitaire, the Cuban green woodpecker, and the Cuban trogon. (See p. 104.)

• **Parque Nacional Viñales,** Pinar del Río Province. Dramatic scenery is a bonus when birding in this reserve, a setting for possible sightings of the zunzuncito and Cuban parrot. (See p. 108.)

• **Reserva Ecológica Los Indios,** Isla de la Juventud. Despite its isolated location, this reserve rewards bird-watchers with the potential of spotting several of Cuba's most sought-after endemic species, including the Cuban sandbill crane and the now endangered Cuban parrot. (See p. 227.)

• **Finca La Belén,** Camagüey Province. The Cuban trogon is relatively easily seen among the semi-deciduous forests of the Sierra del Chorrillo hills. Lucky birders can also set their scopes on the endangered giant kingbird. (See p. 168.)

• **Reserva de la Biosfera Cuchillas del Toa,** Guantánamo Province. Don't expect to spot the ivory-billed woodpecker, but you may see the endemic and endangered royal woodpecker. (See p. 221.)

Guided Birding Tours

• **Ecotur** (*Calle 13 #18005 between 5ta & 182, Playa, tel 7/273-1542, ecoturcuba.tur.cu*) runs all nature trips in Cuba and has regional offices.

• **Worldwide Quest** (*491 King St., Toronto, ON, M5A 1L9, Canada, tel 416/633-5666, worldwidequest.com*)

• **Real Cuba** (*Box 2345, Swan River, MB, R0L 1Z0, Canada, tel 306/205-0977, realcubaonline.com*)

ARCHITECTURE

Cuba's sugar wealth spawned a trove of glorious buildings. The island's varied and distinctive architecture spans four centuries and showcases a dizzying amalgam of styles—from 16th-century colonial asceticism and 17th- and 18th-century baroque to 19th-century neoclassical and neo-Gothic, plus a stunning range of 20th-century designs. Tourism is spurring efforts to preserve the past and providing much needed resources to do so.

Throughout the centuries, Cuban architects have shown remarkable creativity while adapting their vision to local conditions. The greatest concentration of buildings is in Havana, which boasts one of the world's finest bodies of 20th-century architecture in art nouveau, eclectic, beaux arts, Art Deco, and modernist styles. The regional cities and towns tempt visitors, too, with their colonial structures. The entire city of Trinidad is a designated UNESCO World Heritage site, as is Old Havana and the heart of Santiago de Cuba. Though many buildings are in ruins, the

■ **The Gran Teatro, built by Galicians in the early 1900s, showcases Havana's neo-baroque.**

communist system has prevented the kinds of private, for-profit projects that might have demolished architectural treasures. Whole cities are frozen in time, untouched by the wrecking ball or contemporary sprawl.

Early Colonial Structures (16th & 17th Centuries)

The first rustic settlements were built of wood and thatched with palm fronds in indigenous style. These simple *bohíos* are still a staple of rural areas. As towns developed, adobe and later limestone replaced wood. The Laws of the Indies (1537) systemized Spanish plans for colonial settlement and called for plazas to be built every four blocks. These were presided over by a church. Early churches were simple and austere but for the exquisite carved wood altars adorned with elaborate gilt filigree. The period also saw the construction of forts, such as the Castillo de la Real Fuerza, built between 1558 and 1577 and adjoining Havana's Plaza de Armas.

66 **The Laws of the Indies (1537) systemized Spanish plans for colonial settlement and called for plazas to be built every four blocks.** 99

The grid-block pattern decreed by law lent orderliness to city development, with buildings adjoining one another along the narrow streets. The typical 17th-century house was of unadorned Spanish style, with two stories built around an inner courtyard. On the plazas, houses typically boasted a portico and loggia to provide shade and rain protection (see pp. 142–143 for more on the colonial style).

Baroque & Vernacular (18th Century)

By the 18th century, churches had become more ornate, with interiors in the Mudejar style (a blend of Islamic and contemporary European styles, especially Gothic). They had flamboyant baroque facades with portals crowned by scalloped motifs, and huge wooden doors studded with rose-head nails in Spanish style. Havana's Catedral de San Cristóbal (1748–1777) offers the finest example. Major cities also had convents. Most still stand today, their cloistered courtyards hidden behind rammed-earth walls, offering a quiet retreat. Many structures had *alfarjes* (carved wooden ceilings) that in Cuba often showed a nautical influence—not surprising, since many of them had been crafted by shipbuilders.

In Cuba the embellishments of European baroque style were usually reserved for the main front door. Wooden window grilles provided decorative touches, while *vitrales*—stained-glass windows—flooded rooms with tinted light. Cuban cities evolved their own individual styles, such as the projecting turned-wood roof brackets and multicurved *arcos mixtilíneos* (doorway lintels) of Camagüey's houses; the gingerbread of Varadero's wooden beachfront dwellings; and the trompe-l'œil interior wall paintings of Sancti Spíritus Province. Provincial 18th-century houses were typically single story; in Havana, two-story homes prevailed. As Havana expanded, the wide avenues that led out of the city became lined with tall structures fronted by porticoed arcades.

Neoclassical Grandeur (19th Century)

The *ingenio,* or plantation complex, common in rural areas, featured a sugar refinery *(centrale),* a distillery, storehouses, a *barracón* (living quarters) for slaves, and the owner's house. Cuba's plantation economy generated huge wealth and spawned a 19th-century boom in civic and private construction. Havana's *criollo* middle classes and aristocracy built *quintas*—neoclassical villas set in suburban gardens—and grandiose mansions, such as the Palacio Aldama (1840–1884), on Havana's Parque de la Fraternidad. Many were in Palladian style, then popular in Europe. The 19th century also witnessed a return to a more restrained, neoclassical style in church building. Civic structures reflected the growing influence of European neoclassicism. Examples include El Templete, erected in 1828 in Havana's Plaza de Armas to celebrate the city's founding, and theaters such as the Teatro Sauto (1863) in Matanzas, and Teatro Terry (1889) in Cienfuegos. Corinthian columns and lavishly decorated interiors ruled the day; ornate ironwork *rejas* (bars) and railings replaced wooden grilles.

The Palacio de Valle in Cienfuegos was completed in 1917 in neo-Moorish style. Moroccan craftsmen added fretted interiors, stained-glass windows, and balustrades.

Modernist Influences (20th Century)

The end of colonialism ushered in a period of radical change as architects and planners worked to elevate Cuba to the artistic avant-garde in an outpouring of European-inspired architectural styles. Soaring neo-Gothic spires rose above the Havana skyline. Art nouveau, which evolved in Europe from 1905 to 1920, came to Cuba as highly decorative houses in Belgian, French, or, principally, Catalonian styles. In Havana, the style was fostered by Catalans who settled the city. The Palacio Cueto (1906), on the southeast corner of Plaza Vieja, evokes this Gaudiesque influence.

Pride of heritage found expression in Spanish revival as aristocratic Spanish communities vied with one another to build social clubs exhibiting regional influences. Examples are Havana's Centro Asturiano (1927) and Centro Gallego (1915)—now the Museo Nacional de Bellas Artes and the Gran Teatro Alicia Alonso, respectively.

Spanish revival heavily influenced the eclectic style. In Havana, a fine example is the Palacio Presidencial (1920) by architects Paul Belau and Carlos Maruri. Now the Museo de la Revolución, the building's facade is imbued with classical allusions and Spanish revival overtones as seen in its ornate towers and ground-floor portals. The nearby Residencia de Dionisio Velasco (1912), now the Spanish Embassy, and the Cuban Telephone Company (1927) by Leonardo Morales, at Dragones and Aguila, are other fine examples. Eclectic was particularly favored by provincial domestic architects. The streets of Pinar del Río city, for example, are lined with confections dripping with effusive stucco, such as the Palacio de Guasch.

The 1920s brought beaux arts, introduced by the École des Beaux-Arts in Paris. Pompeiian frescoes and Corinthian columns appeared, as did elaborate stained-glass appointments by Tiffany's. During this period, which dominated public buildings until the early 1940s, most Cuban cities erected grand civic edifices in lavish style. Havana gained a monumental look, thanks in no small part to the colossal, symmetrical Capitolio (1912–1929), the country's prime example of the beaux arts style. The neoclassical structure, which emulated the Capitol in Washington, D.C., had a counterpoint in beaux arts statues designed to convey Cuba's newfound confidence and pride. Notable, too, was the classically inspired University of Havana (1902–1940), with an 88-step entrance by French landscape designer Jean-Claude Nicolas Forestier.

By the late '20s, the Art Deco style—terracotta motifs, veneer panels, banded facades—became the rage. Most magnificent of Havana's Art Deco structures is the Edificio Bacardí (1930), by Esteban Rodríguez Castells, Rafael Fernández Ruenes, and José Menéndez, the most completely Art Deco commercial building in Cuba. Its granite exterior is accented by multihued terra-cotta and its interior by lavish decorative art. Cuba's Art Deco heyday coincided with that of the movie theater; one example

Glossary of Architectural Details

Alfarje: Wood-paneled ceiling made of main girders and smaller crossbeams.

Azulejo: Glazed terracotta tiles with a majolica design.

Cenefa: Band of decorative plasterwork on interior walls.

Mampara: Intricately decorated inner door/room divider.

Mediopunto: Wooden or stained-glass arch window designed to filter strong Cuban sunlight.

Portal: Massive doorway featuring elaborate baroque moldings.

Postigo: Smaller door contained within a larger *portal*.

Reja: Elegant, elongated grille protecting a window.

is the pink-pastel exterior of the Cine-Teatro Fausto (1938). Buildings evolved into a sinuous, more streamlined style with a fondness for curves and freestyle strokes. Art Deco designs represented "velocity in motion," as in Havana's National Bus Terminal (1948–1951) on Avenida Rancho Boyeros. The near-complete absence of decoration and sensual nonchalance that marked the style is superbly expressed in movie houses such as Havana's Cine América (1941), where the vaulted auditorium seems to grow from the tiers of curvilinear box seats. The '30s and '40s also saw Art Deco high-rise apartment buildings erected in Havana and Santiago de Cuba. The rounded balconies of the Solimar apartment block (1944), located at Calle Soledad #205 between San Lázaro and Animas in Centro Habana, are fine examples of the style.

The post–World War II boom years ushered in modern rationalism. Austere monumental buildings of fundamentalist proportions went up, such as the Edificio Focsa (1956) apartment complex and the National Library, National Theater, and government buildings of Plaza de la Revolución. Emerging to pioneer the new style was a new generation of gifted young architects, including Mario Romañach, Silverio Bosch, and most significantly Max Borges Recio, who evoked tropical sensuality in his Club Náutico swimming club (1957) and Tropicana nightclub (1951–1956). Each building was characterized by arcing shell vaults and expanses of glass. These architects spearheaded a movement of great importance as Hispanic influence was being swept away by the U.S. model.

Modernity was adopted by the middle classes and spread throughout Havana as new residential districts emerged. In fact, the greatest experimentation took place in the construction of private houses. During the boom years of the early 20th century, Cuba's burgeoning and discerning middle classes sought quality housing in the latest architectural vogues.

The evolution of a huge middle class in the decades between 1920 and 1959 saw lavish single-family residences in eclectic, neoclassical, and revivalist styles go up all over Havana. The most notable examples are in Nuevo Vedado and the upscale suburbs of Miramar and Country Club (today's Cubanacán). Thousands of such gems can be admired simply by walking the streets. On a par with anywhere else in the world, these stunning houses struggle to be acknowledged for their artistic worth as a collective asset of the nation's cultural heritage.

> **Art Deco designs represented "velocity in motion," as in Havana's National Bus Terminal (1948–1951) on Avenida Rancho Boyeros.**

The same time period saw the construction of a new breed of high-rise casino-hotels influenced by the architecture of Miami Beach. The Hotel Riviera's (1957) prodigal use of curves and broad cantilevered eaves aerodynamically complemented the days of finned Cadillacs, while the opening of the landmark Havana Hilton Hotel (1958)—now the Habana Libre—with Hilton's neon-lit name emblazoned across it, confirmed that Havana was indeed enjoying its place in the sun.

Postrevolutionary Architecture (Late 20th Century)

Many Cuban architects fled the island after 1959. The following decades witnessed an upheaval in how architecture was perceived and practiced. Suffering under the rigid yoke of Soviet-influenced post-modernist dictates, the urban landscape was hammered and sickled into disharmony with Cuba's past. Brutish

■ **The famous Art Deco Bacardí Building on Avenida de Bélgica in Havana.**

apartment blocks of prefabricated concrete—a cheap, practical solution to the severe housing shortage—were built by untrained *microbrigadistas* (volunteer construction teams), disfiguring cities throughout Cuba. A brief fling with new forms of artistic expression brought forth Havana's National Arts Schools complex (1961–1965), conceived to be the jewel in the crown of revolutionary architecture. The romance ended, however, when the architects' vision proved too experimental for communist tastes.

As the revolution progressed, resources for construction dwindled. Havana's Coppelia ice-cream parlor (1966) and Las Ruinas restaurant (1972), both of pressed concrete, are among the few postrevolutionary edifices with aesthetic appeal. Santiago de Cuba's post-modernist Hotel Santiago (1986)—a massive assemblage of geometric forms in primary colors—led the way for a new era of stylish, contemporary structures. These have been echoed in new resort projects now sprouting up across the nation. ■

CRUISING TO CUBA

Cuba has become one of the first ports of call for many cruisers. Located about 90 miles (145 km) from Florida, the island is easily accessed by a short flight from the U.S. mainland for trips embarking in Havana, and some cruises even depart from Miami. Loosened travel restrictions have led to a surge of new American visitors, and cruise lines are stepping in to meet the demand.

Cruises around Cuba now offer the first-time visitor a great way to get acquainted with the island.

New Regulations: Why Go Now?

As part of the landmark thaw in diplomatic relations, President Barack Obama eased travel restrictions from the U.S. to Cuba in 2015. Although ordinary sightseeing or beach-going tourism is still illegal, Americans can travel to Cuba if the purpose of their trip falls into one of 12 categories, including educational or cultural programs, professional research, journalistic or religious activities, or visits to close relatives. Visitors must follow a full-time itinerary of activities related to their category of travel.

With a little creativity, Americans can craft a Cuba trip that fits into at least one of the categories, and many organizations and tour operators now offer "people-to-people" trips that satisfy the educational and cultural requirements. With the island opening up to foreign influence, many feel that now is the time to go and experience Cuban culture before it becomes globalized.

Although all of this remains unchanged, fewer and fewer licenses authorizing travel to Cuba have been issued in recent years.

Why Cruise?

Cruises offer travelers the option to circle the entire island in a week—impossible by car—with the bonus of comfortable cabins with modern amenities. Ships are also likely to have some Wi-Fi, which is

INSIDER TIP:
For a land-based journey
that offers an in-depth look
at Cuban culture, see
nationalgeographicexpeditions.com.

—KAREN CARMICHAEL
National Geographic writer

virtually nonexistent throughout Cuba.

Travelers can visit diverse, out-of-the-way ports such as Antilla, Cayo Largo, and Isla de la Juventud. Cruises often offer more flexible excursion choices than land tours (which usually follow a strict itinerary), and can even be cheaper—especially as rates for the limited number of hotel rooms in Cuba have recently skyrocketed.

Cruising Options

Most itineraries include stops in Havana and the colonial cities of Cienfuegos and Santiago de Cuba, which both feature UNESCO World Heritage sites. Popular excursions include walking tours of historic city centers, music and dance performances, visiting artisan workshops, and exploring Guanahacabibes National Park.

Royal Caribbean International *(royal caribbean.com)* offers 6- to 8-night cruise-and-land itineraries, sailing on its 1,600-passenger *Empress of the Seas* and stopping at three Cuban ports (including an overnight stay in Havana) as well as Key West or Miami. Travelers can embark in either Havana or Miami. An appealing choice of authentic shore excursions

Cuba resounds with a rich musical heritage.

(cultural, historical, and culinary) is included.

Carnival *(carnival.com)* offers a variety of 3- to 5-day packages departing from Miami, Fort Lauderdale, or Tampa that include a stop or overnight stay in Havana, with a layover in the Bahamas or Key West.

BeBlue *(beblue.it)* offers 7-day catamaran cruises between Cienfuegos and Cayo Largo that can accommodate from 8 to 12 passengers. Some itineraries are for adults only. Cruises departing from Cienfuegos stop in Rancho Luna and Cayo Sigua or in Cayo Guano Del Est and Punta Sirena.

Longer (up to 15 days) luxury cruises are available on the *MSC Armonia (msc crociere.it)*. These cruises stop in Havana, Jamaica, the Cayman Islands, Mexico, and Belize, depending on the itinerary. They depart from and return to Miami and include a two-night stay in a Havana hotel.

Conserving Cuban Wildlife

Many cruises include a visit to Cayo Largo, a small island off Cuba's southern coast. While there, travelers can meet with scientists involved in coral reef protection and visit the Sea Turtle Breeding Center, where conservationists work to preserve the loggerhead, hawksbill, and green sea turtles that annually nest on the cay's white-sand beaches.

CULTURE

Cuba's vibrant cultural scene stirs the soul and the imagination. Operating in a virtual vacuum for almost six decades, Cuban artists have explored boundaries of self-expression with relatively little outside influence. Cuba's creative performers have set the world abuzz—and not simply with their infectious music; Cuba is also an international trendsetter in the fields of cinema, literature, and the fine arts.

Cuban culture has its historical roots in the fusing of Spanish and African cultures. The national identity and spirit in the arts draw inspiration from a passionate and turbulent history. Cuban culture reflects the centuries-long search for expression of a creative people confined in an authoritarian world. The literary scene,

"Interior of Juan Bautista Sagarra's House," by Manuel Vicens, in the Museo Bacardí, Santiago de Cuba, shows 19th-century upper-class life.

for example, has long found its inspiration in Cuba's continuum of struggle for greater freedom of expression. And Cuba's talented photographers, painters, and sculptors have produced a visceral and dynamic collection of work that provides a visual commentary on Cuban society's aspirations and social tensions.

The revolutionary government's shifting attitude toward the arts has both bolstered and stifled expression. In 1961 the government began to shoehorn artists, writers, and intellectuals into ideological conformity, expressed in Fidel Castro's maxim, "Within the Revolution, everything. Against the Revolution, nothing!"

Today the scene is more liberal, though politically unpalatable works remain subject to official censure. Nonetheless, the Ministry of Culture has been committed to sponsorship of the arts in every field. Budding talent is identified at an early age, and the most gifted students are boarded at special art schools. The Escuela Nacional de Arte, or National School of Art, founded in Havana in 1960, oversees 41 schools across the nation, covering the

> **The national identity and spirit in the arts draw inspiration from a passionate and turbulent history.**

spectrum of fine art, music, theater, ballet, and folkloric and modern dance. The most talented artists attend the Instituto Superior de Arte, Cuba's premier school, in Havana.

Havana has scores of art galleries and museums, and no township is without its museums, Casa de la Cultura, and/or Casa de la Trova. These act as incubators for Cuba's rich cultural heritage under state sponsorship. The Génesis Galerías de Arte exists to promote artists' work. In 1991 artists were granted copyright to their creations and, in a unique arrangement within Cuba, permitted to retain 85 percent of receipts on sales through a state agency.

Fine Arts

Early Cuban painters adopted the Spanish style. It was not until the 1800s that a national Cuban style arose. Led by José Nicolás de la Escalera (1734–1804) and Vincente Escobar (1762–1834), the movement was characterized by an idealized vision of black culture.

The opening in Havana in 1818 of the Escuela de Pintura y Escultura de San Alejandro—the School of Painting and Sculpture—under the direction of French artist Jean-Baptiste Vermay (1786–1833) lent new vigor to the arts community. It was responsible for infusing neoclassicism from the French and Italian schools into romantic landscapes, a direction pursued in the second half of the 19th century by artists such as Esteban Chartrand (1840–1884).

By the turn of the 20th century, Cuba came under the sway of Europe's avant-garde movement. Cuban painters adapted international styles to local themes, notably the

■ Center stage in this Camagüey painting are Che Guevara, Elián González, and José Martí.

emblematic figure of the *guajiro* (peasant farmer) favored by painter Carlos Enrique (1900–1957). Meanwhile, Victor Manuel García Valdés (1897–1969) helped inspire a cadre of Cuban artists who experimented in the style of post-Impressionists such as Gauguin.

The most acclaimed Cuban painter—Wifredo Lam (1902–1982)—was born to a Chinese father and an Afro-Cuban mother. He studied at Vermay's *academía*, then left for Spain in 1936. Lam moved among Havana, Marseille, and Paris. He was influenced by the surrealists—notably Picasso, who took the young Cuban under his wing. Lam immersed himself in African culture and adopted the theme of Afro-Cuban mysticism in his exploration of the magical-surrealist style. His works fetch as much as a million dollars each on today's world market. Many of his paintings hang in Havana's Fine Arts Museum. The influence of Picasso is also felt in the work of Amelia Peláez (1896–1968), known for her abstract ceramic murals. Her 65-yard-long (60 yards) mural "Cuban Fruit" adorns the facade of Havana's Hotel Habana Libre. Inside the hotel, a mosaic by acclaimed contemporary ceramist and sculptor Alfredo Sosabravo (1930–) graces the lobby.

What experts call a true renaissance of Cuban art occurred in the 1980s. The island's artists portrayed ideas in a way they never had. They began to participate in formal exhibits and compete artistically and commercially on an international level. The work of artists such as Los Carpinteros (the collaborative name of Cuban artists Alexandre Arrechea, Marco Castillo, and Dagoberto Rodríguez), Pedro Álvarez, Esterio Segura, and others today forms part of the collections of major museums and art institutions around the world.

Cuba's contemporary art community has evolved a profoundly experimental and easily recognizable genre, not least in a vast and sophisticated body of political poster art and street billboards. The influence of Afro-Cuban religious culture remains

dominant in the wildly imaginative, idiosyncratic works of artists such as Pedro Pablo Oliva (1949–), Nelson Domínguez (1947–), and Manuel Mendive (1944–). Themes of environmental concern and conservation infuse the work of Lester Campa (1968–), known for his evocations of *mogotes*. Themes of eroticism are another constant element of art from this sensual isle. Visitors are often shocked at the highly graphic sexual content on public view, as in the evocatively symbolic works of Chago Armada (1937–1995) and Aldo Soler (1948–). The past decade has also seen a profusion of works catering to the tourist market: Street scenes showing antique Yankee *cacharros* (cars) are a popular theme. Other artists parody the style of Salvador Dalí, whose tortured surrealism serves as a metaphor for their own vision of contemporary Cuba.

Work in sculpture and ceramic arts has been no less expressive. Roberto Fernández Martínez (1933–) finds inspiration in African myth for his totemic oversize sculptures. The exquisitely crafted figures of Rita Longa (1912–2000), Cuba's most famous contemporary sculptor, stand at the entrances to the Riviera Hotel and the Terminal de Omnibus; her ballet dancer has become the emblem of the Tropicana nightclub.

A recent outpouring of contemporary jewelry designs displays a quintessential Cuban passion for creativity—for example, in the use of antique silver cutlery entwining black coral. Nothing is thrown away in Cuba, where recycling is itself an art. And the recent tourism boom has sparked a revolution in crafts such as leatherwork, earthenware pottery, and wood carvings—predominantly of nubile women.

Literature

Injustice and social turmoil are the grist for great literature, and Cuba, with a long history of both, has produced dozens of authors and poets whose works are profound. The *criollo* patriot and national hero José Martí (1853–1895) is revered for his poetry and prose, which passionately decry injustice and espouse the cause of independence. Martí is among a long line of Cuban exiles who produced their best works abroad. Cirilo Villaverde (1812–1894), for example, wrote *Cecilia Valdés* while in exile. Alejo Carpentier (1904–1980) wrote many of his surrealistic novels in Venezuela during the Batista era. Moreover, Virgilio Piñera (1912–1979), author of *Cold Tales,* and Guillermo Cabrera Infante (1929–2005), known for his *Three Trapped Tigers,* set in seedy 1950s Havana, are two of many authors estranged from their country since the 1960s.

One who stayed on the island that inspired him was mulatto poet Nicolás Guillén (1902–1989), who lent lyrical and passionate beauty to his *poesía negra* (black poetry)

> " José Martí is among a long line of Cuban exiles who produced their best works abroad. "

EXPERIENCE: Learn to Dance Salsa

Cuba has taken the world by storm with its sizzling salsa. The red-hot music and dance form is a pervasive undercurrent of Cuban culture, and the staple of almost every nightclub. You'll even hear salsa played in restaurants, causing Cubans to get up and dance to its irrepressible rhythms. Don't be surprised to find yourself dragged onto the dance floor by a Cuban eager to show you the moves. To enjoy the experience fully, take a salsa dance lesson. Here's how:
• **The Instituto Superior de Arte** (Calle 120 #904 corner 9na & 23, Cubanacán, Havana, tel 7/208-0704, isa.cult.cu) offers

a range of intensive dance courses.
• **Plaza Cuba** (P.O. Box 3083, Berkeley, CA 94703, tel 510/848-0911, plazacuba.com) specializes in music and dance workshops, and arranges people-to-people travel to Cuba for U.S. citizens.
• **Real Cuba** (Box 2345, Swan River, MB R0L 1Z0, Canada, tel 306/205-0977, realcubaonline.com) arranges salsa dance classes in Santiago de Cuba.
• **Salón Turquino** (Calle L, bet. 23 & 25, Vedado, Havana, tel 7/834-6100), in the Hotel Habana Libre, offers salsa dance classes on Saturday afternoons.

by drawing on the anguish of slavery. After the revolution, Guillén, a committed socialist, helped found the PCC-controlled UNEAC—Cuban National Union of Writers and Artists—and became Cuba's poet laureate. Alejo Carpentier returned to Cuba in 1959 and remained loyal to the revolution—a prerequisite for being published in contemporary Cuba.

Most of the best writers of the 1960s and '70s fled, however, or were forced to leave. Avant-garde writer José Lezama Lima (1910–1976), author of *Paradiso*, was elevated to literary director of the National Cultural Council before running afoul of Fidel Castro. Similarly, Reinaldo Arenas (1943–1990) and Carlos Franquí (1921–2010), both Castroite guerrillas and brilliant essayists, were later forced into exile.

In the 1980s the works of many forbidden authors were resurrected, and the 1990s saw a new body of literature produced, including works by women. Historically, women have not been well represented in Cuban literature, with the exception of La Avellaneda in the 19th century, famed for her sensitive poems, and Dulce María Loynaz (1902–1997), former director of the Cuban Academy of Language. She was acclaimed as Cuba's finest recent poet.

Unfortunately, material shortages and ideological restrictions have conspired to keep undiscovered an entire generation of Cuban authors. Although Cuba is a country of avid readers (due in large part to the revolution's emphasis on literacy), bookstores and libraries are few and meagerly stocked, and books are recycled until they crumble to dust.

Film & Theater

Cubans are devout moviegoers. Since 1959, Cuba has produced high-caliber movies through the state-controlled film institute, Instituto Cubano de Arte e Industria del Cine. The institute has granted great latitude to intellectuals such as Tomás Gutiérrez Alea (1928–1996), a brilliant producer of populist satires on communist life. His *Fresa y chocolate (Strawberry and Chocolate,* 1994), which portrays the repression of homosexuals, was nominated for an Academy Award.

A respected international film festival takes place annually in Havana.

Theater came to Cuba from Spain during the colonial period. In the 19th century, Teatro Bufo, a vernacular tradition, evolved as Cuba's version of a national theatrical experience. It combined music, dances, and *guarachas* (country ballads), and introduced three popular characters representing Cuban identity: the Spaniard *(el Gallego),* the Mulata *(a* beautiful *mestiza),* and the Black Guy *(el Negrito).* The three characters would sing and interact with the audience, using sarcastic language and often introducing political issues.

In the 1950s, Vicente Revuelta (1929–2012), considered the father of Cuban theater, founded Teatro Estudio. Revuelta's space was a haven for many important actors and directors, including Roberto Blanco, Bertha Martínez, and Abelardo Estorino (1925–2013), the most important Cuban playwright of recent years.

A new generation of Cuban actors, directors, and critics entered the theater in the 1980s. Today there are about 60 professional theater groups and numerous community theater groups across the country. Two important theater festivals take place biennially in September.

Music & Dance

From traditional folk music to rumba and rap, music is Cuba's lifeblood. Since the revolution, the government has promoted folkloric over commercial music and in 1961 founded Conjunto Folklórico Nacional to revive appreciation for traditional music and dance. And Cubans have held fast to their roots: The seductive rhythms and soulful beats pulsing through the streets owe much to the fusion of Spanish and African sounds. Spaniards introduced rural folk music to the isle. Cuba quickly developed a distinctive *criollo* folk music—*guajiras,* or *trovas*—using a tradition of poetry in song. Singing of their sorrows and joys, entertainers improvised to the

Groups such as **Grupo Salsa Matriz infuse Cuba with sensual rhythms.**

musical accompaniment of a guitar, lute, gourd instruments, and *tres* (a Cuban guitar with three sets of double strings). *Guajiras* remain popular today and can be heard performed at Casas de la Trova nationwide. "Guantanamera"—the love song written in 1928 by José Fernández Díaz (1908–1979)—is the most famous. The *nueva trova* has evolved, as performed by Silvio Rodríguez (1946–), with cutting lyrics that focus on contemporary life.

This fusion of sweet folk music with African rhythms and instruments is the basis for modern Cuban popular music, starting with the *danzón,* which evolved from the French *contredanse* in the late 19th century and was popular through the 1920s. Danzón was the basis for *son,* which was popularized in the 1920s by radio and by groups such as the Trío Matamoros. Son derives from the mountains of Guantánamo Province, where it was played with guitar, claves, maracas, bongos, and the *marímbula*—a sound box of Bantu origin played by plucking metal tongues. The music typically uses *décima* verses—octosyllable ten-line stanzas. *Son changuí*—a fast, country version of son as performed by Orquestra Revé—remains popular in Guantánamo.

Beginning in the 1930s, touring U.S. jazz bands influenced Cuban music. The formation of brassy big band sets—*orquestras típicas*—opened the way for the evolution, in the '60s and '70s, of a Latin jazz, dance-oriented sound called salsa. Played by dance bands such as Los Van Van, salsa is a spirited, fast-paced, Cuban fusion of jazz and traditional rhythms. A recent variation is new-wave salsa, or *timba.* This potent blend of keyboards and percussive Afro-Cuban groove is performed by groups such as Bamboleo and ¡Cubanismo!

EXPERIENCE:
Where the Music's At

Havana throbs to sensual rhythms, from traditional *son* to sexy salsa. Here's how to make the most of a few days in the city:
• Sip *mojitos* on the patio bar of the **Hotel Nacional** *(Calles O & 21, Vedado, tel 7/836-3564)* as musicians serenade with son.
• Experience bolero singers crooning tunes at **Café Concierto Gato Tuerto** *(Calle O #14, bet. 17 & 19, Vedado, tel 7/838-2696).*
• Join the salsa fans at **Casa de la Música** *(tel 7/204-1524, promociones.egrem.co.cu)* and dance with abandon.
• Head to **Conjunto Folklórico Nacional** *(Calle 4 #103, Vedado, tel 7/830-3060)* for a vivacious Afro-Cuban rumba.

The success of the 1996 movie *Buena Vista Social Club,* which made international stars of several elderly, half-forgotten masters—Ibrahim Ferrer (1927–2005), Ruben González (1919–2003), Eliades Ochoa (1946–), and Compay Segundo (1907–2003)—has rekindled interest in *son.* Jazz, too, is enjoying a renaissance.

Cuba produces accomplished classical musicians. Composer-pianist Ernesto Lecuona (1895–1963) won acclaim in Europe, writing classical pieces, operas, and songs inspired by Afro-Cuban rhythms. Frank Fernández (1944–), the classical pianist, frequently performs with Cuba's Orquestra Simfónica Nacional. The Ballet Nacional de Cuba, founded in 1940 by Alicia Alonso, performs a yearlong season. The Camagüey Ballet and Ballet Folklórico de Oriente also regularly raise the curtain to ovations abroad.

In Cuba, as elsewhere, art moves much faster than government. Yet, today, even rock-and-roll bands enjoy government sponsorship. In April 2016 the Rolling Stones played a free concert in Havana, a sure sign, as Mick Jagger proclaimed to a vast crowd, that "finally, the times are changing." Hopefully, all of this will not be overcome by the cultural horror called reggaeton that is already invading the entire island. ■

The ethereal excitement of Cuba's history-steeped capital, with its colonial fortresses, cathedrals, and bars still haunted by Hemingway

HAVANA

■ Detail of a restored colonial building in Old Havana

HAVANA

Havana is a gritty, steamy, irresistible city fingering out around a flask-shaped bay. Much of this sprawling metropolis of 2.2 million people has suffered decades of neglect; its decaying buildings and potholed streets bespeak hard times. Yet its historic core is a fairy-tale jewel with intimate streets lined by baroque churches, palaces, castles, and mansions.

Havana is a city rich in history, resembling an abandoned stage set waiting for the curtain to rise. Founded on its current site in 1519, San Cristóbal de la Habana rapidly evolved to become Spain's key to the New World, brimful of architectural gems.

The Pearl of the Antilles remained a prosperous city into the mid-20th century, gradually acquiring handsome parks, leafy boulevards, Belle Époque mansions, streamlined Art Deco blocks, modernist villas, grandiose monuments, and lavish structures that boasted of Havana's wealth and the showy exuberance and sophistication of Cuban culture. Havana's relatively lax morals drew Yankees, tempted by the lures of casinos, *mojitos* (rum cocktails), and more sinful indulgence: live sex shows, cocaine parlors, and other esoteric frontiers of the libertine Latin mystique.

The postrevolutionary era has been hard on Havana. Neglected for six long, hard decades, the once proud city sank into decline. Monstrous Soviet-style apartment blocks replaced the shantytowns of prerevolutionary Cuba with

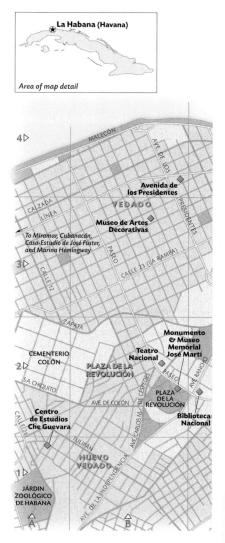

La Habana (Havana)

Area of map detail

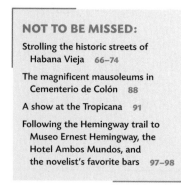

NOT TO BE MISSED:

Strolling the historic streets of
Habana Vieja   66–74

The magnificent mausoleums in
Cementerio de Colón   88

A show at the Tropicana   91

Following the Hemingway trail to
Museo Ernest Hemingway, the
Hotel Ambos Mundos, and
the novelist's favorite bars   97–98

their own form of blight. Though the neglect and dishevelment invoke a profound melancholy, the city has avoided the kind of population onslaught—and shantytowns—that have deluged other cities in developing countries. Greater Havana, comprising 15 *municipios,* or municipalities, retains an amalgam of colonial-era villages, engulfed by the greater metropolis.

The city's colonial core—Habana Vieja (Old Havana)—was declared a UNESCO World Heritage site in 1982. Bit by bit, the government is restoring its venerable structures, a rich blend of architecture dating back 400 years.

Other parts of Havana are on the upswing as tourism blooms in the post-Soviet era. Ritzy

hotels and restaurants have sprouted. Gleaming Mercedes taxis and privately owned Audis now streak past sock hop–era jalopies, and Hungarian buses belching fumes have been replaced with modern air-conditioned buses from China.

Havana's most interesting sites concentrate around the four main plazas of Old Havana. The old city deserves a three-day minimum, and Vedado, Miramar, and outlying districts a day each.

Descriptive exhibits at museums are mostly in Spanish, but English-speaking guides are widely available, and permission to photograph usually costs extra. Petty theft is still common despite a heavy police presence but the *jineterismo* phenomenon (prostitution) has diminished. ■

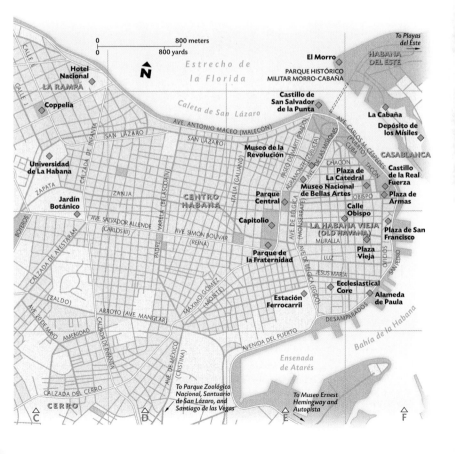

HABANA VIEJA

Replete with culture and history, Old Havana is a 350-acre (142 ha) trove of intriguing attractions guaranteed to enthrall. Its four main squares are graced by palaces, castles, and mansions, many now turned into restaurants, boutique hotels, galleries, and eclectic museums. Much of Old Havana—crammed with 74,000 people—is a lived-in museum: decrepit, yes, and lacking its fortified walls but retaining the earthy, timeworn appeal of life lived in the shadows of Cuba's past.

Like the *dramatis personae* of a Greek play, Havana wears many faces. A performance in Plaza de Armas pays tribute to the government's accomplishments in the arts.

In 1977, Habana Vieja was declared a national monument, and the following year a major restoration project was announced. The need was urgent: Most of Old Havana's 3,157 structures had deteriorated to a point of dilapidation. Three and a half decades on, having been named a UNESCO World Heritage site in 1982, the remarkable effort has lent new vigor to the world's most authentic colonial collection.

The flavor of bygone days is heady along narrow streets, lined with beautiful mansions adorned with graceful *portales* setting off their exquisite facades. The transformation of the colonial center into a remarkable living-history museum has been overseen by city historian Eusebio Leal Spengler, one of the most important figures in postrevolutionary Cuba. Under Spengler's leadershop, historic houses, once abandoned, have been restored and preserved as hotels, cultural centers, nightclubs, and restaurants. The problems of the 21st century are soon forgotten as you stroll the plazas and cobblestoned streets bathed in incandescent light, past buildings whose bright pastels—lemon yellow, guava green, tangerine, like tropical fruits—transport you back 400 years.

A convenient and logical place to start your tour of Old Havana is **Plaza de Armas.** For those who don't want to miss anything important, the point of reference is the **San Cristóbal Agency.**

Plaza de Armas

First laid out in 1519 as a parade ground, Havana's oldest plaza became the center of city life and the seat of government throughout 383 years of Spanish tenure. A small park lies at its heart, framed by tall palms that cast cooling shadows over a statue of the 19th-century revolutionary leader Carlos Manuel de Céspedes. Important 18th-century buildings of coral limestone surround the plaza. Most notable is the **Palacio de los Capitanes Generales**, on the west side, from where the *capitanes generales* (governors) enforced Spanish rule. Fronted by a wide loggia, the three-story structure wraps around a central courtyard. Marble stairs lead up to rooms housing the **Museo**

de la Ciudad (Museum of the City). Its many treasures include the **Sala de los Espejos** (Hall of Mirrors), where the transfer of power from Spain to the U.S. took place on January 1, 1899.

Clockwise around the plaza, the 1772 **Palacio del Segundo Cabo** (Palace of the Second Lieutenant; *tel 7/801-7176, segundocabo.ohc.cu*), in Moorish-inspired Cuban baroque style, was originally built as a post office. Later it housed the vice governor, became the Senate building, and after a restoration, reopened as a cultural space dedicated to Cuban-European relations.

The plaza opens northeast to a pocket-size castle, **Castillo de la Real Fuerza.** The second oldest fortress in the Americas, this was

Shutterbug Etiquette

Cubans adore being photographed and most will happily pose for a snap. However, it is good etiquette to ask permission before photographing individuals.

completed in 1577. Gleaming suits of armor in the foyer beckon you to the **Museo de Navegación** *(tel 7/861-5010, closed Mon., $),* displaying naval uniforms, model ships, armaments, and gold and silver treasures. The weather vane atop the northwest watchtower is a copy of La Giraldilla de la Habana, cast in honor of Isabel de Bobadilla, who served as Cuba's only female governor.

El Templete *($, including guide)* a tiny Greco-Roman–style temple dating from 1828, sits adjacent,

Plaza de Armas
🗺 65 F3 & 71

Agencia de Viajes San Cristóbal
✉ O'Reilly #102 at Tacón
☎ 7/801-7420
viajessancristobal.cu

Museo de la Ciudad
✉ Palacio de los Capitanes Generales, Calle Tacón #1, bet. Obispo & O'Reilly
☎ 7/861-5779
💲 $

Castillo de la Real Fuerza
🗺 65 F3 & 71
✉ Calle O'Reilly #2
☎ 7/861-5010
🕐 Closed Mon.
💲 $

habananuestra.cu

Museo Nacional de Historia Natural

🗺 71

✉ Calle Obispo #61, bet. Oficios & Baratillo

☎ 7/863-9370

🕐 Closed Mon.

💲 $

mnhnc.inf.cu

marking the site of the first Mass held in the then tiny hamlet, in 1519. Votive offerings placed by Santería believers adorn the base of a sacred ceiba tree. The mansion to the south is the former Casa del Conde de Santovenia, today the **Hotel Santa Isabel**.

Located on the south side of the plaza, the informative **Museo Nacional de Historia Natural** displays Cuban flora and fauna in re-creations of their natural habitats.

Caballero de París

The life-size bronze statue that stands outside the entrance to the Iglesia de San Francisco de Asís is made in the likeness of José María López Lledín (1899–1985), a tramp who famously wandered the streets of Havana. The slightly mad but harmless vagabond was known throughout the city, and well liked. He eventually died in a mental hospital and is buried inside the church. Many Cubans touch the statue's long, straggly beard for good luck.

Plaza de la Catedral

The most intimate (and the youngest) of Old Havana's main squares, this compact plaza was originally a swamp. The area was drained and laid out in the late 17th century. From lowly beginnings arose aristocratic mansions and the baroque splendor of the Havana cathedral. Today, troubadours roam the square while *mulattas* in traditional costume add color to

the sense of a *temps perdu*.

Dominating the plaza is **Catedral San Cristóbal** *(tel 7/862-4000)*, built between 1748 and 1777. Dedicated to Columbus, the baroque cathedral once contained a casket thought to hold the explorer's bones; they were returned to Spain in 1899.

The 1720 **Casa del Conde de Casa Bayona**, on the plaza's south side, exemplifies the elegant symmetry of period architecture, with an inner patio surrounded by Tuscan pilasters. Today it holds the **Museo de Arte Colonial** *(tel 7/862-6440, $)*.

On the square's east side stand the **Palacio del Marqués de Arcos** and the **Casa del Conde de Casa Lombillo**, both dating from 1740. The latter became Havana's first post office; you can still insert letters into the mouth of a grotesque face in the wall. On the west side, the **Casa de los Marqueses de Aguas Claras** (1751–1775) is now a restaurant.

The **Centro de Arte Contemporáneo Wifredo Lam** *(tel 7/861-3419, closed Sun.)*, on the northwest side, honors famous artist Wifredo Lam (1902–1982) and exhibits Cuba's contemporary artists. Nearby, at Calle Empedrado #207, is **La Bodeguita del Medio**, where Errol Flynn and Ernest Hemingway quaffed *mojitos*. Directly west, the 1809 **Casa de la Condesa de la Reunión**, the setting for novelist Alejo Carpentier's *The Enlightenment*, now houses the **Fundación Alejo Carpentier** *(tel 7/861-3667 closed Sat. & Sun.)*.

Catedral San Cristóbal on Plaza de La Catedral is dedicated to Christopher Columbus.

Plaza de San Francisco

This open plaza—at Calle Oficios and the foot of Calle Amargura—has changed little since galleons creaked at anchor, holds bulging with treasure bound for Spain. The harbor is hidden by the Aduana, or customs building, erected in 1914 and recently converted, in part, into the new Terminal Sierra Maestra, where cruise ships dock. Horse-drawn carriages still clatter upon relaid cobbles, and the houses of former merchants still gleam like confections in stone.

Commanding the plaza's north side is the five-story **La Lonja del Comercio de La Habana** (Goods Exchange; *tel 7/866-9628*), built in 1909 in a neoclassically inspired eclectic style with a dome topped by a bronze figure of Mercury. Refitted in contemporary vogue, it still functions as a mercantile venue for foreign corporations. To its rear, the **Jardín Diana de Gales** (*Baratillo, cnr Carpinetti*) is a garden honoring Princess Diana.

The **Fuente de los Leones** (Fountain of the Lions), erected in 1836, graces the square on its south side, drawing pigeons and children to its splashing waters. The *fuente* stands in delicate counterpoint to the baroque **Iglesia y Monasterio de San Francisco de Asís**, dating from 1719–1738, which looms behind. It was here that Processions of the Cross once set out each Lenten Friday on a pilgrimage to Plaza del Cristo. The church, built at the end of the 16th century and modified in the 18th century, is topped by a 120-foot-high (36 m) bell tower. The gold-gilt cedar altar was removed after the English invasion of 1762; when a Protestant service was held here, Catholics considered the church defiled and services ceased. Today it hosts classical concerts.

A portion of the crypt is visible beneath glass (people were buried here according to rank; nobles near the altar, baptized black slaves near the door). Note the *trompe* *(continued on p. 73)*

Plaza de San Francisco
🗺 65 F2 & 71

Iglesia y Monasterio de San Francisco de Asís
🗺 71
✉ Calle Oficios, bet. Amargura & Teniente Rey
☎ 7/862-9683
💲 $

WALK THE HEART OF HABANA VIEJA

This circuit follows cobbled streets that echo with history and trace a path through the heart of Havana—a restored seven-by-two-block core with the city's main squares at each quadrant. The walk passes the finest of Old Havana's architectural gems, many now restored. The walk is best done between 8 a.m. and noon to avoid the afternoon heat.

Havana's lively art scene is displayed at Calle Tacón's artisans market.

Start at the southwest corner of **Plaza de Armas ❶** (see pp. 67–68), where Calle Obispo is lined by early colonial houses with exquisite touches: wood balconies, *mediopuntos*, and mahogany carriage doors. The bookstore at Calle Obispo #119 occupies Havana's oldest house, dating from 1598. Next door, the **Museo de la Orfebrería** *(Calle Obispo #113, closed Mon., $)* displays silverwork. After a mineral water at **Casa del Agua "La Tinaja"** *(Calle Obispo #11)*, turn south onto Calle Oficios.

On your right is a fine Moorish inspiration, the **Casa de los Árabes ❷** *(Calle Oficios #16, tel 7/861-5868, closed Mon.)*, celebrating Arab culture in Cuba, with carved saddles, rugs, and other Middle Eastern exhibits. Opposite, the **Museo del Automóvil** *(Calle Oficios #13, tel 7/863-9942, closed Mon., $)* displays vintage autos. Continue south to Calle Obrapía. Here,

NOT TO BE MISSED:

Museo de Ron • Casa de África
• Museo Palacio de Gobierno
• Museo y Farmacia Taquechel

the **Hostal Valencia** *(tel 7/867-1037)*, a classic Spanish-style posada, is worth a stop.

Continuing south on Oficios, you enter **Plaza de San Francisco ❸** (see pp. 69, 73). The block facing the **Iglesia y Monasterio de San Francisco de Asís** contains some of Old Havana's prettiest houses, including the **Galería Carmen Montilla Tinoco** *(Calle Oficios #162, tel 7/866-8786)*. Behind its soft-pink-and-green facade, the cutaway rear wall opens to a sculpture garden highlighted by a 3-D mural by

Alfredo Sosabravo. Follow Oficios two blocks to Calle Muralla and the **Museo Palacio de Gobierno** *(Calle Oficios #211, tel 7/863-4358, closed Mon., $)*, with a neoclassical lobby lit through stunning stained-glass windows. Completed in 1895, it housed the independence-era Chamber of Representatives and, later, the Ministry of Education, then the Municipal Assembly. It now exhibits items related to its history, from uniforms, coins, and original documents to period furniture. Opposite, the **Tienda Museo Reloj** *(tel 7/864-9515)* exhibits antique clocks. Occupying the space between the convent and the Antigua Cámara is an antique presidential railway carriage—the **Coche Presidencial Mambí** *(Callejón de Churruca, $)*.

Kitty-corner is the **Casa Alejandro Von Humboldt** *(Calle Oficios #254, bet. Sol & Muralla, tel 7/863-9850, closed Mon.)*, where displays honor the German explorer who in the early 1800s catalogued the island's flora and fauna. The park opposite features his bust and is backed by the **Casa del Conde de la Mortera**,

> 🅰 See also area map pp. 64–65
> ▶ Plaza de Armas
> 🕓 2 hours
> ⟷ 1.5 miles (2.4 km)
> ▶ Plaza de Armas

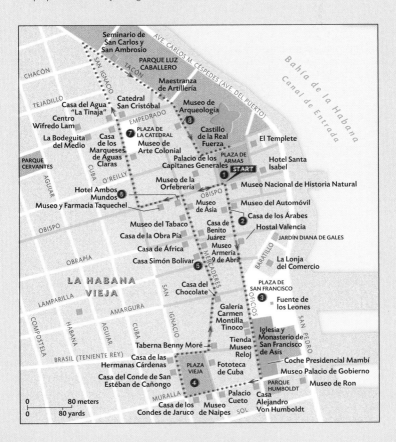

■ **Troubadours serenade diners at La Bodeguita del Medio, off Plaza de La Catedral.**

now housing the **Museo de Ron** *(Museum of Rum; Calle San Pedro #262, bet. Muralla & Sol, tel 7/861-8051, $),* where guided tours explain the stages of rum production. Exhibits include a 1:22.5-scale model of a 1930s rum factory.

Retrace Muralla west to **Plaza Vieja ❹** (see p. 73). Exit north along Calle Mercaderes and stop in at **Casa del Chocolate** *(cnr Calle Amargura, tel 7/866-4431),* selling chocolates made on-site. Cross Calle Lamparilla and stop at **Casa Simón Bolívar ❺** *(Calle Mercaderes #156, tel 7/861-3988, closed Mon.),* dedicated to Venezuelan culture. Note the statue to Bolívar (1783–1830), the great South American liberator, in the *plazuela* (little plaza) opposite. Just north, the **Museo Armería 9 de Abril** *(Calle Mercaderes #157, tel 7/861-8080, closed Sun., $)* is an old armory displaying revolutionary-era small arms. At Obrapía, the **Casa de Benito Juárez** *(Calle Mercaderes #116, tel 7/861-8186, closed Mon.)* celebrates Mexican culture with fine exhibits that include Aztec jewelry.

Fifty yards (46 m) west, on Obrapía, is the lemon-and-cream **Casa de la Obra Pía** *(Calle Obrapía #158, tel 7/861-3097, closed Mon.),* the 16th-century home of a charitable nobleman whose pious acts lent the street its name. Entering through a portal brought from Cádiz in

1686, you stand within a courtyard framed by arched galleries that open to rooms displaying contemporary art and exhibits dedicated to the Swiss-born Cuban author Alejo Carpentier and housing a sewing and embroidery cooperative. **Casa de África** *(Calle Obrapía #157, tel 7/861-5798, closed Mon., $),* opposite, houses artifacts honoring African culture.

Return to Mercaderes and turn left. This block features the **Museo del Tabaco** *(Calle Mercaderes #120, tel 7/861-5795, closed Mon.),* above the Casa del Tabaco on your left. Also, visit the **Museo Casa de Ásia** *(Calle Mercaderes #111, tel 7/863-9740, closed Mon., $)* for mother-of-pearl furniture, weaponry, kimonos, and other delights.

Nearby, at the corner of Calle Obispo, enter the **Hotel Ambos Mundos ❻** *(tel 7/860-9530).* Take the elevator to the fifth floor, where Room 511 *(closed Sun.)* is preserved as it was when Hemingway lodged here in the 1930s and wrote *For Whom the Bell Tolls.* Exit and follow Obispo west 50 yards (46 m) to the **Museo y Farmacia Taquechel** *(Calle Obispo #155, tel 7/862-9286),* an apothecary founded in 1898, filled with jars of potions and herbs.

Turn right on Calle San Ignacio and step north two blocks to **Plaza de La Catedral ❼** (see p. 68). Exit north along San Ignacio to Calle Tacón. Forming Old Havana's boundary, this street runs inside what remains of Havana's fortified wall. Turning right on Tacón, note the **Maestranza de Artillería**, which contains a section of the wall and vestiges of a colonial artillery manufacturer. The wall fronts the former **Seminario de San Carlos y San Ambrosio**, established in 1774 and which features a striking baroque facade.

To return to Plaza de Armas, turn right and follow Tacón one block. En route, stop by the **Museo de Arqueología ❽** *(Calle Tacón #12, tel 7/861-4469, closed Mon., $),* showing pre-Columbian exhibits, plus 18th-century wall murals depicting life of the times.

l'œil that extends the perspective of the nave. The nave opens to the cloisters of the convent, now exhibiting religious treasures in the **Museo de Arte Sacro.** The life-size bronze outside the convent is that of the **Caballero de París,** a stylish Havana tramp of the 1950s. (See sidebar p. 68.)

INSIDER TIP:

In Plaza Vieja, visit the Cámara Oscura ($), a device that projects a 360-degree view of Havana from the Edificio Gómez Villa.

—NEIL SHEA
National Geographic writer

Plaza Vieja

Plaza Vieja—Old Square—was originally the venue for Havana's slave market and fiestas. Until two decades ago, the capacious square was in a sorry state. Today, relaid with cobbles, it shines after a significant renovation. At its heart is a marble fountain, a copy of the one originally designed by the Italian artist Giorgio Massari. It is framed on all sides by gracious colonial homes fronted at their bases by broad loggias. The **Casa de los Condes de Jaruco** *(Calle Muralla #107, closed Sat. afternoon–Sun.),* on the south side, boasts impressive wrought-iron balconies and stained-glass *mediopuntos.* Commissioned in 1832, it now hosts commercial art galleries. Just east, the **Museo de Naipes** displays a collection of

playing cards. Notable on the plaza's southwest corner, the **Casa del Marqués de Casa Torres** today houses a splendid brewpub—**Factoria Plaza Vieja**, *(Calle San Ignacio #368 at Muralla, tel 7/866-4453)*—with copper stills open to view; and on the northwest corner, the neoclassical **Casa de las Hermanas Cárdenas,** with superb baroque woodwork. The latter houses the **Centro de Desarrollo de Artes Visuales** *(Calle San Ignacio #352 at Teniente Rey, tel 7/862-2611, closed Mon.);* beyond its towering doors, a sculpture by Alfredo Sosabravo graces the inner patio.

■ **Diners relax in Plaza Vieja.**

The **Casa de Juan Rico de Mata** was built in 1752 on the plaza's east side, and today hosts photographic exhibitions in the **Fototeca de Cuba** *(Calle Mercaderes #307, tel 7/862-2530).* Next door, the **Planetario de la Habana** features interactive exhibits about the universe. Soaring above the plaza to the southeast is the art nouveau

Plaza Vieja
🅼 65 F2 & 71

Museo de Naipes
🅼 71
✉ Calle Muralla #101
☎ 7/860-1534
🕒 Closed Mon.
💲 By donation

Planetario de la Habana
✉ Calle Mercaderes #309
☎ 7/864-9544
🕒 Closed Mon.–Tues.
💲 $

begun in 1712 and later served as a hospice and government ministry.

Cuba's first convent, **Iglesia y Convento de Santa Clara**, was begun in 1638. Its **Salon Plenario** offers concerts beneath a Moorish-style ceiling. Originally a hermitage for freed slaves, the 1638 **Iglesia Parroquial del Espíritu Santo** (Calles Cuba & Acosta) is Havana's oldest church. The 1867 **Iglesia y Convento de Nuestra Señora de la Merced** (Calle Cuba at Merced) draws devotees of Santería, notably every September 24.

Egido follows the course of the old city walls, razed in 1863. Only fragments remain today, most notably the **Puerta de la Tenaza**, at Egido and Desam-

■ Iglesia de San Francisco de Paula, on Desamparados.

Ecclesiastical Core

🅰 65 E2

Iglesia y Convento de Santa Clara

✉ Calle Cuba #610, bet. Sol & Luz
☎ 7/861-3335
🕐 Closed Sat.–Sun.
💲 $

Centro Cultural Almacenes de San José

✉ Desamparados & San Ignacio
☎ 7/864-7793

Palacio Cuerto, slated to reopen as the Palacio Vienna Hotel.

Ecclesiastical Core

Often overlooked by visitors, the southern half of Old Havana—bounded south and east by Avenida San Pedro (Desamparados) and, to the west, by Avenida de Bélgica (Egido)—abounds in beautiful churches and convents dating from the 1700s.

The area is a residential quarter of sagging walls and makeshift scaffolding. Community-oriented restoration is under way.

One block east of Egido, between Calles Lamparilla and Brasil, is quaint **Plaza del Cristo**, anchored by the **Iglesia del Santo Cristo del Buen Viaje**. This Franciscan hermitage dates from 1640 (it was reconstructed in 1932).

A short stroll away, on Calle Compostela between Luz and Acosta, the **Iglesia y Convento de Nuestra Señora de Belén** was

INSIDER TIP:

Most churches in Havana close between noon and 3 p.m. Check ahead to confirm hours of worship.

—LARRY PORGES
National Geographic Books author

parados, the sole city gate still standing. To its northwest rises the **Estación Central de Ferrocarriles**, the Spanish Revival railway station.

Desamparados curls east from Puerta de la Tenaza, passing the harborfront **Centro Cultural Almancenes de San José**—Havana's main craft market. It's fronted by old steam trains and the quaint **Iglesia de San Francisco de Paula** (tel 7/860-4210), now a chamber music venue. ■

PARQUE CENTRAL & NEARBY

Bustling and pivotally placed Parque Central commands the threshold to Old Havana, accessed via Calle Obispo. A social node for Cubans and a tourist rendezvous, the park is surrounded by important buildings in baroque, Art Deco, and art nouveau styles, including several hotels, major museums, theaters, cigar factories, and important termini for taxis and buses.

Parque Central

Royal palms rise over this two-block-long park, hemmed by Paseo de Martí and Calle Agramonte, and by Calles Neptuno and San Martín. At its heart is a Carrara marble statue of José Martí. Baseball fans gather at the *esquina caliente* (hot corner) for heated discussion.

Four historic hotels stand over the park. Wedged into the northeast corner is the **Hotel Plaza** *(Calle Agramonte #267, tel 7/860-8583)*, in eclectic style, with an exquisite skylight and a triangular lobby supported by Corinthian columns. The **Hotel Iberostar Parque Central** *(Calle*

Neptuno, bet. Agramonte & Prado, tel 7/860-6627) dominates the park's north side; though refitted in contemporary guise, elements of its elegant facade remain. The rooftop bar offers fine views over the square. On the west side, the **Hotel Inglaterra** *(Paseo de Martí #416, tel 7/860-8593)* boasts a lobby flush with patterned azulejos (glazed ceramic tiles). The **Hotel Telegrafo** *(Paseo del Prado #408 at Neptuno, tel 7/861-1010)*, on the northwest corner, recalls yesteryear splendor. On the plaza's east side the **Edificio Manzana de Gómez**, built in 1910 and pitted by bullet holes from the 1934 Machado revolution, has been

Parque Central

▲ 65 E3

Visitor Information

✉ Calle Obispo, bet. Villegas & San Ignacio

☎ 7/863-3333

▪ Leafy Parque Central, with its centerpiece statue honoring José Martí, is a popular gathering place.

Gran Teatro de La Habana Alicia Alonso

- ✉ Paseo de Martí #458 at San Rafael
- ☎ 7/861-7391
- 🕐 Performances held Fri.–Sun.
- 💲 $$

Museo Nacional de Bellas Artes

- 🗺 65 E3
- ✉ Calle Rafael, bet. Agramonte & Monserrate
- ☎ 7/862-0140
- 🕐 Closed Mon.
- 💲 $$

bellasartes.co.cu

Castillo de San Salvador de la Punta

- 🗺 65 E3
- ✉ Ave. Carlos M. de Céspedes, at Prado
- ☎ 7/860-3196
- 🕐 Closed Mon.–Tues.
- 💲 $

converted into the luxurious **Gran Hotel Manzana Kempinski** (*tel 7/86-99100*).

Havana's most exorbitant neo-baroque structure, the adjacent **Gran Teatro de La Habana Alicia Alonso**, resembles a confection in stone. At each corner, four towers are tipped by angels. Initiated in 1907 as the Centro Gallego (a Gala-tian social club), it evolved into an illustrious theater that drew lumi-naries of world opera. The National Ballet and Opera still perform here; rehearsals are open to view.

The grand structure dominat-ing the park's east side is the inter-national division of the **Museo Nacional de Bellas Artes** (Fine Arts Museum). It occupies the **Centro Asturiano**, built in 1927 with a Renaissance facade and a staircase suffused in light from a stained-glass window depicting Columbus's discovery of the New World. Exhibits span the globe and include works by European masters.

Prado (Paseo de Martí)

Spilling north from the park's northwest corner, this tree-lined boulevard slopes down to the mouth of the harbor channel. When laid out between 1772 and 1852, the Alameda de Isabel II (renamed the Prado in 1904) ran outside the old city walls, with an elevated promenade dividing two one-way causeways. It was adopted by the city's nobility, who built their mansions, dance halls, and fencing schools in palatial style. French landscape designer Jean-Claude Nicolas Forestier gave the Prado its current look in 1929, with

bronze lions and marble benches.

Among the baroque gems is the **Palacio de los Matrimonios** (Pal-ace of Civil Marriages; *Prado #306, tel 7/866-0661*), in the old Casino Español. Built in 1914 in Span-ish Renaissance style, its recently restored opulent interior—a mini-Versailles dripping with frescoed stucco—casts its spell over lovers who come to get hitched.

INSIDER TIP:

Be observant in every Cuban home you visit. From the humblest rural abode to Havana's classiest residence you'll find cherished collections of porcelain from Europe and Asia.

—TOM MILLER
National Geographic author

The Prado also boasts fine examples of Moorish style, notably at the 1908 **Hotel Sevilla** (*Calle Trocadero #55, tel 7/860-8560*). The upper-story restaurant-bar, sumptuously neo-classical, is a good spot to settle over a Mary Pickford cocktail (rum, pineapple, grenadine), invented here. The Art Deco style is represented by the **Cine-Teatro Fausto**, at the corner of Calle Colón.

Parque de los Mártires, at the base of the Prado, honors Cubans who have died for the cause of independence. Among them was José Martí, who between 1869 and 1870 was jailed here in the former Prado prison. The park features the **Monumento a los Estudiantes de Medicina**, a small temple honoring eight medical students executed here in 1871, falsely accused of desecrating the tomb of a Spanish loyalist. Across Avenida Carlos M. de Céspedes, the **Castillo de San Salvador de la Punta**, built between 1589 and 1600, commands the stub of land facing **El Morro castle** (see pp. 82–83). In colonial days, a chain was stretched between the two castles each evening to seal the harbor mouth.

Along Agramonte & Monserrate

Calle Agramonte (locally called Zulueta), a block east of the Prado, slopes northeast from Parque Central toward the harbor channel. Avenida de Bélgica (**Calle Monserrate**) runs parallel to Agramonte to the east. Between the two lies **Plaza 13 de Marzo**, merging northward into **Parque de los Enamorados.** Here a bronze monument honors Gen. Máximo Gómez, the Dominican-born commander of the liberation army during Cuba's wars of independence. The art nouveau building at the base of Agramonte is the former **Palacio Velasco**, built in 1912. Today it houses the Spanish Embassy.

Museo de la Revolución

Monserrate follows the course of the old city wall. A remnant watchtower—**Baluarte del Ángel**—still stands to the south side of Plaza 13 de Marzo. Facing it is a Soviet tank supposedly

■ A baroque balcony along the Prado

commanded by Fidel Castro at the Bay of Pigs. Together they guard the Museo de la Revolución, housed in the former Presidential Palace, initiated in 1920 with interior decor by the firm of Louis Comfort Tiffany. In 1957 the palace was the site of an unsuccessful attempt to overthrow General Batista; look for the bullet holes in the foyer.

Sumptuous salons today glorify the revolution that finally toppled Batista, part of a chronology of Cuba's political development, from slave uprisings to joint space missions with the former Soviet Union. Descriptions

Museo de la Revolución

🅰 65 E3

✉ Calle Refugio #1, bet. Agramonte & Monserrate

☎ 7/862-2463

💲 $$

www.cnpc.cult.cu/institucion/436

The interior dome is made of colorful ceramic tiles.

The Museo de la Revolución occupies the former Presidential Palace, built in 1913–1920 by Paul Belau and Carlos Maruri. Today the luxurious mansion houses exhibits related to the revolution.

Enormous mirrors *(espejos)* cover the walls of the Salón de los Espejos, the former reception hall of the Presidential Palace.

Entrance

Main Staircase

are in Spanish and English, but the gory photos, submachine guns, and bloodstained shirts speak volumes. In the grounds to the rear, a glass encasement— **Memorial *Granma***—enshrines the vessel that brought Fidel Castro, Che Guevara, and 80 other rebels from Mexico to launch the revolution. They landed on December 2, 1956, on the southern coast of

Oriente Province, and so began the "Liberation War."

José Martí (for biography, see sidebar p. 188) was baptized on February 12, 1853, in the **Iglesia del Santo Ángel Custodio** *(Calle Compostela #2 at Cuarteles),* to the east of the museum. This gleaming white Gothic church, built in 1846 after a hurricane, features prominently in *Cecilia Valdés,* Cirilo Villaverde's 19th-century novel.

Museo de la Revolución

Memorial *Granma* enshrines the leaky boat in which Castro and 80 other revolutionaries in 1956 returned to Cuba from exile in Mexico.

Around Parque Central

The **Museo Nacional de Bellas Artes**—Museo de Arte Cubano (Fine Arts Museum; Cuban section) is housed in a striking, three-story 1955 modernist structure. This not-to-be-missed museum displays a magnificent collection of Cuban paintings dating back to the early colonial period, arrayed chronologically from the top story down. The full spectrum of artworks includes pieces by Armando Menocal (1863-1942) and Wilfredo Lam (1902-1982) plus a panoply of post-revolutionary artists.

Along **Monserrate** rises the **Edificio Bacardí**. This Art Deco masterpiece, erected in 1929 of coral limestone and pink granite, boasts terra-cotta tilework and a pyramidal roof topped by the Bacardí bat.

A block south is **El Floridita** bar and restaurant *(Monserrate at Calle Obispo, tel 7/867-1300)*. The 1930s Art Deco bar was a favorite of Hemingway's; he sipped his sugarless daiquiri here and now his bronze image props up the bar. ∎

Museo Nacional de Bellas Artes

🗺 65 E3

✉ Calle Trocadero, bet. Agramonte & Monserrate

☎ 7/862-0140

🕐 Closed Mon.

💲 $$

bellasartes.co.cu

HABANA GOLD

A fat cigar is a defining image of Cuba, as quintessential as a bottle of rum and salsa dancing. World-famous brands such as Cohiba, Montecristo, and Romeo y Julieta, made in Cuba's cigar factories, are acclaimed as the finest in the world.

A *torcedor* demonstrates the deft hand skills essential for rolling the world's finest cigars.

The individual character of a cigar depends on its blend of the filler, binder, and wrapper leaves, or *liga*. Every cigar variety and brand has a recipe, and each factory has a tobacco master who ensures the *liga* is appropriate to the specific Havana being rolled.

When dried and fermented leaves arrive in the tobacco factory *(fábrica)*, they are moistened to restore their elasticity, then flattened and stripped of their midribs. The rough leaves are sorted by size, classified according to color, texture, and quality (there are between 11 and 15 grades, and more than 75 colors in each category), then sent to the workshop *(galera)* to be rolled into cigars. First, the *torcedor* rolls two or three *seco* leaves (for strength) in his or her palm. This is then wrapped in *ligero* leaves (for aroma) and *volado* leaves (for even burning) to form the filler. The filler is enfolded by binder leaves, called *capotes*, and rolled until the familiar torpedo shape emerges. After

being pressed in a tubular mold, this cylindrical "bunch" is wrapped in a pliable *capa* leaf, then rolled with the flat of a *chaveta*, a rounded, all-purpose knife that is the torcedor's only tool. Finally, a quarter-size piece of wrapper is folded and sealed at one end.

Manual dexterity is all important to ensure that the cigar is neither too tight nor too loose; otherwise, it won't draw. An experienced roller can roll more than 100 cigars a day. Torcedors are permitted to smoke as many cigars as they wish on the job. For entertainment, a *lector* reads aloud the day's news or literary excerpts.

A guillotine cuts the cigars to size. They are then fumigated, rechecked for quality, and sorted by color according to six categories ranging from greenish brown *(pariso verdoso)* to darkest brown *(oscuro)*. The cigars are then stored in a cool room before being laid out in pine or cedar boxes, sealed with a green-and-white label, signifying *puro habanos*.

PARQUE DE LA FRATERNIDAD

Opening to the southwest of Parque Central, this swath of greenery was laid out for the sixth Pan-American Conference, hosted by Havana in 1928; formerly the city's railway station stood here. The park is anchored by a grand ceiba tree—the Árbol de la Fraternidad Americana (Tree of American Brotherhood)—and by busts of continental heroes, not least Abraham Lincoln.

The domed edifice to the north is the **Capitolio**, soaring 205 feet (63 m). Inspired by Washington's Capitol, this neoclassical structure was erected between 1912 and 1929 to house Cuba's own two-chamber congress. The stone staircase, flanked by bronze figures representing Labor and

---

INSIDER TIP:

In parks and elsewhere, be alive to Havana's sensual soundscapes. Walk to the city's Afro-Cuban beats: spicy salsas, sultry mambos, and haunting rumbas.

—VERONICA STODDART
USA Today *travel editor*

Virtue, ascends to a monumental portal with bronze doors adorned with bas-relief panels depicting historic scenes. The 394-foot-long (120 m) **Hall of the Lost Steps**, aglimmer with gold leaf and marble, features a 59-foot-tall (17 m) statue of La República, with a lance and shield that bears the arms of Cuba. At her feet, inset in the floor, is a 24-carat diamond marking the zero milestone for Cuba's roads. Galleries lead to pavilions that housed the **Senate**

and **Chamber of Representatives**. An accurate restoration was begun in 2013 and is just concluded; the restored building will house the National Assembly.

The **Real Fábrica de Tabaco Partagás**, behind the Capitolio, was founded in 1845 but is now closed long-term for restoration. A cigar store on the ground floor sells all brands of cigars. However, a visit to the modern factory is possible.

To the southeast, a beautiful fountain—the **Fuente de la India**—stands in front of the Hotel Saratoga *(Paseo del Prado #603)*, one of Havana's finest hotels. The neoclassical **Teatro Martí** *(Dragones #58)* reopened as a concert venue. ■

Parque de la Fraternidad

- 🗺 65 E2

Capitolio

- 🗺 65 E2
- ✉ Prado, bet. San Martín & Dragones
- ☎ 7/861-5519
- 💲 $

Real Fábrica de Tabaco Partagás

- ✉ Calle Industria #520, at Dragones (historical headquarters)
- ✉ San Carlos #816, at Penalver (modern factory)
- ☎ 7/833-8060
- 🕐 Closed Sun. (store)

Fun Ways to Explore

For a fun overview of Havana, ride the **HabanaBusTour** *(tel 7/261-9016, $$)*, an open-air double-decker bus that makes a circuit of tourist sites. You can hop on or off at any of 41 stops, beginning in Parque Central.

In Habana Vieja, explore using a *bici-taxi* (see p. 213), the homespun Cuban take on the rickshaw. The frames are handmade from metal pipes and spare parts, then fitted with car seats and an overhead tarp. Your ride will be bumpy and memorable.

EL MORRO CASTLE &
LA CABAÑA FORTRESS

Commanding the rocky peninsula that guards Havana harbor, El Morro castle and La Cabaña fortress together formed the largest Spanish military complex in the Americas. Today, enshrined in the Parque Histórico Militar Morro-Cabaña, the structures echo with the boot steps of soldiers in period costumes, while museums and a nightly firing of the cannon all add to a past that seems cinematic.

■ El Morro guarded Havana with walls 10 feet (3 m) thick until overwhelmed by the English in 1762.

El Morro Castle (Castillo de los Tres Reyes del Morro)

🅼 65 E4 & inside back cover

✉ Parque Histórico Militar Morro-Cabaña, Carretera de la Habana, Habana del Este

☎ 7/861 9706

💲 $

The park, approached via the tunnel that dips beneath the harbor channel, sprawls a mile across **La Cabaña**, the windswept ridge that displays a blunt cliff face toward Old Havana. **El Castillo de los Tres Reyes del Morro** went up between 1589 and 1630 to guard the harbor entrance. Stout and strong, it withstood the English siege in 1762 for 40 days until breached by a massive explosion. When the English departed 11 months later, the Spanish lost no time in securing their precious city with a mightier complex to guard the

land route. Some ten years in construction, the **Fortaleza de San Carlos de la Cabaña** cost so much that Spanish King Charles III jokingly asked for a telescope, saying that such a monstrous structure must surely be visible from Madrid.

El Morro Castle

Named for the knobby promontory on which it was built, this compact castle guards the harbor entrance. Conceived by military engineer Juan Bautista Antonelli (1550–1616), it is shaped in an irregular polygon and surrounded by rock moats. The castle worked in league with the **Castillo de San Salvador de la Punta**, across the bay, to catch enemy ships in a crossfire.

Enter El Morro via a drawbridge that funnels you along the **Tunel Aspillerado** (Loopholed Tunnel) to the **Plaza de Armas**, the military parade ground. The plaza was filled in 1763 with a two-story garrison that now houses the **Sala de Historía de Faro y Castillo**, displaying models of Cuba's lighthouses and castles. A ramp leads to a series of colonial fortifications, including **Baluarte de Austria**, with cannons in their embrasures pointing down at the moat, and **Batería de Velasco**, named for the Spanish general and governor who bravely defended the castle.

The **Surtida de los Tinajónes** displays the great earthenware vases that once held rapeseed to fire the lantern of the 35-foot-tall (10 m) **lighthouse**, erected in 1844. The lighthouse still functions with a flashing electric lantern. You can ascend (*$*) to the balcony for a stupendous view.

INSIDER TIP:

Don't miss the performance of the Malecón and the silhouette of the city from Castillo del Morro at sunset; it's priceless.

–GIANNI MORELLI
Travel guide author

To the south, a ramp leads down from the castle to the **Batería de los Doce Apóstoles** (Battery of the Twelve Apostles), named for the dozen cannons dating from the Spanish-American War. In addition to a refreshment area, there's a small maritime museum to complete your visit.

La Cabaña Fortress

Symbol of Spanish rule for more than three centuries, this awesome bastion, built between 1763 and 1774 in the shape of an isosceles triangle, sprawls over 25 acres (10 ha). Initiated following the English invasion of

Cuba, it was designed and built by French engineers. Its stone ramparts are 40 feet (12 m) thick in places. The fortress comprises successive lines of defense, each higher than the last, with a system of moats, so that the hapless invader who overcomes any line finds himself trapped in the next.

You enter La Cabaña via the monumental baroque portal. Beyond, a drawbridge spans a dry moat carved from solid rock and extending eastward to **El Foso de los Laureles** (Moat of the Laurels), an execution ground for nationalist rebels in the 19th century and, later, for Batista henchmen and suspected anti-Castroites following *"el triunfo de la revolución,"* when Che Guevara set up headquarters here.

The sally port opens to the **Plaza de Armas**, featuring the **Museo de Fortificaciones y Armas**, dedicated to the castle's evolution and to weaponry. At the west end stands the **Capilla de San Carlos**, a simple chapel with an exquisite altar. On the north side of the fortress, the **Área Depósito Crisis de Octubre** displays missiles and anti-aircraft batteries from the time of the Cuban Missile Crisis of 1962.

La Cabaña changes by night, when torches are lit and Cuban soldiers costumed in 18th-century military garb march along the ramparts and touch a spark to a cannon, marking the end of the day. In colonial times, the Cañonazo announced the closing of the city gates and drawing of a chain across the harbor. ∎

La Cabaña Fortress (Fortaleza de San Carlos de la Cabaña)

🗺 65 F3 & inside back cover

✉ Parque Histórico Militar Morro-Cabaña, Carretera de la Habana, Habana del Este

☎ 7/861 9706

💲 $

CENTRO HABANA AND CERRO

Predominantly residential and decrepit, Centro Habana (central Havana) is laid out in a rough grid receding inland from the Malecón, the sinuous shoreline boulevard that links Old Havana to Vedado. The district of Cerro (Hill) sprawls to the south. Here the street life is lively, offering an entrée to fascinating microcosms of city life.

The dense street life around Centro Habana invigorates Calle Neptuno.

**Centro Habana &
Cerro**

⊠ 65 C1, D1, D2, D3

**Casa-Museo
Lezama Lima**

⊠ Trocadero #162,
bet. Consulado
& Industria

☎ 7/863-4161

🕒 Closed Mon.

💲 $

Lying due west of Old Havana, Centro Habana—usually referred to as Centro—evolved during the late 19th century as a residential district. Its block after block of buildings are similar to those of Old Havana, though taller and lacking interior patios. Corroded by sea air, many have been lost to decay. The dilapidated buildings along the Malecón (see sidebar p. 87) are being restored. The first building to metamorphose was the **Centro Hispano-Americano de Cultura** (*Malecón #17, bet. Prado & Capdevila, tel 7/860-6282*), its

facade supported by Art Deco caryatids. Three blocks inland, the former home of author José Lezama Lima (1910–1976) is now the **Casa-Museo Lezama Lima**, celebrating the author's life.

Westward, the Malecón sweeps past the **Monumento a Antonio Maceo**, dedicated to the brilliant black general, second in command under Gen. Máximo Gómez during the wars of independence. A short stroll inland up Calle San Lázaro leads to **Callejón de Hamel**, an alley ablaze with evocative murals and sculptures by the

INSIDER TIP:

In places like Centro Habana, don't haggle over prices for craft souvenirs down to the absolute minimum with artisans who are already struggling to make ends meet.

—NEIL SHEA
National Geographic writer

local artist Salvador González. Barrio Cayo Hueso, south of Calle San Lázaro, has some remarkable 1950s Art Deco apartment buildings, such as **Edificio Solimar** (*Calle Soledad 205*). Its main attraction is **Museo Fragua Martiana**, the prison quarry site—now a memorial garden and museum—where nationalist hero José Martí broke rocks.

Slicing Centro north-south is **Avenida de Italia** (Galiano), which, with Neptuno and San Rafael running perpendicular, form Havana's once elegant, now impoverished shopping streets. The **Cine América** is one of the world's great Art Deco theaters. Intersecting Galiano farther south, Zanja forms Centro's axis. Towering over the junction is the 1927 **Cuban Telephone Company** building (*Calle Aguila #565*), in flamboyant Spanish Renaissance style. The broad arch spanning the road outside is the **Pórtico Chino**, the Dragon Gate announcing the official entry to **Barrio Chino.** Centro's Chinatown was once Latin America's largest (in population). This was the location of the infamous Shanghai Theater,

offering cabarets "of extreme obscenity," according to the English writer Graham Greene (1904–1991). After the revolution, the Chinese fled Cuba en masse. The restaurants along Calle Cuchillo serve a remnant Cuban-Chinese population of about 300 Chinese-born naturals and several thousand descendants; the former **Restaurante Pacífico** was a favored eatery of both Ernest Hemingway and Fidel Castro.

Avenida Salvador Allende forms an axis for Centro and, east of Padre Varela, slopes east to Parque de la Fraternidad as Ave-

Tipping Tips

Cubans who work in tourism rely on tips, being paid a paltry wage. Unless your service was awful, tip fairly: CUC 1 per day for housemaids, CUC 0.50 per bag for bellboys, and 10 percent of a restaurant bill is fair. Musicians will play at your table until tipped, or may ask you to buy a CD (typically CUC 10–15). Cubans who guide you to a site may also expect a tip.

nida Simón Bolívar. Sites of interest include the **Gran Templo Nacional Masónico** (Freemason's Temple), with a museum on Freemasonry, and the neo-Gothic **Iglesia del Sagrado Corazón de Jesús** (1914–1923). Step down Padre Varela to the **Fábrica Romeo y Julieta**, founded in 1875 to make the famous cigars. ∎

Cine América

✉ Ave. de Italia #253 at Neptuno
☎ 7/862-5416

Gran Templo Nacional Masónico

✉ Ave. Salvador Allende, bet. Padre Varela & Lucena
☎ 7/878-5065
🕐 Closed Sat.–Sun.

Iglesia del Sagrado Corazón de Jesús

✉ Ave. Simón Bolívar, bet. Padre Varela & Gervasio
☎ 7/862-4979

Fábrica Romeo y Julieta

✉ Calle Padre Varela, bet. Desague & Peñalver
☎ 7/870-4797
🕐 Closed Sun.
💲 $

VEDADO

Memories of 1950s mobster excess linger on the streets of Vedado, studded by high-rise hotels and commercial offices at its core. Its broad, tree-shaded *calles* (streets), lined with mansions of the erstwhile well-to-do, make for pleasant strolling. To the south, Plaza, or Nuevo Vedado, hosts the government ministries. Museums and architectural attractions abound.

The Malecón is a 24-hour social center of conversation, relaxation, and fishing for *habaneros*.

Vedado
🗺 64 B3

Museo de Artes Decorativas
🗺 64 B3
✉ Calle 17 #502, bet. D & E
☎ 7/832-0924
🕐 Closed Mon.
💲 $

Beginning in 1859, an elegant new district was laid out upon the reserve *(vedado)*, the wide expanse west of Centro that in colonial days served as a buffer zone in the event of an attack on the city. Divided by broad boulevards into a quilt of graceful blocks, this leafy district blossomed in the early 20th century, when wealthy Cubans and other North Americans built small apartment buildings and villas in neoclassical beaux arts style. **Calle 17**—novelist Alejo Carpentier's "row of magnificent mansions"— boasts several stunning exemplars

of beaux arts villas. Among them is the 1927 Casa de José Gómez Mena, which houses the **Museo de Artes Decorativas**, brimming with chinoiserie and gleaming antiques. Eight blocks west at **Parque Lennon** *(Calles 15/17 & Calles 6/8)*, a bronze statue of ex-Beatle John Lennon (1940–1980) by Cuban artist José Ramón Villa draws admirers.

La Rampa & Vicinity

The area around La Rampa, the inclined boulevard that links Calle L with the **Malecón**, is

Havana's business and hotel district, full of cinemas, jazz clubs, and modern high-rises harking back to the 1950s. At its base is the neo-Renaissance–style **Hotel Nacional de Cuba** *(Calles O & 21, tel 7/836-3564)*, inaugurated in 1930 and sitting atop a bluff occupied by a battery of colonial-era cannons. Reached via a palm-lined drive, this graceful grande dame—its lobby agleam with azulejos—was the venue for the mobster get-together depicted in *The Godfather II*.

Minimalism in high-rise 1950s design is epitomized by the **Hotel Capri** *(Calle 21, bet. Calle N & O, tel 7/839-7200)*, where actor George Raft (1895–1980) famously refused entry to a revolutionary mob that came to trash the casino; and by the 25-story **Habana Libre** *(Ave. 23 & Calle L, tel 7/834-6100)*, which started in March 1958 as the Havana Hilton. In January 1959, Castro set up headquarters in suite 2224, on the 22nd floor, and bearded revolutionaries lounged around in its domed lobby, marking the end of the high-rolling heyday. A remarkable mural by Amelia Peláez graces the facade.

Kitty-corner, the beloved **Coppelia** ice-cream parlor, serving 30,000 people daily, is not to be missed. A classically inspired staircase, **Las Escalinatas** leads from Calle L to the Acropolis-like **Universidad de La Habana**. Founded in Old Havana in 1728, it moved to its current location in 1902. During the republican era, the staircase was the setting for violent rallies. The university library boasts

exquisite Art Deco; the **Great Hall** features a splendid mural by Armando García Menocal (1863–1942). The Felipe Poey Science Building houses the **Museo Antropológico Montané**, with a superb collection of pre-Columbian art; and the **Museo de História Natural Felipe Poey**, dedicated to the natural world.

Nearby, the Renaissance home (1910–1912) of Orestes Ferrara is now the **Museo Napoleónico**, displaying a magnificent collection devoted to the French emperor amassed prior to the revolution by Cuban millionaire Julio Lobo. Decor includes period furniture.

Along the Malecón

From the base of La Rampa, the Malecón (see sidebar above) sweeps westward past the **Monumento a las Víctimas del Maine**, erected in 1926 in homage to the 288 sailors killed when the U.S.S. *Maine* exploded in Havana harbor in 1898, sparking the

---

The Malecón

Havana's serpentine seafront drive, the Malecón was laid out in 1901 by the U.S. governor, Gen. Leonard Woods (1860–1927); it twines 5 miles (8 km) west from the base of the Prado to the Río Almendares. The seawall is the great meeting point for *habaneros*, notably lovers, and for children who come to swim in the square baths *(baños de mar)* hewn from the shoreline rocks. In inclement weather, waves cascade over the seawall; the once glorious colonial structures facing the ocean have proven incapable of withstanding the corrosive assault. Many are currently being restored.

Museo Antropológico Montané

✉ Universidad de la Habana, Calles L & San Lázaro

☎ 7/879-3488

🕐 Closed Sat.–Sun. & Aug.

Museo de História Natural Felipe Poey

✉ Universidad de la Habana, Calles L & San Lázaro

☎ 7/863-9361

🕐 Closed Sat.–Sun. & Aug.

Museo Napoleónico

✉ Calle San Miguel #1159, bet. Ronda & Masón

☎ 7/879-1412

🕐 Closed Mon.

💲 $

Cementerio de Colón

🅰 64 A2 & B2

☎ 7/830-4517

$ $

Plaza de la Revolución

✉ 64 B2

Spanish-American War. Nearby is the **Tribuna Antiimperialista José Martí**, inaugurated in 2000 as a setting for anti–U.S. demonstrations. Here, erected in response to the Elián González tug-of-war, a bronze statue of José Martí holding the boy in his arms points an accusatory finger at the **U.S. Embassy** (reopened as such in 2015), one block west.

EXPERIENCE: Cruise Havana in a Classic Car

There's no more nostalgic way to explore historic Havana than in a 1950s convertible. It can be arranged through **Gran Car** *(Calle Marino at Santa María, Nuevo Vedado, tel 7/855-5567, email: grancardp@transtur.cu),* which rents chauffeur-driven classic cars, or another possibility is to ask your concierge.

The **Monumento a Calixto García**, at the base of palm-shaded Avenida de los Presidentes (Calle G), was erected in 1959 to honor the hero general of the wars of independence. Mobster Meyer Lansky owned the **Hotel Riviera**, farther west at the base of Paseo. Opened in 1958 and still displaying its original kitschy decor, it remains a monument to modernism. The seafront boulevard ends at **Torreón de la Chorrera** fortress, built in 1645 at the mouth of the Río Almendares.

Cementerio de Colón

Havana's vast and remarkable necropolis, at Zapata and San Antonio Chiquito, was laid out from 1871. It spans some 125 acres (50 ha) of fabulous statuary and mausoleums representing a flamboyant array of styles. Cuba's finest lie here: from novelist Alejo Carpentier and world chess champion José Raúl Capablanca (1888–1942) to Gen. Máximo Gómez and revolutionary heroines Haydée Santamaría and Celia Sánchez. Collective pantheons include those of martyrs, such as the students who died in the 1958 attack on the Presidential Palace.

Suppliants attribute miraculous healings to **La Milagrosa**, the tomb of Amelia Goyri de la Hoz, who died in childbirth in 1901. The grave draws women who ask for a baby by knocking three times on the tomb.

Plaza de la Revolución & Vicinity

Originally called Plaza Cívica when laid out in the 1950s, this vast open swath is surrounded by government ministries in monumental style, plus the **Biblioteca Nacional José Martí** (National Library; *tel 7/855-5442*) to the east; and **Teatro Nacional** *(tel 7/878-0769),* with a glazed convex facade, to the west.

Looming over the 11-acre (4 ha) square is the 59-foot-tall (17 m) **Monumento a José Martí**, hewn of granite and marble and showing the Cuban hero of independence. The statue, by Juan José Sicre (1898–1974), is dwarfed by a granite obelisk towering 423 feet (129 m). At its base—shaped as a five-pointed star—is the **Museo Memorial José Martí**. An elevator *($)* whisks visitors to the top of the tower,

■ Cubans celebrate the revolution at the towering Monumento a José Martí.

where an observation platform offers a spectacular 360-degree view of Havana from its highest point.

The labyrinthine government building to the rear is the enormous **Palacio de la Revolución**, erected as the Palace of Justice in 1953–1957 with a monumental gravitas inspired by the fascistic 1942 Universal Exhibition in Rome and the Trocadéro in Paris. Off-limits to visitors, this is the seat of government.

The facade of the stark stone **Ministerio del Interior**, on the plaza's north side, bears a ceramic mural by Amelia Peláez overshadowed by a five-story-tall face of Che Guevara—the universally recognized image photographed by Alberto "Korda" Gutiérrez (1928–2001), cast in iron and inscribed with the motto "*Hasta la victoria siempre*–Toward victory,

always." In 2009 a similar face of fellow revolutionary hero Camilo Cienfuegos was erected on the facade of the **Ministerio de Informática y Comunicaciones**, on the plaza's northeast corner. Its **Museo Postal Cubano** displays postage stamps from around the world. Time your visit for the rallies held January 1, May 1, and July 26, when Cubans carrying banners troop by to demonstrate their loyalty to the revolution.

Avenida Boyeros runs north from the plaza to the **Monumento a José Miguel Gómez**, commanding the crest of the broad avenue. To the east, Avenida Salvador Allende (Carlos III) fronts the **Quinta de los Molinos**, commissioned in 1837 as the summer palace of the *capitanes generales*. The villa, today a botanical garden, was gifted to Gen. Máximo Gómez in 1899. ■

Monumento & Museo Memorial José Martí

🅰 64 B2
✉ Plaza de la Revolución
☎ 7/859-2347
🕐 Closed Sun.
💲 $

Museo Postal Cubano

✉ Ave. Independencia at 19 de Mayo
☎ 7/881-5551
🕐 Closed Sat.–Sun.
💲 $

MIRAMAR & CUBANACÁN

West of the Río Almendares lies the sprawling *municipio* of Playa, a region of supreme architectural charm divided into districts *(barrios)* that include the tony seafront precinct of Miramar—full of grandiose, green-lawned mansions—and, to the west, Cubanacán, where exclusive houses of the wealthy line leafy hills. The areas are perfect for touring by car.

■ The legendary Tropicana cabaret is an exhilarating experience in open-air entertainment.

Miramar & Cubanacán

🗺 64 A3 & inside back cover

Visitor Information

✉ Infotur, Ave. 5ta & 112, Miramar

☎ 7/204-7036

Maqueta de la Habana

🗺 Inside back cover

✉ Calle 28 #113, bet. Ave. 1ra & 3ra, Miramar

☎ 7/202-7303

🕐 Closed Sun.– Mon.

💲 $

Miramar

The '30s, '40s, and '50s live on in the eclectic architecture of Miramar, from classical interpretations of colonial architecture to uninhibited free-form compositions. Anchoring Miramar is **Quinta Avenida** (Avenida 5ta), the main east-west boulevard and the westerly extension of the Malecón, beyond a tunnel beneath the Río Almendares. Stunning beaux arts, Art Deco, and modernist villas edge this shaded thoroughfare, known as "Embassy Row." Many mansions have metamorphosed in recent years such as the green-roofed, German Renaissance–style **Casa de las Tejas Verdes** *(Calle 2 #308, tel 7/212-5282, by*

appointment), brought back from dereliction as a cultural center dedicated to architecture.

Remarkable for its giant *jagüey* trees (banyans) dripping their roots to the ground, **Parque Mahatma Gandhi** and **Parque Emiliano Zapata** *(Ave. 5ta, Calles 24/26)* boast busts of the Indian pacific philosopher (1869–1948) and Mexican revolutionary (1879–1919). The **Maqueta de la Habana** (Havana Model) displays a 1:1,000-scale reproduction of the city made of recycled cigar boxes.

Ecclesiastical sites of interest include the **Iglesia de Santa Rita** *(Ave. 5ta at Calle 26, tel 7/205-2001),* with parabolic arches; the Romanesque **Iglesia San Antonio** de Padua *(Calle 60 #316 at Ave. 5ta)*, built in 1949 and today overshadowed by the towering cubist **Russian Embassy** *(Ave. 5, Calles 22/66)*; and **Basilica Jesús de Miramar** *(Ave. 5ta, Calles 80 & 82)*, a 1953 Byzantine-style cathedral.

Avenida Primera parallels the shoreline and leads west to the **Acuario Nacional**, the National Aquarium. The dolphin and sea lion shows are impressive. West of Miramar, the shore-front of **Flores** is lined with erstwhile private clubs and *balnearios* (beach resorts) established in the early 20th century to serve the upper classes and, since the revolution, a more democratic clientele. It is one of the few restaurants where Fidel ate dinner in public. **Casa-Estudio de José Fuster**—the home and studio of the world-famous artist—is itself a flamboyant work of art extending throughout the community, the heart of **Fusterlandia**, an extensive park full of street art. Fidel Castro's home—Punta Cero—is nearby, out of sight on Avenida 5ta.

Cubanacán

Cubanacán—nicknamed Cuba's Beverly Hills—was developed beginning in the 1920s, when the city's wealthy built posh country estates along sinuous, sloping streets. Many homes were seized by the government when their occupants fled to Miami after Castro took power. Many homes are now embassies or protocol houses for use by Cuban officials and visiting foreign dignitaries.

In 1960 the former Havana Country Club was converted into a site for the **Instituto Superior de Arte** (today the University of Arts), conceived by Castro to be an exemplar of the possibilities of revolutionary architecture. The complex was partially built between 1961 and 1965 before being deemed too avant-garde and cancelled. Since 2001, the facility has been partially restored. Art lovers may also enjoy **Kcho Estudio Romerillo**, the studio-gallery of world-renowned artist Alexi Leyva "Kcho" Machado (1970–).

Nearby are the **Palacio de las Convenciones** *(Calle 146, bet. 11 & 13, tel 7/202-6011)*, Cuba's premier convention site, and the mansion of the **Marques de Pinar del Río**. Abounding with 1930s Art Deco glass and chrome, this villa functions as **Fábrica el Laguito**, where the finest of Cuban cigars—the Cohibas—are rolled. ■

Acuario Nacional

- ▲ Inside back cover
- ✉ Ave. 1ra #6001 & Calle 60, Miramar
- ☎ 7/203-6401
- 🕐 Closed Mon.
- 💲 $$

acuarionacional.cu

Casa-Estudio de José Fuster

- ✉ Calle 226 at Ave. 3ra A, Jaimanitas
- ☎ 7/271-2932
- 🕐 By appt. only

Instituto Superior de Arte

- ▲ Inside back cover
- ✉ Calle 120 at Ave. 9na
- ☎ 7/208-0704
- 🕐 Closed July–Aug.

isa.cult.cu

Kcho Estudio Romerillo

- ✉ Ave. 7ma & Calle 120
- ☎ 7/279-1844
- 🕐 Closed July–Aug.

Fábrica el Laguito

- ✉ Calle 146 #2302, Cubanacán
- ☎ 7/208-2486
- 🕐 By appt. only

Cabaret Tropicana

- ▲ Inside back cover
- ✉ Calle 72 #4504, Marianao
- ☎ 7/207-0110
- 💲 $$$$

cabaret-tropicana.com

Tropicana

The Tropicana's nightly show is world famous for its flashy cabaret routines and the showgirls' stupendous costumes. The club opened on New Year's Eve, 1939, in an open-air theater in the Buena Vista district south of Miramar. Max Borges Recio designed the current theater in the '50s, blending modernism with the tropics in his "mambo-style" club. The central stage is open to the sky. Though expensive (*from $75*), shows are often sold out; reserve ahead.

KEEPING THE FAITH

About three-quarters of Cubans profess some kind of Afro-Cuban religious belief. Followers of Santería—the most popular of these religions—come from all walks of life. The Castro government discouraged religion during three decades, but relented in the 1980s. Today many Cubans practice both Santería and Roman Catholicism. Other popular religions with roots that twine back to Africa include Palo Monte and Abakuá.

During centuries of colonial rule, West African slaves in Cuba clung to their ancestral religions. The Spanish permitted slaves to practice their religion, believing it would help avoid rebellions. Practice was restricted, however, to ethnic social clubs, or *cabildos,* and each cabildo was required by law to be patronized by a Roman Catholic saint. As a result, the various African cults unified as *la regla de ocha* (the way of the saint). The resulting syncretic religion—Santería—hid behind a facade of Catholicism, with various saints representing the *orishas,* the spiritual emissaries of Olofi (God) in the traditional Yoruba religion of what are now Nigeria and Benin.

There are more than 200 *orishas* recognized in Africa; 56 are worshipped in Cuba. Among them, Changó, god of passion and lightning, is represented by the colors red and white;

he embodies manhood and virility, and his Catholic equivalent is Santa Bárbara. His femme fatale equivalent is Ochún, goddess of sweet water, fertility, and love; she is represented by La Virgen de la Caridad, whose color is yellow. Yemayá, symbolizing motherhood and the sea, wears blue and white; her equivalent is the Virgen de Regla. Obbatalá, who symbolizes creation and peace, is associated with the Virgen de la Merced, and dresses all in white. Santería balances the moral proscriptions of Roman Catholicism; orishas are hedonistic, licentious, and fallible.

Orishas are thought to play a role in each individual's destiny and can be called upon for both miracles and to solve everyday problems. Every *santero* or *santera,* or practitioner of Santería, has a spirit altar where offerings such as rum, fruits, and flowers are made to one's

EXPERIENCE: Santería

Santería, or Afro-Cuban saint worship, is an entrenched and fascinating part of Cuban culture. Everywhere throughout Cuba you're likely to witness *santeros* or *santeras* (individuals who have been initiated in *la regla de ocha*—the way of the saint) dressed all in white.

The complexities of this syncretic religion take some fathoming. The following experiences will aid in your understanding of Santería:

• **Asociación Cultural Yoruba de Cuba** *(Paseo de Martí #615, bet. Dragones & Monte, Habana, tel 7/863-5953).* This Afro-Cuban cultural center has a museum on Santería and hosts Santería-themed

music and dance each Thursday and Friday evening.

• **Casa Templo de Santería Yemayá** *(Calle Real del Jigüe, Trinidad)* is a small temple that hosts Santería performances.

• **Iglesia de Nuestra Señora de Regla** *(Calle Santuario #11 corner Máximo Gómez, Regla, tel 7/797-6228).* The Church of Our Lady of Regla is the most important Santería chapel in Havana. The black virgin stands for Yemayá, the goddess of the sea.

• **Rumba del Callejón de Hamel** *(Callejón de Hamel, Centro Habana, tel 7/878-1661).* This Sunday afternoon music and dance session is inspired by Santería, and shrines adorn Hamel's Alley.

A Santería priestess performs a ceremony to honor deceased ancestors.

personal orishas, who "live" in clay or porcelain pots kept in one's home. Each pot, arranged in hierarchical order, contains consecrated stones thought to embody the spirit of the orisha.

Santeros and santeras—often identified by their necklaces of colorful beads–use divination to communicate with their orishas. Simple questions can be answered using a fresh coconut divided into four sections. More complex oracles are interpreted by an *oriaté,* who elucidates prophecies through divination with cowrie shells; or one's *babalawo* (high priest), who offers counsel and guidance.

At ritual ceremonies, three *batá* drums are used to invoke the orishas, who may "mount" a santero or santera, who goes into trance. Such ceremonies are private. Tourists can experience faux ceremonies at theaters, museums, and tourist complexes, but to experience the real thing, you will need to evolve a close friendship with a santero.

Palo Monte, similar to Santería, but deriving from the Congolese Bantu religion, believes in the redemptive power of the dead, which, as in voodoo, may be used to affect the destiny of another person. Abakuá, from Nigeria, is a monotheist cult practiced by all-male secret societies dedicated to social justice and welfare. Members *(ñañigos)* worship representations of the spirits, called *iremes* or *diabolitos,* who dance dressed in hooded burlap outfits. Initiates *(ekobios)* hear sacred voices in sacred drums.

REGLA & GUANABACOA

These contiguous *barrios*, rising on the east side of Havana harbor, are centers of Santería (see pp. 92–93), where community life is infused with the spirit of ancient African rhythms. Shrines dedicated to the Afro-Cuban pantheon abound, as do centuries-old Roman Catholic churches.

Museo Municipal de Regla
- ⊠ Calle Martí #158
- ☎ 7/797-6989
- 🕐 Closed Mon.
- 💲 $

Museo Histórico de Guanabacoa
- ⊠ Calle Martí #108
- ☎ 7/797-9117
- 🕐 Closed Mon.
- 💲 $

The harbor town of Regla evolved as a smuggling port for slaves. It is reached by a rustic passenger ferry *(lanchita)* from the Muelle de Luz on Old Havana's **Avenida del Puerto**. The ferry deposits you beside the **Iglesia de Nuestra Señora de Regla** *(Calle Santuario #11, closed Mon.)*, an endearing hermitage dating from 1687 that draws adherents of Catholicism and Santería alike. A gilt altar gleams within the simple church, where devotees mumble bequests to statues of saints, and to the black Virgen de Regla (the Roman Catholic equivalent of Yemayá, goddess of the sea). Nearby, the **Museo Municipal de Regla** provides a grounding in Regla's Santería associations. Nearby, **Colina de Lenin** (Lenin Hill) has a 10-foot (3 m) visage of the Russian revolutionary inset in rock, surrounded by 12 human figures. **Guanabacoa**, uphill east of Regla, was founded in 1607 and became an important bastion in protecting the approach to Havana. In the 18th century, it gained popularity among the nobility for its mineral springs and as an ecclesiastical center. The **Iglesia Parroquial Mayor de Nuestra Señora de la Asunción** *(Calle Division #331)*, on the main square, has a fine baroque altar. Adjoining, the **Museo Histórico de Guanabacoa** is devoted to the theme of Santería.

The **Iglesia y Convento Santo Domingo** *(Calle Santo Domingo #407 at Lebredo)*, erected in 1728, boasts an *alfarje* ceiling in Mudejar style. A rare restored gem is the tiny **Ermita de Potosí** *(Calzada de Guanabacoa at Calle Potosí)*.

As in Regla, the practice of African-derived cults is a long-held tradition, earning Guanabacoa the nickname the *"pueblo embrujado"* (bewitched village). Watch for performances by the **Guaracheros de Regla** carnival dance troupe. ∎

■ A bronze sculpture of Lenin's face created by the Cuban artist Thelma Marín in 1984

HABANA DEL ESTE

Extending east of the city, miles of contemporary suburbs compose Habana del Este. Making amends are a quaint fishing hamlet which Hemingway frequented regularly and the scintillating beaches of Playas del Este, to which *habaneros* flock in droves on sun-splashed weekends.

Habana del Este is accessed via the tunnel that burrows beneath the harbor channel and widens into the Via Monumental. Rising over the highway are various sports stadiums custom built for the 1991 Pan-American Games. **Villa Panamericana** is a residential town that was originally built to house the athletes and press.

Two miles (3 km) east of Villa Panamericana begin the sprawling twin dormitory cities of **Alamar** and **Celimar**. Although helping ease the acute housing shortage, together they are a postrevolutionary blight entirely lacking requisite services. The high-rise accommodations, covering more than 6 square miles (15.5 sq km), were erected by untrained volunteers (*microbrigadas*) to provide laborers with housing.

Worth the visit, however, is **Organipónico Vivero Alamar**, an organic urban farm run by a workers cooperative. Fascinating guided tours are given by founder Miguel Salcines or his daughter Isis María.

While here, seek out the surreal **Jardín de los Afectos** (Garden of Endearment; *Edificio 11C, Micro X),* a baroque miscellany of items conjured into dedications of love by local artist Héctor Pascual Gallo.

■ **All smiles at Playa Bacuranao**

Cojímar

Much more engaging for travelers is the village of Cojímar—squatting in a cove between Villa Panamericana and Alamar. A diminutive fortress—**El Torreón** (*closed to the public)*—was built in 1649 and guards the entrance to the cove where the English came ashore in 1762 to capture the isle for King George. In front of this is located the **Monumento a Ernest Hemingway**, a classical rotunda surrounding a limestone pedestal bearing a bust of the

Habana del Este

⚑ 65 F4 & inside back cover

Visitor Information

✉ Infotur S. María del Mar, Ave. de las Terrazas at Calles 10 & 11

☎ 7/797-1261

Organipónico Vivero Alamar

✉ Calle 160C & Parque Hanoi

☎ 57/763-0532

🕐 By appt. only

American writer, molded from brass items donated by local fishermen.

Hemingway frequented **La Terraza de Cojímar** *(Calle Real #161 at Candelaria, tel 7/766-5151)*, a bar with restaurant overlooking the cove where he berthed his boat, *Pilar.* The author's memory lingers at the

---

INSIDER TIP:

Just east of Playas del Este, you can book a tour to dive the *City of Alexandria* shipwreck. The ship dates from the late 1800s.

—FABIO AMADOR
*National Geographic Society
Grants Officer*

---

mahogany bar and on the walls, adorned with black-and-white photos of "Papa" proudly displaying his prize trophy fish.

Playas del Este

Popular with Cubans for sands like pulverized sugar, this series of beaches unspools for several miles, drawing *habaneros* to flirt beneath the palms and swim in the warm turquoise sea. The beaches are accessed via the **Vía Blanca**, the main east-west coast highway, beginning with **Playa Bacuranao**, crowded with impecunious youths from Alamar.

Playa Tarará *(passport required, $)* extends eastward and is the setting for an all-villa tourist resort, **Villa Tarará**

(tel 7/798-2072), famous as the former setting for **José Martí Pioneer City**, once dedicated to the treatment of child victims of the 1986 Chernobyl nuclear catastrophe (today it houses Chinese students). It was here, in 1959, that Che Guevara came to recuperate from three years of fighting; and that Fidel Castro, using his visits as a pretext, established a secret government to undermine President Urrutia's democratic government after Batista's ouster.

Beyond Tarará are **Playa El Mégano** and lovely **Playa Santa María del Mar**, the most renowned in Este, with palm-shaded white sands backed by hotels and villas that are popular holiday venues for Cubans and tourists. Other than the gorgeous beaches, the hotels and restaurants are lackluster, and the entertainment desultory. Thatched *ranchitas* (small huts) serve grilled seafoods, and water sports are offered, including sportfishing.

A lagoon—**Laguna Itabo**—and mangrove swamp, good for bird-watching, extend behind **Playa Boca Ciega**, also known as Playa Mi Cayito (for a now-defunct restaurant).

Farther east, **Playa Guanabo** fronts the old village of **Guanabo**, which offers *casas particulares* (see p. 238) for rent and a small naturalistic museum. Although the beaches here are less appealing than those farther west, the village is lent vitality by the presence of vacationing Cubans ∎

HAVANA'S OUTSKIRTS

Neglected to a large degree by tourists, Havana's outer reaches offer genuine delights, not least colonial-era outposts that still move at a 19th-century pace. Hemingway's former home is a de rigueur attraction for travelers, and the district of Arroyo Naranjo-Boyeros offers the bucolic charms of a vast recreational park and the national botanical garden.

Museo Ernest Hemingway

For pilgrims, the highlight of the **Hemingway Trail** is this 20-acre (8 ha) estate, dominated by a colonial house perched atop a hill in **San Francisco de Paula**, 8 miles (12 km) southeast of Havana. Appropriately, it is called **Finca Vigía**–Lookout Farm.

The author lived here in between his travels for nearly 20 years, making it his most permanent home. Remodeled and now the Museo Ernest Hemingway, it remains much as Hemingway left it when he departed Cuba in 1960.

The simple, Spanish-style house is strewn with trophies, firearms, more than 9,000 books and magazines, and artworks by Picasso. The heads of antelope,

impalas, and buffalo that Hemingway killed on safari look down from the walls. A four-story tower, adjacent, was intended as Hemingway's study. He thought it too isolated and continued to write in the main house, often standing on a kudu rug with Boise, his favorite cat, at his feet (he had 50–70 cats). Guides follow your every move.

Hemingway's well-varnished sportfishing cruiser–*Pilar*–is docked in a pavilion overlooking the swimming pool, where it is said that Ava Gardner used to bathe naked.

In 2011, his long-lost 1955 Chrysler convertible was found; once restored, the classic car will be exhibited in the *finca*'s former garage.

Finca Vigía
 Inside back cover

Museo Ernest Hemingway
✉ Calle Vigía *&* Singer, Km 12.5, San Francisco de Paula

☎ 7/691-0809

💲 $

◾ Hemingway left Finca Vigía in 1960, the year following the revolution.

Hemingway's Cuba

Ernest Hemingway lived in Cuba for the better part of 20 years, drawn initially by its "great, deep blue river" teeming with billfish. He arrived in April 1932 and made the Hotel Ambos Mundos his first pied-à-terre. Handily, it was a stone's throw from what would become his favorite bar, El Floridita. Later, the irascible author would drive into town from Finca Vigía to carouse with politicians, movie stars, bullfighters, and ordinary folk, who found their way into his novels, including *The Old Man and the Sea*. In 1960, Hemingway was forced to decide between divided loyalties. He donated his Nobel Prize for Literature to his adoptive island. In November 1960 he left for Spain, then Key West, never to return to Cuba.

Parque Lenin
- Inside back cover

ExpoCuba
- Inside back cover
- Carretera del Rocio Km 3.5
- 7/697-4269
- Closed Mon.–Tues. & Sept.–Dec.
- $$

Jardín Botánico Nacional
- Inside back cover
- Carretera del Rocio Km 3.5
- 7/697 9159
- $

Parque Lenin

This vast park located in **Arroyo Naranjo** and **Boyeros** boroughs, 14 miles (23 km) south of central Havana, is popular with Cuban families, attracted on weekends to the carousels, a narrow-gauge steam-train ride, rodeos, horseback riding, and boating. Concentrated at the south end are a series of monuments, museums, and galleries, including **Galería de Arte Amelia Peláez**, on Calle Cortina, displaying works by this famous Cuban ceramist. Nearby, the **Monumento a Celia Sánchez** honors the revolutionary heroine (see sidebar p. 193) who conceived the park; she ran the secret network that supplied Castro's guerrillas with arms and became Castro's closest confidante. Honoring the park's namesake is the 30-foot-tall (9 m) **Monumento Lenin**,

carved of marble by Soviet sculptor L. E. Kerbel (1917–2003).

The facilities are meager. An exception is **Las Ruinas** *(tel 7/643-7743)* restaurant, a prefab built in 1972 around the remains of an 18th-century sugar mill. Shady bamboo copses and greenswards are good for picnics.

ExpoCuba

Carretera El Globo leads south from Parque Lenin to this complex—a self-congratulatory cross between a trade fair and museum—that pays homage to Cuba's accomplishments in industry, sports, science, and culture. Its 25 pavilions span the nation's provinces, with live music, crafts displays, and exhibits that profile Cuba's diversity. ExpoCuba boasts a large display of vintage rolling stock, plus a maritime pavilion with various seacraft.

Jardín Botánico Nacional

Laid out between 1968 and 1984, and extending over 1,480 acres (600 ha), Cuba's national botanical garden appeals for its sheer grandness. More than 20 miles (32 km) of road thread the park, partitioned by tropical regions and divided into zones that reflect Cuba's own varied ecosystems. A highlight is the exquisitely landscaped Japanese garden centered on a lake full of koi. The **Rincón Ekman**, named for the Swedish Erik Leonard Ekman (1883–1931), who pioneered the study of botany in Cuba, features separate greenhouses exhibiting mountain plants, cacti, and epiphytes, bromeliads, and ferns. ∎

More Places to Visit in & Around Havana

Alameda de Paula

Rising alongside Avenida del Puerto, this 200-yard-long (183 m) elevated pedestrian causeway makes for pleasant strolling. Marble benches and wrought-iron lamps add a romantic note. **Columna O'Donnell**, a carved column spouting from a fountain and erected in 1847, honors the Spanish navy; it was named for a *capitán general*. Before the revolution, the area was an infamous red-light district. Hints of the past still linger at **Dos Hermanos** *(Ave. del Puerto #304 at Sol)*, a bar where Ernest Hemingway sipped many a *mojito*, his famed rum cocktail. The bar adjoins a Russian Orthodox church—the **Sacra Catedral Ortodoxa Rusa**—topped by spectacularly gilded onion domes. ◾ 63 F2

▪ **The revolution is one subject that has inspired many of Cuba's artists.**

Avenida de los Presidentes

Ascending all the way from the Malecón to the Monumento a José Miguel Gómez (see p. 89), this broad boulevard is lined with monuments to Latin American presidents; that of Cuba's first president—Tomás Estrada Palma—was toppled after the revolution; he was considered a U.S. puppet. Ascending past the **Casa de las Américas** *(at Calle 3ra, tel 7/832-2706, casa.cult.cu)*, a cultural institution in a soaring Art Deco edifice, you'll see monuments to Ecuador's Eloy Alfaro *(between Calles 15 & 17)*, Mexico's Benito Juárez *(between Calles 17 & 19)*, the "Great Liberator" Simón Bolívar and Panama's Omar Torrijos *(between Calles 19 & 21)*, and Chilean president Salvador Allende *(between Calles 21 & 23)*.

Cuba's fine dance tradition is celebrated at the **Museo Nacional de la Danza** *(Calle Linea #365, tel 7/831-2198, closed Sun.–Mon, $)*, housed in a neoclassical mansion. Exhibits include the personal wardrobe of Alicia Alonso (1921–), the founder of Cuba's National Ballet. ◾ 64 B4

Calle Obispo

Linking Parque Central to Plaza de Armas via the city's former financial district, narrow and pedestrian-only Calle Obispo—Havana's busiest thoroughfare—is thronged with strollers drawn to the many art galleries, boutiques, and bars. Toward the eastern end, the **Museo Numismático** *(Calle Obispo #305, tel 7/861-5811, closed Mon, $)* occupies the former neoclassical Banco Mendoza. Its superb coin collection spans the Roman, Greek, Spanish colonial, and Republican eras. One block beyond soars the neoclassical former **Banco Nacional de Cuba** *(Calle Obispo #211)*, where Che Guevara once presided as minister of banking and industry. ◾ 65 F2

Centro de Estudios Che Guevara

Opened in 2014, the Center for Che Guevara Studies is dedicated to studies and public education about the Argentinian revolutionary who became a *comandante* in the armed struggle against Batista (see pp. 35–36) and, later, Cuba's minister of banking and industry. The center occupies a purpose-built structure opposite the 1950s modernist home where

Santuario de San Lázaro draws supplicants from far and wide.

Che lived in 1962–1964. It has an auditorium, library, and displays dedicated to Che and fellow revolutionaries Camilo Cienfuegos and Haydée Santamaría. ✉ Calle 47 #772, bet. Conill & Tulipán, Nuevo Vedado ☎ 7/881-4113 $ 🅼 63 A1

Santa María del Rosario

Steeped in bucolic charm, Santa María del Rosario, in the *municipio* of Cotorro, some 12 miles (20 km) southeast of Central Havana,

---

INSIDER TIP:

As many as half of Cubans profess atheism or agnosticism. Travelers should refrain from attempting to convert Cubans—the government doesn't like it.

—STACIE PIERPOINT
Annenberg Learner educational editor,
learner.org

---

harks back to a quieter era. Its red-tile-roof houses are typical of the country style. **Plaza Mayor** is dominated by the **Iglesia de Nuestra Señora del Rosario** (*tel 7/682-2183, closed Mon.*), a national monument dating from 1720 and boasting a glorious gilt baroque altar. The **Casa de la Cultura** (*Calle 23 #202, tel 7/682-4259*), on the west side of the plaza, has the added attraction of an impressive mural by acclaimed artist Manuel Mendive. 🅼 63 E1

Santuario de San Lázaro

Cuba's foremost pilgrimage site is the **Santuario de San Lázaro**, on the western outskirts of Rincón, about 18 miles (30 km) south of central Havana drawing supplicants year-round. They come seeking cures from San Lázaro, patron saint of sickness and disease (his African equivalent is Babalú Ayé, god of healing in Santería). Holy powers are ascribed to the waters that flow from a fountain behind the church. Try to time your visit for December 17, when thousands of believers flock here for the feast day, many crawling along the road and some even dragging rocks tied to their feet.

Gen. Antonio Maceo (1845–1896), the mulatto hero of the wars of independence, is buried in a hilltop mausoleum at **El Cacahual**, 3 miles (5 km) southeast of Rincón, where he died in battle in 1896. ✉ Carretera de San Antonio de los Baños 🅼 65 D1 & inside back cover

Stunning limestone formations, pristine coral reefs, and broad valleys in the home of the world's finest tobacco

FAR WEST

A delicate *Ralonia* at Orquideario Soroa

FAR WEST

Almost every tourist who ventures from Havana heads to the Valle de Viñales, the crown jewel of Cuba's scenic attractions. Here, broad valleys are quilted with tobacco farms, and oxen till loamy, red fields framed by sheer-sided *mogotes*. The Cordillera de Guaniguanico mountain spine runs east-west through Pinar del Río Province. Paved, albeit potholed, roads twist through western Cuba, and carry you back through the centuries.

■ **Exploring Cueva del Indio by boat**

Just west of Havana, newly created Artemisa Province (2010) is relatively flat and fertile, and intensely farmed, mostly lacking sites of interest for travelers. Exceptions are found in time-worn colonial towns such as Artemisa and San Antonio de los Baños; and in *presas* (reservoirs) stocked with largemouth bass.

Pinar del Río ("pine forest by the river") Province, farther west, is largely mountainous. Prior to the Spanish arrival, the area was a retreat for the various Indian tribes driven west by succeeding invasions that culminated with conquest by Spain. The region's development came relatively late in the day when settlers (predominantly from the Canary Islands) planted tobacco in the early 18th century. The following century, French settlers planted several coffee plantations in the Sierra del Rosario; the coffee industry later fell into ruin, but the first glimmers of revival now show. Heavily forested, the sierra also formed a base for counterrevolutionary bands in the early years following Castro's takeover. Peaceful today, the mountains lure hikers and birders, notably to the ecotourism sites of Soroa and Las Terrazas, and spelunkers tempted to cool off in the many underground caverns—one cave system in the Valle Santo Tomás comprises more than 15 miles (24 km) of underground passages.

The scenery builds westward, culminating in the splendor of the Valle de Viñales and neighboring vales, where the intrepid hiker might find patches of endemic cork palm, tracing a lineage back more than 200 million years. The eponymous provincial capital is a draw for its colonial structures.

To the south sprawls a vast alluvial plain, smothered in a rippling ocean of sugarcane. The marshy shore is popular with hunters who come to down waterfowl. Tantalizing beaches

are few, although the Bahía de Corrientes offers scintillating sand and superb diving, as does the necklace of coral cays—the Archipiélago de los Colorados—off the north shore. As yet none of the upscale resort hotels planned for the archipelago have opened. Westward, the land peters down to an arid peninsula protected as the Parque Nacional Península de Guanahacabibes, selected as a UNESCO biosphere reserve.

Three routes access the far west region. The Circuito Norte twines along the north coast, delivering marvelous mountain and ocean vistas. The Carretera Central, once the main highway linking Havana with the city of Pinar del Río, runs along the mountains' southern flank, connecting a string of colonial towns. These days, most travelers opt for the *autopista*—a fast highway that cuts straight through the countryside, but is devoid of markings—and there is no shortage of Cubans desperately beseeching rides. Drive carefully! ■

NOT TO BE MISSED:

Hiking the Sierra del Rosario Reserva de la Biosfera at Las Terrazas 104

A visit to the Finca El Pinar tobacco farm in San Luís 105

Boat rides on the subterranean lake at Cueva del Indio in Viñales 109

The wonder of underground dripstone formations at Cuevas de Santo Tomás 109

Scuba diving in search of whale sharks at María la Gorda 113

Snorkeling in the calm turquoise waters off Cayo Levisa 115

SIERRA DEL ROSARIO RESERVA DE LA BIOSFERA

Pine forests clad the hills of the Sierra del Rosario, rising to 1,640 feet (500 m) and beneficiary of two decades of reforestation of teak, mahogany, cedar, and pine. Named a UNESCO biosphere reserve in 1985, this 61,775-acre (25,000 ha) park is alluring to hikers and to botanists drawn, not least, to a fine orchid garden.

Sierra del Rosario Reserva de la Biosfera
🗺 103 D2 & 115

Las Terrazas
🗺 103 D2 & 115
☎ 048/57-8555
lasterrazas.cu

Soroa
🗺 103 D2

This reserve protects an area that over the centuries had been heavily logged and cleared for coffee estates. The Castro government initiated a pine replanting program in 1967. Rich in biodiversity, the forests are habitat to at least 98 species of birds that include parrots, trogons, and the *tocororo*. Deer and *jutías ratas* (large rodents) are common, as are harmless snakes and amphibians, including *Sminthillus limbatus,* the world's second smallest frog.

Las Terrazas

Touted as Cuba's prime ecotourism site, this *complejo turístico* (tourist complex; $) is centered on a delightful peasant village

■ Las Terrazas offers the traveler Cuba's finest eco-retreat.

built around **Lago San Juan** in 1971. Several residents work as artists; worth a visit are the **studio of Léster Campa** (Edificio 4, tel 53/5272-0477) and **Casa-Estudio Henry Aloma** (Edificio 34B, tel 48/57-8692), both of whom are inspired by environmental issues. You can swim in the natural pools of **Baños de San Juan**, where a thatched restaurant overlooks cascades. The restored **Cafetal Buena Vista** coffee plantation, dating from 1801, is now a restaurant, adjoining the ruins of a 19th-century plantation displaying slave quarters and an ox-powered grinder. You can hire guides for hikes at **La Moka** (tel 48/57-8555), a fine hotel amid woods overlooking the village and lake. One of the few **zip line** tours ($$$$) in Cuba is here.

Soroa

This eco-retreat dates from colonial days. The **El Salto cascades** are refreshing, and the **Baños Romanos** offer relaxing massage. A prime draw is **Orquideario Soroa** (tel 048/52-3871, $), an orchid garden created in the mid-1940s. More than 700 species of plants (some 250 endemic to Cuba) are displayed on the craggy hillside. ■

VUELTA ABAJO

While lacking the grandeur of the Valle de Viñales, the flat but fertile soils of Vuelta Abajo produce unequivocally the finest tobacco in Cuba—outclassing even that of Viñales. One of the *vegas* (tobacco farms) is so revered that cigar aficionados from around the world flock there like devout pilgrims to Mecca.

A *torcedor* practices his age-old craft.

At the region's heart is the colonial town of **San Juan y Martínez**, 15 miles (24 km) southwest of Pinar del Río. Its main street is lined with colonnaded arcades. The sleepy town floats in a sea of dark green tobacco fields that produce the choice wrapper leaves for Cuban cigars. The persistence of ox-drawn plows still evokes bucolic images of yesteryear.

Among the most famous of the plantations is **Hoyo de Monterrey**, which has its own cigar label and has been producing fine smokes since 1865. At **San Luís**, the **Finca El Pinar** is renowned for the very best leaves, carrying on a tradition of tobacco production that dates back to 1845. The private 48-acre (16 ha) finca is the best place in Cuba for

an immersion in Tobacco 101, as demonstrated by Hirochi Robaina, grandson of Alejandro Robaina (1919–2010), the "godfather of cigars," who traveled the world as Cuba's official cigar ambassador and was the only Cuban since the revolution to have a brand named after him. Guided tours begin in a reception room displaying cigar paraphernalia. You then progress to the plant nursery, tobacco fields, and curing sheds. The plantation is 9 miles (15 km) west of Pinar del Río; turn south off the highway for San Luís, from where the unmarked farm is reached via a maze of country lanes.

Vuelta Abajo is framed to the north by the **Sierra de los Órganos**, a compelling venue for scenic mountain drives. ∎

Finca El Pinar

🗺 103 B1
✉ Cuchillas
de Barbacoa,
1.3 miles (2 km)
E of San Luís
☎ 48/79-7470
or 5291-2764
🕐 Closed Sun.
💲 $ (guided tour)

TOWERING TOPOGRAPHY

Much of Cuba comprises what geologists call classic karst topography: irregular limestone terrain studded with conical mountains, divided by flat valleys and precipitous ravines, and underlain with labyrinthine caves. The most striking component of this geology, the signature feature of Cuba, is the conical mountains called *mogotes* **(haystacks). They speckle the landscape, adding to Cuba's surreal beauty.**

The product of uplift and erosion over millennia, *mogotes* owe their genesis to an erstwhile limestone seabed formed during the Jurassic period, beginning some 160 million years ago, when the compressed remains of myriad shells and other aquatic life accumulated on the ocean bottom. Gradually the great plateau was thrust from the sea.

Limestone is extremely porous and succumbs to the dissolving action of rainwater and underground streams as water drains through structural joints. Rainwater also interacts with limestone to form a mild carbolic acid. In Cuba, heavy tropical rains and high temperatures speed the acidic assault on the permeable rock. Eventually, chemical action erodes the limestone into a network of huge underground passages and caves. In due course, the roofs of the largest caverns collapse, forming the *mogotes'* accompanying great valleys, some measuring as much as half a mile (0.8 km) across.

Flora & Fauna of the *Mogotes*

Many *mogotes* are freestanding and conical in shape, like upended bullets soaring as high as 1,000 feet (305 m). Others, as seen from above, wind for miles in sinuous chains. All are rounded and sheer-sided and rise above the flat, fertile valleys whose vertical walls give a sense of being walled in. Many *mogotes* are undercut at their bases, as if by the action of waves. In fact, it's a result of erosion by groundwater whose acidity content is increased by decomposed vegetation.

The *mogotes* are further broken down by plants whose roots expand incipient cracks

in the rock. Vegetation roots in hollows where soils accumulate, forming natural bowls and hanging planters, like densely packed arboretums. Since rainwater drains rapidly, the surface soil is dry. Hence, the dome-shaped hilltops themselves are sparsely vegetated. But the *mogotes'* sheer sides are overgrown with luxuriant greenery: thick brush, epiphytes, lianas, and mountain species that have adapted to tough conditions, such as caiman oaks, sierra palms,

and the rare cork palm, which grows only in the karst terrain of Valle de Viñales. North-facing slopes typically are lusher, with a heavier preponderance of epiphytes, ferns, and mosses. More than 20 species of flora are endemic to the *mogotes* of Viñales.

So specialized is the environment that specific *mogotes* often harbor species of fauna absent even on neighboring hummocks. This is especially true of certain species of mollusks: Each elevation holds several unique species of land snails. One snail genus, *Chondropomete,* whose long eyestalks blaze a fluorescent orange, has evolved a unique defense against predators: It glues itself beneath rocky out-crops and hangs by a homemade elongated suspender. Similar terrain exists elsewhere,

notably in neighboring Puerto Rico and Jamaica, as well as the Guangxi region of southern China and the karst region of Croa-tia's Dalmatian Coast.

INSIDER TIP:

To capture the *mogotes* at their most dramatic, set up your camera and tripod before dawn or dusk and be ready to shoot in the spectacular lighting that nature provides twice daily.

—CHRISTOPHER AUGER-DOMÍNGUEZ
*National Geographic
Latin America photographer*

The sheer *mogotes* add drama to the valley's timeless landscapes.

VIÑALES

The Valle de Viñales claims stupendous scenery—unequivocally Cuba's finest. Cut into the Sierra de los Órganos and ringed by *mogotes,* the valley is quilted with red, fertile soils and green *vegas* (fields), where the world's finest tobacco is grown. Cast in a quintessential Cuban time warp, the valley's one main town, Viñales, resounds to the creak of ox-drawn carts and the clip-clop of hooves. Hotels perched atop *mogotes* offer the most absorbing of views.

A fruit stop at day's end in Viñales

Viñales

103 C2 & 114

Museo Municipal

Calle Salvador Cisnero #115

048/79-3395

Closed Mon.

$

Tobacco farmers—*vegueros*—tend the fields, dressed in straw hats and white linens or well-worn army fatigues. They have no machinery to help with their work, only white oxen to draw wooden plows and comb the rich soil into rows. Many of the farmers own the land they till (although they must sell their entire crop to the government at a fixed rate). Feel free to enter the *vegas* and tent-shaped thatched curing sheds to ask for a lesson in the basics of tobacco farming.

Chickens, horses, pigs, and cattle wander about the fields and roads, while snowy white egrets jab for insects. Palm fronds and the orange blossoms of *Spathodea* burst over the scene. The valley is splendid for hiking. Take a guide if you scale a *mogote.*

Valley views are best at dawn and dusk, when the *mogotes* glow molten and the *bohíos* (thatched huts) below are lit by the warm glow of lanterns. The best vantages are from the **Hotel Los Jazmines** and **Hotel La Ermita** (see p. 245).

Viñales Village

A spell seems to have been cast over Viñales, a sleepy cowboy village founded in 1607. The village is centered on a small colonial plaza that boasts a fine 19th-century church and the **Casa de la Cultura** *(tel 48/77-8128).*

The main street, **Calle Salvador Cisneros**, is lined with pine trees, statues, and colonial houses. The former home of independence heroine Adela Azcuy (1861–1914) is now a **Museo Municipal.** The **Jardín Botánico de Viñales** *(tel 48/79-6274)* at the east end of Cisneros is a garden festooned with oddities such as Santería dolls.

Parque Nacional de Viñales

The Viñales National Park incorporates a series of narrow, interconnected valleys that open up to include the larger Valle de Viñales. Begin your visit at the **Centro de Visitantes** *(tel 48/79-61444),* with a sensational view from atop a *mogote* on the road that leads to Pinar del Río; it has a bas-relief map and excellent displays on flora, fauna, and geology. West from Viñales, the road to the village of Pons passes through the **Valle de Santo Tomás**, whose walls are riddled with miles of connected chambers—the **Cuevas de Santo Tomás** (see sidebar below). South of Pons, you find the **Valle de San Carlos**.

One mile (1.6 km) west of Viñales, a side road leads into the **Valle de los Guasas**, a vast amphitheater where the road dead-ends beneath the sheer-faced **Mogote Dos Hermanas**. The cliff is interrupted by the **Mural de la Prehistoria**, a 300-foot-long (180 m) mural in naïve style commissioned by Castro in 1961. The rustic restaurant

(tel 8/79-6260) at its base also offers horseback rides. The nearby campsite **Campismo Dos Hermanas** *(tel 8/79-3223)* has a small **Museo de la Prehistoria** *(closed Mon.)*. This is a good place to begin hikes that loop around Mogote Dos Hermanas.

North of Viñales, the *mogotes* close in to form the **Valle de San Vicente**. The **Cueva de San Miguel** *(tel 048/79-6290)*, 2 miles (3 km) north of Viñales, is a curiosity for its dripstone formations that act as a backdrop to the nightly cabaret-disco. Guided tours are offered.

More interesting is the nearby **Cueva del Indio** *(tel 048/79-6280, $$)*, a system of underground caverns that in places attain heights of 300 feet (91 m). Boats tour through the dripping stygian gloom. ∎

Fun for the Family

In Viñales and elsewhere, Cuba proves a great place for family travel. Cubans—and the Cuban government—dote on children, who are indulged in all manner of ways. Theme parks do exist, but entertainment venues are far fewer and much simpler than those of North America and Western Europe. Here are five venues to consider for family fun:

• **Cuevas de Santo Tomás, Viñales** *(tel 48/79-3145, guided tours $$)*. Adolescents will thrill to adventurous exploration of these vast caverns.

• **Acuario Nacional** *(Ave. 3ra corner 62, Miramar, Havana, tel 7/202-5871, acuarionacional.cu)* has live exhibits of marine creatures, from corals to sharks. The highlight is the three-times-daily shows featuring sea lions and dolphins.

• **Circo Trompoloco** *(Ave. 5ta at 112, Miramar, Havana, tel 7/206-5609, $$)*. Inside the Parque de Diversiones Isla del Coco see Cuba's National Circus under a "big top," Thursday to Sunday.

• **Delfinario** *(Carretera Las Morlas Km 12.5, Varadero, tel 45/66-8031, adults $$$, children under five free)*. Children can swim with dolphins and see "Flipper" perform.

• **Parque de Diversiones Isla del Coco** *(Ave. 5ta at 112, Miramar, Havana, Fri.–Sun.)*. Havana's only amusement park, it has a small roller coaster, carousel rides, and even go-carts.

• **Playas del Este.** Cuban families love these beaches east of Havana. Don't let your children swim unattended, as riptides are a frequent threat; so too are small jellyfish in winter (see p. 96).

TOBACCO ROWS

It is appropriate that the world's finest tobacco is Cuban. *Nicotiana tabacum* has been cultivated in Cuba since pre-Columbian times. It was hallowed by the indigenous Taino, who smoked it through tubes made of hollowed wood called *cohibas*. Today, the image of a mustachioed tobacco farmer *(veguero)* attentively coddling his tobacco plants is a quintessential image that personifies Cuba.

Viñales's ideal climate and rich soils are perfect for growing tobacco.

A cousin of the potato, tobacco is a member of the nightshade family. Two varieties are grown in Cuba. The *corojo,* which provides the cigar's large, thin wrapper leaves, is grown under fine sheets of mosquito netting *(tapados)* to protect against harsh sunlight and ensure leaves that are smooth and pliable. The *criollo,* used for filler leaves, is grown in direct sunlight, which brings out the fullest of flavors derived from oils that are a protective response to the sun.

Tobacco requires near-constant sunlight and minimal rain during its growing season. October to January are the prime months, after the rains have ceased. Seeds are planted in a mix of sand and ashes under beds of straw that are removed upon germination. After about 45 days, seedlings are laid out in rows in the fields.

The maturing plants are handled with great tenderness—*vegueros* are even known to talk to their leaves to stimulate growth. When the plant attains a height of 5 feet (1.5 m), the central bud is nipped off before flowering to encourage leaf growth.

The leaves grow in pairs, with six or more pairs on each plant. They are harvested January through March in six phases according to the leaves' respective positions. The lowest leaves are snicked off first, two by two, with a small sickle. The leaves above them are gathered in one-week intervals as they mature, until the *corona,* the top leaf of the plant, is taken.

The harvested leaves are sewn together and strung up on long poles, or *cujes,* arranged in rows in thatched barns *(casas de tabaco* or *secaderos);* the barns are aligned east to west for exposure to even sunlight. Here the leaves are left to dry for about 60 days, during which time they lose about 85 percent of their water and turn a reddish gold color, the green chlorophyll having turned to brown carotene.

Once cured, the leaves are taken down and bundled into wooden cases to be sent to a sorting house, where they are left to ferment for as long as three months. This reduces the resin and nicotine content. The leaves are then graded and sent to the factories to be moistened and fermented again for 60 days to remove

ammonia and other impurities. After drying, the leaves are packed in bales wrapped in palm bark, which keeps the leaves at a constant humidity. After aging for as long as four years, they are ready to be rolled into the world's finest cigars (see p. 80).

EXPERIENCE:
Holy Smoke!

How to light and smoke a cigar is an art. Here are a few dos and don'ts.

• Trim the draw end with a cutter, and don't bite off the cap as cowboys do in Hollywood Westerns.

• Light your cigar with a lighter, not a match, which will impart soot that can affect the flavor.

• First "warm" the end of the cigar with the flame, then twirl the cigar while drawing for an even light all around.

Finca El Pinar (see p. 105), in Vuelta Abajo, includes a demonstration as part of your visit, as does **Casa del Habano** *(Ave. 5ta at Calle 16, Miramar, Havana, tel 7/214-4737).*

■ **Leaves hang like smoked fish in a *secadero.***

PINAR DEL RÍO

The sleepy, down-at-heels provincial capital offers limited appeal for tourists other than as an overnight stop. It is known, however, for its neoclassical structures graced by art nouveau facades, and a miscellany of modest attractions—including a tobacco factory and esoteric museum—are worth a visit before moving on.

■ Pinar del Río's Restaurante Rumayor features a jazzy Afro-Cuban folkloric show and cabaret.

Pinar del Río

🅰 103 C2

Visitor Information

✉ Infotur, Hotel Vueltabajo, Calle Martí #117

☎ 48/75-4803

🕓 Closed Sat.–Sun.

Fábrica de Tabacos Francisco Donatién

✉ Calle Antonio Maceo #157 at Ajete

☎ 48/77-3069

🕓 Closed Sat.–Sun.

💲 $

Pinar del Río, 90 miles (145 km) west of Havana, was founded in 1669. It thrived in the 18th century as a center for cigar production, but when the factories moved to Havana in the 19th century, its fortunes declined.

Today, this town of 143,000 retains a laid-back rusticity, despite modern amenities such as a university and stadium. Its dusty streets boast colonial beaux arts and Art Deco facades, notably along the main street, **Calle Martí.** An architectural delight is the **Teatro José Jacinto Milanés** (Calle Martí #160 at Calle Colón, tel 48/75-3871), built in 1898 in Italianate Renaissance style.

The most interesting site is the **Fábrica de Tabacos Francisco Donatién**, a diminutive cigar factory where you can watch rollers behind glass conjure cigars for domestic consumption. Guayabita, a brandy made of the guayaba fruit, has been distilled at the tiny **Fábrica de Bebidas Guayabita/ Casa Garay** (Calle Isabel Rubio #189, bet. Cerefino Fernández & Frank País, tel 48/75-2966, closed Sun., $) since 1892; tastings and tours are offered.

Peer into the **Palacio de Guasch**, built by a local doctor between 1909 and 1914, with a gauche baroque frontage incorporating Gothic gargoyles, Athenian columns, and other travel-inspired elements. Inside, the **Museo de Ciencias Naturales** (Calle Martí #202 at Ave. Comandante Pinares, tel 48/77-9483, $) offers a truly eclectic array of exhibits, including seashells and a motley assortment of dinosaurs cast in cement. The modest **Museo Provincial de Historia** (Calle Martí #58, tel 48/75-4300, $) presents weapons and period furnishings illustrating the history of the town and province. **Catedral de San Rosendo** (Calle Maceo Este #2 at Calle Gerardo Medina) has a beautiful gilt altar. Outside the town, **Finca La Guabina** (Carretera de Luis Lazo, km 9.5, tel 48/75-7616), a farm and horse-breeding facility, welcomes visitors. ■

PARQUE NACIONAL PENÍNSULA DE GUANAHACABIBES

Extending like a witch's finger into the Gulf of Mexico, the 60-mile-long (96.5 km) Península de Guanahacabibes is virtually uninhabited. Smothered in cacti and scrubby woodland, and edged by a corona of sugar white beaches, the slender promontory is a pristine refuge best known for its superlative diving in the translucent waters of Bahía de Corrientes.

Prior to the Spanish conquest of Cuba, this remote region had become a point of refuge for the indigenous Siboney (also known as the Guanahatabeys), driven west by the Taino. Several archaeological sites attest to the tenure of these early residents. Today, the small community of **Villa San Juan** raises bees, while impoverished charcoal-burners cut mangroves on the swampy north coast. Otherwise, the

---

INSIDER TIP:

Watch the sun set at Cabo de San Antonio, at Cuba's far western tip. But ask before photographing the lighthouse, as this is a military site.

—VIRGILIO VALDÉS
National Geographic Latin America editor

---

region is mostly left to wild pigs, deer, *jutías ratas* (large rodents), iguanas, and copious birdlife, including parakeets, Cuban trogons, and endangered great lizard cuckoos.

The flat, semiarid peninsula is enshrined as a 250,806-acre (101,500 ha) national park and UNESCO biosphere reserve. This is divided into the **El Veral Cabo Corrientes** and the **Cabo de San Antonio** reserves. There are facilities for tourists and three hiking trails. Obligatory guides can be hired at the **Centro Ecológico**, an ecological research station at the tiny community of La Bajada. The road splits here. To the left, you'll swing around the east end of Bahía de Corrientes to the **María la Gorda Hotel** (*tel 48/77-8077*), a dive resort with a modest beach. The bay extends south to Cabo Corrientes and offers prime diving, with coral formations and sightings of dolphins and whale sharks. There are also sunken galleons to explore. The bay was a haven for pirates, and the most prominent physical feature hereabouts is named, according to local lore, for the endowments of their favorite madame (María la Gorda, or Fat Mary).

West from La Bajada, a dirt road extends 34 miles (54 km) along the peninsula's southern shore and deposits you at a lighthouse at **Cabo de San Antonio** (Cuba's westernmost point). The lighthouse is backed by a military outpost. Beyond lies the mediocre beach of **Playas las Tumbas** and **Punta Cajón**, with fine fishing. ∎

Parque Nacional Península de Guanahacabibes

🗺 102 A1

Visitor Information

✉ Estacion ecológica, La Bajada

☎ 48/75-0366

💲 $$

DRIVE THE NORTH COAST

Although most travelers heading west from Havana opt for the fast *autopista*, which sweeps through the southern lowlands of Pinar del Río, the Circuito Norte, which hugs the north shore, is far more appealing. This roller-coaster ride offers seductive vistas of peacock-colored waters and dramatic *mogotes,* and the bucolic calm of sleepy coastal towns interspersed among rolling cane fields.

The eco-resort of Las Terrazas nestles in the Sierra del Rosario Reserva de la Biosfera.

The 90-mile (145 km) drive along Route 1-1 (the Circuito Norte) begins at **Mariel ❶**, 28 miles (45 km) west of Havana, an excellent natural port that has now become a mega-port and is attracting a lot of foreign investors. It's known as the departure point for the "boat lift" of 1980, when 120,000 Cubans (many of them criminals released from jail) fled Cuba for Florida. This event and its aftermath were fictionalized in the 1983 Hollywood film *Scarface,* starring Al Pacino.

West of Mariel, the sense of urban enclosure gives way to more calming sensations as the road narrows down to do a twisty two-lane tango along a ridgetop between lime green sugarcane fields and the rich blue Atlantic. *Centrales* (sugar factories) rise over the fields. Traffic is limited, with a preponderance of tractors and creaking wooden carts pulled by white oxen dropping long stalks of cane as they go. Potholes are numerous, as are the usual obstacles—bicycles,

cattle, and, during the *zafra* (sugar harvest), steam trains shunting to and from *centrales*. You'll pass through forlorn fishing villages, with signs pointing to various *campismos*—holiday camps. Gradually the Sierra del Rosario rises to the south. Numerous side roads lead into the cool, pine-clad mountains.

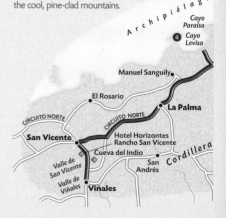

NOT TO BE MISSED:

Sierra del Rosario Reserva de la Biosfera
• Cueva del Indio • Valle de Viñales

At **San Diego de Núñez ❷**, you might opt to detour inland and follow the twisting road up to **Soroa** and **Las Terrazas**, two ecological tourist communities in the **Sierra del Rosario Reserva de la Biosfera** (see p. 104). A visit to these sites will add several hours to your journey.

Back on the Circuito Norte, you pass through the unremarkable town of **Bahía Honda.** Seven miles (11 km) farther west, turn south for a brief detour for a close-up view of **Pan de Guajaibón ❸**, a dramatic, mauve-colored sugarloaf soaring 2,294 feet (699 m). The detour—which snakes 9 miles (14 km) up through coffee country, with glossy-leafed bushes aligned in neat rows—peters out at the ramshackle hamlet of **Rancho Canelo**. From

here, you can hike to the base of the mountain.

West of Las Pozas, the coastal views open to the cays of the **Archipiélago de los Colorados** floating in the turquoise shallows offshore. Inaccessible Cayo Paraíso was once used by Ernest Hemingway as a base for antisubmarine operations from his yacht—*Pilar*—during World War II. Farther west, a signed turnoff leads 2 miles (3 km) north to the ferry berth for **Cayo Levisa ❹** (*tel 48/75-6501*), a prime dive site with sparkling beaches (*ferries run twice daily*). This tiny, exquisite isle is a perfect place to relax and has a fine hotel plus water sports.

The road pitches in sweeping curves as it leads southwest to **La Palma.** At **San Vicente**, 20 miles (32 km) farther, turn south for Viñales. You'll pass the **Horizontes Villa Rancho San Vicente** (*tel 48/79-6201*), a spa hotel with a fine restaurant, and **Cueva del Indio** (see p. 109). Beyond, the valley opens dramatically into the **Valle de San Vicente** (see p. 109), an amphitheater that you exit via a narrow passage that deposits you in the **Valle de Viñales** and the eponymous village (see pp. 108–109).

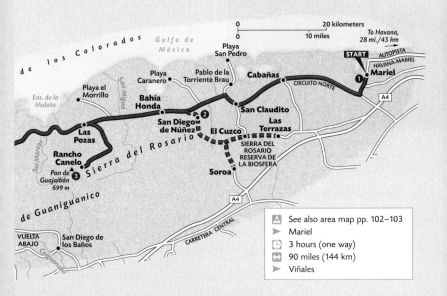

See also area map pp. 102–103
Mariel
3 hours (one way)
90 miles (144 km)
Viñales

More Places to Visit in the Far West

Antiguo Cafetal Angerona

This *finca,* 10 miles (16 km) west of Artemisa, was built in 1813 and became one of the largest coffee and sugar estates in Cuba, with 450 slaves. You can explore the subterranean cisterns, and the watchtowers that shadow the *barracón,* where slaves were kept when not toiling the fields. The finca was famously used by the author James A. Michener as a setting in his 1989 novel, *Caribbean.* **Finca Charco Azul** *(tel 7/649-1055),* at Cayajabos, 9 miles (14 km) west of Artemisa, breeds Gertrudis cattle and Percheron draft horses. It has a small boutique hotel. ⚑ 103 D2

■ **The ruins of Antiguo Cafetal Angerona, once one of Cuba's largest coffee and sugar estates**

Parque Nacional La Güira

Spanning 54,000 acres (21,850 ha) of the **Sierra de los Órganos**, the park is approached from its south side, off the Carretera Central, via a mock fortress that opens to **Hacienda Cortina**, a once imposing medieval–style mansion now mostly in ruins.

Cuevas de los Portales *($),* some 10 miles (16 km) north of Hacienda Cortina, forms the hollow of a sheer-sided *mogote* cut through by the Río Caiguanabo. The cathedral–like vault forms a dark habitat for bats. Ornate dripstone formations resemble giant organs. Che Guevara set up headquarters here during the Cuban missile crisis, when he commanded the Western Army. His bedroom and makeshift "office" are maintained. A *campismo* (basic camping facility; *tel 48/63-6749)* offers cabins. This is best reached from the *autopista* at Entronque de Herradura, 12 miles (20 km) west of San Diego de los Baños. ⚑ 103 C2

San Antonio de los Baños

Despite its forlorn appearance, this small town, 19 miles (30 km) south of Havana, clings to its colonial charm, concentrated around the main plaza. Its main draw is the **Bienal Internacional del Humor**, a comedy festival held every two years. The festival has spawned the **Museo del Humor** *(Calle 60 #4116, tel 47/38-2817, cnpc.cult.cu, closed Mon., $),* displaying cartoons from around the world—with a strongly anti-imperialist slant. ⚑ 103 D3

San Diego de los Baños

This sleepy, down-at-heels place, half a mile (0.8 km) north of the Carretera Central, about 38 miles (61 km) east of the town of Pinar del Río has been an important spa town since the late 19th century. The mineral springs, which hover around 100°F (38°C), feed subterranean whirlpool baths at the **Balneario San Diego** *(tel 48/54-8880).* Tourists lodge at the handsome **Hotel Mirador** (see p. 245), a restored 1950s mansion now specializing in medical treatments. The Greek orthodox—style church in the main square is an architectural curiosity but nature is the main attraction here. ⚑ 103 C2

Slender beach-fringed peninsulas, rugged tobacco country, and mausoleum and monuments to the memory of Che

WESTERN CUBA-NORTH

Festive mask at the Museo de las Parrandas, Remedios

WESTERN CUBA—NORTH

East of the Cuban capital, the island fattens out, with the limestone uplands of Havana Province shouldering against the broad plains, or *llanuras*, of Matanzas Province. Green and flat as a billiard table, these plains possess Cuba's richest soils, ideal for growing sugarcane. Narrowing eastward, they edge along the coast in the cusp of low hills that compose the soft, rolling landscape of Villa Clara Province.

Scenic only at the hilly extremes, the northwest offers scant delights along the shore. Mangroves creep into the calm waters of the Archipiélago Sabana-Camagüey, an unbroken necklace of coral cays between 5 and 15 miles (8–24 km) offshore.

The cays extend east of the Península de Hicacos, a thin sling cast from the mainland of Matanzas Province. The peninsula hosts Varadero—Cuba's Cancún—drawing package tourists to its famous 7-mile (11.5 km) beach lined with more than 50 hotels. Despite a bagful of offerings—water sports, scuba diving, and golf, to name a few—Varadero disappoints, not least because few Cubans are present, sapping resorts of the vivacity and passion that are the hallmarks of the Cuban spirit. A new resort playground is emerging farther east, at Cayo Santa María and neighboring Cayos de Villa Clara.

East of Varadero, a broad plain extends inland from the coast. Since the 19th century, this area has been Cuba's most fertile sugar-growing region, a landscape of Day-Glo green cane fields with tornadoes of black smoke whirling from *centrales* (sugarcane-processing plants). During the *zafra,* or sugar harvest, the idyll is tainted with the cloying smell of molasses. "White gold"—sugar—paid for towns such as Matanzas and Cárdenas. There are caverns to explore in the hills and vales surrounding Matanzas, where a once popular spa destination—San Miguel de los Baños—still awaits restoration to its former splendor.

The cities are linked to Havana by the Carretera Central, built between 1926 and 1931 as the country's main highway and today connecting dusty farming towns whose former prominence has since been usurped by the Autopista Nacional, farther south.

The Vía Blanca, or Circuito Norte, accesses the north coast. Rising eastward into the Alturas del Nordeste, it offers an entrée to the beauty of upland Villa Clara south of the rich coastal plain. Royal palms stud the valleys where *vegueros* (tobacco growers) lovingly tend

their plants and till the fields with oxen in the time-honored way.

Most travelers visit Villa Clara to pay homage to Che Guevara in the provincial capital of Santa Clara. The city, scene of the decisive battle that toppled the Batista regime, has adopted the Argentine revolutionary as one of its own. The heavily industrialized city now hosts a towering statue and a mausoleum to Che. His remains were laid to rest here on October 17, 1997, along with those of fellow combatants from the Bolivian campaign.

Santa Clara draws the three main highways to itself and spins the Circuito Norte shooting back toward the coast via Vuelta Arriba to Remedios, steeped in colonial charm. Remedios is enticing for its year-end *parrandas*—battles of fireworks that erupt during Christmas week. ■

NOT TO BE MISSED:

Relaxing on Varadero beach   123

Santa Clara's mausoleum and the museum of Che Guevara 125

The end-of-year excitement of the *parranda* celebration in the colonial city of Remedios   129

Boning up on Cuban history at Cárdenas's Museo Oscar María de Rojas   130

The spectacular 30-mile (50 km) causeway across the Caribbean lagoons to the Cayos de Villa Clara   130

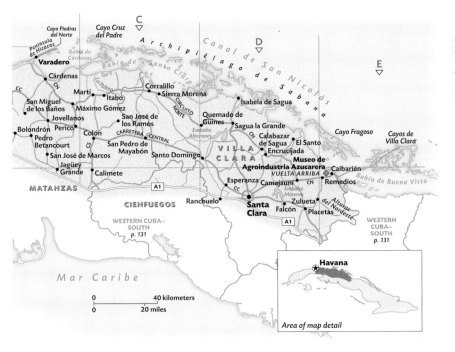

HAVANA TO MATANZAS

A coastal zone of prim coves and golden beaches extends between the cities of Havana and Matanzas. Uninspiring stretches of raised coral, some marred by oil derricks and overpowered by the stench of sulfurous fumes, meld into more graceful vistas that reveal the beauty of inland valleys studded by *mogotes* (see pp. 106–107). A venerable sugar-processing town and a scenic canyon make intriguing stops on any journey between the two cities.

The Puente Bacunayagua sweeps traffic high over a canyon.

Havana to Matanzas

![map] 118 A2 & B2

Eastward, beyond Playas del Este, the Vía Blanca (Rte. 2-1.3) hugs the shoreline, offering little of note for the first 10 miles (16 km). Beyond Boca de Jaruco,

the mouth of the Río Jaruco, oil derricks appear. Looming beyond is an oil-fed electrical-generating plant at the edge of Santa Cruz del Norte. Here the taint of molasses emanates from Fábrica Cubaron *(closed to the public)*, which produces Havana Club rums.

Swoop south 3 miles (5 km) to **Camilo Cienfuegos**, a community built around a now closed *centrale* (sugarcane-processing plant). Before the revolution in 1959, the Pennsylvania-based Hershey chocolate company owned 44,500 acres (18,000 ha) of land here to farm sugarcane; it was centered on the purpose-built village— christened "Hershey"—complete with movie theater, baseball field, and hotel. Though ramshackle, the town is worth a quick browse.

On the **Puente Bacunayagua**, 66 miles (106 km) east of Havana, travelers trundling along the highway are treated to a spectacular vista. Here, a 1,030-foot-long (314 m) bridge hangs over a canyon at the mouth of the Río Bacunayagua, 361 feet (110 m) below. To the south is the Valle Yumurí, its rolling green landscape dotted with palms. No stopping is allowed on the bridge. A *mirador* (viewing platform) overlooking the highway offers a chance to photograph the picture-postcard setting. ■

EXPERIENCE:
Cuba's Vintage Rails

Experience the beauty of rural Cuba aboard the electric-powered **Hershey train**, originally built by the chocolate firm in 1916 to transport workers. This train runs between Casablanca (on the north shore of Havana harbor) and Matanzas. As it wends through the **Valle Yumurí**, it stops at remote stations where *guajiros* (peasant farmers) get on or off. A highlight is a stop at the old **Hershey estate**, where you can explore the now tumbledown village. Antique Spanish cars provide the current service, originally inaugurated in 1916 as a steam train. The train operates five times daily *(tel 45/24-4805, schedule varies)*.

MATANZAS

Long known as the "Athens of Cuba," the port city of Matanzas offers its share of neo-classical structures of note. It is hardly a picturesque city, however, despite its dramatic location on a sweeping bay—Cuba's largest—enfolded by hills. Matanzas is known for its traditional music, strongly influenced by African rhythms.

A bronze statue of José Martí overlooks Plaza de La Libertad.

Matanzas (pop. 140,000) was founded in 1693 between the mouths of the Yumurí and San Juan rivers. Before that, it was best known for Dutch pirate Piet Hein's attack on the Spanish treasure fleet in 1628; two dozen gold-laden galleons were sent to the bottom of the bay.

The city was named for either a massacre (*matanza*) of Spaniards by Indians in 1510 or that of pigs killed to supply fleets of ships. It became a hub for the disembarkation of slaves and grew wealthy during the mid-19th-century heyday of sugar. It evolved a café society that found its expression in civic construction, music, and dance—the *danzón*, a

derivative of the quadrille, was invented here in 1879, and the city is considered the "queen of rumba."

Today, tankers and freighters anchor in the bay, surrounded by sugar-loading and oil-refining facilities and industrial factories. For a splendid view, head up Calle 306 to **Ermita de Monserrate**, a restored hilltop hermitage; and **Parque René Fraga**, at Bonifacio Byrne and Calle 312.

The Historic Core

Reparto Matanzas, the early colonial core, is laid out in a grid west of Plaza de la Vigía, the original town plaza. Its pride is the

Matanzas

118 B2

Museo Provincial Palacio de Junco

- ✉ Calle 83 (Milanés) & Calle 212, bet. Magdalena & Ayón
- ☎ 45/24-3195 or 45/24-3464
- 🕒 Closed Mon.
- 💲 $

Museo Farmacéutico

- ✉ Calle 83 (Milanés) #4951, bet. Santa Teresa & Ayuntamiento
- ☎ 45/24-3179
- 💲 $

cnpc.cult.cu

Museo de la Ruta del Esclavo

- ✉ Castillo de San Severino, half mile (0.8 km) NE of Puente de la Concordia
- ☎ 45/28-3259
- 🕒 Closed Mon.
- 💲 $

Cuevas de Bellamar

- 🅰 118 B2
- ☎ 45/25-3538 or 45/26-1683
- 💲 $$

Teatro Sauto *(tel 45/24-2721)*, built in neoclassical style in 1863. Once one of the finest opera theaters, its tiered balconies and hardwood floor have been recently restored. To learn something of local history, stop by the splendid **Museo Provincial Palacio de Junco**, in a neoclassical structure with arcades built in 1840 by a wealthy planter.

The plaza merges into **Parque de los Bomberos** (Firemen's Square), where antique fire engines are on display in the

---

INSIDER TIP:

Going to Matanzas aboard the Hershey train is a must-do: An intimate engagement with Cubans, from schoolkids to farmers, is guaranteed.

—STACIE PIERPOINT
Annenberg Learner educational editor, learner.org

---

quaint neoclassical firehouse, now the **Museo de los Bomberos** *(tel 45/24-2363, closed Sun.)*. Opposite, an esteemed publishing house, **Ediciones Vigía** *(tel 45/26-0917, closed Sat.–Sun., $)* still produces fine hand-printed books.

Parque de La Libertad, four blocks west, has a bronze statue of José Martí. To each side are buildings of note: to the north, the **Biblioteca** (library) and adjoining **Casa de la Cultura**, in the former Lyceum Club and Casino Club, respectively; and to the south, **Museo Farmacéutico** (Pharmaceutical Museum) that occupies a

preserved 1882 pharmacy. Carved wooden shelves are lined with ornate porcelain jars and crystal flasks containing cures. The partially restored **Catedral de San Carlos Borromeo** *(Calle 282, bet. Calles 83 & 85)*, built in 1878 and restored in 2016, boasts a beautiful frescoed ceiling.

Reparto Versalles

Settled by French refugees from Haiti in the early 19th century, this district lies north of the Río Yumurí. To get there, cross the arched **Puente de la Concordia**, built of stone in 1878 with decorative columns. Worth perusal is the **Iglesia de San Pedro Apóstol** *(Calles 57 & 270)*.

Castillo de San Severino rises over the port at the east end of Reparto Versalles. The castle, completed in 1735, was a prison in the wars of independence; bullet holes where 61 nationalists were executed scar the dry western moat. The castle hosts the **Museo de la Ruta del Esclavo** (Slave Route Museum), with exhibits on pre-Columbian, colonial, and slave-trade history; two rooms feature displays on Santería. The terminus of the Hershey train is here (see sidebar p. 120; *Calle 262 at 67, tel 45/24-4805)*.

Cuevas de Bellamar

A mammoth cave system, at **Finca la Alcancía**, 3 miles (5 km) southeast of Matanzas, has more than 2 miles (3 km) of viewable chambers full of dripstone formations and marine fossils. Hour-long guided tours are offered. ■

VARADERO

Cuba's lodestone of tourism, Varadero, located 88 miles (141 km) east of Havana, lures many vacationers with a diamond-dust beach edging the length of an 11-mile-long (17 km) peninsula. Half of the nation's hotels are here—from budget options to international-chain resorts. If sun, sand, and sea are your thing, this is for you. But Varadero caters mainly to Canadian and European package tourists and, being a pipe dream to Cubans, is somewhat soulless for it.

Jutting out into Bahía de Cárdenas, the pencil-thin **Punta Hicacos** is being developed as a Cuban Cancún. The beaches on the north shore shelve into turquoise waters whose coral reefs tempt divers—notably in **Parque Marino Cayo Piedras del Norte**, with its sunken plane and frigate. **Gaviota Diving Center** *(Marina Gaviota, Autopista Sur Km 21, tel 45/66-7755)* offers trips, while a "**Seafari Cayo Blanco**" *(tel 45/66-7550)* catamaran excursion departs Marina Chapelín.

Varadero village evolved in the 1880s as a summer resort; the red-roof wooden houses can still be seen along Avenida 1ra. In the 1920s, U.S. industrialist Irénée du Pont developed much of the peninsula. By the 1950s, grand hotels and casinos had sprung up.

Du Pont's Spanish-style mansion, now a hotel and restaurant called **Mansión Xanadú** *(tel 45/66-8482)*, commands a headland at the east end of the main beach. Du Pont's 9-hole golf course is now the 18-hole **Varadero Golf Club** *(tel 45/66-7788, varaderogolfclub.com)*.

Parque Retiro-Josone *(Ave. 1ra & Calle 59)* offers a bucolic retreat with a lake and rowboats *($$)*. The **Museo Municipal de Varadero** *(Ave. 1ra at Calle 57, tel

⬛ **Flying above the tourist paradise of Varadero**

45/61-3189, $)* displays exhibits on aboriginal culture, flora and fauna, and Varadero's historic regattas. The **Taller de Cerámica** *(Ave. 1ra bet. Calles 59 & 60)* produces and sells pottery.

Reserva Ecológica Varahicacos *(tel 45/66-8018, $)*, a 730-acre (296 ha) swath at the island's east end, has trails leading to caves, including **Cueva Ambrosio**, which contains Indian drawings. ■

Varadero
🗺 119 B2
Visitor Information
✉ Infotur,
    Ave. 1ra at
    Calle 13,
    Hotel Acuazul
☎ 45/66-2966
    or 45/66-2961

SANTA CLARA

This important industrial and university city, capital of Villa Clara Province and gateway to the eastern provinces, lies at the heartland of Cuba. The city (pop. 216,000) has strong associations with Che Guevara (see pp. 126–127), who here led the final, successful battle of the revolutionary war to topple Batista.

A boxcar from the train derailed by Che Guevara in 1958

Santa Clara

119 D1

Visitor Information

Infotur, Calle
Cuba #66, bet.
San Cristóbal &
Candelaria

42/20-1352

**Teatro
La Caridad**

Parque Vidal,
bet. Máximo
Gómez & Marta
Abreu

42/20-5548

$

Santa Clara, 170 miles (274 km) east of Havana, was founded in 1689 when residents of nearby Remedios relocated to escape the Inquisition (see p. 128). The city was fought over fiercely during the wars of independence and later proved critical in the ouster of General Batista when it was attacked in 1958 by Che Guevara's men. After three days of battle, Santa Clara was captured and Batista fled Cuba the next day. Che's remains were interred here in October 1997.

Worth seeking out are **Iglesia de Nuestra Señora del Buen Viaje** *(Calle Unión & Buen Viaje)* and **Iglesia del Carmen**, in Parque del Carmen.

Parque Vidal

This park—named for independence hero Col. Leoncio Vidal—lies at the city core. Shaded by poinciana and *guásima* trees, the square is ringed by a two-tier walkway divided by a rail that separated colonial whites from blacks. Neoclassical buildings surround the square, including (on the east side) the **Palacio del Gobierno Provincial**, the former town hall now housing the **José Martí library**. On the northwest corner stands the **Teatro La Caridad**, built in 1885 for the poor of Santa Clara and funded by local noblewoman-philanthropist Marta Abreu de Estévez (1845–1909); her bronze bust looks over the plaza.

A fresco by Spanish-Philippine artist Camilo Salaya graces the theater's dome.

Next door, an 18th-century mansion contains the **Museo de Artes Decorativas**, displaying a sumptuous collection of paintings and antiques spanning three centuries. The tall structure on the southwest side of the plaza is the **Hotel Santa Clara Libre**. Bullet holes from the battle of 1958 can still be seen on its facade.

The **Museo Provincial Abel Santamaría**, in Reparto Osvaldo Herrera, is a curiosity. Its eclectic exhibits range from natural history to colonial furniture. It is housed in the city's former military barracks—now a school, **Escuela Abel Santamaría**—where Che accepted the surrender of the city.

Homage to Che

Calle Independencia slopes downhill to the Río Cubanicay and the remains of the **Tren Blindado**, an armored train sent to reinforce Batista's forces. On December 29, 1958, a rebel band led by Che derailed the train loaded with munitions and 408 men. After a battle, the troops surrendered. The monument comprises four carriages arrayed as they came to rest in a tangle; one is now a museum. One block east is the **Estatua al Che** (pictured on p. 8) showing Che holding the Child of the Revolution. Now head to **Plaza de la Revolución.** The vast concrete plaza is dominated by the **Conjunto escultórico comandante Ernesto Che Guevara**, artist José Delarra's colossal bronze statue of Che bearing a rifle.

The **Museo del Che** is at the rear. Photographs and mementos trace Che's life, from his childhood to his death in Bolivia in 1967. No photos are allowed. Adjacent is a mausoleum where Che's remains are inset in the wall. An eternal flame—lit by Fidel Castro in 1997—adds to the stirring effect. ∎

Museo de Artes Decorativas
- ⊠ Parque Vidal #3 at Luis Estévez
- ☎ 42/20-5368
- 💲 $

Museo Provincial Abel Santamaría
- ⊠ Escuela Abel Santamaría, Calle Esquerra at Central
- ☎ 42/20-3041
- 🕐 Closed Sun.
- 💲 $

Museo del Che
- ⊠ Plaza de la Revolución at Ave. de los Desfiles
- ☎ 42/20-5878
- 🕐 Closed Mon.

Know Your Revolutionary Heroes

• **Camilo Cienfuegos (1932–1959).** A radical student activist, he participated in the *Granma* landing, was named Fidel's chief of staff, and commanded the fourth front in Castro's Rebel Army. The extremely popular guerrilla leader died when his plane mysteriously disappeared at sea in October 1959.

• **Frank País (1934–1957).** He founded the National Revolutionary Movement in Santiago de Cuba and merged it with Castro's M-26-7 revolutionary organization. He then headed the M-26-7 in Oriente and oversaw the movement's plans and activities in Cuba in the months preceding the *Granma* landing. He led an attack on police headquarters in Santiago de Cuba to coincide with the landing, and was assassinated in July 1957.

• **Celia Sánchez (1920–1980).** She operated the secret supply route to Castro's Rebel Army in the Sierra Maestra. Later she became Fidel's secretary (and, it is rumored, his lover) and helped moderate his most mean-spirited tendencies.

• **Abel Santamaría (1927–1953).** He was named as number two in the M-26-7 movement. He helped lead the attack on the Moncada barracks. He was captured and tortured to death by Batista's forces.

WHAT IS IT ABOUT CHE?

Ernesto "Che" Guevara is Cuba's most revered revolutionary hero. His steely visage—the famous image of the "Heroic Guerrilla" in signature beret with five-pointed star—is seen across Cuba on everything from billboards to key chains. A chief architect of the Cuban revolution, this Argentine is still invoked as the model for the "New Man," someone unselfishly committed to socialist ideals.

Ernesto Guevara (1928–1967) was born in Rosario, Argentina, to an intellectual middle-class family. He trained as a doctor, then, seeking to sow some wild oats, set out to explore South America on his Norton motorcycle. The poverty and injustice he saw awakened his socialist passions. In 1954 he witnessed the CIA's overthrow of Guatemala's socialist Arbenz Guzmán government. Embittered, he fled to Mexico City, where he met Fidel Castro and signed on with Castro's guerrilla army-in-training—the Movimiento 26 de Julio. In time, he became Castro's closest friend and was known simply as "Che," the Argentine equivalent of the American "buddy." Che was one of only 17 rebels who survived the *Granma* landing in December 1956.

A daring and reckless fighter, Che proved himself a brilliant field commander; he was beloved by his troops, many of whom committed to him for the rest of their lives—*los hombres del Che*. In the decisive battle at Santa Clara in December 1958, Che won a stunning victory that sealed the fate of the Batista dictatorship. After *el triunfo*, Che led the tribunals that sent thousands of counterrevolutionaries to be executed at the wall. He was given Cuban citizenship and shaped the revolution hand in hand with Castro.

Che negotiated key treaties with the Soviet Union, supervised agrarian reform, and oversaw the transformation of the economy as head of the national bank (from 1959) and minister of finance and industry (from 1961).

EXPERIENCE: Follow Che's Trail Through Cuba

In 1997, the remains of Che Guevara were brought back from Bolivia to rest in the mausoleum in Santa Clara. So this is the perfect place to start your islandwide trail of the Argentine revolutionary hero:

• **Museo del Che, Santa Clara:** The memorial museum in Santa Clara gives Guevara the pop sanctity of James Dean or Jim Morrison. You'll see Che's pistol, plus other memorabilia from his days as a revolutionary (see p. 125).

• **Ministerio del Interior (Ministry of the Interior), Havana:** In Plaza de la Revolución, with its bronze mural of Che.

• **Casa-Museo del Che, Havana:** Che's former headquarters, overlooking Casablanca immediately east of La Cabaña fortress, is kept as it was when in use, with

his armaments and other memorabilia (see p. 83).

• **Museo de la Revolución, Havana:** The *Granma* boat that brought Che and his comrades to Cuba from Mexico in 1956 is enshrined here (see pp. 77–79).

• **Centro de Estudios Che Guevara, Havana:** Dedicated to studies and public education about Che (see p. 99–100).

• **Playa Las Coloradas, Granma Province:** In December 1956, Fidel, Che, and fellow revolutionaries stumbled ashore in the south of the island to launch the revolution. A pathway and concrete pier make it easy to retrace their route through a sweltering mangrove swamp. You'll share the path of revolution with crabs, mosquitoes, and biting flies—just as Che and his *compañeros* did (see p. 194).

A mosaic in Matanzas honors the "Heroic Guerrilla."

The committed Marxist denied himself any privileges and scorned individualism. He espoused replacing the drive for material gain with moral incentives inspired by altruism and collective welfare. A brilliant intellectual, Che wrote poetry and authored several books.

An anti-imperialist, the restless romantic clung to his fervid dream of inspiring international revolution. In 1965, he renounced his Cuban citizenship and departed Cuba in secret to train leftist rebels in the Congo. The following year he appeared in Bolivia with a Cuban force, intent on sparking continent-wide insurrection. Disaster ensued. Bolivian peasants betrayed him, and in 1967 Che was executed by the Bolivian army and buried in a secret grave.

Castro built a cult of the dead hero. A 1960s "Be Like Che" campaign still stokes revolutionary fervor. His motto—*Hasta la victoria siempre* (Toward victory, always)—is splashed across Cuba.

REMEDIOS

Second only to Trinidad in provincial colonial charm, Remedios—one of Cuba's oldest settlements—clings to its well-preserved past. Spruced up after being named a national monument, its streets vibrate with color and never more than at year's end, when the otherwise somnolent town explodes in firework fever.

■ Taking a break: students at Remedios's Escuela Mártires de Barbados

Remedios
🖼 119 E1

**Museo de la
Música Alejandro
García Caturla**
✉ Parque Martí #5
☎ 42/39-6851
🕐 Closed Mon.
💲 $

Remedios was founded in 1513 close to the Atlantic and, due to predation by pirates, relocated in 1544 to its present position, 26 miles (42 km) northeast of Santa Clara. The town grew to become the region's most important until the late 17th century, when catastrophe befell. It was almost completely destroyed by fire in 1692. Local legends embellish the event with stories of demons and exorcists. Many villagers abandoned Remedios to found a new township—today's Santa Clara (see pp. 124–125).

Remedios, untouched by modernity, is replete with venerable buildings spanning the past 300 years. Simply wandering the streets is its own reward.

Your starting point is **Plaza Martí**, an intimate square graced by tall palms shading a bandstand and wrought-iron benches. The ocher **Parroquia Mayor de San Juan Bautista** rears over the plaza. Dating from 1682, the church's interior features a baroque gilt altar and a vaulted mahogany ceiling, noteworthy for its stylized floral decoration. To the north, the **Museo de la Música Alejandro García Caturla** honors the musical prodigy Alejandro García Caturla (1906–1940), a foremost composer and liberal social activist.

On the plaza's southwest corner stands the **Hotel Mascotte** *(tel 42/39-5144)*. A plaque on the exterior wall recalls that on February 1, 1899, Gen. Máximo Gómez and Robert P. Porter, acting on behalf of President William McKinley, negotiated the honorable discharge of the Mambí army following the Spanish-American War. A stone's throw east is the historic and lovely **Hotel E Barcelona** (see p. 246) with a remarkable courtyard. Also worth a visit is the tiny **Iglesia del Buen Viaje** *(Calle Alejandro del Río #66),* occupying a small *plazuela* facing east onto Plaza Martí. Fronting it is a marble statue of Cuba's Indian maiden. Be sure to visit the **Museo de las Parrandas**,

---

INSIDER TIP:

If attending the Parrandas Remedianas, wear nonflammable clothing and avoid wearing nylon, which can easily melt.

—STACIE PIERPOINT
Annenberg Learner educational editor, learner.org

---

one block east, to learn of the fascinating *parrandas* unique to the region (see sidebar above). Exhibits include flags, parade costumes, floats, and samples of fireworks used for the Christmas festivities, when the two sides of

Noisy Nights

At year's end, the sky over Remedios and neighboring villages literally explodes in bright lights, when communities divide into rival sections to do battle for status in an orgy of pyrotechnic insanity. The Mardi Gras–style festival, called Parrandas Remedianas, dates from the early 19th century. Lasting through the night, the *parranda* begins when neon-lit murals towering 90 feet (27 m) over the plaza are lit, and the entire town crowds onto the plaza. Rum flows freely as a barrage of homemade fireworks is unleashed. Each side also presents a parade float, which emerges around 3 a.m. Points are added up, but it is the bombast of fireworks rather than any artistic creativity that takes precedent in deciding the winner.

town and neighboring villages do battle. To learn more about Remedios's intriguing history, stop by the **Museo Municipal de Remedios**, housed in a beautiful mansion.

Caibarién

This once wealthy port town, 5 miles (8 km) east of Remedios, exudes a faded colonial splendor, centered on **Parque de La Libertad**. Worth a peek is the **Museo Municipal María Escobar Laredo**, on the southwest corner of the square. Don't miss the **Museo de Agroindustria Azucarera** (Sugar Industry Museum; *on the way to Remedios, km 3.5, tel 42/36-3286, closed Sat.–Sun., $),* adjoining a now defunct sugar mill. This excellent museum includes more than 20 antique steam trains. ∎

Museo de las Parrandas

- ✉ Máximo Gómez #71
- ☎ 42/39-5677 or 42/39-5400
- 🕐 Closed Mon.
- 💲 $

cnpc.cult.cu

Museo Municipal de Remedios

- ✉ Calle Antonio Maceo #56, bet. Ave. General Carilla & Fe del Valle
- ☎ 42/39-6792
- 🕐 Closed Mon.

More Places to Visit in Western Cuba–North

Horse-drawn buggies in front of the Catedral de la Concepción Inmaculada in Cárdenas

Cárdenas

Founded in 1828, this sprawling port town is located some 8 miles (13 km) southeast of Varadero. The Cuban flag was first flown here in 1850, when Venezuelan adventurer Narciso López launched an ill-fated invasion to spawn Cuban independence. Worth a visit are the **Catedral de la Concepción Inmaculada,** in Parque Colón; and the **Plaza Molokoff,** a domed market hall at Calle 12 and Avenida 3.

Parque Echeverría hosts the **Museo Casa Natal de José Antonio Echeverría** *(Ave. 4, bet. Calle 12 & 13, tel 45/52-4145, closed Mon., $),* dedicated to the revolutionary student leader (1932–1957). On the park's south side is the superb **Museo Oscar María de Rojas** *(Calzada #4, bet. Echeverría & Martí, tel 45/52-2417, closed Mon., $$),* with expansive and eclectic displays portraying the city's and Cuba's history. Cárdenas is most famous as being the home of Elián González, the child who became the object of a custody battle after being rescued at sea off Florida in November 1999. The story is regaled in the **Museo a la Batalla de Ideas** (Museum of the Battle of Ideas; *Ave. 6, bet. Calles 11 & 12; tel 45/52-7599, closed Mon., $).* 119 B2

Cayo Santa María

This is the last of a 35-mile-long (56 km) parade of cays sprinkled across the **Bahía de Buena Vista,** off northeast Villa Clara. Gorgeous beaches gird the isles' seaward side, with inshore fishing and scuba diving being offered at **Marina Gaviota** *(tel 42/ 35-0013).* Linked to the mainland by a toll *pedraplén* (raised causeway), **Cayo Santa María** *(passports required for access)*–the largest and principal cay–is now lined by all-inclusive resort hotels erected in the past decade. Dolphin shows are performed at the **Acuario-Delfinario** *(tel 42/35-0013).* 119 E2

San Miguel de Los Baños

The once fine spa town lies nestled in the hills some 25 miles (40 km) southeast of Matanzas. The Muslim-style **Balneario San Miguel** is now sadly in a state of near ruin, but the traveler will find many intriguing traces of its former elegance. The tumbledown, mostly wooden homes found here are of a gingerbread style that is unique in Cuba. 119 B2

Sugar white beaches, cobbled plazas, beautiful Trinidad, and a time-warp colonial town that's a UNESCO World Heritage site

WESTERN CUBA-SOUTH

Young Cubans at the Ismadillo camp, between Trinidad and Cienfuegos

WESTERN CUBA–SOUTH

Spanning the provinces of Matanzas, Cienfuegos, and Sancti Spíritus, this region leaves an indelible impression on those who venture here. The Autopista Nacional—the nation's sole freeway—cuts a swath through the western lowlands and skirts more easterly mountains, linking Havana with the city of Sancti Spíritus and enabling swift access to all sites via paved roads that feed south from the arterial highway.

The west comprises a vast plain farmed in sugarcane and citrus. It is also home to the pristine wetlands of the Ciénaga de Zapata, unparalleled in the Caribbean as a refuge for rare bird and other animal species. Spoonbills and neon pink flamingos forage in the shallows while crocodiles bask on the mudflats. Anglers are hooked on the lure of Zapata, but the area has a place in

history as well. Here is the swampy Bay of Pigs, the spot where in April 1961 CIA-trained Cuban exiles sworn to overthrow Castro attempted to invade their former homeland. Today, tourists relax and sun themselves along the string of white-sand beaches that edge the famous shore. Playa Ancón, near Trinidad, is the finest beach on the coast. There and at Playas Larga

and Girón, dive facilities will outfit you to take the plunge to admire groves of black coral and spectacular sponges.

Pockets of Old World charm can be savored in the once prosperous cities of Sancti Spíritus and Cienfuegos. The latter is a charming port city with a well-regarded botanical garden and a small castle (the only one in the region).

Trinidad, a 19th-century living museum, enchants visitors who metaphorically step back in time. Its status as a UNESCO World Heritage site is testament to its unique importance. Adding to the calming sense of a *temps perdu*, mules and donkeys clip-clop through the cobbled streets and plazas.

Cienfuegos and Trinidad unfold against a backdrop of kelly green—the Guamuhaya

NOT TO BE MISSED:

Birding at Parque Nacional Ciénaga de Zapata   134–135

The Cuban perspective on the 1961 Bay of Pigs invasion at the Museo Girón   137

Hiking to El Nicho waterfall in the Sierra del Escambray   140

The cobbled colonial streets of Trinidad   146–147

Scuba diving amid the corals off Playa Ancón   148

An ascent of Torre de Manaca Iznaga for a bird's-eye view over the Valle de los Ingenios   149

mountains, colloquially called the Sierra del Escambray. Perched amid these cool heights is a spa hotel; from here hiking trails radiate through lush forests of pine and eucalyptus, cut through by tumbling rivers. To the east, the fertile Valle de los Ingenios was the setting during past centuries for dozens of sugar plantations and today is also a UNESCO World Heritage site. The landscapes grow larger as the coast highway—Circuito Sur—swings up through the Alturas de Banao, where wild, whiskey brown crags resemble those of the Scottish Highlands. Horseback riding is offered at working *fincas*.

In the southeastern quarter of the region, the wetlands of Sancti Spíritus Province are full of limpid lagoons. Migratory waterfowl flock to these vital reserves, including those surrounding the man-made lake Presa Zaza. Along the north shore, an endemic crane species inhabits coastal wetlands that are slated for development as an ecotour site. Overall, tourist facilities in the region are scarce. However, boutique city hotels complement a fistful of beach hotels now sprinkled along the southern shore. ■

PARQUE NACIONAL CIÉNAGA DE ZAPATA

Crocodiles. Flamingos. Antediluvian garfish. The vast Ciénaga de Zapata swamp—the Caribbean's largest wetland ecosystem—harbors a veritable Noah's ark of wildlife within its 1,893-square-mile (4,904 sq km) swath of mangroves, saw grass, *marabú* brush, and lagoons.

Crocodile farm at La Boca de Guamá

Parque Nacional Ciénaga de Zapata

132 A2 & B2

Visitor Information

Oficina del Parque Nacional, Playa Larga

45/98-7249

Mirroring the Everglades of Florida, Zapata unrolls across a vast triangular peninsula that comprises a virtually unexplored wilderness, where sloughs and lagoons speckle a spread of tall saw grass punctuated with clumps of hardwoods and palms. The tan carpet yields to mangrove jungle along the fringe. The wetlands surround the 13-mile-long (21 km) **Bahía de Cochinos** (Bay of Pigs) inlet, incised into a limestone plain honeycombed with *cenotes*, or water-filled sinkholes. The park protects more than 900 species of flora, 171 bird species, 31 reptile species, and 12 mammal species. Many, such as the rare Zapata rail, are found only here. The Ciénaga de Zapata also protects a rare population of Cuban parrots. Sandhill cranes, ibises, and flamingos are among the stilt-legged waders. Crocodiles slosh about in the shallows. Ancient *manjuarí* (Cuban Gar) and equally endangered manatees live in the brackish lagoons, notably around the mouth of the Río Jatiguanico. Migratory waterfowl are abundant October through April. **Laguna de las Salinas** is recommended for fishing—tarpon, bonefish, and snook ply these waters–or observe the nearly 100 species of birds that stop here.

Route 116 links the Bay of Pigs with the Autopista Nacional (the turnoff is at Jagüey Grande) and leads past the **Criadero de Cocodrilos** (see next paragraph). The road meets the shore at **Playa Larga**, a small fishing village (with plenty of *paladares*—family-run restaurants—and private B&B rentals) and landing site during the 1961 Bay of Pigs invasion (see sidebar p. 137). Guides are required and can be hired at the Playa Larga ranger station; you'll need your own car.

La Boca de Guamá

This tourist complex *(tel 45/91-5551)*, located some 11 miles (18 km) south of the autopista is highlighted by the **Criadero de Cocodrilos** (crocodile farm; *tel 45/91-5666, $$*), where endemic Cuban crocodiles are bred for release to the wild. You might also spot these fearsome reptiles on a boat ride to the large lake called **Laguna del Tesoro**, replete with feisty game fish; fishing trips are offered. At its heart is **Villa Guamá**; 13 islands connected by boardwalks form a hotel complex with a theme of a Taíno village. ■

The Magnificence of Mangroves

Mangroves are halophytes—plants that thrive in salty conditions. Four species are found in Cuba, and the areas they inhabit teem with wildlife.

The dense, glutinous mud that mangroves live in contains almost no oxygen. Most mangroves form aerial roots, drawing in oxygen through spongy bark. One species sends out underground roots that sprout long lines of offshoots; these poke through the surface of the ground like upturned nails.

Mangroves propagate swiftly. The mangrove blooms briefly in spring, then produces a fruit from which sprouts a fleshy seedling shaped like a plumb bob. This pendulous seed grows to a foot (30 cm) in length, germinates on the branch, then drops like a dart. The seeds stick upright in the mud and send out roots. A seedling can grow 2 feet (60 cm) or more its first year. By the third year it has become a mature bush, sprouting seeds that establish themselves around the parent's roots. The web of roots helps protect land against erosion by waves,

and builds land by filtering out silt brought to the sea by rivers. As the land builds up in their lee, the mangroves eventually strand themselves and die on land they've created.

Mangroves are vital aquatic nurseries for creatures such as oysters, sponges, crustaceans, fish, and even stingrays and baby sharks. So important are these habitats that the destruction of mangroves has an inordinately harmful effect on the marine ecosystem. The nutrient-rich muds also foster the growth of micro-organisms that are a food source for larger species, such as shrimps and snails.

The redolent mangroves are favored by scores of bird species, not least white ibises, flamingos, roseate spoonbills, and the great blue heron (one of ten heron species inhabiting the halophyte wetlands of Cuba). Cormorants, pelicans, and frigate birds favor the mangroves for nesting. The Cuban parrot and bee hummingbird are also present, as is the common black hawk. *Jutías,* lizards, crocodiles, and snakes also abound.

PLAYA GIRÓN

Playa Girón has lovely beaches and great diving; *cenotes* (limestone sinkholes) and coves filled with warm waters offer prime snorkeling. But the area is best known for a single event: The 1961 Bay of Pigs invasion, which aimed to topple the young Castro regime, took place at Girón Beach.

Playa Girón today; in 1961 it was the Bay of Pigs battlefield.

Playa Girón
🔺 132 B1

Beyond Playa Larga, Route 116–then 122–unfurls toward the mouth of the Bahía de Cochinos, then swoops eastward along the rugged limestone shore. As you drive along the route, take note of the 161 obelisks placed alongside the road—these commemorate the Cuban nationals killed during the invasion of 1961.

Beaches are few and far between in this region; here the shore is lined with mangroves (see sidebar p. 135). Before the revolution, impoverished *cenagueros* (swamp people) eked out a meager living by burning and selling mangroves as charcoal. In 1960, Castro ordered a highway built into the swamp, and a hospital and teachers soon followed, but the isolated communities remain impoverished.

INSIDER TIP:

After visiting the Bay of Pigs Museum (Museo Girón), stroll through the lobby of the nearby hotel and step out onto the beach, where the ill-fated, CIA-sponsored invasion force landed.

—NEIL SHEA
National Geographic writer

Today, the community is thriving off tourism, and almost every family rents out rooms.

To cool off, stop at **Cueva de los Peces**, 5 miles (8 km) east of Playa Larga, for a dip in the 60-foot-deep (18 m) *cenote*; the turquoise ocean waters nearby are popular with scuba divers. **Caleta Buena**, an exquisite coral cove 5 miles (8 km) east of Playa Girón, offers snorkeling in waters teeming with fish. You can rent snorkel and scuba diving gear on-site.

The beach at Playa Girón is one of the finest along the island's south coast, although marred by a concrete barrier (erected since the 1961 invasion) that stretches across the bay, cutting off both the tide and the view.

The mediocre hotel here is uninspired, but local room rental (albeit simple) offers a chance to engage with families.

The sole site of interest is the splendid **Museo Girón**, which displays a Sea Fury fighter, Soviet T-34 and SAU-100 tanks, and other armaments from the 1961 battle; maps trace the course of events. Political commentary mocks the Cuban exiles and portrays the hardships of the *cenagueros* on the eve of the ill-fated invasion.

In spring, millions of red land crabs migrate 125 miles (200 km) to the sea to lay their eggs. The coast road becomes a swarming crustacean carpet and eventually turns into a hazard to motorists as the crushed 6-inch (16 cm) diameter carapaces of the unluckier crabs can cause tire punctures (see sidebar p. 151). ∎

Museo Girón
- ✉ Playa Girón
- ☎ 45/98-4122
- 💲 $
- cnpc.cult.cu

Bay of Pigs Invasion

In 1959, the CIA conceived a plan to land Cuban exiles in Cuba to topple Castro's regime. President John F. Kennedy vetoed an initial plan for a landing at Playa Ancón as too ambitious. Thus, on April 17, 1961, about 1,400 heavily armed exiles were put ashore at the Bay of Pigs. The attack started badly and only got worse.

The landing craft grounded on coral that CIA analysts had dismissed as seaweed, and most heavy armor was lost.

The supply ships were sunk by Cuban aircraft (which survived a preemptive strike), as Castro directed the defense. Although U.S. jets flew reconnaissance, President Kennedy refused to order air strikes (however, six U.S. pilots did fly combat; four were killed).

After 72 hours of ferocious fighting, the U.S. task force withdrew, abandoning most of the exiles—who were later traded back to the U.S. in exchange for $53 million in food and medicines.

CIENFUEGOS

Imbued with French influences, Cienfuegos is one of Cuba's loveliest and liveliest cities, well worth a visit. Officials have put a shine to the colonial core, and sites of architectural interest dot the city, neat and pristine like no other on the island. Stifling hot due to its sheltered position within a vast bay, it is Cuba's third largest port city (pop. 150,000).

■ Parque Martí's bandstand

Cienfuegos
🗺 132 C1
Visitor Information
✉ Ave. 54, Calles 29 & 31, Cubanacán
☎ 43/55-8840

Although the city's name appropriately means "100 fires," it was actually named for Don José Cienfuegos, the Cuban governor at the end of the 19th century. The city was founded in 1819 as a settlement for emigrés from France and Louisiana. Located 151 miles (244 km) southeast of Havana, the city prospered as a port for sugar and cattle. Today the sprawling city boasts Cuba's largest oil refinery and bulk sugar terminal.

A broad boulevard—**Paseo del Prado** (Calle 37)—runs north–south through the city center. Its promenade, lined with busts of distinguished people, bustles at night and on weekends. Avenida 5 de Septiembre, which leads east to Trinidad, passes by the **Cementerio Tomás Acea** (tel 43/52-5257, $).

This grand cemetery is notable for its entrance gate, which boasts 64 columns, and for its grand neoclassical tombs. At Calle 25 and Avenida 46, catch the ferry to **El Perche**, a scenic fishing village at the entrance to Cienfuegos Bay. The community nestles in the shadow of the **Fortaleza de Nuestra Señora de los Ángeles de Jagua**, built between 1738 and 1745 to protect against pirates.

Pueblo Nuevo

Pueblo Nuevo, the colonial core, extends west of the Prado. Avenida 54 links the Prado with **Parque Martí**, the palm-shaded main plaza laid out in 1839 with a bandstand, a triumphal arch, and a statue of José Martí guarded by marble lions. To the east is the **Catedral de la Purísima Concepción**, dating from 1869, with its Corinthian altar, vaulted ceiling, and French stained-glass windows.

A counterclockwise tour passes the **Teatro Tomás Terry** *(tel 43/51-3361)*, opened in 1890 and worth a peek inside for the exquisite bas-relief of Dionysus in the proscenium and the 950-seat, Italian-style auditorium. In its heyday, Enrico Caruso and Sarah Bernhardt performed here. Adjoining is the **Colegio San Lorenzo**, with a gracious neoclassical facade. On the south side, the **Casa de la Cultura** *(tel 43/51-6584)*, located in the baroque **Palacio Ferrer** *(Calle 25 #5403)*, has a *mirador* offering a view of the town. Lining the west side of the square are the **Galería Maroya**, displaying art; the **Museo Histórico**

Provincial, brimful of period furnishings; and the red-domed **Ayuntamiento de Cienfuegos**, the seat of local government. Slake your thirst at the **Palatino**, a colonial-era bar.

The **Museo Histórico Naval** at the old naval base has excellent exhibits on local naval history.

INSIDER TIP:

Attend a rehearsal or concert by the Cantores de Cienfuegos in Catedral de Cienfuegos. This choral group, conducted by the gifted Honey Moreira, makes transcendent music.

—JEFF GREENWALD
Author and director of ethicaltraveler.org

Punta Gorda

South of the colonial core, the Prado becomes the **Malecón**, extending along the once exclusive Punta Gorda Peninsula, where Detroit classics occupy the driveways of Art Deco bungalows. This is a pleasant 1.5-mile-long (2.4 km) stroll. At its base is the town's architectural jewel—the **Palacio de Valle** *(tel 43/55-1003, cienfuegoscity. org)*, now a restaurant. It was built between 1913 and 1917 by Acisclo del Valle Blanco, who imported Moroccan craftsmen to design in Mudejar and Gothic style. Midway, admire the beaux arts **Club Cienfuegos**—the old yacht club, with restaurant and a swimming pool. ∎

Museo Histórico Provincial
✉ Ave. 54 #2702 at Calle 27
☎ 43/51-9722
🕐 Closed Mon.
💲 $

Museo Histórico Naval
✉ Ave. 60 & Calle 21
☎ 43/51-9143
🕐 Closed Mon.
💲 $

SIERRA DEL ESCAMBRAY

The sawtooth Escambray, Cuba's second highest mountain chain, rises precipitously from the coast east of Cienfuegos. Pine studded and a luscious green, this sierra—reaching 3,762 feet (1,147 m) atop Pico San Juan—offers breathtaking views of the landscape below.

Sierra del Escambray

🗺 132 C1
  & 132/133 D1

Visitor Information

✉ Complejo Turístico Topes de Collantes

☎ 41/54-0330

The thickly forested Guamu-haya mountains, aka the Sierra del Escambray, sheltered Che Guevara's Second Front in the late 1950s. It is cool and moist at these heights (visitors should bring a jacket), and air plants weigh heavily on the moss-laden boughs of Caribbean pine and eucalyptus. The many bird species include *cotorras* (parrots).

Tumbling rivers have gnawed deep ravines into the precipitous southern flanks, where coffee is farmed. For scenery, follow the **Valle de Yaguanabo**, offering waterfalls and Cueva Martín Infi-erno, with exquisite gypsum flow-ers (*flores de yeso*) and a stalagmite soaring 220 feet (67 m).

Northward, the sierra eases into Villa Clara Province. The long grades coil down through valleys carpeted in rows of cof-fee bushes, descending through a landscape of *bohíos* (thatched huts) and lime green tobacco fields to the tidy agricultural town of **Manicaragua**. Inset in the slopes southwest of Manicaragua is **Embalse Hanabanilla**, a lake favored by anglers. Fishing and scenic boat trips are offered at **Hotel Hanabanilla** (*tel 42/20-8461*).

Excursions from Hanaba-nilla also lead to **El Nicho** (*tel 43/43-3351, $$*), where a stun-ning waterfall tumbles into a forest-fringed, unbelievably turquoise pool. A thatched restaurant serves lunch, and horseback rides are offered. It can be reached by car (8 miles/14 km) from the Manicaragua-Cumanayagua highway. En route you'll pass through **El Jovero** hamlet, famous for its peasant theater group.

Gran Parque Natural Topes de Collantes

This ecotour and spa complex nestles in the mountains, 13 miles (21 km) northwest of Trinidad. In its midst stands the towering **Kurhotel** (*tel 42/54-0180*), a spa-hotel erected in 1936 as a sanatorium for victims of tuberculosis. Nearby, the **Museo de Arte Contemporá-neo** (*tel 42/54-0231, $*) displays works by some of Cuba's leading artists.

A short hike from the Kurho-tel leads downhill to a touristic recreation of a traditional farming village; the **Casa de Café** has a display on coffee growing. The park is laced with steep hiking trails that lead to the lovely **Salto Vega Grande** and **Salto de Caburní** waterfalls. Treks and guided tours are offered through Gaviota (*tel 42/54–0330, gaviota hotels.com*). These include excur-sions to **Hacienda Codina**, a center for birders and hikers. ∎

TRINIDAD

Tucked between the Sierra del Escambray and the Caribbean Sea, Trinidad is Cuba's colonial treasure. Its recently restored historic core is unequaled for its trove of pastel houses from the isle's golden age. Designated a UNESCO World Heritage site in 1988, Trinidad and the Valle de los Ingenios are living monuments to a way of life going back nearly 500 years.

Traditional musicians play in Trinidad. The town became a UNESCO World Heritage site in 1988.

Trinidad (pop. 75,000) nestles against a breeze-swept hillside, with views toward both mountain and sea. Founded by Diego Velázquez de Cuellar in 1514, it was Cuba's third settlement. A short-lived gold mine cast a warm glow on the town and its port of Casilda, point of departure for conquistador Hernán Cortés, who set out for Mexico in 1518 to conquer the Aztec Empire for Spain. Fleets bearing the spoils of Mexico soon filled Trinidad's vaults. But Havana eclipsed the southern city, which became an outpost for smugglers, pirates, and slave traders. The abundance of slaves stimulated the local sugar industry, and Trinidad entered its golden age as profits from the 18th-century sugar boom bankrolled the construction of fine houses, churches, and convents. Eventually, however, the town was overshadowed by developments elsewhere in the country, and it began a slow demise.

In the 1950s, Trinidad was decreed a national monument. A restoration project was begun.

(continued on p. 144)

Trinidad

🔺 132 D1

Visitor Information

✉ Infotur, Gustavo Izquierdo #101, bet. Simón Bolívar & Piro Guinart

☎ 41/99-8257

COLONIAL LEGACIES

Cuba's colonizers brought with them a Spanish aesthetic that they adapted to the tropical clime. Glorious buildings from centuries past display the evolution of an architectural heritage influenced by Mudejar style.

This typical 18th-century home has *postigos* (smaller doors set within larger ones), *rejas* (ornate window grilles), and a balcony with turned wooden railings.

Cuba's first colonial settlements were of single-story adobe dwellings with palm fiber roofs. By the 17th century, houses had become much more complex. Typically built of local limestone, with two stories and tiled wooden roofs, they followed the Moorish convention of having an inner courtyard that permitted air to circulate through the house—a design that was to last for the following four centuries.

The ground floor of the typical Cuban colonial house was devoted to commerce, while the upper stories served as private apartments. Relatively austere, their facades were softened by turned wooden balconies and by ornamental *portales,* doors with elaborate baroque moldings that through the years grew large enough to admit a horse and carriage. Typically, these massive doors contained smaller doors—*postigos*—set at face level.

The patio was accessed by an inner archway of intricate multifoil design. The hall *(zaguán)* between portal and patio was usually open to the public; inner arcades provided access to *dependencias*—commercial rooms that opened to the street. The rooms around the patio's perimeter were given to offices and storage, while those at the rear of the house surrounded a *traspatio* and were devoted to stables and domestic activities.

Houses facing the plazas and main boulevards featured facades that were fancifully embellished by porticos—galleried walkways with arches supported by columns, providing shelter from the climatic extremes of the Cuban sun and rain.

Interiors & the Evolution of Decoration

A staircase led to the private quarters— a chapel, kitchen, dining room, and bedrooms. Rooms were divided by *mamparas*, intricately decorated inner doors something like saloon swing doors, to provide privacy while retaining a sense of communal living.

By the 18th century, the typical Cuban town house had added a low-ceilinged mezzanine level *(entresuelo)*, either below or above the second story and given over to offices and slave quarters.

The greatest evolution of form was in ornamentation, notably in windows, which were initially protected by wooden panels and later by the addition of ornate grilles— *barrotes*—of lathe-turned wood.

By the 19th century, when neoclassical forms were adopted in town house design, elaborate metal grilles *(rejas)* had replaced wood. Colored glass began to appear on the engraved panels, which featured slatted shutters *(persianas)*. These decorative windows evolved into fanciful geometric patterns, with larger windows topped by *mediopuntos*—arches that support the windows. The stained glass filtered the sun and cast diffused colors into household interiors. Additional artistic touches were lent by *cenefas*—bands of decorative plasterwork— on interior walls.

■ Decorative *mediopuntos* top windows at the Hotel Tejadillo in Havana.

Roofs & Ceilings

The beamed roofs on many of Cuba's colonial houses were often built by shipbuilders and frequently enhanced by *alfarjes*—wooden ceilings featuring angled beams that were set in exquisite star patterns in Mudejar fashion. These were usually elaborate in style and decoratively painted, taking their inspiration from Spain's long tradition of Moorish architecture; they bring an unexpected Middle Eastern thread to Cuba's colonial legacy.

Museo Romántico

🏛 147

✉ Calle Fernando Hernández Echerrí #52 at Calle Simón Bolívar

☎ 41/99-4363

🕐 Closed Mon.

💲 $

Museo de Arqueología Guamuhaya

✉ Calle Simón Bolívar #457

☎ 41/99-3420

🕐 Closed Mon.

💲 $

While the city now thrives on tourism, life moves at a yesteryear pace. About 6,000 Trinitarios still inhabit the colonial core, where the clip-clop of horses' hooves echoes down cobbled streets. It is a joy to wander the traffic-free lanes—laid out higgledy-piggledy to thwart pirates—especially at dawn and dusk when sunlight gilds the timeworn, red-tile-roof houses. (Note the caged songbirds hung on exterior walls.)

Plaza Mayor

The old town's compact main square is dominated by a simple cathedral and five exquisite

A colonial-era bedroom displayed at the Museo Romántico

Museo de Arquitectura Colonial

🏛 147

✉ Plaza Mayor, Calle Ripalda #83, bet. Cristo & Calle Real del Jigüe

☎ 41/99-3208

🕐 Closed Sun.

💲 $

colonial mansions painted in pastel yellow, pink, green, and blue. At its heart is a park with a statue of Terpsichore, the muse of dancing and song, and bronze greyhounds in the shade of royal palms, framed by wrought-iron fences draped with hibiscus.

The **Iglesia de la Santísima Trinidad** (Holy Trinity Church),

today known as the **Parroquial Mayor**, was rebuilt in 1892. Inside, it has a simple Victorian-Gothic motif. But note the marble altar and statuary, including the 18th-century "Cristo de la Vera Cruz" ("Christ of the True Cross"). Just west, the **Palacio Brunet**, built in 1808, is Trinidad's most beautiful mansion. Now restored, it houses the opulent **Museo Romántico**, brimful of period furnishings and bespeaking 18th-century wealth.

To the southwest is **Casa Padrón**, fronted by iron railings. The mansion houses the **Museo de Arqueología Guamuhaya**, which displays exhibits ranging from pre-Columbian culture to local flora and fauna. German explorer Alexander von Humboldt stayed here during his sojourn to Cuba in 1801. Facing it on the east is the pale blue **Casa de los Sánchez-Iznaga**, former home of a wealthy sugar baron and today the **Museo de Arquitectura Colonial**, tracing Trinidad's evolution of architectural styles.

Colonial Treasures

The streets fanning out from Plaza Mayor are replete with colonial treasures. The El Futuro district, west of the plaza, is highlighted by the **Antiguo Convento de San Francisco de Asís**, dating from 1813. Climb the original bell tower for a fine view. Today the convent houses the **Museo de la Lucha contra Bandidos** (Museum of the Fight Against Bandits), where exhibits portray the fight to eradicate counterrevolutionaries based in the Sierra del Escambray from 1959 to 1966. Nearby,

Casa-Estudio Carlos Mata Pich *(Piro Guinart #80, tel 41/99-4380)* is the gallery-home of a renowned artist—"the painter of the night."

The **Palacio Cantero** was acquired by Justo Cantero, a powerful plantation owner. Still filled with stylish period furnishings, it is today the **Museo Histórico Municipal**. Tracing the town's history, it displays miscellany such as slave stocks and a fountain that supposedly spouted champagne.

Other mansions that speak of the glittering 18th-century lifestyle include **Casa de González Gil** *(Calles Maceo at Bolívar)*, **Casa Meyer**, today a *casa particular* *(Calle Izquierdo #111)*, and **Casa de Aldemán Ortiz** *(see p. 146)*, with its yellow walls and petrol blue shutters overlooks the west side of the Plaza Mayor. It is home to the **Galería de Arte** and its modern art, jewelry, and embroidery. Several cobbled streets hereabouts serve as open-air crafts markets, while art galleries abound, particularly on triangular **Plaza Segarte**, to the northeast of Plaza Mayor and the setting for the ever-lively **Casa de la Trova** *(Echerrí #29, tel 53/41-99-6445)*. Be sure to view, and perhaps buy, the unique hand-carved bas-relief art at **Estudio-Galería Lázaro Niebla** *(Calle Real del Jigüe #11)*, one block east of Plaza Mayor.

Farther Afield

A stroll east from Plaza Mayor brings you to **Plaza Santa Ana** *(Calles Camilo Cienfuegos & José Mendoza)*, overlooked by the ruins of **Iglesia Santa Ana**. On the east side stands the fortress-like **Cárcel**

EXPERIENCE:
Get Married in Cuba

The streets of Trinidad, like much of Cuba, offer couples a romantic wonderland. To marry in Cuba, you'll need your birth certificate, a divorce certificate (if applicable), and/or proof of single status. The documents must be translated into Spanish and verified by the Cuban consulate in your home country. **Cubanacan** *(cubana can.cu)* offers wedding packages at beach resorts. The **Bufete Internacional** *(Ave. 5ta #4002, Miramar, Havana, tel 7/204-5126)* handles civil marriages, with offices in all major cities.

Real (Royal Prison), newly restored as a cultural center containing artisans' workshops and restaurants beneath the shaded arcade of its inner courtyard. Five blocks east and one south is **El Alfarero Cerámica** *(Calle Andrés Berro Macias #51, at Pepito Tey & Rubén Batista)*, where a family cooperative shapes clay into fine pottery.

Parque Céspedes *(Calle José Martí at Calle Lino Pérez)* is the town's main square; it is ringed by government buildings such as the town hall—**Ayuntamiento**—and by the diminutive **Iglesia San Francisco de Paula**; peek in at the statuary. Overlooking the town is the **Ermita de Nuestra Señora de la Candelaria de la Popa**, built in 1740. The gravel road that leads to the retreat crosses the town's most run down outskirts. The **Academía de Artes Plásticas** *(Calle Lino Pérez at A. Rodríguez, tel 41/99-6798, closed Sat.–Sun.)*, in the crenellated former army barracks, has art galleries. ■

Museo de la Lucha contra Bandidos

 147

✉ Calle Echerrí #59 at Piro Guinart

☎ 41/99-4121

$ $

Museo Histórico Municipal

✉ Calle Simón Bolívar #423, bet. Francisco Gómez Toro & Gustavo Izquierdo

☎ 41/99-4460

🕐 Closed Fri.

$ $

STROLL COLONIAL TRINIDAD

Exploring the heart of colonial Trinidad, this walk follows narrow cobbled streets winding from the main plaza into the ancient *barrio* of Tres Cruces. This quarter features the city's prime concentration of exquisitely restored colonial mansions turned into museums. There are some short but steep grades, with the ground uneven underfoot, but the ambling is peaceful and traffic free.

Brunet Palace and San Francisco Church on the Plaza Mayor

Begin your walk at the **Antiguo Convento de San Francisco de Asís**. It now houses the **Museo de la Lucha contra Bandidos ❶** (see p. 144). Exiting the museum, walk south 80 yards (70 m) to the palm-shaded **Plaza Mayor** and the newly restored **Palacio Brunet**, now the **Museo Romántico** (see p. 144), on your left.

Proceed south 50 yards (46 m) and enter the **Iglesia de la Santísima Trinidad ❷** (see p. 144) to admire the vaulted ceiling, carved statuary, and sacred icons. Kitty-corner to the cathedral, facing you on your left as you exit, is the **Casa de los Sánchez-Iznaga**, now housing the **Museo de Arquitectura Colonial ❸** (see p. 144). Descend the south face of the square 50 yards (46 m) to Calle Rubén Martínez

> ## NOT TO BE MISSED:
>
> Museo Romántico ● Plaza Real del Jigüe ● Casa de la Música

Villena and pause to admire the facade of the grand mansion before you. The home of local art critic Carlos Sotolongo, it is full of period furnishings *(visits by request)*. Next door, the **Casa de Aldemán Ortiz**, at the corner of Calle Simón Bolívar, beckons you upstairs to look at artwork in the **Galería de Arte del Fondo Cubano de Bienes Culturales** *(Calle Simón Bolívar #418, tel 41/99-3590)*.

Exiting, head west up Rubén Martínez

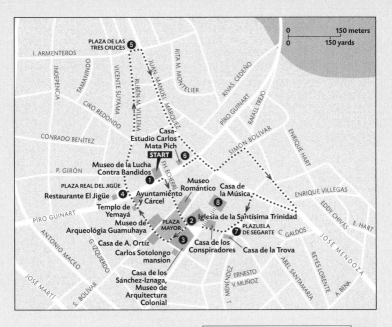

See also area map pp. 132–133
▶ Plaza Mayor
🕒 2 hours
↔ 1.5 miles (2 km)
▶ Plaza Mayor

Villena to the plaza's west corner, and **Casa Padrón**, housing the **Museo de Arqueología Guamuhaya** (see p. 144). Proceed along Villena, noting the **Templo de Yemayá** *(#59)* on your left; it features Santería altars and hosts occasional religious ceremonies. A few steps farther is **Plaza Real del Jigüe ❹**, an enchanting plaza where the **Restaurante El Jigüe** *(tel 41/99-6476)* wears a facade of ceramic tiles. Note the original stone-and-lime masonry exposed in a portion of the **Ayuntamiento y Cárcel**—the old town hall and jail—on the opposite corner.

After three more blocks you'll emerge on **Plaza de las Tres Cruces ❺**, an undeveloped area of bare earth in the heart of Trinidad's oldest neighborhood. Turn right and right again on Calle Juan Manuel Márquez. Turn right on Piro Guinart to visit **Casa-Estudio Carlos Mata Pich ❻** to admire his unique art style. Retrace your steps, climb uphill and turn right on Calle José Mendoza. After three blocks, turn right onto Calle Juan

Manuel Márquez, which descends 70 yards (60 m) past a trio of houses with photogenic elevated galleries. Turn left at Calle Jesús Menéndez into intimate, triangular **Plazuela de Segarte ❼**, surrounded by venerable houses fronted by *barrotes* and tall carriage doors. At the junction with Calle Fernando Hernández Echerrí is the **Casa de la Trova** (see p. 145), where traditional music performances are hosted. You will see Plaza Mayor 100 yards (90 m) east. En route, on your right, pause to admire the **Casa de los Conspiradores**, with an impressive ocher facade and wooden balcony. Reentering Plaza Mayor, ascend the wide staircase to the **Casa de la Música ❽** *(tel 41/99-6622)*, where often live music is played.

PENÍNSULA DE ANCÓN

Curling around the sheltered waters of the Ensenada de Casilda like a shepherd's crook, the pencil-thin Península de Ancón is fringed by fine beaches whose white sands shelve into warm, tranquil green-blue waters. The longest and most beautiful beach—a stone's throw from Trinidad—hosts several hotels.

Península de Ancón

🗺 132 D1

La Boca

This charming fishing village, beside the mouth of the Río Guaurabo, 5 miles (8 km) west of Trinidad, is favored by Trinitarios on weekends for its proximity and for its pocket-size beaches. Exposed coral heads provide pedestals for enjoying vistas of the **Sierra del Escambray** while cooling your heels in jade waters.

Trinitarios cool off at La Boca.

Bougainvillea bowers spill over simple, timeworn red-tile-roof cottages—many offering rooms for rent. A string of beaches unspools south along the peninsula and awaits development. Facilities are limited—bring a packed lunch.

The **Casa Museo Alberto Delgado** *(closed Mon.),* 2 miles (3 km) east of La Boca, honors a Castro sympathizer killed during the counterrevolutionary war. Nearby, **Finca Dolores** *(tel 41/99-6481)* is an ancient farm offering horseback rides and folkloric shows.

Playa Ancón

This 2-mile-long (3 km) sliver of beach washed by turquoise Caribbean waters proves perfect for snorkeling and scuba diving. The **Cayo Blanco de Casilda** reef boasts the largest black coral grove in Cuba. The **Hotel Ancón** *(tel 41/99-6120)* and **Hotel Brisas Trinidad del Mar** *(tel 41/99-6500)* both offer scuba diving and water sports, including sailboats, as does the **Marina Marlin** *(tel 41/99-6205),* which also runs a "seafari" to Cayo Blanco, an offshore cay with superb corals.

A shuttle runs regularly between Trinidad and the beach, 10 miles (16 km) away. ■

VALLE DE LOS INGENIOS

Nicknamed Valle de los Ingenios for the sugar mills *(ingenios)* that once dotted this broad sprawling valley, the Valle de San Luís draws its appeal from its scenic beauty and historic value as an open-air museum recalling the heyday of sugar. Some of the estate houses and mills still stand; others are being restored to their former grandeur, broadening the appeal of the bucolic landscape.

The Carretera de Sancti Spíritus, linking Trinidad with the city of Sancti Spíritus, cleaves a path through the Valle de San Luís, which was named a UNESCO World Heritage site for its *ingenios* legacy.

Fields of sugarcane, green as limes, carpet the valley, framed to the north by a crescent of mountains and to the south by the Caribbean Sea. During the 18th century, this was Cuba's most productive sugar-growing region, with 40 mills. By the mid-19th century, the aging mills proved unable to compete with the more advanced central plantation system that had been introduced elsewhere in Cuba.

Hacienda Manaca Iznaga is the most comprehensive estate in existence, with a 148-foot-tall (45 m) tower that serves as the valley's emblem. The main house, completed in 1845, sits atop a breeze-swept hillock 8 miles (13 km) east of Trinidad. It features period costumes and other exhibits, and a restaurant serves up food and vistas across the valley. The slave quarters and warehouses still stand. You can ascend the 136 tower stairs of the **Torre de Manaca Iznaga** *($)* for the sweeping view. Local artisans sell lace items at its base.

A commuter train offers an enjoyable way to savor the scenery from the Trinidad terminal into the valley via Iznaga, stopping at **Casa Guachinango**. Horseback rides and *criollo* fare are offered at this restored 18th-century *hacienda*, where cows can also be milked.

One of the mills worth visiting is the **Sitio Histórico Guáimaro** with its sugar cane press: Follow the signed turnoff from the highway. Also off the highway is **Sitio Histórico San Isidro**, recently reopened though still under restoration. The site will eventually house a **Museo de Caña de Azúcar** (Sugarcane Museum). ∎

Cockfights

Cuban society, with its deep-rooted farming culture, has a long tradition of cockfighting, and many Cubans raise gaming cocks (the Cuban state also breeds fighting cocks for export). Virtually every rural community has a *valla* (cockfighting ring). Cocks reach fighting age at eight months. They are exercised to build muscle and stamina. Crests and wattles are removed to prevent bleeding. The birds' legs and abdomens are plucked and massaged with rum, and the legs are fitted with artificial spurs. Fights to the death, while often abhorrent to tourists, whip the all-male crowds into a frenzy.

**Valle de San Luís
(Valle de los
Ingenios)**
🗺 133 D1

**Hacienda Manaca
Iznaga**
✉ Iznaga
8 miles/13 km
E of Trinidad
☎ 41/99-7241

SANCTI SPÍRITUS

Despite its size and regional import as provincial capital at the midpoint of Cuba, Sancti Spíritus is limited in its tourist appeal and can be fully explored in a day. Quaint colonial streets are worth browsing, bolstered by a historic church of note.

Judas Martínez Moles statue, Sancti Spíritus

Sancti Spíritus

133 D1

**Fundación
de la Naturaleza
y el Hombre**

✉ Calle Cruz Pérez
#1 at Céspedes
& Independencia

☎ 41/32-8342

🕐 Closed Sat.–Sun.

💲 $

This city of 108,500 straddles the Carretera Central, 245 miles (394 km) east of Havana. Founded in 1522 on the east bank of the Río Yayabo, Sancti Spíritus prospered on sugar and the slave trade. It has an expansive colonial core that has been partly restored.

At the city's heart is the bustling **Parque Serafín Sánchez,** named for a local patriot killed in 1896. The **Biblioteca** (library) and **Centro Provincial de Patrimonio Cultural** (Provincial Center of Cultural Heritage), on the west side, and the **Hotel Plaza,** to the east, and the **Teatro Principal,** four blocks south, have neoclassical facades of modest appeal. Note the statue of local hero Judas Martínez Moles (1861–1915) in the *plazuela* tucked off the northeast corner of the square.

Follow Calle Independencia north three blocks to **Parque Maceo,** an intimate plaza anchored by a simple church—**Iglesia de Nuestra Señora de la Caridad.** On the park's southeast corner is the **Fundación de la Naturaleza y el Hombre,** a small museum celebrating the fantastic journey of a team of Cubans between 1987 and 1988, who paddled in a dugout canoe for 10,820 miles (17,420 km), from the source of the Amazon to the Bahamas. Returning to the Parque Sánchez via Calle Céspedes, stop at the **Museo Casa Natal de Serafín Sánchez**, where the local hero of the wars of independence was born.

The Colonial Core

Most sites of interest are concentrated southwest of Parque Sánchez. Stroll 200 yards (180 m) along Calle Máximo Gómez to **Plaza Honorato del Castillo,** a triangular *plazuela* anchored by a statue of local doctor Rudesindo Antonio García Rojo. To the north and east are ancient arcades where shoe-shine stands abound and a giant brass bell is displayed. The **Casa de la Trova**, on the west side, hosts performances of traditional music and dance.

Dominating the plaza, to the south, is the splendidly preserved **Parroquial Mayor de Sancti Spíritus**, dating from 1680. The triple-tiered, 98-foot-tall (30 m) bell tower, topped by a cupola, was added in 1764. The church is simple within, with an *alfarje* ceiling of intricately crossed beams.

Following Avenida Menéndez as it curls south, you drop to the Río Yayabo, spanned by a triple-arched stone bridge completed in 1825. En route you'll pass the two-story **Palacio del Vallé Iznaga**, the town's finest mansion and home to the **Museo de Arte Colonial**. The rooms are crammed with period furnishings and decorative pieces portraying the lavish lifestyle of an earlier time, when the mansion was owned by one of Cuba's wealthiest families. More modest abodes line **Calle el Llano**, an exquisitely restored cobbled street due east of Menéndez. Llano and the surrounding streets vibrate with color: Venerable low-roof houses fronted by hanging lanterns and *rejas* of lathe-spun wood and wrought-iron are painted in every shade of soft pastel. At dusk, slanting rays splash the scene in fiery

orange and violet. Calle el Llano slopes to the river, where a grand mansion—Quinta de Santa Elena—hosts the **Casa de la Guayabera** *(Llano at Padre Quintano, tel 41/32-2205, guayabera@hero.cult.cu),* a small museum honoring Cuba's national dress. This not-to-miss site features *guayaberas* worn by Fidel, Raúl, and former Venezuelan president Hugo Chávez, among other famous personalities. ■

Museo Casa Natal de Serafín Sánchez

- ✉ Calle Céspedes #112 at Sobral & San Cristóbal
- ☎ 41/32-7791
- 🕐 Closed Sun.– Mon.
- 💲 $

Museo de Arte Colonial

- ✉ Calle Plácido #74 at Boquete de Guairo & Ave. Jesús Menéndez
- ☎ 41/32-5455
- 🕐 Closed Mon.
- 💲 $

Crab Invasion

If you're driving to Sancti Spíritus or other southerly destinations in spring, be forewarned. In this season the coast roads of southern Cuba are dramatically swarmed by legions of land crabs. Millions of the giant purple-and-black and orange *cangrejos* **emerge from the mangrove and dry forests to march to the sea to spawn. So dense are the swarms that many roads are impassable due to broken crab shells and pincers. Soon enough, the crabs return to their burrows inland, followed a few weeks later by millions of smaller newborns.**

More Places to Visit in Western Cuba–South

Royal palms stand sentry over Sancti Spíritus Province.

Jardín Botánico de Cienfuegos

This 232-acre (94 ha) garden near Guaos, 10 miles (16 km) east of Cienfuegos, boasts more than 2,000 species of tropical plants. Rubber trees, bamboos, palms, and cacti are represented. Edward Atkins, a New Englander and local sugar plantation owner, created the garden in 1899 to propagate more productive sugarcane strains. Harvard University later administered the garden. Today the Cuban Academy of Sciences maintains the site. It is approached via an avenue of palms that extends across the highway to **Pepito Tey**, a fascinating village centered on the remains of a now defunct sugar mill. ▲ 132 C1 ✉ Calle Central 136, Pepito Tey 🖇 $

Museo Memorial Comandancia de las FAR

The Central Australia sugar-processing factory, founded in 1863 on Route 3-1-18, is located on the nearby Jagüey Grande. It was the site of Castro's headquarters during the Bay of Pigs invasion and defensive actions were planned here. The museum displays relics of local history and of the attack, as well as newspapers of the era. ▲ 132 B2 ☎ 45/91-2504 🕑 Closed Mon. 🖇 $

Playa Rancho Luna

This flaxen beach shelves into calm turquoise waters with coral. Two hotels are up to international par, the **Club Amigo Rancho Luna** (tel 43/54-8012) also offers scuba diving. Dolphins and sea lions cavort at the **Delfinario** (closed Wed., $$). ▲ 132 C1

Presa Zaza

Cuba's largest man-made lake supplies Sancti Spíritus Province with water and anglers with trout and bass. The wetlands host multitudes of waterfowl. The **Hotel Zaza** (tel 41/32-7015) is a base for hunting and fishing. ▲ 133 E1

Yaguajay

This small town, 25 miles (40 km) east of Remedios, boasts the impressive **Monumento y Museo Camilo Cienfuegos** (tel 41/55-2689, $), honoring the revolutionary commander who led a decisive battle here in December 1958. The museum sits beneath a large statue of the eponymous hero, who died in a mysterious plane crash in 1959. To the museum's rear, an eternal flame flickers beside a tomb reserved for Cienfuegos. **Parque Nacional Caguanas**, 31 miles (50 km) northeast of Yaguajay, is home to a big population of endemic cranes. ▲ 133 E2

Home to Cuba's most spectacular beaches, beckoning divers to clear blue waters and fabulously healthy coral reefs teeming with life

CENTRAL CUBA

Cayo Coco

CENTRAL CUBA

The heartland of Cuba—comprising Ciego de Ávila and Camagüey Provinces—is sparsely populated beyond the two namesake cities, which offer sites of historical interest. Visitors come mainly to sun themselves on glorious beaches or dive the coral reefs of the Cayerías del Norte off the north shore. The Carretera Central speeds through the region's center, offering forays afield. More scenic is the Circuito Norte, which parallels the north coast.

Under a rainbow in the central Cuban town of Manicaragua, where tobacco is king

Ciego de Ávila Province, the narrow waist of Cuba, is pancake-flat and lushly green. Citrus and sugarcane farms dot the landscape, and pineapple is grown around the eponymous capital city. Freshwater lakes offer prime fishing for bass. The heat builds gradually as you travel eastward, until the verdant landscape withers to a featureless plain shaded by broad trees spreading their gnarled branches long and low to the ground.

Neighboring Camagüey Province is the color of honey, a rolling upland plain where hot winds whistle through tall, rain-starved grasslands and *vaqueros* (cowboys) survey the land from their saddles. A forested region when Columbus came ashore, during the 17th and

18th centuries, it evolved as the center of cattle breeding. Camagüey Province is still dominated by state-owned *ganaderías* (ranches).

The south coast is sparsely populated. Much is swampy, providing a habitat for large bird populations and crocodiles that slosh along the mangrove-lined shore. A few paved roads slice through the bright green carpet of sugarcane and sedge and lead to humble fishing villages, such as Júcaro and Santa Cruz del Sur. These serve as jumping-off points for forays to the Jardines de la Reina (Queen's Gardens)—a vast archipelago of coral cays and turquoise ocean shallows. Tourist facilities are meager, but scuba diving and sportfishing are offered. New eco-focused hotels are in the works.

NOT TO BE MISSED:

Lazing the day away on the powdery white sands of **Cayo Coco and Cayo Guillermo** 158–159

Wandering through the colonial plazas of **Camagüey** 162–165

A performance by the world-acclaimed **Camagüey Ballet** 163

A dive in the shark-infested waters off **Santa Lucía** 166

Bonefishing in the **Jardines de la Reina** 167

A hike of the forest trails at **Finca La Belén**, with binoculars and bird book in hand 168

Cayo Coco and Cayo Guillermo are favored by Canadians, Europeans, and South Americans. Coco and Guillermo are part of the Jardines del Rey (King's Gardens), a larger system of cays and isles off the north coast. The hotel star ratings are generous, but the diving here and off Playa Santa Lucía (in northeast Camagüey) is fabulous; more than 50 coral species thrive in one of the world's longest reefs. Flamingos inhabit the inshore lagoons, looking like feathered roses atop spindly stalks. The cays do not have public transportation, and the only Cubans here are hotel workers.

Ciego de Ávila can be seen in half a day. Save your urban outing for Camagüey, where many plazas have been impressively restored. ∎

CIEGO DE ÁVILA

The recently spruced-up provincial city of Ciego de Ávila (pop. 119,000) attracts few visitors despite its strategic location midway between Sancti Spíritus and Camagüey. Cuba's main highway—Carretera Central (in town it is called Calle Chicho Valdés)—cuts through the heart of the city, where horse-drawn wagons predominate.

Ciego de Ávila
- 🗺 155 B2

Visitor Information
- ✉ Infotur, Calle Honorato del Castillo, bet. Libertad & Independencia
- ☎ 33/20-9109

Museo de Artes Decorativas
- ✉ Calle Marcial Gómez #2 at Independencia
- ☎ 33/20-1661
- 🕐 Closed Fri.
- 💲 $

Museo de Historia Simón Reyes
- ✉ Honorato del Castillo at Máximo Gómez
- ☎ 33/20-4488
- 🕐 Closed Mon.
- 💲 $

Officially founded in 1840, today Ciego de Ávila is known as the "pineapple town" for the acres of sweet, juicy *piñas* grown locally. The city is laid out in a grid centered on **Parque Martí**, graced by shade trees and Victorian-style lampposts. A small bust (1920) of national hero José Martí stands in the center. Buildings of note include, on the south side, the **Poder Popular**—the old town hall—dating from 1911. The fine colonial mansion on the southeast corner houses the **Museo de Artes Decorativas**, a treasure trove of antique furnishings and other colonial delights in the manner of a lived-in home. One block north, the **Museo de Historia Simón Reyes** offers excellent displays on local history.

Head one block south, where Calle Joaquín Agüera crosses Calle Honorato del Castillo, and you can find the baroque **Teatro Iriondo** *(tel 33/22-2086)*. The

theater's interior is elaborately decorated in a mix of baroque and neoclassical styles, highlighted by statuary and a marble staircase. The **Fortín de la Trocha**, at the west end of Calle Máximo Gómez, is a remnant of Cuba's own Maginot Line. This is the only fortress along the line still standing (see sidebar below). ∎

Defense! La Trocha Fortresses

During Cuba's first war of independence (1868–1878), a defensive line of 43 forts extended for 42 miles (67 km), from Morón in the north to Júcaro in the south. These fortresses blocked the westward advance of the rebel army. The line, conceived by Spanish Gen. Blas Villate y de la Hera, was called La Trocha. It was finally penetrated in 1875 but fortified during the country's second war of independence (1895–1898). Rebel forces under Gen. Antonio Maceo broke through the line again in 1895 and ravaged western Cuba.

MORÓN & NEARBY

Gateway to the Jardines del Rey, Morón is a crossroads town linking Ciego de Ávila to the Circuito Norte—the north coast highway. A place to stock up on supplies rather than a sightseeing destination in its own right, the City of the Rooster nonetheless boasts some intriguing architecture and adjoining wetlands to lure anglers and birders.

Morón (pop. 64,000) was settled in 1643 by Andalusians, who named it after their hometown in Spain. Its nickname derives from early days, when a corrupt judge who had earned the unflattering sobriquet "the cock of Morón" was banished from town. In the 1950s, Fulgencio Batista presided over the unveiling of an emblematic rooster at the southern entrance to Morón. It was toppled following the revolution, but a **bronze rooster** replaced it in 1981; it stands beside the clock tower outside the **Hotel Morón** on Avenida Tarafa.

Tarafa runs north past a 1923 Teutonic-style railway station and becomes Calle Martí. The **Museo Caonabo** has a small, well-displayed collection spanning the pre-Columbian to revolutionary eras. Lined with columned porticoes, Martí leads into the old quarter, centered on **Parque Agramonte**, at the north end of town. This tiny square is surrounded by a simple church—**Iglesia de Lourdes**—and quaint houses painted in soft pastels. A vast wetland system of sedges and mangroves spreads over the coastal plains north of town. At its heart is **Laguna de la Leche** (Lagoon of the Milk), a jade jewel lent its opaque complexion by deposits of gypsum.

Morón's metal rooster crows automatically at dawn and dusk.

Gawky flamingos tiptoe around. The former Patria o Muerte sugar mill houses the **Museo de Azúcar** (Sugar Museum). Anglers flock to **Centro Pescadores la Redonda** (tel 33/30-2489), a fishing lodge on the shores of Laguna la Redonda, with functioning machinery to inform on sugar processing.

A 1917 Baldwin steam train offers rides, and 17 other locomotives are displayed. Boat rides and fishing trips of up to four hours can be organized at the lagoon (which is more touristic than the one in Leche). Lazier travelers can kick back and have a cool drink on the shore. ■

Morón
- ⓐ 155 B3

Museo Caonabo
- ✉ Calle Martí #374 at Sergio Antuña
- ☎ 33/50-4501
- 💲 $

Museo de Azúcar
- ✉ Patria, 3 miles (5 km) SE of Morón
- 🕐 Closed Sun.
- 💲 $

JARDINES DEL REY

Spanning the width of Ciego de Ávila and Camagüey Provinces, this wilderness of sandy coral islands crouches 5 to 15 miles (8–24 km) offshore in a great line that parallels the coast for some 248 miles (400 km). These island jewels beckon with whiter-than-white sands washed by waters of startling turquoise hues.

Royal palms sway on their namesake beach, Playa Palma Real, Cayo Coco.

Jardines del Rey

⚠ 155 B3 & C3

Visitor Information

✉ Infotur, Aeropuerto Internacional de Jardines del Rey, Cayo Coco

☎ 33/30-9109

The Jardines del Rey (King's Gardens) are one of the least disturbed areas of Cuba. Few among the 400 or so low-lying isles and cays are inhabited or even accessible, and only two—Cayo Coco and Cayo Guillermo—have been developed for tourism so far. The cays are smothered in scrub and mangrove marshes that harbor *jabalí* (wild pigs), iguanas, and more than 150 species of birds. Reefs run virtually unbroken the entire length of the cays' north shores, offering superb snorkeling

and diving. Be sure to pack insect repellent against the mosquitoes that abound especially at sunset and are insatiable.

Cayo Coco

On Cayo Coco, 56 miles (90 km) northeast of Ciego de Ávila, about a dozen resort hotels operate under foreign management, and Cuba plans to build 13,000 hotel rooms. Twelve miles (19 km) of frosted sands line the 20-mile-long (32 km) Atlantic shore of the isle, divided westward into **Playa Colorada**, **Playa Larga**, and **Playa Prohibida**. To escape the crowds, venture to **Playa Los Flamencos** or hire a catamaran or Windsurfer. On the smaller **Cayo Paredón Grande**, northeast of Cayo Coco, visit the **Faro Diego Velázquez**, an 1859 lighthouse at the cay's northern tip. You reach Cayo Coco from the mainland via a 17-mile-long (27 km) causeway *(pedraplén)* across Bahía de Perros (Bay of Dogs). At a security checkpoint *(toll),* show your passport. The bay hosts the Caribbean's largest flock of flamingos. At sunrise and dusk they fly over the tombolo; watch them at the **Parador La Silla** restaurant, midway along the pedraplén.

Much of the cay is within **Parque Nacional el Bagá**. Guided birding and other tours are offered through the **Centro de Investigaciones de Ecosistemas Costeros** *(tel 33/30-1161),* east of the Hotel Tryp. Within its fold is **Cueva del Jabalí** *(tel 33/30-1206),* a dank cave with cabarets at night. Plan guided horseback rides at **Sitio la Güira** *(tel 33/30-1208).* Sportfishing and diving are offered at **Marina Marlin Aguas Tranquilas** *(tel 33/30-1328),* on **Playa Las Coloradas**, and at major hotels.

Cayo Guillermo

Two miles (3 km) west of Cayo Coco is Cayo Guillermo. Its chief draw is **Playa El Paso**, a 3-mile-long (5 km) beach. Farther west are **Playa El Medio**, backed by huge dunes, and **Playa Pilar**, named for Hemingway's

sportfishing vessel. Water sports are available, and **Marina Marlin** *(tel 33/30-1737)* offers "seafari" excursions and boat rentals. The **Delfinario** *(tel 33/30-1529, $$$$),* set amid mangroves at the east end of the cay, offers dolphin shows several times a day.

Cayo Sabinal

The easternmost cay, **Cayo Sabinal** is reached from the port town of Nuevitas by a rugged and often muddy 4WD track with a police checkpoint *(passports required),* or by boat excursions from Playa Santa Lucía (see p. 166). Sabinal is

---

INSIDER TIP:

The Jardines del Rey were used as a setting for Ernest Hemingway's *Islands in the Stream*, based on his WWII exploits hunting Nazi U-boats. It's the perfect beach book.

—JUSTIN KAVANAGH
National Geographic Travel Books editor

---

soon due to receive 12,000 new hotel rooms. The finest beach is the usually empty **Playa los Pinos**. Food is served at a beach bar. Smaller **Playa Brava** and **Playa Bonita** extend west and east, respectively; the latter has a rustic bar. **Faro Colón**, a 1848 lighthouse, and the remains of an 1831 fortress—**Fuerte San Hilario**—guard the island's eastern tip. ∎

REEF WORLD

Among the most biologically productive ecosystems on Earth, a string of coral reefs encircles Cuba's shores—luring scuba divers and snorkelers from afar.

Coral reefs are built by tiny organisms called polyps—the corals. Each polyp, some the size of a pinhead, secretes calcium carbonate from its base to form an external skeleton—a protective chamber in which it lives. But it is strength in numbers that produces a reef. New polyps can bud off the old, securing their own skeletons in the interstice and atop older polyps; some species beget offspring that smother their parents and use those skeletons as foundations on which to cement their own. Over thousands of generations, millions of polyps create an intricately structured limestone reef.

Reefs are divided into life zones defined by depth, water temperature, and light. Distinct corals inhabit each zone. They come in a profusion of forms: massive brain coral; translucent saucer coral; gracefully curled wire coral; elkhorn coral (named for its resemblance to an elk's antlers), which can span 10 feet (3 m); and pillar coral, which sends its perfectly cylindrical columns shooting sunward as high as 15 feet (4.5 m).

Each reef is a subaqueous metropolis that also hosts a multitude of other creatures: sea urchins, moray eels, lobsters, octopuses, anemones, tubular sponges, and, of course, fishes large and small. Huge groupers and *cubera* snappers hang suspended as if by invisible strings. Manta rays and hawksbill and loggerhead turtles cruise leisurely by. Sharks lurk beneath ledges and inhabit tunnels. Schools of permit and *crevalle jacks* stream past. And an endless parade of brightly colored fish add their beauty: blue tangs, queen angelfish, yellow-and-purple fairy basslets, and iridescent blue chromis.

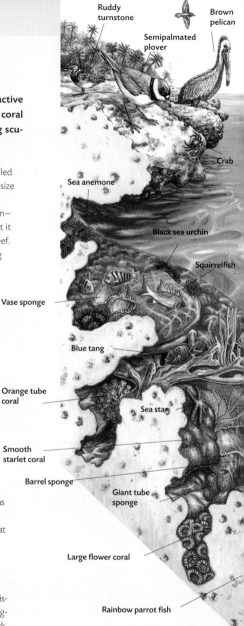

Ruddy turnstone
Brown pelican
Semipalmated plover
Crab
Sea anemone
Black sea urchin
Squirrelfish
Vase sponge
Blue tang
Orange tube coral
Sea star
Smooth starlet coral
Barrel sponge
Giant tube sponge
Large flower coral
Rainbow parrot fish

CAMAGÜEY

One of the island's original seven settlements, Camagüey is a labyrinth of winding lanes and cul-de-sacs; its defensive layout, once meant to thwart pirates, now often confounds tourists. Persistence pays off, however, revealing Camagüey's charms—its restored buildings, colonial plazas, and ubiquitous *tinajónes*, the earthenware rain collectors that are a symbol of the city.

■ The Historic Center of Camagüey became a UNESCO World Heritage site in 2008.

Camagüey
🗺 155 B2
Visitor Information
✉ Infotur, Ignacio Agramonte Airport
☎ 32/26-5807

Casa Natal Ignacio Agramonte
✉ Calle Ignacio Agramonte #459
☎ 32/29-7116
🕐 Closed Mon.
💲 $

Founded in 1514 under the name Santa María del Puerto del Príncipe, Camagüey moved to its present site on the north bank of the Río Jatibonico in 1528. The town prospered from its position at the heart of cattle country—attracting pirates on numerous occasions—and by the 19th century it was the second largest city in Cuba. It has since been superseded by Santiago de Cuba and now, with 306,000 residents, it is the second city on the island.

Colonial Plazas

The heart of the city is compact **Parque Agramonte**, named for

Maj. Gen. Ignacio Agramonte (1841–1873), who led the city's rebel forces against Spain during the first war of independence. He is honored in bronze, riding his charger. On the south side of the park is the austere **Catedral de Nuestra Señora de la Candelaria** *(tel 32/29-4965)*, dating from 1617. First erected in 1530, the original structure was felled by an earthquake.

Plaza de los Trabajadores (Workers' Plaza) is an irregular polygon centered on an aged ceiba tree. It is dominated by **Iglesia de Nuestra Señora de la Merced** *(tel 32/29-2740)*, built in 1748. This stately church boasts a neo-Gothic gilt altar, baroque balconies, and a frescoed ceiling. Supplicants pray beside the silver coffin of Santo Sepulcro, made of thousands of coins. Skeletons are still on view in the catacombs below.

On the square's west side stands the **Casa Natal Ignacio Agramonte**, birthplace of the aristocratic war hero. The 18th-century mansion, heavy with hardwood balustrades, was seized by the government during the war; it later served as the Spanish consulate. Impressively restored, it displays an array of sumptuous period furnishings.

Photogenic **Plaza San Juan de Dios**, the most intimate

INSIDER TIP:

In Camagüey's streets look out for the camels (*camellos*)! These giant articulated buses were designed to transport Cubans during the gasoline crisis and can carry up to 220 people. Beware of pickpockets!

—JUSTIN KAVANAGH
*National Geographic
Travel Books editor*

square, is now a national monument surrounded by 18th-century houses gaily painted in bright pastels.

The **Convento y Hospital de San Juan de Dios** dates from 1728 and features handsome arcaded cloisters added in 1840; the adjoining church boasts a splendid mahogany ceiling and commanding bell tower. The **Centro Provincial de Patrimonio**, which oversees the city's restoration, is housed here, as is the **Museo San Juan de Dios**, with exhibits on the evolution of the city.

Six blocks west of Parque Agramonte, on Plaza del Carmen, stands the restored **Iglesia de Nuestra Señora del Carmen**. The intimate cobbled plaza is lined with 18th-century houses and features life-size ceramic figures reflecting scenes from daily life. Be sure to visit **Galería-Estudio Martha Jiménez** (*tel 32/25-7559*), displaying other fabulous pieces of art by the sculptor.

Farther Afield

The **Teatro Principal** (*Calle Padre Valencia, tel 32/29-3048*), which once drew operatic luminaries, is open intermittently; pop in to admire the marble staircase, gilt chandeliers, and truly magnificent stained-glass windows (*vitrales*). The acclaimed Ballet de Camagüey performs here.

Bustling Calle República leads north to **Museo Provincial Ignacio Agramonte**, housed in the former cavalry garrison. Its eclectic exhibits span natural history to local culture.

The neoclassical **Instituto de Segunda Enseñanza** (Institute of Secondary Education) stands on the south bank of

Rain Catchers

The earthenware jugs called *tinajónes*, modeled on Spanish wine jars, were used in Camagüey in colonial times to collect water during a drought. Up to 5 feet (1.5 m) tall and 10 feet (3 m) in diameter, the jugs were sunk into the ground to keep the water cool. Legend suggests that visitors who accept a drink from a *tinajón* offered by a girl will fall in love and never leave town. Sip cautiously!

the Río Jatibonico, at Avenida de la Libertad. Adjacent to the Institute is the **Casino Campestre**, a spacious park with statuary and a bandstand. To its north, the vast **Plaza de la Revolución** features an impressive sculpture dedicated to Ignacio Agramonte. ∎

Museo San Juan de Dios

✉ Plaza San Juan de Dios
☎ 32/29-1388
🕐 Closed Mon.
💲 $

Museo Provincial Ignacio Agramonte

✉ Ave. de los Mártires #2
☎ 32/28-2425
🕐 Closed Mon.
💲 $

WALK COLONIAL CAMAGÜEY

This walk leads you down side streets linking hidden churches, small museums, and the city's three major plazas. You'll see much of the city's most intriguing colonial architecture. Some sites are tumbledown, but pockets of renovation lift the spirit. Take time to stop and talk to locals, who, with luck, might invite you into their homes, through ancient timber doorways to cool patios in the rear. Set out in late afternoon to miss the midday heat.

Sculptures made by Martha Jiménez in Plaza del Carmen, Camagüey

NOT TO BE MISSED:

Iglesia Nuestra Señora de la Soledad • Plaza San Juan de Dios • Casa de la Trova

Your starting point is the **Gran Hotel** ❶ *(tel 32/29-2314)*, midway down Calle Maceo, a pedestrian-only thoroughfare. The hotel deserves a look for its gleaming 19th-century decor. Walk north 50 yards (46 m) to the junction with Calle República, the city's central thoroughfare, also now pedestrian-only. You stand facing **Iglesia de Nuestra Señora de la Soledad** ❷, built in the 18th century and recently restored. Its redbrick facade belies the exquisite interior, which showcases baroque frescoes and a fine vaulted ceiling. The church's lofty tower is a city guidepost.

Turn right and follow República to Calle Martí; turn left and walk two blocks to tiny **Parque Martí**. On its south side, on Calle Luaces, is **Iglesia del Sagrado Corazón de Jesús** ❸, a neo-Gothic church built in 1920. Slip through the church's enormous mahogany

doorway to admire the *trompe l'œil* interior gleaming with gold and marble.

Follow Luaces west to República, turn left, and walk 400 yards (366 m) to **Puente Jatibonico**, a metal bridge over the Río Jatibonico that dates from 1773. Note the **Instituto de Segunda Enseñanza** on the south side of the Carretera Central. The tiny triangular plaza on the north side of the bridge has an intriguing revolutionary mural. Now turn west along Matadero, then right on Independencia, and left on Varona. This opens to cobbled **Plaza San Juan de Dios** ❹ (see pp. 162–163), edged with brightly hued houses with red-tile roofs. Explore the **Convento y Hospital de San Juan de Dios**, which served as a hospital until 1902 and in various capacities since.

Exit the plaza to the northwest and turn left onto Calle Hurtado, then right onto Calle Raúl Lamar for 50 yards (46 m), then left onto Calle Cisneros. Follow this north to **Catedral Metropolitana de Nuestra Señora de la Candelaria** ❺ on your right and then to **Parque Agramonte** ❻ (see p. 162), where you might want to sit awhile and admire the *tinajónes,* the Victorian lamp stands, and the fine facades. A statue of General Agramonte presides. The palm trees at each corner of the square were planted by locals in secret tribute to four Cuban independence fighters executed by the Spanish in 1851. Be sure to call in at the **Casa de la Trova** (*Calle Cisneros #171, tel 32/29-1357*), where most nights folkloric music performances take place on the rear patio, and at the **Casa de la Diversidad Cultural** (*Calle Cisneros #69*), with its beautiful blue façade. The house shows visitors the array of cultures that make up the city's community, from the Andalusian colonizers to the Haitian minorities. The building, from the 1700s, belonged to the Rubirosa family through the first years of the revolution but its current appearance is the work of a Catalan architect who was called in by the family to renovate the building in the 1900s.

Head west along Martí four blocks to cobbled **Plaza del Carmen ➐** to admire the charming life-size ceramic statues of local residents shown gossiping, reading a newspaper, and pushing a cart. Peruse the art and perhaps meet the artist at work in **Galería-Estudio**

Martha Jiménez (*tel 32/25-7559, marta-jimenez.com/news*), then return east along Calle Hermanos Agüero (10 de Octubre) four blocks to the **Casa Natal Nicolás Guillén ➑** (*Calle Hermanos Agüero #58, tel 32/29-3706, closed Sat.–Sun.*), the birthplace, in 1902, of poet, nationalist, revolutionary, and co-founder of the National Union of Cuban Writers and Artists. Guillén, who championed the cause of Afro-Cubans, was poet laureate until his death in 1989. The small home contains his library and possessions.

Return to Cisneros and go north two blocks to **Plaza de los Trabajadores ➒** (see p. 162), anchored by the **Catedral Nuestra Señora de la Merced**, where your walk ends.

> 🅰 See also area map p. 155
> ➤ Gran Hotel
> 🕒 3 hours
> ↔ 1.5 miles (2 km)
> ➤ Plaza de los Trabajadores

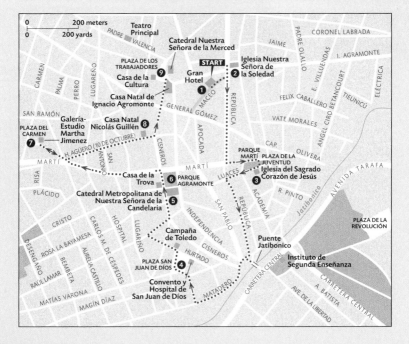

SANTA LUCÍA

One of Cuba's historic resorts has much to offer if your idea of a great getaway includes 12 miles (19 km) of sun-washed sand and great diving amid magnificent offshore coral reefs. There aren't a lot of amenities, nearby attractions, or even much local color to soak up. But there is the sun, the sand, and the sea.

■ Playa Los Cocos and the hamlet of La Boca

Santa Lucía

⚑ 155 C2

Visitor Information

✉ Cubatur, Hotel Brisas Santa Lucía

☎ 32/33-6291

Santa Lucía boasts the island's third longest beach and pristine turquoise shallows that are splendid for swimming and snorkeling. Sea grasses smother much of the seabed.

Divers will not be disappointed here either. Imagine huge gardens of black coral, massive sponges, nurse sharks, and an infinite number of zebra-striped, polka-dotted, rainbow-hued fish. Numerous shipwrecks litter the mouth of the **Bahía de Nuevitas**, including the doomed steamship *Mortera,* which sank to a depth of 20

feet (6 m) in 1898. A range of diving and sportfishing can be booked through **Shark's Friend Dive Center** *(tel 32/36-5182),* which also offers excursion by catamaran to Cayo Sabinal (see p. 159).

The region is semiarid and flat as a pancake. Two mangrove-edged lagoons—**Laguna Daniel** to the south and **Laguna El Real** to the northwest—harbor a diversity of birdlife, and the spectacle of flamingos is a daily delight. The lagoons have yet to be tapped for ecotourism.

Currently Santa Lucía, 70 miles (112 km) northeast of Camagüey, offers only a half dozen mediocre hotels and some ancillary services along 3 miles (5 km) of beachfront. Cubans vacation in *campismos* and bungalows, a considerable distance east of the tourist hotels. You can rent a *casa particular* (licensed room rental) here. A highway runs along the shore; bicycles and mopeds share it with horse-and-carriage taxis. The road extends, unpaved, to **La Boca**, a colorful, ramshackle fishing hamlet 2 miles (3 km) north. The hamlet enfolds **Playa Los Cocos**, where the snorkeling and diving are sublime. Cubans are permitted access without restriction—an excellent chance to mingle freely with locals. ■

PARQUE NACIONAL JARDINES DE LA REINA

An unexplored frontier awaiting discovery, the chain of almost 700 islets and cays lying off the southern coast of central Cuba is one of the world's most pristine marine zones. This string of coral jewels in a sapphire sea is a mecca for divers, boaters, and self-reliant types who are undeterred, or even drawn, by a lack of facilities.

Three subgroups extending across 200 miles (322 km) of shallow sea compose the archipelago called the Jardines de la Reina (Queen's Gardens). The largest islands—the so-called Labyrinth of the Twelve Leagues—gather in a long line about 50 miles (80 km) offshore of Ciego de Ávila Province and taper east into the neighboring province of Camagüey. This chain of stepping-stone isles shields the Golfo de

INSIDER TIP:

Scuba diving at Jardines de la Reina offers a real thrill— dive masters sometimes clamber aboard the backs of sharks, riding them like cowboys at a rodeo!

—VIRGILIO VALDÉS
National Geographic Latin America editor

Ana María, a sea that is about as shallow as the islands are high; it is bounded along the south by a continuous coral reef. Beyond it, barely a mile (1.6 km) from shore, the plateau drops off to a dark 6,000 feet (1,829 m).

Eastward, scores of smaller cays scattered across the western extent of the Golfo de Guacanayabo make up the second group. A third group, the **Cayos Ana María**, clusters close to the shores of Ciego de Ávila Province. All are flat, sandy, and covered with swampy mangrove pools.

The vast flats are a supreme bonefish habitat, and catching them requires little skill. These waters literally boil with tarpon also, guaranteeing anglers the thrill of a lifetime. Fidel Castro once frequented the area, flying down to his personal isle—Cayo Piedra—to fish, dive, and entertain friends.

Scuba divers are drawn by the diversity of sea life, including marine turtles and sharks, which feature in shark-riding exhibitions by trained dive masters. The convoluted passages through the archipelago became a graveyard for Spanish galleons—the seabed is a trove of doubloons and precious trinkets. More treasure probably lies buried in the sand, courtesy of pirates such as Sir Francis Drake.

Facilities are few and far between. The only permanent accommodation is in six live-aboard boats dedicated to fishing and scuba diving, operated by **Avalon Cuban Diving Centers**. ∎

Jardines de la Reina

🗺 155 A1 & B1

Visitor Information

✉ Centro de Investigaciones Medio Ambientales de Camagüey, Calle Céspedes & Carretera Central, Camagüey

☎ 32/29-6349

Avalon Cuban Diving Centers

✉ Marina Júcaro

☎ 338/732-0517

cubandiving
centers.com

More Places to Visit in Central Cuba

Área Protegida de Recursos Manejados Sierra del Chorrillo

The Sierra del Chorrillo rise over southeastern Camagüey Province and feature dramatic limestone formations called *mogotes*. The semideciduous and tropical montane ecosystems are protected with the **Área Protegida de Recursos Manejados Sierra del Chorrillo**, a 10,168-acre (4,115 ha) reserve centered on **Finca La Belén**, where horseback rides and guided hikes are offered. The *finca* is also a working farm and has water buffalos and even zebras. Make reservations through Ecotur *(Calle San Esteban #453 bet. Lope Recio*

■ Craftsmen at work in the Fábrica de Violines in Minas

& Popular, Camagüey, tel 33/224-3693, e-mail: comercial@cmg.ecotur.tur.cu). 155 C1

Minas & Around

This small village is 23 miles (37 km) northeast of Camagüey. Its draw is the **Fábrica de Violines** *(tel 32/69-6232, closed Sun.)*, a small factory producing guitars, violins, cellos, and other musical instruments. Worth a look, too, is **Ingenio de Santa Isabel**, the remains of a historic sugar mill, about 10 miles (16 km) east of Minas, in the village of San Miguel, which has a café. The Criadero de Cocodrilos (crocodile-breeding center) outside the village of **Senado**, about 5 miles (8 km) northwest of Minas, breeds American crocodiles for their skins (the Cuban crocodile—*Crocodylus rhombifer*—is not raised here). You can see about 350 animals, from newborns to 15-year-old crocs. 155 C2

Rancho King

Prior to the revolution, this cattle *finca,* about 5 miles (14 km) west of Camalote and 1 mile (1.6 km) south of the coast highway, was one of Cuba's largest. Once part of the Texas-based King Ranch empire, it still operates as a cattle-breeding station and welcomes visitors to its rodeo *(tel. 32/48-115)*. You can also ride horses or take a buggy ride, which includes a visit to a local village. Hotel tour desks in Camagüey and Santa Lucía offer excursions. 155 C2

Sitio Arqueológico Los Buchillones

At this coastal archaeological site, 20 miles (30 km) north of Chambas *(on the Circuito Norte 20 miles/30 km west of Morón),* the remains of a Taíno village are being excavated from the mud. Declared a National Historic Monument, the one-of-a-kind site includes several dozen wooden houses that once stood atop posts. A museum displays a dugout canoe, pottery, and indigenous artifacts. 155 A3

In a region of contrasts, colonial cities, sugar white beaches, steam-train rides, and Fidel Castro's guerrilla headquarters

WESTERN ORIENTE

At the Museo Celia Sánchez, Media Luna

WESTERN ORIENTE

The sweeping, palm-studded plains of the western Oriente region encompass Las Tunas, Holguín, and Granma Provinces. With a backdrop of mountains that reach 6,475 feet (1,974 m) at Pico Turquino, Cuba's highest peak, the flatlands range in terrain from swamp to semidesert. The region is often overlooked by visitors, despite its many draws, which include fine beaches, ecosystems rich with bird species, and key historic sites.

The province of Las Tunas lies to the east of Camagüey. It is cattle country in the south, flat and dry, easing to verdant green farther north. The eponymous capital city comes alive each June for a folklore festival, and the area plays host to a large cattle fair. Just to the east, Holguín Province boasts a sprawling city of the same name, with quaint colonial streets at its core. The area's

economy is dominated by sugar: During the *zafra*, or sugar harvest, the air is filled with the cloying odor of molasses emanating from the sugar mills. To the northeast the Sierra del Cristal mountains are being developed for ecotourism, with trails and lodges atop the misty heights where Fidel Castro played as a boy—his birthplace, Finca Manacas, is nearby. The mountains are laced with cobalt, manganese, and nickel, which generate almost one quarter of the island's export earnings.

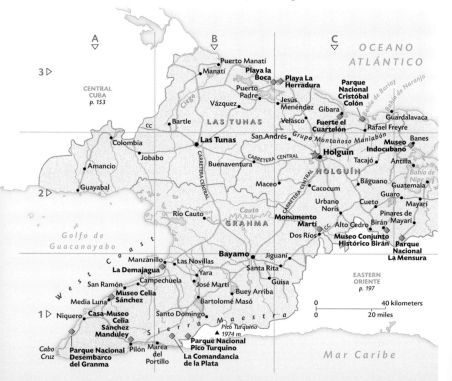

The beauty of Holguín Province as seen from Mirador de Mayabe

Mangrove forest lines much of the north coast, but it is the ribbons of talcum-fine beaches that attract the most attention, especially at Guardalavaca and at Playa Pesquero, with its all-inclusive resorts offering water sports and a host of local excursions. These include a trip by steam train through the dramatic Grupo Montañoso Maniabón mountains, known for Cuba's foremost pre-Columbian site. This is where Christopher Columbus stepped ashore in 1492, near what is now the coastal town of Gibara.

Granma, extending south of Las Tunas and west of Holguín like a great arrowhead jutting into the Caribbean, comprises fertile plains watered by the Río Cauto, Cuba's largest river.

NOT TO BE MISSED:

The cool uplands and pine forests at Pinares de Mayarí 186

Strolling Parque Céspedes in Bayamo and learning about the war of independence sparked by Carlos M. de Céspedes 187–188

A visit to Fidel Castro's former guerrilla headquarters at La Comandancia de la Plata 191

A trek to the summit of Pico Turquino, Cuba's highest peak 191

Touring the former Castro family estate at Museo Conjunto Histórico Birán 196

The vast delta that opens to the Golfo de Guacanayabo is a swampy no-man's-land where crocodiles are king. Granma is steeped in history: Independence was born at the city of Bayamo and at Carlos Céspedes's estate La Demajagua. You can also visit the site where national hero José Martí was martyred, and where Castro and his comrades came ashore to launch the decisive stage of the revolution. Cactus-studded Parque Nacional Desembarco del Granma is laced with trails. So, too, is the Sierra Maestra, a sheer mountain chain where trails ascend to Castro's former guerrilla head-quarters and Pico Turquino. ■

LAS TUNAS

This unassuming and intimate city straddling the Carretera Central is the gateway to the Oriente region. Though it is not a stand-alone attraction, you can easily spend a half day in this quiet provincial capital while passing through. Sites include handsome colonial buildings, a museum to a homegrown revolutionary hero, and contemporary ceramic murals.

The small-time capital of Las Tunas boasts a tidy, restful town center.

Las Tunas
170 B2

Victoria de las Tunas—a name adopted in 1869 following a Spanish victory here during the Ten Years' War—was once a territory of Bayamo, but became a city in its own right in 1852. Las Tunas is small in scale, with a compact town center that lost many original structures in an 1897 fire. The somnolent town of 170,000 has traditionally served as a regional center for the surrounding cattle industry; Cuba's largest annual horse and cattle fair is held here. It is also known as the City of Sculptures for the unique terra-cotta art

forms found on the exteriors of many buildings.

The Historic Core

At its heart, at the top of Avenida Vicente García, is **Parque Vicente García**, the town's intimate main square honoring Maj. Gen. Vicente García González. A rebel leader who commanded nationalist forces during both wars of independence, it was he who ordered the city of his birth set ablaze in 1876. Admire his marble bust from marble benches set in the shade of begonias that ring the square. The park opens to smaller **Plaza Martiana de las Tunas**, home to a large, contemporary sundial sculpture that points to an embossed head of José Martí.

On the northeast side of Parque Vicente García stands the **Museo Provincial**, housed in the old *ayuntamiento*, or town hall—an attractive white-and-blue structure with a handsome clock tower. The museum's displays include historical artifacts and photos, with a section on slavery and another profiling the life of Juan Cristóbal Nápoles Fajardo (see sidebar below), the town's famous 19th-century poet. Slip upstairs for a brief look at the timeworn natural history collection. The **Centro Histórico**, one block west, offers its own lean exhibits. Seek out the terra-cotta wall plaque showing the old city in bas-relief.

Avenida Vicente García, the bustling main street, slants west and is lined with aged buildings fronted by columned *portales*. Pop into the **Casa de la Cultura** (*Vicente García #8, tel 31/34-3500*), where poetry readings and music recitals are offered. Despite the conflagration that swept the city in 1897, the **Casa de Vicente García González**, where García was born, survived the blaze and—fully restored—now serves as a museum recalling those dramatic events. Exhibits include the homegrown hero's ceremonial swords.

About Town

At the foot of Avenida Vicente García, step across narrow Río Hormiguero. Facing you, on the north side of Calle Luca Ortíz, is a venerable wooden home that is now the **Memorial Mártires de Barbados**, dedicated to the 57 Cubans and 16 others who died in 1976 when a Cubana airliner was blown up by Cuban-exile terrorists. The museum is housed in the former casa of Carlos Leyva González, Cuba's champion *florete* (fencer), who died along with the Cuban team. Leyva's medals and fencing gear are displayed. Note the metal sculpture of a clenched fist, to the side of the house.

Reparto Aurora, northeast of the historic core, is the setting for the austere **Plaza de la Revolución**, dominated by the **Monumento del Mayor General Vicente García**; beneath, the **Salón de los Generales** (*tel 31/34-7751, $*) features busts of García and other generals of the wars of independence. ■

Museo Provincial

✉ Calle Francisco Varona at Lucas Ortíz Angel de la Guardia

☎ 31/34-8201

🕐 Closed Mon.

💲 $

Casa de Vicente García González

✉ Ave. Vicente García #5

☎ 31/34-5164

🕐 Closed Mon.

💲 $

Memorial Mártires de Barbados

✉ Calle Luca Ortíz #344

☎ 31/34-7213

🕐 Closed Mon.

💲 $

El Cucalambé

If possible, time your visit for June, when Las Tunas hosts the annual Jornada Cucalambeana (Cucalambé Folkloric Festival), drawing Cubans to hear *trovadores* (troubadours) celebrate the tradition of rhyming song. The festival is named for local poet Juan Cristóbal Nápoles Fajardo (1829–1862), nicknamed El Cucalambé. Nápoles was Cuba's preeminent composer of *décimas*—rhyming, eight-syllable verses that form the lyrics for songs. In 1856, Nápoles published a booklet of verses that celebrated the creole Cuban *guajiro* (peasant). His poems were enthusiastically received and contributed to the nationalist spirit of the times. The festival is held at Motel El Cornito, 4 miles (6 km) west of town; cabarets are also hosted here throughout the year.

BASEBALL FEVER

Cubans are a peaceable people, though you'd never know it on a sunny afternoon in Havana's Parque Central. Here baseball fanatics gather at *la esquina caliente* (hot corner) to debate the finer points of the national sport. Arguments break out. The odd fight is not unknown, so passionate are the Cubans for *pelota*, or *béisbol*. Cubans have been *locos* for baseball ever since the game was introduced by the U.S. in the 1860s.

Cuba's baseball team celebrates reaching another World Cup final in Panama City, 2011.

In 1872, the Habana Baseball Club was founded as Cuba's first professional team. The first league was formed six years later. North American clubs headed south as early as 1881 to take on Cuban teams, and in the decades that followed, major league heroes chased the sun to play "winter ball." Willie Mays and Tommy Lasorda both played baseball for Cuban clubs. The exchange of talent went both ways. "The rush of Cubans to the big leagues may cause an appeal for an amendment to the immigration laws," joked sports columnist W. O. McGeehan in 1919 after Cuban pitcher Oscar Teuro led the St. Louis Cardinals to a victory over the New York Giants. Even the Cuban revolution came to a halt during the 1957 World Series, when guerrilla commanders stopped operations to catch the final game. (It is said that Fidel Castro once tried out, unsuccessfully, for the Washington Senators.)

Cubans are known for playing the game with fierce determination. Boys grow up swinging a bat, which in Cuba means any stick they can get their hands on. No one has money for real bats, which in any event are as rare as gold in the stores. And no one has spikes or helmets. Bottle tops serve as stand-ins for baseballs. An entire school or neighborhood team might share a worn Cuban-made Batos glove. But what they lack in equipment, they make up for in talent.

Cuba's Baseball Season

Sixteen championship teams play in a split season (45 + 42 games), which runs from September to June. The top six teams go on to play the National Series. Regional fans are assured of seeing their favorite team play live—the last game of each three-game series is played in a rural township.

Cuba has seventeen major baseball stadiums. The largest, Havana's simple 55,000-seat Estadio Latinoamericano, is the yin to L.A.'s Dodger Stadium's yang, with none of its flashing scoreboards. And while the fans may be fiercely partisan, they're also applauding when the opposition scores, in the name of sportsmanship.

Talent Flies North

In this land of endless egalitarianism, even the professional baseball players earn only about 1,000 pesos (US$40) a month, although since 2013 they also get bonuses based on performance and may keep a percentage of prize money in foreign competitions. Not surprisingly, the U.S. professional leagues have been snapping up the best Cuban talent like stolen bases. Cuban national team pitchers, in particular, have caught home-run fever. Hundreds of Cuban professionals have defected in recent decades. José Abreu, Cuba's top player, fled the isle in August 2013 to sign a US$68 million, five-year deal with the Chicago White Sox. To stem the flow, the following month Cuba began to permit its star players to sign with foreign teams under terms negotiated by Cubadeportes (the state retains 20 percent). Thus, eight Cubans played in the 2015 Japanese professional league season. In December 2018, the United States and Cuba signed an historic agreement that states that any Cuban player over the age of 25 is free to sign with MLB teams. The Cuban federation receives compensation equaling at least 15–20 percent of the amount stipulated in the player's contract. The goal is to limit the unchecked flow of athletes out of Cuba, a number that in 2014 reached nearly 350.

EXPERIENCE:
Take in a *Béisbol* Game

During the September–June season, visit one of Cuba's baseball stadiums to experience all the energy and passion that Cubans display for their teams. Havana's team, the Industriales (colloquially called the Lions), plays at **Estadio Latinoamericano** (*Ave. Consejero Aranjo & Pedro Pérez, Cerro, Havana, tel 7/870-6752*). Some seats are reserved for foreigners. The following offers baseball tours:
• **Baseball Adventures** (*1001 Dove St., Newport Beach, CA 92660, tel 949/525-0920, baseballadventures.com*).

HOLGUÍN

Lying within the fold of surrounding hills that offer their own sites of interest, Holguín is a modern city with modest tourist facilities. But it is home to some of Cuba's most charming plazas and, for that reason alone, it is worth a visit.

The city is adorned with numerous statues of well-known Holguiñeros.

Holguín

🗺 170 C2

**Visitor
Information**

✉ Infotur, Edificio
Cristal, Calle
Martí & Libertad

☎ 24/42-5013

**Casa Natal de
Calixto García**

✉ Calle Miró #147,
bet. Calles Martí
& Luz Caballero

☎ 24/42-5610

🕐 Closed Sun.–
Mon.

💲 $

In 1535 the Spanish granted the land around Cubanacán, a major Taino Indian settlement, to conquistador Capitán García Holguín, who founded a cattle estate that would eventually become Cuba's fourth largest city (pop. 295,000). During the 19th century, the city grew in prominence and was fought over in the wars of independence. But industrialization—Cuba's major brewery and a sugarcane harvester factory are here—and urban expansion in dour communist style have defaced the contemporary city. Its saving grace is that its concentrated colonial core is attractive and the city has a vital culture, with mechanical organ groups a prominent feature.

Loma de la Cruz (Hill of the Cross) shoulders up to the north side of the city, providing a panoramic view over the great sweep of Holguín Province. You can ascend by car or attempt a leg-trembling climb up the 458-step staircase that begins at the head of Calle Maceo. The hill is named for the wooden cross erected here on May 3, 1790; a religious procession—the Romería de la Cruz (Pilgrimage of the Cross)—ascends the steps on the anniversary of that day.

City Parks

The logical starting point for exploring is **Plaza Calixto García**, the town's expansive main square, which is laid out in ornamental pink and green marble. At its heart is a statue of the revered Gen. Calixto García Iñiguez sitting on horseback (see sidebar p. 178). García was born one block east, in the **Casa Natal de Calixto García**. Today it is a museum displaying meager personal effects and exhibits tracing his role in the fight for independence. For more about regional history, check out the **Museo Provincial**, housed in the former Casino Español (a social club founded by Iberians), graced by delicate wrought-iron balconies. Erected in 1860–1862, the building later became a barracks and is mockingly called "La Periquera"—parakeet's cage—after Spanish troops dressed in yellow, green, and blue uniforms were barricaded behind the grilled windows during the fighting of October 1868. It has a fine collection of pre-Columbian artifacts, including a polished peridot ax (the *hacha de Holguín*) carved in the shape of a human. José Martí's ceremonial sword is there also, encased in glass.

Be sure to take in the **Casa de la Trova**, on the park's west side, where *música campesina* (country music) performances are hosted on the patio, and the **Centro Provincial de Artes Plásticas Galería Holguín**, a stone's throw south. Note, too, the Art Deco facade of the **Teatro Comandante Eddy Suñol** (named for a revolutionary hero), on the plaza's south side.

The **Museo de Historia Natural Carlos de la Torre**, 50 yards (46 m) south of Plaza Calixto García on Calle Maceo, displays a ragtag collection of mounted Cuban fauna, including a manatee, plus *polymites*—the dazzling colored snails endemic to Oriente (see sidebar p. 46).

Museo Provincial
- ✉ Calle Frexes #198
- ☎ 24/46-3395
- 🕐 Closed Mon.
- 💲 $

Centro Provincial de Artes Plásticas Galería Holguín
- ✉ Calle Maceo #180
- ☎ 24/45-3302
- 🕐 Closed Sat.–Sun.

Museo de Historia Natural Carlos de la Torre
- ✉ Calle Maceo #129, bet. Calles Martí & Luz Caballero
- ☎ 24/42-3935
- 🕐 Closed Mon.
- 💲 $

EXPERIENCE: Learn Spanish in Cuba

Speaking Spanish isn't a prerequisite for enjoying a visit to Cuba, but the history and culture of the island are easier to appreciate with at least some basic grasp of its mother tongue. Many children speak English (a compulsory part of their school curriculum), even if their parents don't. In the countryside, far fewer speak English. Wherever you are in Cuba, even a little Spanish will ease your way and guarantee more meaningful interactions. Not least, Cubans will delight in discovering that you speak their language. The following institutions offer Spanish language instruction:

- **Universidad de Holguín** (University of Holguín; *tel 24/48-1690, uho.edu.cu*) offers 2- to 6-week courses.
- **Universidad de la Habana** (University of Havana; *Calle J #556, bet. 25 & 27, Vedado, Havana, tel 7/870-4667*) offers "quickie" Spanish immersion classes, plus intensive (as much as 480 hours) "Spanish and Cuban Culture" courses, which begin on the first Monday of every month.
- **GoAbroad** (*goabroad.com*) offers a compendium of companies with Spanish language programs in Cuba.

Museo del Deporte

✉ Ave. XX Aniversario

☎ 24/47-1448

💲 $

The museum building itself melds Moorish elements into the neoclassical style.

Maceo opens onto the intimate **Parque Julio Grave de Peralta**, anchored by a marble statue of Gen. Grave de Peralta (1834–1872), who led the rebel assault in 1868 that captured Holguín from the Spanish. The venerable church on the east side is the recently restored **Catedral de San Isidoro**, built in 1720 in dedication to the town's patron saint and recently restored. Peek in to admire the wooden ceiling.

Holguín's Hero

Born in Holguín on August 4, 1839, Calixto García Iñiguez rose to become commander in chief of the rebel army during the Ten Years' War. On December 19, 1872, the general led the rebel assault that seized his hometown from Spanish forces. He was captured in 1874 and taken to Spain. When the second war of independence broke out in 1895, García returned to Cuba from New York, where he had escaped in 1880. In 1898 he again attempted to capture Holguín, but abandoned the siege to lead rebel forces in the battle for Santiago de Cuba following U.S. intervention. He died later that year and was reinterred in Holguín in 1980.

Holguín's most pleasing square is cobbled **Parque San José**, two blocks north of Plaza Calixto García. It is surrounded by old colonial houses and the charming **Iglesia de San José**, which dates from 1819 and features a domed neoclassical clock tower. Romantic tunes waft over the square each Sunday evening, when a mechanical organ is played.

Beyond the Core

The city claims the nation's sole mechanical organ factory—**Fábrica de Órganos** (Carretera de Gibara #301, tel 24/42-6616 or 42-4162, closed Sat.–Sun.)—where artisans craft organs, guitars, and other musical instruments in traditional fashion. Baseball fans might want to head to the **Estadio Calixto García** in the modern **Reparto Plaza de la Revolución**, situated east of downtown. The stadium features a **Museo del Deporte** with exhibits of sports memorabilia, including some interesting historical shots of Che Guevara and Castro playing baseball. Calixto García slumbers in a mausoleum, which is located opposite the provincial headquarters of the Communist Party. A broad boulevard—**Avenida de los Libertadores** (Carretera a Mayarí)—leads east from downtown and celebrates Cuban and continental "liberators" with monuments to Benito Suárez, Simón Bolívar, Máximo Gómez, Antonio Maceo, and Che Guevara.

Mirador de Mayabe

Mirador de Mayabe (tel 24/42-2160), 5 miles (8 km) southeast of Holguín, has a lookout with views across Valle de Mayabe, a fine hotel and restaurant, plus a faux farmstead with animals on view in pens, and a valla (cockpit) for cockfights. Horseback rides are offered. Do not buy Panchito the burro (donkey) a beer, as is tradition. His papa Pancho died of cirrhosis! ■

GIBARA & NEARBY

The sleepy, weather-beaten coastal town of Gibara is a trove of salt-preserved architectural treasures. It is also famous as the site of Christopher Columbus's landing in Cuba. The presumed spot of the explorer's first footfall, in sparkling, flask-shaped Bahía de Bariay, is enshrined within a national park that also encompasses beaches, mangroves, and mountains.

The beautiful statue of liberty in front of the Iglesia de San Fulgencio is the work of an Italian artist who used a young local woman for his model.

Gibara, 21 miles (34 km) north of Holguín, dates from 1817. The ruins of the **Fuerte el Cuartelón** fortress (a 30-min. hike from the town plaza) overlook elegant colonial buildings that earned Gibara the nickname Perla del Oriente (Pearl of the Orient). Waves break over the coral foreshore alongside Gibara's seafront promenade, which leads to **Playa de Caletones,** a white-sand beach 9 miles (15 km) north of town.

Parque Calixto García—the main plaza, lined with *robles africanos* (African oaks)—boasts a small statue of Cuba's Indian maiden representing the freedom gained when the Spanish left in 1898. To one side of the plaza is the Byzantine-style **Iglesia de San Fulgencio,** completed in 1950. On the park's west side is the small yet impressive **Museo de Historia Natural,** exhibiting various stuffed birds and beasts. The **Museo de Artes Decorativas** exhibits period furnishings and paintings in a restored colonial mansion.

Take note of the beautiful *mediopuntos.* If you happen to be in the area in July, don't miss the **Festival Internacional de Cine** *(ficgibara.com).*

The flat-topped **Silla de Gibara** (Saddle of Gibara) rising over the bay was recorded by Columbus on his arrival on October 28, 1492, and lies at the heart of **Parque Natural Cristóbal Colón,** an ecological megapark. ■

Gibara & Nearby

🗺 170 C3

Museo de Historia Natural

✉ Calle Luz Caballero #23

☎ 24/84-4458

💲 $

Museo de Artes Decorativas

✉ Calle Independencia #19

☎ 24/84-4687

🕐 Closed Mon.

💲 $

DRIVE HOLGUÍN TO BANES

Dipping down to the shore and into the lush vales of the Grupo Montañoso Mani-abón mountains (see p. 183), Route 6-241 carves a superbly scenic path through a landscape punctuated with an irregular pattern of limestone hummocks and ridges running to all points of the compass. Although the road is mostly in good condition, the usual hazards—potholes, bicycles, and ox-drawn carts—require constant caution.

Departing **Holguín** ❶ can be confusing. Exit Plaza Calixto García along Calle Martí and veer right along Avenida de los Libertadores; immediately beyond the baseball stadium (visible on your left), turn left onto Avenida XX Aniversario, which leads to Route 6-241 and Guardalavaca. The road dips and rises

NOT TO BE MISSED:

Playa Mayor, Guardalavaca
• Museo Aborigen Chorro de Maíta, near Yaguajay • Iglesia de Nuestra Señora de la Caridad, Banes

Statue of José Martí in Banes

through wide-open rangeland, with steep-faced *mogotes* (see pp. 106–107) studding the landscape. Bright red crotons flame alongside the road, and you'll pass *bohíos* (thatched huts) fenced by tightly packed cacti shaped like candelabras, neatly and lovingly trimmed. For 10 miles (16 km), the mark of the hedge clipper can be seen on every bush.

About 20 miles (34 km) northeast of Holguín, turn left for Rafael Freyre. Bypass the town and continue straight to Frey Benito; turn right and follow the road north to **Parque Monumento Nacional Bariay** *($$).* This 509-acre (206 ha) park has a small pre-Columbian museum, enactments of Taino lifestyle in a re-creation of an Indian village, and a motley monument commemorating Columbus's landing. Retrace your route to Rafael Freyre and turn left in town, passing Central Rafael Freyre, a now defunct sugarcane-processing factory. Continue to **Playa Blanca** ❷, a lovely white-sand beach and humble fishing community as yet unde-veloped for tourism but with a plaque at the southern end of the beach that proclaims this "the site of the first landing of Christopher Columbus in Cuba."

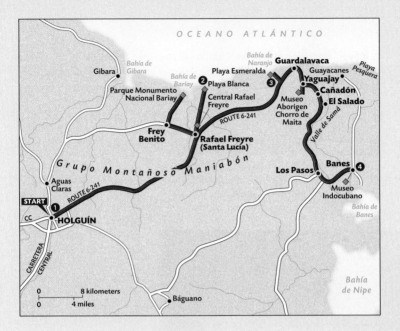

Ten miles (16 km) beyond Rafael Freyre you'll pass the turnoff for **Playa Esmeralda** ③ and, a short distance farther, for **Bahía de Naranjo**. Three miles (5 km) farther on, turn left off the *carretera* and take a rest in the resort of **Guardalavaca** (see pp. 182–183). After sunning yourself and swimming in the warm turquoise waters, return refreshed to the highway and continue east. The road immediately heads south and cuts inland over the northernmost *mogotes* of the **Grupo Montañoso Maniabón** mountains. At the village of **Yaguajay**, turn right at the sign for **Museo Aborigen Chorro de Maíta** (see p. 183), Cuba's largest pre-Columbian archaeological site; it's 2 miles (3 km) uphill. After visiting the museum and the re-creation of an Indian village, head back to Route 6-241.

Beyond Yagaujay, the road drops down to the village of Cañadón, in the **Valle de Samá**. Tousled royal palms stand sentry over lime green tobacco fields in the lee of sensuously rounded hills. You'll soon pass through

> ⛰ See also area map pp. 170–171
> ► Holguín
> ⏱ 4.5 hours (one way)
> ⟷ 60 miles (96 km)
> ► Banes

the community of **El Salado**, where the freestanding knolls tower over the highway. The road snakes in and out of lush vales and deposits you, 18 miles (29 km) beyond Guardalavaca, on a broad plain that sweeps east to the **Bahía de Banes**. Sugarcane stretches out before you, rippling in the breeze like folds of green silk.

Follow the road as it curves northeast to **Banes** ④, with a well-preserved colonial core (travelers should note that the town has no hotels). Fulgencio Batista was born here in 1901, and Fidel Castro was married in 1948 in the **Iglesia de Nuestra Señora de la Caridad**. The **Museo Indocubano** (see p. 183) is also worth a visit.

GUARDALAVACA & NEARBY

As a resort destination, pocket-size Guardalavaca has been overtaken in recent years by Cayo Coco. But what it lacks in size it makes up in beautiful beaches and water. Adjacent *playas* are being developed with showy all-inclusive hotels, ecotour projects are evolving, and the area is rich with worthy excursions.

Guardalavaca

🏔 170 C3

Visitor Information

✉ Cubatur, Centro Comercial Los Framboyantes

☎ 24/43-0170

Guardalavaca (the name means "watch the cow") was created in the 1970s, when the area became popular with Soviet officials. Since their departure it began to launch itself as a tourist destination. The basic amenities are present—car rental, liquor store, souvenirs—but not much else. However, you can mingle with local Cubans, who gather for family picnics. The beaches—**Playa Guardalavaca** to the west and **Playa Las Brisas** to the east—are beautiful, and water-sports outlets rent equipment, including sailboards. Divers justifiably rave about the riotous glories of the undersea world: Giant groupers and sponges, for example, and even swordfish are commonly seen slicing along a wall called **The Jump**. The reef begins just 200 yards (183 m) from shore. **Eagle Ray Dive Center** *(tel 24/43-0316),* tucked beneath the cliffs on Playa Guardalavaca, offers dive trips.

Parque Natural Bahía de Naranjo

This horseshoe bay, approximately 5 miles (8 km) west of Guardalavaca, is surrounded by mangroves and woodland, parts of which have been developed for ecotourism. **Reserva Ecológica Las Guanas**, on the eastern headland at the mouth of the bay, has trails that lead from an interpretive center; one deposits you at **Cueva Siboney**, a cave displaying Indian petroglyphs. You can rent horses at **Rancho Naranjo**, an equestrian center, and view

The beautiful Playa Guardalavaca is slated for development.

Hop a Steam-train Ride

During the sugar harvest season, from January through June, the countryside resounds around the clock with the whistles, hissing, and clanking of steam trains as sugarcane is unloaded at *centrales*. A decade ago, Cuba had more than 100 steam trains in operation—the largest collection of working steam trains in the world. Some date back more than a century, but in recent years many have been retired. Although most are destined to become museum pieces, some have been converted to haul passengers along scenic countryside rides. The following are among the best trips:

• Short rides are offered on a 1917 Baldwin at the **Museo de Azúcar** *(tel 33/50-3309),* outside Morón (see p. 157).

• A 1914 steam train offers nostalgic trips, starting from the **Museo de Agroindustria Azucarera** *(tel 42/35-3864)* in Caibarién (see p. 129), to Remedios.

exhibits of local flora and fauna at **Rancho Mongo**, a re-creation of a country *finca*. **Bioparque Rocazul**, at the bay's northwest extreme, offers hiking trails and horseback rides along dry forest trails and a hokey faux farm that children will enjoy.

The beaches around the shore on either side of the bay—**Playa Esmeralda** to the east, and **Playa Pesquero** to the west—are being gilded with upscale, all-inclusive resorts, but beware the dangerously strong currents at Pesquero.

A very small island—**Cayo Naranjo**—sits in the bay. Its main draw is **Acuario Cayo Naranjo** *(tel 24/43-0439),* an aquarium where sea lions and dolphins perform daily. You can swim with the dolphins for an extra charge. Excursions run from nearby hotels. Catamaran excursions, including sunset cruises, depart from here.

Grupo Montañoso Maniabón

These dramatic mountain formations rise south of Guardalavaca and are made up of *mogotes* (see pp. 106–107). These geographic wonders are arranged in a bizarre topography that is among the most beautiful in Cuba. The valleys, with their rust red soils, are cultivated in sugarcane and tobacco.

Tucked into these heights is **Museo Aborigen Chorro de Maíta**, the site of a Taino cemetery and the largest aboriginal burial site found in the West Indies. A pit in the center of the hilltop museum displays some of the more than 100 skeletons unearthed here since 1930 (note the malformed skulls, which the Taino intentionally flattened at birth). Ceramics, jewelry, and other artifacts can be viewed here (many of the finest remains are displayed at the **Museo Indocubano Bani**, in nearby Banes; see p. 181).

To experience a living sense of the Taino culture and lifestyle, venture across the road to **Aldea Taína** *($),* which offers visitors an interesting, although idealized, re-creation of life in an Indian village. ∎

Museo Aborigen Chorro de Maíta

⊠ Route 6-241, near Yaguajay

☎ 24/43-0201

$ $

Museo Indocubano Bani

⊠ Calle General Marrero #305, Banes

☎ 24/80-2487

⊕ Closed Mon.

$ $

SWEET HARVEST

Cuba is a gently undulating sea of chartreuse. Rippling fields of *azúcar*—sugar—cover 3 million acres (1.2 million ha), or about 35 percent of all arable land. The local saying *"sin azúcar, no hay país*–without sugar, there's no country" reflects Cuba's economic dependence on the crop. Recently income from tourism has exceeded income that derives from sugar, which is still the island's primary export.

Macheteros cut the grass beside cane fields in preparation for the *zafra*.

Sugarcane was brought to Spain by the Moors. It was introduced to Cuba in 1512 by Diego Velázquez, at a time when "white gold" was one of Europe's most valued commodities. Cuba's humid tropical climate and deep, fertile soils proved perfectly suited to growing *Saccharum officinarum*—a tall, reedlike grass whose hard, multijointed stalk is filled with spongy pulp containing sweet, juicy sucrose.

The plant requires plentiful rainfall during the growing season and a dry season to bring in the crop. It is propagated from cuttings, which are laid lengthwise about 12 inches (30 cm) apart in furrows, then covered with soil.

The cuttings sprout multiple stems that grow in clumps. The thick stalks grow to more than 9 feet (3 m) high and mature about 12 to 18 months after planting, strewing the lime green cane fields with wispy white blossoms.

In preparation for the *zafra*—the harvest— of the January–June dry season, the fields are set afire to burn off the long, scimitar-sharp, sword-shaped leaves. Today, most cane is cut by mechanical harvesters. Smoke-smudged *macheteros* dressed in straw hats and coarse linens have not been replaced entirely, though, and still wield their sharp blunt-nosed machetes to fell the charred stalks on hillsides and in valleys. A skilled *machetero* can cut more than 4 tons (3.6 tonnes) of cane a day; a Cuban-designed combine-harvester cuts twice that amount in one hour. The stalk is cut off close to the ground, where the sucrose concentrates, while the leafy top is lopped off and the leaves stripped from the stalk. The plant is left to regrow; after three crops, the field is plowed over and replanted.

Processing Sugar

The stems are transported to Cuba's 44 dilapidated sugar-processing factories *(centrales)*. Here, the stems are shredded and crushed between huge rollers that squeeze out the juice *(guarapo)*. The liquid is boiled in a clarifier, where impurities settle out. A filtering step is next, then the clear sucrose is evaporated in a vacuum pan to remove excess water. This produces a viscous yet crystalline syrup. A centrifuge spins out the molasses syrup and leaves raw brown sugar crystals, which are sent to shipping terminals for refining abroad. Nothing is wasted. The mud—*vinasse*—from the clarifier is used as a fertilizer. The molasses goes to make rum. And the fibrous, pulpy cane waste *(bagasse)* is used as cattle feed, for cardboard and wallboard, and to fuel *centrale* boilers.

Cuba's early, labor-intensive sugar industry relied on simple mills *(trapiches)* driven by oxen, mules, or slaves. It remained relatively backward for almost two centuries. The industry was also held back by a shortage of slaves. Spain had been slow to engage in the slave trade dominated by the British, who in 1762 seized Cuba, opened the island to trade, and introduced advances such as water-powered sugar mills *(ingenios)*, which they had pioneered on their Caribbean island possessions. The brief British occupation gave Cuba's sugar industry a boost.

Sugar had its heyday in Cuba in the 19th century, when the first railroads were laid and steam power and mechanization were introduced to the mills. It became the foremost crop, accounting for about 70 percent of Cuba's revenue, and Cuba became the world's largest producer. The wars of independence, however, ravaged the industry, which passed largely into the hands of U.S. corporations after Cuba's independence in 1898. The industry was modernized and the U.S. government made guarantees to buy Cuba's sugar; the nation became bound economically to the United States.

In 1960, Fidel Castro nationalized the sugar industry. Soon after, sugar was supplied to the Eastern bloc in exchange for rice, grain, and other staples, locking the island nation into a

EXPERIENCE:
Make a Classic *Mojito*

In the land of sugar and rum, why not make a *mojito*? Using a highball glass, mix together a half tablespoon (7 g) of sugar and the fresh-squeezed juice of half a lime. Add a sprig or two of fresh-cut mint, then crush the stalks to release the flavor. Next, add two ice cubes followed by 1.5 ounces (40 mL) of white rum. Fill the glass with soda water, add a dash of angostura bitters, then dress with some fresh mint sprigs.

dependency on the Soviets. The *zafra* became the measure of the economy. In 1970, Castro announced Cuba would produce 10 million tons (9,072,000 tonnes) of sugar that year. The entire economy was reorganized as city people worked in the fields. The effort failed, and the economy ground to a halt. The attempt to wean the economy off its sugar dependence also failed; Cuba remained the world's largest producer, averaging 8 million tons (7,258,000 tonnes) annually. Since the Soviet Union's collapse, Cuban production has slumped, averaging less than 4 million tons (3,630,000 tonnes) annually since 1990. In 2002 the government scaled back its sugar lands and closed inefficient centrales. More than half have since closed, and production has continued to plummet.

SIERRA DEL CRISTAL

Verdant and virginal, the Sierra del Cristal rises east of Holguín, inland of the narrow coastal plain. Pine-clad and home to myriad species of flora and fauna, including many rare birds, these refreshing, unsullied heights beckon hikers and nature lovers undaunted by the lack of facilities.

The Cuban parrot, colorful resident of the Sierra del Cristal

Sierra del Cristal

171 D2

Visitor Information

✉ Gaviota

☎ 7/869-5774

gaviota-grupo.com

Few roads penetrate these mountains, which rise eastward and attain 4,346 feet (1,231 m) atop Pico de Cristal, where clouds swirl through the mist-sodden montane forest. Many endemic species thrive amid the lush landscapes, including, at drier lower elevations, orchids that have uniquely adapted by growing neither leaf nor flower.

Pinares de Mayarí, located 10 miles (16 km) south of the town of Mayarí, draws visitors for birding and forest hikes at the **Parque Nacional La Mensura**, high in the Altiplanicie de Nipe. The climate is almost alpine (so bring a warm jacket). You can take an organized excursion through Gaviota, which runs an alpine-themed eco-resort called **Villa Pinares de Mayarí** (*tel 24/50-3308*). This rustic yet cozy Teutonic-style stone-and-timber lodge is surrounded by scenic pine forest. There are trails and horses for guided rides to the **Salto de Guayabo**, a 280-foot (85 m) waterfall with a fabulous view north to the Bahía de Nipe.

INSIDER TIP:

Locals in the Sierra del Cristal may try to sell you jewelry of colorful *polymite* shells. Refrain from buying, as these snails are endangered.

—JENNIFER ALLARD
National Geographic contributor

The birding is superb here, with the endemic Cuban parrot, Cuban parakeet, Cuban trogon, Cuban tody, Cuban screech owl, and Cuban pygmy owl all among the resident avian fauna.

Nearby is **La Plancha**, a horticultural garden alive with colors and scents. Also nearby, the **Orquideario La Mensura** (*$*)—an orchid garden run by the Cuban Academy of the Sciences—has a short self-guided nature trail. ■

BAYAMO & NEARBY

Bayamo, dating from 1513, is one of the original seven settlements founded by Diego Velázquez. Its central plaza has been restored, and sites of great importance in Cuba's history now gleam. Nearby, several sites associated with the long struggle for independence provide intriguing forays afield.

The early settlement of Bayamo was built atop a bluff overlooking the Río Bayamo (today lily clogged), in the lee of the Sierra Maestra. The town thrived as a center for smuggling and later prospered from the sugar trade.

By the mid-18th century, Bayamo had become a hotbed of independence sentiment—and the setting for some consequential events. On October 10, 1868, a *criollo* landowner, Carlos Manuel de Céspedes, initiated revolt against Spain (see sidebar below). Ten days later, rebel forces led by Céspedes seized Bayamo, where a revolutionary junta was formed. In January 1869, with Spanish troops at the door, the rebels torched the city; it was finally recaptured by Gen. Calixto García Íñiguez in April 1898. Today the city's central core is designated as a national monument.

The Carretera Central skirts the north side of Bayamo, which lies midway between Holguín and Santiago de Cuba. The city's heart is the expansive main square—**Parque Carlos Manuel de Céspedes**—which is named for the nationalist revolutionary who was born here. Note the granite column in the center of the square, topped by a larger-than-life bronze effigy of a dignified yet solemn Céspedes in frock coat, with bas-reliefs depicting scenes from his life. A bust, inscribed with the national anthem, "La Bayamesa," honors composer Perucho Figueredo (1819–1870).

On the plaza's north side is Céspedes's birthplace, **Casa Natal de Carlos Manuel de Céspedes**, a house that, remarkably, survived the conflagration. It is now a museum tracing Bayamo's history

Bayamo

🗺 170 B1

Visitor Information

✉ Infotur, Plaza del Himno

☎ 23/42-3468

Casa Natal de Carlos Manuel de Céspedes

✉ Calle Maceo #57

☎ 23/42-3864

🕐 Closed Mon.

💲 $

Carlos M. de Céspedes & the "Grito de Yara"

Carlos Manuel de Céspedes (1819–1874) is called the Father of the Nation. The estate owner, poet, and lawyer published the first journal of the independence movement—*El Cubano Libre (Free Cuba)*. On October 10, 1868, Céspedes freed his plantation's slaves at La Demajagua, near Manzanillo, and, in an oration known as the "Grito de Yara" ("Cry of Yara"), called for open revolt against colonial rule. This led to the Ten Years' War (1868–1878), Cuba's first concerted attempt at independence. Céspedes was named head of a rebel army and of the first Assembly of the Republic. The Spanish captured his son Oscar, but Céspedes refused to give himself up, and Oscar was shot. Céspedes was deposed in 1873 in a leadership coup. Spanish troops killed him in 1874 in his Sierra Maestra refuge.

Museo Provincial

✉ Calle Maceo #55

☎ 23/42-4125

⊕ Closed Tues.

$ $

and Céspedes's rise from law student to revolutionary president. Original furnishings still grace the upstairs bedrooms; and the exhibits include Céspedes's law books and sword.

Next door, the **Museo Provincial** also features period furnishings, plus the original Cuban

Revolutionary Poet

The "spiritual father of the revolution," José Martí is the most revered figure in Cuban history. Born in Havana to Spanish immigrant parents in 1853, the young Martí agitated against Spanish rule and was exiled for sedition. He graduated in law and philosophy from Spanish universities and began a luminous journalistic, academic, and literary career, working in Mexico and Guatemala before settling in New York. Martí founded the Cuban Revolutionary Party in 1892 and went on to form La Liga de Instrucción to train guerrillas in preparation for the day when he would put his revolutionary ideas of Cuban independence into action.

José Martí published the *Manifesto de Montecristi* as a blueprint for the second war of independence (1895–1898). On the stormy night of April 11, 1895, Martí and his comrades pulled ashore in a rowboat on a beach at Cajobabo, in eastern Cuba. On May 19, in his very first skirmish as a revolutionary soldier—the Battle of Dos Ríos—Martí rushed headlong into the conflict and was instantly killed by Spanish troops, thus becoming an inspirational martyr for the cause to which he had dedicated his life.

national anthem score, initially composed as a stirring martial song. On the square's eastern side, Céspedes proclaimed Cuban independence in front of the

ayuntamiento (town hall). This historic building was also the site of the first meeting of the Assembly of the Republic.

The *parque* opens to the northwest onto the cobbled **Plaza del Himno Nacional**, surrounded by cream-colored colonial houses. The revolutionary anthem was first sung by a choir of women in the **Catedral de San Salvador** *(tel 23/42-2514)* on November 8, 1868. The beautifully restored church, rebuilt after the 1869 fire, features an exquisite mural above the altar depicting the town's dramatic events. Slip into the **Capilla de la Dolorosa**; this side chapel, featuring an impressive Mudejar-style ceiling, dates from 1740. The first flag of the republic, sewn by Céspedes's wife, is displayed here; note also the baroque gilt altar to the Virgen de Dolores, ornately adorned with faux fruit.

Moving southward along **Calle de Céspedes**, you'll pass several old buildings worth noting. Tomás Estrada Palma, first president of independent Cuba, was born at **Casa de Estrada Palma** *(Calle de Céspedes #158);* today it hosts the cultural and artistic organization **UNEAC** *(tel 23/42-3670).*

Notable personalities—the eclectic mix ranges from physicist Albert Einstein (1879–1955) to Cuban musician Compay Segundo (1907–2003)—are honored at the **Museo de Cera** (Wax Museum), Cuba's only such museum, on the pedestrian-only main drag of Bayamo, General García. Across the street, scale models of the city can be viewed at **La Maqueta** *(tel 23/42-3633, closed Sat.–Sun.).* Next

The musical group La Familia rehearses in Bayamo.

door, and worth a browse, is the **Gabinete de Arqueología** *(tel 23/42-1591, closed Mon.)*, which displays a range of pre-Hispanic artifacts.

Follow General García south three blocks to **Parque Ñico López** *(at Calle Martí and Amado Éstevez)*, a leafy plaza where a bas-relief monument of bronze and marble—the **Retablo de los Héroes**—honors various local revolutionary and nationalist heroes, including Ñico López, the revolutionary hero who led a fateful attack on Bayamo's army barracks on July 26, 1953. The medieval-style barracks, one block west, today house the **Museo Ñico López** *(tel 23/42-3742, closed Mon.)*.

Dos Ríos

The site where independence leader and national hero José Martí met his death in 1895 (see sidebar opposite) is set in the midst of a semiarid alluvial plain, on the north bank of the Río Contramaestre, located some 14 miles (23 km) northeast of Jiguaní and 32 miles (52 km) northeast of Bayamo. A path lined by a wall with a bronze bas-relief of Martí leads through a garden of white roses—an allusion to his famous poem "Cultivo una rosa blanca ..." ("Cultivate a white rose"). The wall here is inscribed with another Martí quote: "When my fall comes, all the sorrow of life will seem like sun and honey."

Here, the **Monumento Martí**—a 30-foot-tall (9 m) concrete obelisk—is shaded by palms. A bronze plaque notes: "He died at this place on 19 May 1895." Martí devotees arrive each May for anniversary celebrations.

It's better to approach Dos Ríos from the south road. ∎

Museo de Cera
- ✉ General García #173, bet. Perucho Figueredo & General Lora
- ☎ 23/42-5421
- 🕐 Closed Mon.

Dos Ríos
- 🗺 170 C2

SIERRA MAESTRA

The Sierra Maestra, Cuba's highest and most daunting terrain, runs along the southern shore in a serried spine rising to 6,476 feet (1,974 m). Sparsely inhabited, incised with precipitous ravines, and thickly forested, it's a hiker's delight—and ideal guerrilla terrain: Castro set up rebel headquarters here, and the sierra became the main battlefront in the war against Batista.

■ A view over the Sierra Maestra, where Fidel Castro headquartered the rebel army

Sierra Maestra
🗺 170 A1, B1, & C1

Cruce de los Baños
🗺 198 C1

El Saltón
🗺 198 C1

The brooding mountains rise from Cabo Cruz in the west and run to the city of Santiago de Cuba, 100 miles (160 km) to the east. Most people living here lead a simple lifestyle, raising coffee and traversing narrow trails that link remote hamlets. Many houses have bare-earth floors and no running water.

In the east, access to the Sierra Maestra is via **Cruce de los Baños**, where the **Museo Tercer Frente Guerrillero** (Ave. de los Mártires, closed Mon.) is dedicated to the "Third Front"—led by Comandante Juan Almeida Bosque (1927-2009)—in the Armed Struggle against Batista;

Bosque and 216 guerrilla fighters who lost their lives in the struggle are buried in the **Mausoleo del Tercer Frente Oriental**, outside town. From here a badly potholed road winds up to **El Saltón** (tel 22/56-6326), a popular eco-resort and spa that originally served the communist elite. Trails lead to waterfalls and pools for swimming; you can also rent horses. To the west, the main gateway is the sugar-processing town of **Bartolomé Masó**, where a road begins to climb to the village of **Providencia**, set in an exquisite valley. From here, a left turn at the T-junction leads you to the hamlet of **Santo Domingo**, nestled above the Río Yara at the base of Pico Turquino. Santo Domingo—accessed by a log bridge spanning the river—was the setting for a fierce battle between Batista's and rebel forces in June and July 1958. The tale is told in the rustic **Museo Santo Domingo** ($). Trails lead to the battle sites. Refreshments and cabin accommodations are available at **Villa Santo Domingo** (tel 23/56-5613, comercial@islazul. grm.tur.cu).

Parque Nacional Turquino

This 56,800 acre (23,000 ha) national park centers on **Pico Real del Turquino**. A permit ($$, passports are required) and guide are required and can be requested at the Centro de Visitantes (Visitors Center), beside the park entrance 100 yards (91 m) uphill from Villa Santo Domingo. Reservations can also be made through Ecotur (tel 23/48-7006, Bayamo).

From Santo Domingo, the road spirals uphill, with spectacular views through plunging ravines. After a steep final ascent, you arrive at **Belvedere Alto del Naranjo**. From here, a 2-mile-long (3 km) trail climbs westward to **La Comandancia de La Plata**, Castro's guerrilla headquarters, located atop a ridge in a forest clearing. Here, a series of wooden huts are preserved as a museum, including an infirmary run by Che Guevara. In Castro's hut is a bedroom, office, kitchen, and deck. A transmitter from which Radio Rebelde broadcast to the masses still sits here, long silent.

Trails also lead to the summit of Pico Turquino. En route you'll pass through several ecosystems replete with wildlife. Near the top, mists swirl and the alpine weather varies dramatically.

INSIDER TIP:

For the ultimate high, take two days to hike Pico Turquino, timing your summit arrival for dawn. Cuba's highest peak (6,476 feet/1,974 m) gets cloudy during the day.

—NEIL SHEA
National Geographic writer

The northerly **Sendero Pico Turquino trail** begins at Alto del Naranjo and leads 8 miles (13 km) via the mountain communities of La Platica and Palma Mocha. Most hikers stay overnight at **Aguada de Joaquín**, a tent camp 2.5 miles (4 km) below the summit.

A second, extremely steep trail leads north from the **Estación Biológica Las Cuevas**, on the Santiago de Cuba–Marea del Portillo coast road. It's a stiff 8-mile (13 km) hike. The fit can hike round-trip in one day, or you can camp at 5,445 feet (1,660 m) on **Pico Cuba** (6,177 feet/1,883 m). The weather is fickle; take warm, waterproof clothing. Two sets of guides are required by prearrangement for hikes between Alto del Naranjo and Las Cuevas. ■

WEST COAST

Cuba's remote southwestern shore is off the beaten tourist path, but nonetheless offers a few intriguing sites. Manzanillo boasts beautiful ceramic murals and a museum paying homage to a revolutionary heroine, and nearby are remains of an original sugar mill.

The Gulf of Guacanayabo at sunset

West Coast

📍 170 A1 & B1

**Museo Casa
Natal de
Celia Sánchez
Manduley**

✉ Ave. Podio #11,
Media Luna

☎ 23/59-3466

🕐 Closed Sun.–
Mon.

💲 $

Manzanillo

📍 170 B1

The highway from Bayamo meets the Gulf of Guacanayabo at Manzanillo and runs south a short distance inland of the shore. The local economy is fueled by sugarcane, and during the harvest, smoke-smudged field hands slash at the charred stalks, and black plumes swirl over the fields. **Media Luna**, 32 miles (52 km) southwest of Manzanillo, a sugar-dependent town, is also the hometown of revolutionary heroine Celia Sánchez (see sidebar opposite). Visit the **Museo Casa Natal de Celia Sánchez Manduley** in the gingerbread wooden home

where she was born. Farther south, **Niquero** is distinct for its wooden architecture in French Caribbean style.

Manzanillo

This somewhat down-at-heels fishing town, 41 miles (67 km) west of Bayamo, is known as a sugar port and a center for lobster and shrimp.

The historic core of the city is centered on **Parque Céspedes**, highlighted by a *glorieta* (bandstand), with cupola, arches, and *azulejos*—delicate tilework in Andalusian style. The square is ringed by wrought-iron lampposts and royal palms, with small stone sphinxes at each corner. Many of the nearby buildings also bear Moorish influences, notably the **Edificio Quirch** and the **Casa de la Cultura** (*Calle Masó #82, tel 23/57-4210*). In the courtyard of the latter, see the *azulejo* mosaics of Don Quixote and of Columbus coming ashore. Stop by the **Museo Histórico Municipal**, on the square's east side, to view cannon and antiques and learn about regional history. Also visit the **Iglesia de la Purísima Concepción**, on the east side, to see its gilded altar.

Walk south along Calle Martí to Calle Caridad and ascend the staircase lined with *azulejos* of sunflowers and doves, which pay homage to Celia Sánchez. The **Monumento a Celia**, featuring a visage of the revolutionary heroine, stands at the top. Immediately south is **Barrio de Oro**, where cobbled streets are lined with wooden houses, each with a cactus planted on the red-tile roof for good luck. On the south side of the barrio, Celia Sánchez and other revolutionary heroes

(not least Fidel) are honored with a huge bas-relief monument in the **Plaza de la Revolución** (*Ave. Camilo Cienfuegos*). The **Criadero de Cocodrilos** (crocodile farm; *tel 23/53-2211, closed Sun., $*), lies 3 miles (5 km) south of town.

La Demajagua

Eight miles (13 km) south of Manzanillo, leave the highway and head west to La Demajagua, the former estate of Céspedes, who sparked the first war of independence by freeing his slaves on October 10, 1868 (see sidebar p. 187). A week later his home was destroyed. A museum displays weaponry, edicts, and *banderas* (flags). A stone path leads to the mill ruins. Here, *calderos*—cauldrons used to boil sugarcane—cogwheels, and a steam-operated *trapiche*—sugar press—are encircled by a stone amphitheater inset with the La Demajagua bell, rung by Céspedes when he freed his slaves. ∎

Museo Histórico Municipal
✉ Calle Martí #226, Manzanillo
☎ 23/57-2053
🕐 Closed Mon.
💲 $

Museo Histórico La Demajagua
✉ 8 miles (13 km) S of Manzanillo
☎ 5219-4080
🕐 Closed Mon.
💲 $

PARQUE NACIONAL DESEMBARCO DEL GRANMA

Tucked into the island's southwest corner, this little-visited national park is named for the "landing of the *Granma*"—the boat that brought Castro and his rebel band to the island in 1956 to launch the revolution. Today, trails access wetland and semiarid ecosystems that shelter 170 species of birds.

Parque Nacional Desembarco del Granma

🅰 170 A1
☎ 72/09-0600
💲 $

Lying in the rain shadow of the mountains that rise from the arrowhead point of Cabo Cruz, this area is notably dry. Cacti punctuate the woodlands that cover 80 percent of the 64,000-acre (26,000 ha) park, which harbors exquisite endemics such as the Cuban Amazon butterfly

■ The rising tide at Cabo Cruz

and the blue-headed quail-dove. The mostly limestone terrain is pocked by caverns, such as **Hoyo del Morlotte** and **Cueva del Fustete**. Hike to them from the highway via the **Sendero Morlotte-Fustete** trail. Another trail, the **Sendero Arqueológico Natural El Guafe**, passes sites of pre-Columbian antiquity (including a cavern with stalagmites carved into Indian totems). Bring adequate water supplies whenever you set out on any of the trails in this region.

The park entrance at **Playa Las Coloradas**, where the *Granma* landed, has a visitor center. A reproduction of the *Granma* is displayed here at the **Monumento del Desembarco** (*$*), where a small museum displays a map of battles fought by the rebels immediately after their landing; and a boardwalk through the mangroves leads to the exact spot where the famous boat ran aground (bring insect repellent).

Southward, the coast road curls around **Laguna de Cabo Cruz**, full of wading birds, and deposits you at **Cabo Cruz**, where a quaint fishing village is marked by an 1871 lighthouse—Faro Cabo Cruz. A plaque records that Christopher Columbus supposedly landed here in May 1494.

The snorkeling is excellent amid reefs close to shore. Watch for white-tailed and red-billed tropic birds. ■

PILÓN & MAREA DEL PORTILLO

Northern snowbirds flock to this isolated, sun-drenched pocket of far southwestern Cuba. Though the beaches aren't the most beautiful that Cuba offers, the seclusiveness and the stunning mountain backdrops offer a unique appeal, best enjoyed by forays along the coast and into the Sierra Maestra.

Getting a quick trim in Pilón

To the west, the broad coastal plain occupies a basin carpeted in sugarcane and centered on the town of Pilón. Embraced by sea and mountains, Pilón is defined by tumbledown wooden houses and unpaved, potholed streets. One such house is now the **Museo Municipal de Pilón Celia Sánchez Manduley** *(Calle Benítez #20, tel 23/59-4107, closed Sun.–Mon.)*, from where the revolutionary heroine (see sidebar p. 193) ran a secret supply route to Castro's army. You can negotiate with a local fisherman to take you out to offshore cays, with coral reefs good for snorkeling.

Farther east, the landscape changes abruptly. The mountains wring rain from the clouds, and the narrow shore is a virtual desert. You'll pass Brahman cattle munching in cactus-studded, stony pastures. The sierra clambers down to a broad bay that shelters a tourist resort at Marea del Portillo. The brown beach is of modest appeal, though its setting in the lee of the Sierra Maestra is fabulous. A white-sand beach, **Cayo Blanco**, lies offshore. Schedule scuba diving at the **Albacora Dive Center** *(tel 23/59-7034)*. The resort tour desks can book guided horseback trips to the **El Salto** waterfall, and excursions to Bayamo and Santiago de Cuba. ■

Pilón & Marea del Portillo

▲ 170 A1 & B1

More Places to Visit in Western Oriente

African zebras get a new lease on life at Cayo Saetía, a former communist hunting reserve.

Cayo Saetía

This 16-square-mile (42 sq km) cay lies off the north shore of Holguín Province and occupies the east side of Bahía de Nipe. It is billed as an ecotour destination, although for many years, Fidel Castro brought politicians and businessmen here as his hunting guests in pursuit of zebras, antelope, and other African beasts. Zebras graze, ostriches bound across the grasslands, and water buffalo wallow in the mangroves. Jeep safaris and horseback rides are offered from **Villa Cayo Saetía** *(tel 24/51-6900, villacayosaetia.com)*, which has a bar, restaurant, and rental cabins, plus trails leading to sugar-fine beaches. 🗺 171 D2 💲 $$

Museo Conjunto Histórico Birán

The country estate where Fidel Castro Ruz was born on August 13, 1926, is at Birán, 38 miles (61 km) southeast of Holguín, at the foot of the Altiplanicie de Nipe. The *finca* was part of a 65,000-acre (26,000 ha) domain owned by Castro's father, Ángel Castro y Argiz. Castro's father and mother (the family maid, Lina Ruz González) are buried here. Finca Las Manacas was opened to the public in 2003, and guided tours, which include the village schoolhouse (relocated here) with Fidel's desk front and center, give a not wholly accurate profile of Fidel's early life here. Eleven of the original 27 structures of Finca Las Manacas still stand, including the *valla* (cockfighting pit). The Model A Ford that Ángel gifted Lina is also shown. Fidel's personal effects include his basketball, baseball glove, and hunting rifle. 🗺 170 C2 ✉ Birán, 37 miles (60 km) SE of Holguín ☎ 24/28-6114 🕐 Closed Mon. 💲 $$, cameras $$

Puerto Padre

Once an important colonial port town, charming Puerto Padre, some 31 miles (50 km) northeast of Las Tunas, is located well off the tourist trail. **Fuerte de la Loma**, an independence wars–era fortress, guards the city. The main attraction is a twin beach community, consisting of **Playas La Herradura** and **La Boca**, about 6 miles (10 km) northeast of town. Here, sugar white sands dissolve into blue seas. North of Puerto Padre, the excellent resort **Brisas Covarrubias** *(tel 31/51-5530)* is located in a small bay. There are also room rentals and several simple restaurants. 🗺 170 B3

A region that is rugged and remote, from Cuba's oldest settlement to Santiago de Cuba, "cradle of the revolution"

EASTERN
ORIENTE

The towering Monumento Antonio Maceo, Santiago de Cuba

EASTERN ORIENTE

In far east Cuba, in the eastern part of the region called Oriente, the sun burns down with crushing intensity. The three major cities—Santiago de Cuba, Guantánamo, and Baracoa—each occupy a bowl surrounded by mountain topography that has played a key role in Cuban history. The appeals of city life, and their varied histories and cultural influences, combine with those of some of the island's wildest terrain.

Santiago de Cuba, Cuba's second largest city, predates Havana and, though lacking the latter's stature and grandeur, offers notable monuments and attractions befitting its unique history as the "birthplace of the revolution." The Cuartel Moncada, for example, is a de rigueur stop on the revolutionary trail. The city is wholly unique in character—lent an infusion of French-Caribbean influences following the 1791 rebellion in Haiti, notably in its tradition of music and dance. The region has a distinctive folk culture, and it is considered the cradle of *son*, a mixture of old Spanish songs

and African choruses. Santiago de Cuba is also known for its cabarets and for its carnival, held in July.

Beyond the city lie a fortified castle; the pilgrimage site of El Cobre; and Parque Baconao, a UNESCO biosphere reserve thus far undeveloped for ecotourism. The latter hosts a bevy of one-off attractions, not least a classic car museum and the Valle de la Prehistoria, a kitschy take on Jurassic Park. Beaches allayed along the narrow coast prove popular with Santiagueros escaping the city, and west of Santiago the dramatic shoreline delivers one of Cuba's preeminent drives.

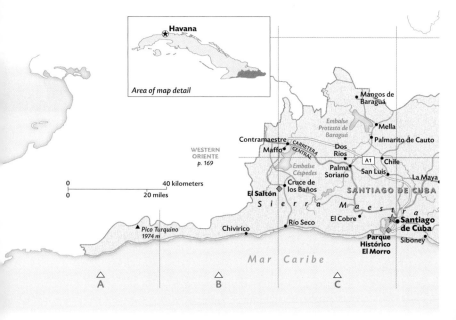

The city of Guantánamo has an intriguing colonial core, deep Jamaican and Haitian roots, and a large military presence. A "stone zoo" in the nearby foothills is worth the excursion, and the famous U.S. naval base can be viewed from a lookout. Most appealing is Baracoa, Cuba's oldest city, with its sense of otherworldly remove. Baracoa languishes in the lee of mountains now being developed for ecotourism: There's a heart-catching loveliness to the rain forest–covered heights of the Cuchillas del Toa, drawing birders and hikers to their cobalt-green heights.

Cuba's extreme Oriente is a mountainous region. The Sierra Maestra in the west, and the Sierra del Cristal and Sierra del Purial eastward, rise in an immense chain stretching across Santiago de Cuba and Guantánamo Provinces. The vegetation grows lusher moving eastward: The northeast coast around Baracoa faces the prevailing trade winds and is lavished with Cuba's heaviest rainfall. Note, however, that Santiago de Cuba and Guantánamo cities

lie in hot rain shadows and that their lowland temperatures are markedly higher than elsewhere in Cuba. ■

SANTIAGO DE CUBA

Cuba's second largest city (pop. 434,000) has beguiling and enigmatic appeal. The architecture is unique, as are regional expressions of music and dance. Varied museums, imposing monuments, and a compelling cemetery hold visitors spellbound. The city is also where Castro launched his revolution in July 1953 with an ill-fated assault on the Moncada barracks.

Catedral de Nuestra Señora de la Asunción, the centerpiece of Parque Céspedes

Santiago de Cuba

📍 198 D1

Visitor Information

✉ Infotur, Felix Pena 562 at Aguilera

☎ 22/66-9401

After Diego Velázquez founded the original settlement in 1515, it was named Cuba's capital and thrived on the port trade and on copper mined at nearby El Cobre. In 1553, however, the capital was transferred to Havana, which was to become the main connecting port between America and Spain. In 1639 Santiago de Cuba was fortified and in time became a major slave port. The city became the center of intense fighting during the wars of independence; it was here, on July 1, 1898, that U.S. and Mambí forces ended 400 years of colonial rule with the destruction of the Spanish fleet and a famous charge up San Juan Hill.

This city of broad boulevards and intimate plazas has its share of museums. The main draw is its old town, laid out in a grid tilting down to the harbor. History echoes in the narrow streets graced by timeworn buildings painted in sun-bleached pastels.

In many ways, Santiago de Cuba—a major port and industrial city—is more Caribbean than Havana. The city's proximity to Santo Domingo and Jamaica fostered close links with both, and thousands of English- and French-speaking immigrants have stitched their customs into the city's cultural quilt. Even the lilting tongue of the Santiagueros and the sensuality of their music hint at a Caribbean potpourri.

Parque Céspedes

Ground zero in Santiago de Cuba's antiquity, the former Plaza de Armas, or military parade ground, lies at the heart of the historic city center. The cosmopolitan square is named for Carlos M. de Céspedes (1819–1874), who launched the wars of independence with his "Grito de Yara" in 1868 (see sidebar p. 187). His bronze bust now oversees the square atop a pedestal shaded by trees.

The boot steps of Hernán Cortés and Diego Velázquez echo across the square. Beautifully maintained, the Andalusian-style **Casa de Don Diego Velázquez**—dating from 1516 and thereby said to be the oldest structure still extant in Cuba—stands on the northwest corner. Today it houses the **Museo de Ambiente Histórico Cubano** (Museum of Historic Cuban Ambience), full of period furnishings, armor, and, to the rear, a small gold foundry. Moorish-style *rejas* and wood shutters hang dark and heavy on its somber facade. To the

north you will find the white-and-blue **Ayuntamiento**, or town hall, with a tiny balcony from which Castro gave the victory speech on January 1, 1959, following Batista's flight from Cuba. The building was erected in the 1950s in neocolonial style, after its antecedent was toppled by an earthquake.

INSIDER TIP:

Several blocks east of Parque Céspedes, submit to the sensual sway of *son* music at the Patio de Los Dos Abuelos (*Calle Pérez Carbo #5, Plaza de Marte, tel 22/64-4788*).

—OMAR LÓPEZ VERGARA
National Geographic
Latin America editor

The plaza is dominated to the south by the **Catedral de Nuestra Señora de la Asunción** (*tel 22/62-8502*), initially constructed in 1522. It was destroyed by earthquakes and pirates four times and was reconstructed each time. The remains of Diego Velázquez are supposedly interred in the floor. A statue of the Angel of the Annunciation, with trumpet, stands between the twin towers of the neoclassical facade. Note the exquisitely carved choir stalls and impressive organ. Severely damaged by Hurricane Sandy in 2012, the cathedral has been recently deeply restored. The **Museo Arquidiocesano**, entered on the east side, exhibits religious art and statuary.

Museo de Ambiente Histórico Cubano
🅰 205
✉ Calle Felix Peña #612
☎ 22/65-2652
$ $

Museo Arquidiocesano
☎ 22/65-4586
🕐 Closed Sun.
$ $

Colegio Jesuita de Dolores
☎ 22/62-4623

Savor the square's ambience from the **Hotel Casa Granda**, which rises over the east side. Its first-floor terrace bar overhangs the plaza and makes for a great vantage as you sip a cocktail under the shade of Parisian-style awnings. The rooftop bar affords splendid views down over the old city, best enjoyed at night, when floodlights dramatically illuminate the square.

■ A *comparsa*—musical group—competes during carnival.

Museo Municipal Emilio Bacardí Moreau
🅰 205
✉ Calle Pío Rosado at Aguilera
☎ 22/62-8402
🕐 Closed Sun.
💲 $

The square is graced by wrought-iron seats, buildings with original wrought-iron balconies, and a column supporting a statue of Francisco Vicente Aguilera (1821–1877), who wrote Cuba's national anthem.

One block west, Calle Aguilera opens to a quaint *plazuela* lorded over by a neoclassical structure fronted by Corinthian columns. The **Museo Municipal Emilio Bacardí Moreau**—Cuba's oldest museum—was founded in 1899 by Emilio Bacardí y Moreau (1844–1922), city mayor, revolutionary, and son of the founder of the Bacardí rum distillery. Colonial artifacts relating to the wars of independence grace the first floor (and include personal effects of Antonio Maceo, Carlos Manuel de Céspedes, and José Martí); upstairs, an art gallery

Plaza de Dolores

Smaller and more intimate than Parque Céspedes, the former market square called Plaza de Dolores is shaded by tamarinds and ablaze with bougainvillea spilling their tropical hues into the square. It is named for the **Iglesia de Nuestra Señora de los Dolores**, commanding the hill to the east side; the church adjoins the old **Colegio Jesuita de Dolores**, the once prestigious school that Fidel Castro attended between 1937 and 1942; today it is a concert hall.

Carnaval

Santiago de Cuba's *Carnaval* dates from the 18th century, when slaves were permitted a carousal once a year. Today's annual Festival of the Caribbean, held in July, is based on parades of secret societies of ancient Africa, transformed in Cuba into neighborhood *comparsas*—musical groups parading in musical melees. Revelers dress as *orishas* (gods), and the blare of Chinese cornets and the beat of *bata* drums echo as conga lines and floats wind their way down Avenida Jesús Menéndez.

EXPERIENCE:
The Dance Moves of Afro-Cuban *Comparsas*

Numerous *comparsas* (musical groups) welcome visitors to their year-round workshops in Santiago de Cuba, where they practice routines for their big day at the annual carnival. You'll witness performances of *conga oriental, tumba francesa,* and *carabali obulo,* and maybe learn a few slick moves. The choreography is based on the black Haitian tradition. Among the many Afro-Cuban troupes that host rumbas are:

• **La Tumba Francesa** (*Calles Los Maceos #501 & General Bandera*)
• **Ballet Folklórico Cutumba** (*Cine Galaxia, Av. 24 de Febrero at Santa Ursula, tel 22/65-5173*)
• **Foco Cultural El Tivoli** (*Calle Desiderio Mesnier #208, tel 22/62-0142*).

spans colonial to contemporary works. Pre-Columbian curios such as shrunken heads, plus Peruvian mummies and an Egyptian one are also displayed. The neoclassical **Palacio Provincial** also rises over the *plazuela.*

North of Parque Céspedes

The streets immediately north of Parque Céspedes offer a medley of modest attractions for visitors with an ecclesiastical or historical bent. The area boasts four 18th-century churches within a 20-minute walk of the plaza.

Head up Calle Félix Peña (Calle Santo Tomás) two blocks to **Iglesia de Nuestra Señora del Carmen** (*Calle Félix Peña #505 at Tamayo Fleites*), known for its statuary. Two blocks farther north on Félix Peña, turn left for the 18th-century **Iglesia de San Francisco** (*Calle Juan Bautista Sagarra #121*). Félix Peña also leads to another 18th-century church, **Iglesia de Santo Tomás** (*Calle Félix Peña #314*), at the junction with Calle General Portuondo. Five blocks east on Portuondo is **Iglesia de la**

Santísima Trinidad (*Calle General Portuondo #661, bet. Gral. Moncada & Porfirio Valiente, tel 22/62-2820*), notable for its ceiling and neoclassical features.

History buffs might call in at **Museo Frank y Josué País**, where exhibits pay homage to brothers Frank and Josué País, the revolutionary heroes born in this house. On November 30, 1956, Frank led the ill-fated assault on the police headquarters in Santiago de Cuba, timed to coincide with Castro's arrival in Cuba aboard the *Granma.* Frank was assassinated in July 1957, one month after his brother was gunned down, inspiring mass demonstrations against the Batista regime. **Calle Sánchez Hechavarría** between Calles Hartmann and Valiente is lined with colonial homes. Plaques dedicated to members of Fidel's 26th of July Movement mark the walls, including at **Museo Memorial Vilma Espín Guilllois**, the former home of Vilma Espín, the revolutionary who married Raúl Castro and founded the Federación de Mujeres Cubanas (Federation *(continued on p. 207)*

Museo Frank y Josué País

✉ Ave. General Banderas #266, bet. Trinidad & Habana
☎ 22/65-2710
🕐 Closed Sun.
💲 $

Museo Memorial Vilma Espín Guilllois

✉ Calle Sánchez Hechavarría #473, bet. Porfirio Valiente & Pio Rosada
☎ 22/65-5464
🕐 Closed Sun.

WALK HISTORIC SANTIAGO DE CUBA

This walk, sloping downhill most of the way, takes in Santiago de Cuba's most colorful street, passing a bevy of attractions that define Santiago's culture, including the once fashionable enclave of Tivoli, and ending with a fine vista that puts your walk in perspective.

A walk through the heart of colonial Santiago de Cuba is a stroll through times past and present.

Begin in **Plaza de Marte ❶**, between Calle Aguilera and Avenida Victoriana Garzón, which leads to Reparto Vista Alegre. The park itself, which was known during the wars of independence as an execution ground for nationalists, is of modest interest. Note the bust of José Martí at the southern end. The old city falls away as you stroll westward along Aguilera, once the city's foremost commercial thoroughfare; it still bears street signs from the 1950s.

After three blocks, you'll enter tree-shaded **Plaza de Dolores ❷** (see p. 202), overshadowed by the former **Iglesia Nuestra Señora**

NOT TO BE MISSED:

Museo Municipal Emilio Bacardí Moreau • Casa de la Trova • Catedral de Nuestra Señora de la Asunción • Museo de Ambiente Histórico Cubano

de los Dolores. Proceed west one block on Aguilera to Pío Rosado, where you should pop in the **Museo Municipal Emilio Bacardí Moreau ❸** (see pp. 202–203), with broadranging displays and an impressive art gallery.

Exiting, turn south and follow Pío Rosado 50 yards (45 m) to **Calle Heredia**, a lively street that reverberates to the clack of the claves and beat of the African drum. A cultural fair is hosted on weekend evenings, when traffic is barred and troubadours and other street performers entertain.

The house at the corner of Heredia and Pío Rosado is adorned with typical 19th-century balconies. The brick stairs lead up to the **Museo del Carnaval** (*Calle Heredia #304, tel 22/62-6955, $*), exhibiting lavish costumes and other paraphernalia tracing the past and celebrating the present of Santiago de Cuba's famed carnival.

Turn right and stop in at the **Galería de Arte UNEAC** (*Calle Heredia #266, tel 22/65-3465*), displaying vibrant artwork; and, a stone's throw west, the **Casa José María Heredia** ❹ (*Calle Heredia #260, tel 22/62-5350, closed Mon., $*), an 18th-century town house where the independence fighter and romantic poet José María Heredia (1803–1839) was born. Heredia paid tribute to the beauty of the Americas in verse, most famously in his "Ode to Niagara." Today, his

house is a museum and cultural center in his honor.

Continue west on Heredia and push through the doors of the **Casa de la Trova** (*Calle Heredia #208, tel 22/63-3892*), formerly the home of revered composer Rafael Salcedo (1844–1917), who founded a troubadour tradition carried through to today. Afternoons and evenings you can still swing your hips to *son*, plaintive boleros, and other classic sounds from groups such as the Trío Matamoros. A similarly heady atmosphere can be enjoyed on Saturday evenings at the **Casa de los Estudiante** (*Calle Heredia #204*), which showcases sensual Afro-Cuban rhythms.

After exploring the sites of nearby **Parque Céspedes** ❺ (see p. 201), including the **Catedral de Nuestra Señora de la**

🅰	See also area map pp. 198–199
➤	Plaza de Marte
🕐	2 hours (one way)
↔	1.3 miles (2 km)
➤	Casa de las Tradiciones

The Plaza de Dolores offers a shady rest for walkers.

Asunción and the **Museo de Ambiente Histórico Cubano**, follow Calle Félix Peña one block south to Calle Bartolomé Masó. Turn right. After one block, turn left onto Corona for the **Maqueta de la Ciudad de Santiago** *(tel 22/65-2095, closed Sun., $)*, a huge scale model of the city and bay, with every building in situ. The city's evolution is regaled in maps and exhibits. Continue south one block and turn right on Joaquín Castillo Duany. After one block turn left to climb the broad flight of stairs—**La Escalinata de Padre Pico**—that you may recognize from many a tourist poster.

Ascend the stairs and follow the crenellated wall as you climb 50 yards (46 m) up Calle Rabí to the **Museo de la Lucha Clandestina** ❻ *(Museum of the Clandestine Struggle; tel 22/62-4689, closed Mon., $)*, dedicated to the tale of the 26th of July Movement and the fight to topple Batista. It is housed in the former police barracks that was attacked on November 30, 1956, by a group of revolutionaries led by Frank País. Three

members died as they fled down Padre Pico. Exhibits on two floors revolve around País. Now lovingly restored, the bright yellow building has a courtyard and good views of the city.

Continuing south along Rabí, you'll pass **Fidel Castro's former lodging** *(Calle Rabí #6)* and a series of **carnival murals** *(Calle Rabí at Calle Rafael Salcedo)*. Three blocks farther is **Casa de las Tradiciones** *(Calle Rabí #154, bet. Santa Rosa & Princesa, tel 22/65-3892)*, an old house turned into a club hosting traditional music and dance. Your walk ends here.

of Cuban Women) sustaining the revolution. The struggle for independence is recalled at the **Museo Casa Natal de Antonio Maceo**, where the astute tactician was born on June 14, 1845. Maceo was second-in-command of the Mambí forces during the wars of independence.

Reparto Sueño

You might do a double take at first sight of the **Cuartel Moncada**, its crenellated walls and turrets an incongruous vision of beau geste in the leafy suburb of Sueño. The opening shots of the revolution were fired here in 1953, when 26-year-old Fidel Castro led 122 lightly armed rebels in an assault on the military barracks, as bullet holes in the exterior walls attest (Batista had the walls repaired, but the holes were faithfully reconstructed once Castro took power).

Established as a Spanish fortress, the former barracks of Moncada is now a school, Ciudad Escolar 26 de Julio. Seven rooms have metamorphosed as the **Museo Histórico 26 de Julio** (*Calle General Portuondo & Ave. Moncada, tel 22/62-0157, $*), with maps, bloodstained uniforms, and other memorabilia from that fateful day. English-speaking guides are on hand.

Moncada is bound on the west by **Avenida de los Libertadores**, lined with bronze busts of independence-era heroes. Facing Moncada across the boulevard is **Complejo Histórico Abel Santamaría**, a park with a column

The Moncada attack is marked at Ciudad Escolar 26 de Julio.

bearing a large granite cube carved with bas-reliefs of Abel Santamaría and José Martí. To the rear of the park, the former hospital from where Abel Santamaría and 22 fellow rebels fired on Moncada now houses the **Museo Abel Santamaría** (*tel 22/62-4119*).

The Reparto Sueño is graced by many creaky wooden houses in Caribbean vernacular style—a carryover from the French Creole immigrant influx dating from 1791. In counterpoint, and dominating the skyline, the **Hotel Santiago**, on Avenida de las Américas, is a 15-story modernist structure,

Museo Casa Natal de Antonio Maceo

⊠ Calle Maceo #207, bet. Corona & Rastro

☎ 22/62-3750

🕐 Closed Sun.

💲 $

Museo Abel Santamaría

⊠ Ave. de los Libertadores at General Portuondo

☎ 22/62-4119

🕐 Closed Sun.

💲 $

Revolutionary Attack

Fidel Castro launched his revolution to topple Batista at dawn on July 26, 1953, with an attack on the barracks of Moncada. Lightly armed, the revolutionaries struck during the *Carnaval* celebration. The alarm was raised and the rebels were caught in a crossfire. Eight were killed. Fifty-nine were captured and tortured to death. Castro was caught a week later and sentenced to 15 years in prison. Photos of the tortured Fidelistas unleashed a wave of disgust and lent legitimacy to Castro's 26th of July Movement (M-26-7), the group that would evolve into Cuba's preeminent opposition.

Casa de las Religiones Populares

✉ Calle 13 #206, bet. Calles 8 & 10

☎ 22/64-2285

💲 $

Museo de la Imagen

✉ Calle 8 #106, bet. 3ra & 5ta

☎ 22/64-2234

🕐 Closed Sun.

💲 $

gaudily painted and appearing more cubist than Cuban. The **Bosque de los Héroes**, opposite the hotel, is a 1973 bas-relief monument honoring Che Guevara and his Cuban guerrillas who died in Bolivia.

Plaza de la Revolución

This plaza, capable of holding a crowd of 200,000, sprawls at the junction of Avenida de las Américas and Avenida de los Libertadores.

On the plaza's north side towers the **Monumento a Antonio Maceo**, paying homage to the general (1845–1896) who rose to second-in-command of the rebel Mambí forces. Considered the godfather of Santiago de Cuba, the "bronze titan" rides upon a rearing charger, in front of 23 big steel machetes pointing upwards.

The bowels of the monument house the **Sala de Exposición de Holografía** (closed Sun., $). Maceo's role in the wars of independence is told using holograms and an illuminated bas-relief model depicting the battles.

Reparto Vista Alegre

To the southeast of the plaza, the eastern suburb of Vista Alegre boasts grand houses ranging in style from neoclassical villas to Caribbean vernacular clapboards to mid-20th-century California-style houses. Most are in sad disrepair. Vista Alegre is split down the center by Avenida Manduley, lined with some of the more grandiose houses. **La Maison** (Ave. Manduley #52, tel 22/64-3449) is superbly maintained and hosts

boutiques and a nightly fashion show. Note the pink, baroque **Casa de Don Pepe Bosch** (Ave. Manduley, bet. Calles 9 & 11), the former home of the head of the Bacardi rum empire and now a school for Young Pioneers.

Mysteries of Santería are revealed at the **Casa de las Religiones Populares**. A stone's throw away, the **Casa del Caribe** (Calle 13 #154, tel 22/64-3609), which studies Caribbean cultures, has exhibits from the region. Stop off at the **Museo de la Imagen**, whose collection of 500 cameras includes CIA espionage cameras.

Avenida Raúl Pujol borders Vista Alegre to the south. Follow Calle 11 and you'll emerge opposite the **Loma de San Juan**.

INSIDER TIP:

Ascend the marble plinth of the Monumento a Antonio Maceo for a dramatic view of the plaza.

—VIRGILIO VALDÉS
National Geographic Latin America editor

San Juan Hill

It was at Loma de San Juan, the famous San Juan Hill, where, on July 1, 1898, a charge led by Theodore Roosevelt's Rough Riders sealed the Spanish-Cuban-American War. Today the hill is **Parque Histórico de San Juan y Árbol de la Paz**.

The treaty ending the war was signed on July 17, 1898, at the **Árbol de la Paz** (Peace Tree)—

a *ceiba* surrounded by cannon at the foot of Calle 11, 100 yards (91 m) west of the hill.

Cementerio de Santa Ifigenia

Santiago de Cuba's vast cemetery is graced by scores of important tombs, many of Carrara marble adorned with angels. Luminaries of Cuban history are here: Carlos de Céspedes (1819–1874), José Martí (1853-1895), and Fidel Castro Ruz (1926-2016).

José Martí slumbers in the **Mausoleo de Martí**. His tomb is draped with the Cuban flag beneath a crenellated hexagonal tower designed so that, during the day, sunlight always shines on him. A changing of the military honor guard occurs every 30 minutes, when uniformed youths goosestep past. Fidel Castro's ashes are buried beside the mausoleum in an enormous, boulder-shaped granite reliquary that has a simple plaque with his name on it. Other notables buried here include Emilio Bacardí (1844–1922), in the pyramid-shaped tomb to the right of the entrance; Tomás Estrada Palma (1835–1908), Cuba's first president; and Compay Segundo (1907-2003), singer of the famous Buena Vista Social Club. The many graves marked by red-and-black flags denote members of Castro's revolutionary M-26-7 movement who died for the cause, including Frank and Josué País (see p. 203). To get there, hop in a horse-drawn carriage on Avenida Jesús Menéndez. En route, opposite the railway station, you'll pass

the **Fábrica de Ron Caney** *(Ave. Peralejo #103, tel 22/62-5576),* the former Bacardí rum factory; dating from 1868, it is Cuba's oldest extant rum factory. It was seized by the Castro regime in 1959, when the Bacardí family went into exile. It is not open to view, but you can tipple *tragos* (shots) of the rums made here in a tasting room. Four blocks north, your horse will draw past the **Fortín de Yarayó**, an ocher-colored hexagonal fort at the junction of Avenida Crombet and Avenida Juan Gualberto Gómez. The encasement is one of 116 such fortresses (most long demolished) that formed a cordon around Santiago de Cuba. ■

Cementerio de Santa Ifigenia

✉ Calzada Crombet

☎ 22/63-2723

💲 $

José Martí's mausoleum

RUM NATION

Cuba's national drink is *ron*, rum. It infuses island culture. Rum is made from the fermented juice of sugarcane or a mix of cane juice and molasses, the dark brown residue left after crystallized sugar has been processed from cane. The basis for almost every island cocktail, rum is amazingly versatile and comes in a broad range of colors and flavors.

A multitude of cellars in Havana contain rooms full of oak barrels of aging rum.

The man to thank for Cuba's fine rums is Christopher Columbus, who first brought sugarcane from the Canary Islands on his second voyage in 1493. Soon after, rudimentary ox-powered mills *(trapiches)* were producing sugarcane juice *(guarapo)* and molasses that 16th-century Spanish settlers turned into a crude type of "molasses wine." In 1838 the introduction of steam power and of distilleries in the manufacturing process led to an increase in sugar production while dramatically improving rum quality. By the mid-19th century, the cities of Havana, Matanzas, Cárdenas, and Santiago de Cuba produced large quantities of export-quality rums, sold under world-famous

labels such as Bacardí, Bocoy, Havana Club, and Matusalem. The most important company by far was Bacardí, which was founded by Don Facundo Bacardí, a Catalan migrant, who established his first rum factory in Santiago de Cuba in 1868.

After the 1959 revolution, the state took over the rum industry (the Bacardí family fled the island, and took their name and their brand with them). Today, some dozen distilleries throughout the island produce about 60 brands of Cuban rum. The most notable label is Havana Club, produced today at Santa Cruz del Norte, a town heady with the sweet smell of fermentation.

Rum provides the base for a host of Cuban cocktails.

Process & Product

Rum has four stages of production: fermenting, distilling, aging, and blending. First, molasses is fermented with yeast (present in the raw material), which transforms the sugar into ethanol. Compressed vapor then heats the fermented brew, which is diluted with distilled water and fed into a copper distillation vat, where the alcohol concentration is increased to about 75 proof; the pleasant flavors are separated out and the unpleasant ones eliminated. The distillate is then aged from 1 to 15 years in oak barrels. All distilled rums are clear. Darker rums attain their distinct flavor and color from the tannins of the oak barrels, and, in some rums, from the addition of caramel during the aging process. The rum is then diluted to reduce the rum to commercial strength before it is bottled.

Cuban rums are traditionally light in flavor. Of export-quality rums, the title *carta blanca* denotes a clear "white rum" aged for three years, with an alcohol content of 40–60 proof. It is used in most cocktails, including the *cuba libre* (rum and cola), *daiquiri* (rum, lime juice, sugar, and maraschino liqueur blended with crushed ice), and *mojito* (rum, lime juice, sugar, soda water, mint leaves). Dorado rums, aged for five years, are fuller bodied with an amber color. They make cocktails such as the *mulatta,* with lime and cocoa liqueur. Premium rums are darker and smoother *añejos,* aged for seven years and distilled in copper tanks to enhance aroma and flavor. Añejos, drunk neat, are as distinct as single-malt whiskeys; the best—such as the 15-year-old Havana Club Gran Reserva—rank with fine cognacs.

INSIDER TIP:

Of many fine rums made in the Fábrica de Ron Caney (see p. 209), one of the best is Ron Santiago, aged 11 years and tasting like a fine cognac. Savor it in the tasting room at Avenida Peralejo #103.

—VIRGILIO VALDÉS
*National Geographic
Latin America editor*

PARQUE HISTÓRICO EL MORRO

The eastern heights overlooking the bottleneck entrance to Santiago Bay are guarded by this clifftop colossus in stone, formally known as the Castillo de San Pedro de la Roca. The imposing castle, a striking embodiment of Spanish military might, dates back to 1643, though much of its current bulk was added in ensuing decades following depredations by pirates. Cannon point menacingly from massive batteries, and the powder magazines are still filled with cannonballs.

In age-old tradition, a cannon is fired nightly at El Morro castle.

Parque Histórico El Morro

🏔 198 C1

✉ Carretera del Morro, 6 miles (10 km) S of Santiago de Cuba

☎ 22/69-1569

💲 $

You are free to roam at leisure, although guides are on hand to make sense of the befuddling maze of dark passageways. From the bastions, magnificent vistas open up westward along the coast, where the relics of Spanish vessels have lain submerged since the fleet's destruction during the Spanish-American War. A splendid exposition regales the tale of the naval engagements, plus piracy, with blunderbusses, cutlasses, and other colonial-era relics. U.S. efforts to destabilize the Castro regime are given prominence. Note, too, the simple chapel with a large wooden statue of Christ. The **Faro del Morro** pins the headland and can be climbed ($) to admire the view and Fresnel lens. Nightly, soldiers in period costume march from the lighthouse to **El Morro** to enact the *cañonazo*— the lighting of a cannon and raising of the Cuban flag.

Cayo Granma

Sheltered within the neck of the harbor, this picturesque island makes for a pleasant excursion when combined with a visit to El Morro. The isle, which you can walk around in 30 minutes via the island's sole road, is fringed by red-tile-roof houses overhanging the water. Be sure to ascend to the hilltop **Iglesia de San Rafael**, offering a fine bay view. The island is most famous for the **Restaurante El Cayo** *(tel 22/69-0109)*, a waterfront seafood eatery on the cay's northeast side.

In order to reach Cayo Granma, pick up the passenger ferry from Parque Alameda, on Avenida Jesús Menéndez in Santiago de Cuba; or you can depart from Embarcadero Cayo Granma, a wharf on Carretera Turística a short distance north of El Morro.

INSIDER TIP:

When photographing the *cañonazo* ceremony, set your camera for as many frames per second as possible; this will maximize your chances of capturing the millisecond blast of the cannon.

—CHRISTOPHER AUGER-DOMÍNGUEZ
National Geographic Latin America photographer

The once fashionable **Punta Gorda** district, 3 miles (5 km) north of the wharf, now boasts an international marina and a statue of the eponymous revolutionary in **Parque Frank País**. ∎

EXPERIENCE: Transportation in Timeless Cuba

Visitors to Cuba can be forgiven for feeling like Alice after she tumbled down the rabbit hole. Especially so when it comes to Cuban transportation, where wacky homespun contraptions will often force you to do a double take. "What was that?" you may well ask as a *lada limosina*—two Lada sedans welded together—rumbles past. Riding around in a medley of motley taxis adds an only-in-Cuba dimension to your travel experience.

Here are three rides not to miss:
• *Bicitaxis:* These crude Cuban versions of Asian rickshaws are pedal-powered, three-wheeled cycle cabs made by welding together a metal frame and baseboard supporting two side-by-side passenger seats from a car. Use them for short-haul journeys in major cities, but only if you're in no rush. (See sidebar p. 81.)

• *Cocotaxis:* Resembling an oversize children's toy, these motorized tricycles feature a fiberglass body shaped like a hollow egg. The wind (and rain) whips your face as you whiz through the tourist zones of Havana and the island's other major resorts.

• *Colectivos:* Weary and weathered *cacharros* (prerevolutionary U.S.–made cars) are the workhorses of the local taxi system. Since 2009, foreigners have been permitted to flag them down and hop aboard. Like buses, these shared taxis run along fixed routes, pick up and drop off people along the route. Agree upon the fare in advance.

EL COBRE

Cuba's most important pilgrimage site and the island's only basilica makes for a fulfilling excursion from Santiago de Cuba. Dramatic in its setting and fascinating for its historical associations twined in legend, El Cobre traces a lineage back to the 1530s, when the Spanish established a copper *(cobre)* mine here.

Thousands of pilgrims flock annually to El Cobre.

El Cobre
198 C1

The slaves who worked the mine were granted freedom in 1801, some 75 years before their brethren in the cane fields. The small town their descendants occupy today is backed by the thickly forested Sierra del Cobre, 12 miles (20 km) northwest of Santiago de Cuba. It is dominated by the **Basílica de Nuestra Señora del Cobre** *(tel 22/34-6118)*, erected in 1927 and dedicated to the miracle worker Virgen de la Caridad del Cobre, officially named Cuba's patron saint in 1916.

To the right of the main nave, the side nave is filled with offerings spanning 200 years, including *milagros* (adornments in the shape of limbs) left in bequest of healing.

An effigy of the black **Virgen de la Caridad del Cobre** is displayed in a glass case above the altar, her yellow robes the same color as those of Ochún, the Santería goddess. Try to time your visit to be here on September 8, when thousands of pilgrims descend on El Cobre and the Virgin is carried in a procession. ■

Virgen del Cobre

In 1606, legend dictates, two *indio* men and a black boy were caught in a storm in the Bay of Nipe. Just as their boat nearly capsized, a plank appeared bearing a statue of a *mulatta* Virgin holding a baby Jesus and bearing the inscription "*Yo soy la Virgen de la Caridad*—I am the Virgin of Charity." The waves subsided, and the men declared it a miracle. The figure was taken to El Cobre mine, where a hermitage was built. Miracles were ascribed to the Virgin, who soon came to occupy a pivotal role in the Cuban psyche. The cult of worship is strengthened by the Virgin's associations with Ochún, the Santería goddess of love, femininity, riches, and sweet water. She is usually shown standing atop the waves, with the men at her feet.

PARQUE BACONAO

This 209,050-acre (84,600 ha) park extends from the eastern suburbs of Santiago de Cuba to the border with Guantánamo Province. Part of Baconao has been named a UNESCO biosphere reserve, including more than 6,000 species of higher plants. A popular weekend getaway for Santiagueros, the park offers beaches, a valley with prehistoric re-creations, and museums.

Baconao is accessed from Santiago de Cuba via Carretera de Siboney, the same route taken by invading U.S. forces in 1898, and later by Castro and his revolutionaries en route to the

INSIDER TIP:

After visiting Parque Baconao, drive west to catch the scenic Santiago–Marea del Portillo road (see pp. 216–217). But note it is often impassable after storms; and the bridge over the Río Macio is near collapse.

—CHRISTOPHER P. BAKER
National Geographic author

Moncada barracks in 1953. Along the road, 26 monuments honor the revolutionaries who died in the Moncada assault.

Fidel Castro and his men set out for Moncada on July 26, 1953, from **Granjita Siboney**, a small farmhouse that is now a museum. The farmstead shows bullet holes blasted by Batista's troops, who placed the bodies of captured revolutionaries here and riddled them with gunfire to portray them as having been caught while plotting. Nearby, the **Museo de la Guerra**

Hispano-Cubano-Norteamericana de Baconao (Museum of the Spanish-Cuban-Northamerican War) displays photos, exhibits, and battle maps.

The beach at **Siboney** has long been a favorite with Santiagueros. A war memorial recalls the landing of U.S. troops here on June 23, 1898. A couple of miles farther you'll spot **El Oasis**, an artists community, and, still farther ahead, after the turnoff for Playa Daiquirí, is the **Comunidad Artística Verraco**. Halfway between the two, lies the **Valle de la Prehistoria** *($)*, a valley laid out with life-size dinosaurs; a small **Museo de Historia Natural** offers exhibits of local fauna. Farther on, the **Museo Nacional del Transporte Terrestre** features a motley collection of classic cars, plus a display of 2,700 miniature cars. At **Playa Verraco**, divert into **Comunidad Artística Los Mamoncillos**, a community dedicated to sculpture.

Farther east, you pass a **cactus garden** *($)* and a display of Mesoamerican sculptures. Three hotels are served by beaches and by **Acuario Baconao**, an aquatic park. At the border with Guantánamo Province, the road ends at **Laguna Baconao**, a large lake with a restaurant and lovely mountain backdrop. ∎

Parque Baconao
🗺 199 D1

Granjita Siboney
✉ Carretera de Siboney Km 3.5, just before Siboney town
☎ 22/39-9168
💲 $

Museo de la Guerra Hispano-Cubano-Norteamericana de Baconao
✉ Carretera de Siboney
☎ 22/39-9119
🕐 Closed Sun.
💲 $

Museo Nacional del Transporte Terrestre
✉ Carretera de Baconao
☎ 22/39-9197
💲 $

Acuario Baconao
✉ Carretera de Baconao
☎ 22/35-6264 or 35-6176
💲 $

DRIVE SANTIAGO DE CUBA TO MAREA DEL PORTILLO

One of Cuba's preeminent drives, this scenic, lonesome road hugs the shore beneath the Sierra Maestra. The beauty of the looming mountains and the stark low-desert country and teal-blue sea make for a picture-perfect day's outing.

Exit **Santiago de Cuba** westward along Paseo de Martí, which leads past a slew of dockside factories and, after about 9 miles (15 km), meets the coast at **Playa Mar Verde ❶**, a beach that draws Santiagueros on weekends. The main road slices ruler-straight 13 miles (21 km) west to **Aserradero**, one of a dozen tiny communities along the route. Here, watch for a gun turret of the Spanish warship *Vizcaya* poking above the surf; it was sunk by U.S. warships on July 3, 1898 (the barrels of another Spanish cruiser, the *Almirante Oquendo*, can be seen just 50 yards/45 m offshore at **Ensenada Juan González**, 5 miles/8 km west of Playa Mar Verde).

Mountains to the north ascend prominently above the broad coastal plain. About 8 miles (13 km) west of Aserradero, at the Río Seco, you'll pass a turnoff to the right that leads over the mountains to **Cruce de los Baños**; 4WD is recommended. Continue straight, with the road rising and dipping between headlands. Eventually you'll pass through **Chivirico ❷**, the only town along the entire route. You'll

NOT TO BE MISSED:

Uvero • Pico Turquino • Marea del Portillo

also pass beaches of variegated colors, including **Playa Blanca** (6 miles/10 km before Chivirico) and **Playa Sevilla Guamá**, about 40 miles (64 km) west of Santiago de Cuba and dominated by the **Brisas Sierra Mar Los Galeones** (*tel 22/32-9110*), an all-inclusive hotel atop Punta Tabacal.

Now the scenery begins to stagger, while the road deteriorates markedly. Copper-colored cliffs loom out of the sea as the mountains close in on the shore. Settlements whittle down to a few rustic rural communities, most notably at **Uvero ❸**, 14 miles (22 km) west of Chivirico. This is the site of the first battle won by Fidel Castro's rebel army, on May 28, 1957, when a military outpost was captured. A glade of royal palms leads to a monument honoring the

A beach near Chivirico. The beauty only increases as you drive westward.

event. Ahead rises **Pico Turquino**, Cuba's highest peak at 6,475 feet (1,974 m), dipping down to the dancing blue waters. Though the cloud-draped peaks that rise from the shore are lushly forested, the narrow coastal littoral hereabouts receives little rain. Cacti begin to appear on penurious hillsides nibbled by goats.

At **Las Cuevas ④**, 16 miles (25 km) beyond Uvero, you'll pass the trailhead to Pico Turquino and, 2 miles (3 km) beyond, **La Plata ⑤**. A dirt road leads south to the tiny **Museo Municipal de Guamá Combate de la Plata** *(closed Mon., $)*, which celebrates events here on January 17, 1957, when Castro's rebels made their first strike against Batista's troops since Moncada in 1953. From here westward, it's just you and the buzzards and goats as the road wrinkles up into sharp curves, claws its way over great headlands,

and hangs suspended in air before cascading steeply to the next valley. Eventually, you arrive at **Marea del Portillo ⑥**, with its resort hotels and welcome refreshments. Continuing west, you'll arrive in the village of **Pilón**, after which, the road turns toward the interior.

In spring, crabs migrate en masse (see sidebar p. 151). Crushed by passing vehicles, they form a smorgasbord of crabmeat for vultures. The road is occasionally closed due to landslides or wave erosion. Retrace your steps to return to Santiago de Cuba.

🗺 See also area map pp. 198–199
➤ Santiago de Cuba
🕓 4 hours (one way)
↔ 100 miles (160 km)
➤ Marea del Portillo

GUANTÁNAMO

Known for the Cuban folk song "Guantanamera" and as the setting for the contentious U.S. naval base, Guantánamo lies about 20 miles (32 km) inland of the coast, at the head of a deep bay. The sprawling city, laid out in a near-perfect grid, occupies a barren plain and functions primarily as a military town but, newly restored, one with plenty of touristic appeal.

Guantánamo
- 🗺 199 E1

Visitor Information
- ✉ Infotur, Calixto García bet. Emilo Giro & Crombert
- ☎ 21/35-1993

British West Indian Welfare Center
- ✉ Serafín Sánchez #663, Paseo y Narciso López
- ☎ 21/32-5297

Tumba Francesa
- ✉ Calle Serafín Sánchez #751

Museo Histórico Provincial
- ✉ Calle Martí #804
- ☎ 21/32-5872
- 🕐 Closed Sun.
- 💲 $

This historic town got a late start in life, boosted in 1791 by the slave rebellion in nearby Santo Domingo, when French settlers and their slaves washed ashore. In the early 1900s, migrant workers from English-speaking Caribbean islands arrived. The French- and English-speaking cultures remain strong, nurtured by the **British West Indian Welfare Center** and **Tumba Francesa**, which promote their mother tongues and regional music and dance.

Guantánamo's few sites are found around **Parque Martí**, a small square graced by the 1863 **Iglesia Parroquial de Santa Catalina**. Nearby, the rose pink, neoclassical market—**Plaza del Mercado** (Calles Los Maceos & Prado)—is Guantánamo's architectural gem. To learn of the town's history, head to the **Museo Histórico Provincial**. The **Plaza de la Revolución Mariana**

INSIDER TIP:
The British West Indian Welfare Center works to keep alive the English-speaking Caribbean culture in Guantánamo. Visitors are welcome.

—CHRISTOPHER P. BAKER
National Geographic author

Grajales (Ave. 13 de Junio and Calle 11 Norte), on the northwest side of town, features the massive concrete **Monumento a los Héroes** showing revolutionary heroes in bas-relief.

Some 16 miles (26 km) northeast of Guantánamo, in the forests of the Sierra del Cristal foothills, **Zoológico de Piedra** (Stone Zoo; $) offers visitors a menagerie of life-size beasts, hewn in situ from giant rocks by farmer Angel Iñigo Blanco. ■

The U.S. Presence

Since 1903, the U.S. has held an indefinite lease on 45 square miles (116 sq km) of headland at the entrance to Guantánamo Bay. The property comprises a naval station and naval air station, served by several thousand military and civil service personnel, plus contractors. The facility includes a movie house, a golf course, and the only McDonald's in Cuba.

The Cuban government refuses to cash the annual $4,085 lease check and demands that the U.S. vacate the base, which was granted via the Platt Amendment to the Cuban Constitution in 1903. The base can be viewed from the hilltop **Mirador La Gobernadora** (tel 21/57-8908), 13 miles (20 km) east of Guantánamo.

BARACOA

Cuba's oldest and easternmost settlement, Baracoa counts also among the island's most charming cities. Small and compact, it claims a magnificent setting—embraced by mountains and surrounded by rain forest. Brought into the national fold only within recent decades, it clings fast to a sense of lifestyle steeped in the past.

■ Panoramic view of the bay of Baracoa

Diego Velázquez founded this picturesque town in 1512, making it the oldest colonial city in the Americas. Its remote location did little to favor the settlement. Cut off from the rest of the island, it paid the serious consequences of Hurricane Matthew in 2016. After the revolution, a dramatic switchback road—**La Farola**—over the Sierra del Purial mountains was completed, linking Baracoa to Guantánamo township.

Baracoa feels its age. Its narrow streets are lined by red-tile-roof wooden houses fronted by eaves supported by creaking timbers. The town's setting, too, seems fitting for a Hollywood epic: It spread-eagles below a dramatic flat-topped formation—**El Yunque**, the "anvil"—hovering above the surrounding hills that form an amphitheater flowing down to the Bahía de Miel (Bay of Honey), where fishing boats bob at anchor.

In the 18th century, three small fortresses went up to guard against predation by pirates. Rising over Baracoa from atop a soaring outcrop is **Fuerte de Seboruco**, built in the 1730s and later converted into a fine hotel that offers a bird's-eye view over town. Guarding the eastern entrance to town is the well-preserved **Fuerte Matachín**,

Baracoa
🗺 199 F2
Visitor Information
✉ Infotur, Maceo #129A
☎ 21/64-1781

Columbus Conundrum

Locals are highly partisan about claims that Columbus landed at Baracoa. Although evidence suggests Columbus actually landed farther west, near Gibara, most Baracoans point to their Cruz de la Parra (Cross of the Vine) as proof that the Genoese explorer came ashore here in 1492. In the 1980s, Belgian scientists analyzed samples of the wooden cross. Carbon dating confirmed the relic's antiquity, although tests show that it is hewn of a local hardwood—*Coccoloba diversifolia*—abundant around Baracoa. Thus, doubt was cast on the legend. The venerable relic is tipped with silver, added over ensuing centuries.

Museo Municipal de Historia

✉ Fuerte Matachín

☎ 21/64-2122

💲 $

dating from 1802. Today it houses the **Museo Municipal de Historia**, tracing the region's history since pre-Columbian days. From here, you can follow the **Malecón**, a decrepit wave-washed promenade extending westward to the semicircular **Fortaleza de la Punta**, guarding the harbor entrance.

The center of affairs is leafy, triangular **Plaza Independencia**, on Calle Antonio Maceo, dominated by the simple, ocher-colored **Catedral de Nuestra Señora de la Asunción** *(tel 21/643352)*. A church has occupied the site since the town's inception. This one, however, dates only from 1833 and was restored in 2012 after being badly damaged by Hurricane Ike in 2008. The church has traditionally displayed the silver-trimmed, 3-foot-tall (1 m) **Cruz de la Parra** (see sidebar left), which locals claim was left on the beach here by Christopher Columbus in 1492 and later found by Diego Velázquez and used to convert the Indians. Local resistance to the arrival of the Spanish was led by the Dominican-born Taino chieftain Hatuey. Burned at the stake in 1512, his noble visage is honored in bronze in Plaza Independencia.

To gain a real taste of the local flavor, check out the **Casa de Chocolate** *(Calle Maceo #121, tel 21/64-1553)*, which makes chocolates from local cocoa. At night, stop by **Plaza Martí**, where townsfolk gather to watch TV alfresco, sitting in neat rows facing the television that by day is kept locked inside its case.

Caves that riddle the cliffs south of town were used as pre-Columbian funerary chambers. In-situ skeletons and aboriginal artifacts can be seen at the **Museo Arqueológico La Cueva del Paraíso** *($)*, at the west end of Calle Moncada. ■

Playing ball on Playa de Barigua

CUCHILLAS DEL TOA BIOSPHERE RESERVE

Baracoa is hemmed by verdant mountains. This wild northeast corner—Cuba's wettest region—is deluged by rains and cloaked in virgin rain forest that smothers the Cuchillas del Toa, a rugged coastal mountain chain that is among the least explored terrains in Cuba. The region's unique flora and fauna have evolved in isolation—a godsend for birders and hikers. Some 514,000 acres (208,000 ha) of these lands are protected as the Reserva de la Biosfera Cuchillas del Toa.

The Toa River, Cuchillas del Toa

The reserve was officially created in 1987 to protect the only known habitat of the ivory-billed woodpecker, a mainland native considered extinct since the 1940s. Then, in the mid-1980s, the bird was sighted in these mountains, prompting the Cuban government to declare the region a protected area. Facilities for ecotourists are as yet minimal.

Parque Nacional Duaba includes **El Yunque** (1,886 feet/575 m), the flat-topped mountain above Baracoa. You can hike or drive to the summit with a guide from Finca Duaba, where a restaurant serves *criollo* dishes. The park also incorporates the mouth of the **Río Duaba**; a monument here marks the site where mulatto general Antonio Maceo came ashore on April 1, 1895, to relaunch the wars of independence. Nearby, the white-sand beach at **Playa Maguana**, 14 miles (22 km) west of Baracoa, shelves into sheltered teal waters.

Reserva de la Biosfera Cuchillas del Toa protects the interior mountains, whose inhabitants still bear the physical features of Indian forebears. Farther west, the 187,720-acre (76,000 ha) **Parque Nacional Alejandro Von Humboldt** has been a World Heritage site since 2001, with manatees living in its mangrove lagoons. All visits are handled by Ecotur, in Baracoa. ∎

Cuchillas del Toa Biosphere Reserve
- 199 F2
- Ecotur, Antonio Maceo
- 21/64-3665
- Closed Sun.

More Places to Visit in Eastern Oriente

Cajobabo

This lonesome beach, 62 miles (100 km) east of Guantánamo, is hallowed ground to Cubans. Here, on April 11, 1895, nationalist hero José Martí (see sidebar p. 188) returned from exile, along with Gen. Máximo Gómez, to incite the second war of independence. The tiny **Museo Municipal de Imías 11 de Abril** *($)* honors Martí and recounts the tale. Guides will lead you 1 mile (1.6 km) along the shingly beach to a marble monument built into the cliffs. 199 F1

El Güirito Comunidad Kiriba-Nengón

Scant remnants of the Taino bloodline remain in Cuba. An exception is clearly visible at this tiny farming hamlet some 9 miles (15 km) east of Baracoa, where the facial features of community members bear distinct hallmarks of indigenous DNA. A cultural group performs traditional *kiriba* and *nengón* music and dance and serves regional dishes. 199 G2

INSIDER TIP:

Raúl Castro's prepped grave can be viewed at the Mausoleo del Segundo Frente Oriental Frank País, at Mayarí Arriba.

—NEIL SHEA
*National Geographic
magazine writer*

Mayarí Arriba

This bucolic mountain town lies at the center of a coffee-producing area in the heart of forested mountains. The town, 34 miles (55 km) northeast of Santiago de Cuba, is remote: Raúl Castro established his headquarters here when he commanded the Second Front in the war to topple Batista. The **Museo Comandancia del II Frente** *(Ave. de los Mártires, tel 22/42-5749, closed Mon., $)* tells the tale, while the nearby **Mausoleo del Segundo Frente Oriental Frank País** honors those killed. Raúl Castro's grave is also prepared and marked by a plaque attached to a huge boulder, where his former wife and Cuban Republic's heroine, Vilma Espín, is buried. 199 D2

Parque Nacional Gran Piedra

Approximately 8 miles (13 km) east of Santiago de Cuba, a spur road off the Carretera de Siboney switchbacks sharply uphill through shifting ecosystems to Parque Nacional Gran Piedra, with dramatic vistas en route. At the top, a 459-step staircase delves through exotic vegetation to **La Gran Piedra** (4,048 feet/1,234 m), a mammoth boulder that can be scaled by a staircase. The former **La Isabelica coffee estate** today features a museum *(closed Sun., $)* with period furnishings and exhibits of farm implements. Nearby, a series of cascading gardens—**Jardín Ave de Paraíso**—bloom spectacularly year-round; visits are arranged through various tour agencies in Santiago de Cuba. 199 D1

Punta Maisí

Land's end at the eastern tip of Cuba is this cactus-studded promontory pinned by a 115-foot-tall (35 m) lighthouse, **Faro de Punta Maisí** built in 1862. Approximately 30 miles (45 km) east of Baracoa, it's reached by a coast road that crosses the Río Yumurí and makes a daunting switchback ascent to the mountain community of **La Maquina,** where the land is farmed in coffee. You can ascend to the top of the lighthouse *($)*. 199 G1

A long string of tiny isles stretching across western Cuba, a paradise escape of sand, sea, and sun

ARCHIPIÉLAGO DE LOS CANARREOS

Preparing to set sail at Playa Rojas

ARCHIPIÉLAGO DE LOS CANARREOS

Wearing a necklace of coral, these islands claim some of Cuba's finest beaches and diving venues. One major island anchors the rest—1,180-square-mile (3,056 sq km) Isla de la Juventud. To the east, a string of 350 coral cays scatters across the Caribbean Sea. The latter are uninhabited but for Cayo Largo, catering to beach-minded package vacationers.

The Golfo de Batabanó separates the archipelago from the mainland; ferries link Isla de la Juventud to Batabanó, in Havana Province.

Isla de la Juventud's earliest inhabitants, the Siboney, left their mark in petroglyphs on the walls of Cuevas de Punta del Este. Christopher Columbus, who landed on June 13, 1494, called the isle Evangelista. Pirates taking refuge here gave it the name Parrot Island for the vast

flocks of birds that today exist in lesser numbers. Beginning in the 19th century, the Spanish used the remote island they called Isle of Pines as a prison for Cuban nationalists, including José Martí. Fidel Castro was also jailed in the 20th-century prison, the Presidio Modelo.

The island's present name, which translates as "Isle of Youth," recognizes its role as a special municipality for students from developing

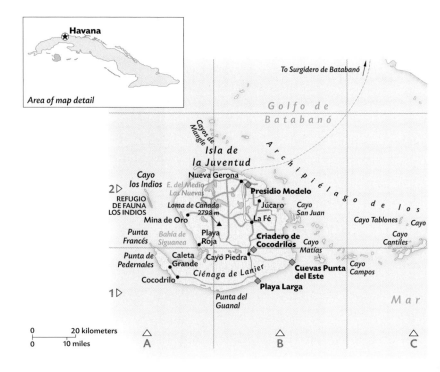

The coral cays around the archipelago offer a tropical world of diving delights.

countries whom socialist Cuba hosted and educated for free. In exchange, the students helped bring in the citrus harvest. The program, initiated in 1971, has been discontinued, though about 61,750 acres (25,000 ha) are still planted in ill-tended citrus. Juventud's entire southern half is a wilderness region of scrub and swamp—a habitat for Cuban crocodiles and for endangered sandhill cranes and Cuban parrots. This southern half is a military zone, although you can visit by permit easily obtained in Nueva Gerona.

The archipelago's waters are littered with shipwrecks; dive boats depart for outlying cays. Flamingos abound in the waters around Cayo Pasaje, while iguanas inhabit Cayo Iguana.

Cayo Largo offers some of Cuba's finest beaches and resort hotels—perfect for overnight packages from Havana. ■

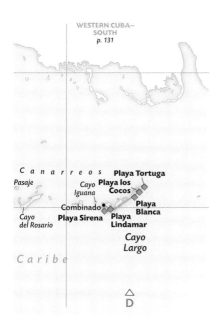

NUEVA GERONA

Steeped in historical charm, Isla de la Juventud's sleepy capital moves at a yesteryear pace. The few sites can be seen in half a day's leisurely browsing.

Nueva Gerona's somnolent main street

Nueva Gerona
🗺 224 B2
Visitor Information
✉ Ecotur, Calles 24 & 31
☎ 46/32-7101

Museo Municipal
✉ Calle 30 at 37
☎ 46/32-3791
🕐 Closed Mon.
💲 $

Museo de la Lucha Clandestina
✉ Calles 24 & 43 at Calle 45
☎ 46/32-4582
🕐 Closed Mon.

Museo de Ciencias Naturales y Planetario
✉ Calles 41 & 46
☎ 46/32-3143
🕐 Closed Mon.
💲 $

Founded in 1830, this port town exists primarily on the export of citrus and marble. Recently restored, the historic core's main artery is **Calle Martí** (Calle 39). Anchoring the main square— **Parque Julio Antonio Mella**— is the **Iglesia Nuestra Señora de los Dolores**, an ocher-colored church built in 1929. The **Museo Municipal**, on the square's south side, traces the region's history, with a focus on piracy. Calle 28 slopes east two blocks to the **Río Las Casas** and the paltry remains of **El Pinero**, the ferry that carried Fidel Castro to freedom in 1955.

Three other museums might fill a rainy day. The **Museo de la Lucha Clandestina** relates the town's history of underground warfare against Batista during the 1950s. At the town's south end, the **Museo de Ciencias Naturales y Planetario** has

motley archaeological and natural history exhibits. Continue strolling south and, after a mile (1.6 km), you'll arrive at the **Museo Finca El Abra** (*tel 46/39-6206, closed Mon., $*): A farmhouse doubles as a museum honoring José Martí, who lived here under house arrest for three months during his six-year term for sedition.

Hikers might head west of town (take Calle 24) to **Loma de Cañada** (1,020 feet/310 m), the highest point of the Sierra de las Casas. At its base, three caves contain pre-Columbian petroglyphs.

INSIDER TIP:

Archipiélago de los Canarreos is often hit by hurricanes; avoid them by visiting December through June.

—JUSTIN KAVANAGH
National Geographic Travel Books editor

The island's main site is **Presidio Modelo**, 3 miles (5 km) east of town. Built in 1931, this was a prison until 1967. Its most illustrious occupant was Castro himself, held in its hospital after the 1953 Moncada barracks attack. The hospital is now the **Museo Presidio Modelo** (*tel 46/32-5112, closed Mon., $*). ∎

BAHÍA DE SIGUANEA & NEARBY

The country's premier diving is the key draw of the Bay of Siguanea, off the coast of Isla de la Juventud, where pirate ships and Spanish galleons can be explored a few fathoms down. Much of the shore along Siguanea is a precious wildlife habitat of particular appeal to birders.

The glassy waters of the Bay of Siguanea, enclosed to the south by a long spit that ends at **Punta Francés**, are now a marine reserve. This is served by the **Hotel El Colony** *(tel 46/39-8181),* on **Playa Roja**, about 20 miles (32 km) southwest of Nueva Gerona. Today the hotel, formerly a Hilton, operates primarily as a scuba resort; it is served by the adjoining **Centro Internacional de Buceo** *(tel 46/39-8181),* which offers scuba certification courses. No diving within the reserve is permitted without an official guide, and drop-in visitors wishing to dive must sign up for an organized program.

The zone between Punta Francés and Punta Pedernales is called the **Costa de los Piratas** (Pirate Coast), where several sunken Spanish galleons and pirate vessels are preserved in pellucid waters. Three galleons at **Cayo de los Indios**, about 25 miles (40 km) northwest of Siguanea, are worth exploration. Divers can hand-feed stingrays at **Stingray Paradise**. And the wall off the Pirate Coast is beset with canyons and caves and coral parapets, including the **Catedral del Caribe**—among the world's tallest underwater coral columns.

Trails lead north from the Colony Hotel into the **Reserva Ecológica los Indios**,

a 9,880-acre (4,000 ha) reserve extending along the shore of the Bay of Siguanea. Its ecosystems include mangroves, grasslands, and palm forest. Los Indios harbors at least six species of endemic reptiles. Its 153 bird species include the *tocororo*—the national bird. The inland waters offer superb angling for bonefish and tarpon; the Hotel El Colony offers fishing. ■

Bahía de Siguanea
- 🗺 224 A2

Reserva Ecológica los Indios
- 🗺 224 A2
- ✉ Ecotur, Calles 24 & 31, Nueva Gerona
- ☎ 46/32-7101
- 💲 $$$ (compulsory guided tour)

Harvesting oranges at La Granja Patria, near Siguanea

EXPERIENCE: # Dive! Dive! Dive!

The translucent waters around Cuba offer some of the most rewarding scuba diving in the Caribbean. The island has everything for the adventurous diver, from the world's tallest coral column, off Isla de la Juventud—the main island in the Archipiélago de los Canarreos chain—to a Soviet-era frigate off Varadero. Welcome to a diver's paradise, teeming with marine life.

Cuba has dozens of world-class dive sites. The best are clustered in five principal zones, beginning with the **"Blue Circuit"** extending along 6 miles (10 km) of shoreline east of Havana. Also along the north coast are the coral-rich sites of the **Archipiélago de los Colorados** (see p. 115), centered on **Cayo Levisa** off Pinar del Río Province; and the **Jardines del Rey** (see pp. 158–159), off Ciego de Ávila and Camagüey Provinces. Off the south coast, the two main zones are the **Jardines de la Reina**, off Ciego de Ávila and Camagüey Provinces; and the scintillating waters off **Punta Francés**, to the southwest of Isla de la Juventud. Water temperatures average a balmy 75–83°F (24–28°C) and, although advisable, wet suits aren't required.

Cuba has more than 40 dive centers, with many located in resort hotels. Most centers are modestly equipped, but Cuba's dive masters are trained to global standards. Most centers offer resort courses and open-water certification. A diving guide is compulsory. The following are the principal dive sites:

• **"Blue Circuit,"** Havana Province. Rich in coral formations, the zone is also littered with the tempting wrecks of several Spanish galleons. **Centro de Buceo La Aguja** (Ave. 5ta at Calle 248, tel 7/204-5088), in Marina Hemingway, offers dives.

• **Bahía de Corrientes**, at Cuba's western tip, offers sheltered waters with whale sharks, coral canyons, and Spanish galleons on view. Dives depart the **Centro Internacional de Buceo María la Gorda** on Peninsula de Guanahacabibes, Pinar del Río (tel 48/77-8131). (See p. 113.)

INSIDER TIP:
Cayo Largo has Cuba's only nudist beaches. Divers should be ready to share the seas and the sands with those in the buff.

—VIRGILIO VALDÉS
National Geographic Latin America editor

• **Punta Francés**, at the southwestern tip of Isla de la Juventud, is Cuba's premier dive destination. Its calm waters shelter almost 60 sites along **La Costa de los Piratas**—a 10-mile-long (16 km) axis offering everything from "Stingray Paradise" to Spanish galleons and modern naval vessels. Dives depart the **Centro Internacional de Buceo Siguanea** (tel 46/32-8438), at the Hotel El Colony. Cayo Largo, far to the east of Isla de la Juventud, offers 39 further dive sites to explore. (See p. 230.)

• **Varadero** has more than 30 dive sites. Sites in **Parque Marino Cayo Piedras del Norte** (1-hour boat ride) excel in sunken military vessels plus a Soviet military aircraft. Contact **Gaviota Diving Center** (Marina Gaviota, Autopista Sur Km 21, tel 45/66-4115). (See p. 123.)

• **Jardines de la Reina**. Hundreds of coral cays dot the shallows of the **Golfo de Ana María**, protected by a barrier reef. Diving with sharks is a major draw. All dives can be booked through **Avalon Dive Center** (tel 33/49-8104, divingincuba.com), an Italian company that operates six live-aboards.

• **Playa Santa Lucia**. The prime draws are shark feeding and the wreck of the steamship Montera, lying barely 22 feet (7 m) down in the **Bahía de Nuevitas**. The **Shark's Friend Dive Center** (tel 32/36-5182) offers twice-daily dives.

JUVENTUD'S SOUTHERN ZONE

Although smothered in its entirety by inhospitable terrain, the remote southern half of Isla de la Juventud claims glorious white-sand beaches, a turtle farm, and a cave known for its Indian petroglyphs. Access is via a military post at Cayo Piedra, 24 miles (39 km) south of Nueva Gerona. A guide is compulsory.

The isle's southern half comprises the **Ciénaga de Lanier**—the Lanier Swamp—a vast swath of sedge wetlands and paperbark swamps that shelters wild pigs, deer, and *jutías* (large rodents). You can hire the compulsory guide via Ecotur *(Calles 24 & 31, Nuevo Gerona, tel 46/32-7101)* or the **Hotel El Colony** *(Playa Roja, tel 46/39-8181),* which offers tours that include the **Criadero de Cocodrilos** *(no facilities),* 19 miles (30 km) south of Nueva Gerona. Here, the reptiles are bred for mass release into the wild. You can get close to scores of crocs sunning themselves on the mud banks, motionless as logs. Visit mid-morning to watch the beasts devouring hacked-up cattle.

A dirt road leads east from Cayo Piedra to **Cuevas de Punta del Este**, 37 miles (59 km) southeast of Nueva Gerona. Here, seven caves of archaeological import back a white-sand beach

One of the bunch at the Criadero de Cocodrilos, Cayo Potrero

(no facilities). The caves contain pre-Columbian petroglyphs dating from about 800 B.C. and representing concentric circles and parallel lines thought to constitute a primitive celestial plan. Some 238 have been identified. Alas, many have been damaged. The main road runs south from Cayo Piedra to **Playa Larga**, whence it parallels the shore westward to the community of **Cocodrilo**, peopled by the descendants of English-speaking Cayman Islanders. ■

Juventud's Southern Zone
224 A1 & B1

Cuba's Crocodiles

The endemic and endangered Cuban crocodile—*Crocodylus rhombifer*—was hunted to near extinction during four centuries of colonial rule. The *Lagarto criollo* is found today in the wild only in Ciénaga de Zapata and Ciénaga de Lanier—the most restricted geographic range of any crocodile species in the world. The species, with its truncated snout and yellow-and-black mottled skin, is highly aggressive and is genetically coded to strike at anything that moves. Seven *criaderos* throughout Cuba breed crocodiles: Two breed Cuban crocodiles for reintroduction into the wild; five breed American crocodiles for skins.

CAYO LARGO

Cayo Largo is girded by sparkling sugar-white beaches shelving into jade-colored waters. The boomerang-shaped isle is the only cay in the archipelago accessible by air from the mainland, and the only one developed for tourism (apart from Isla de la Juventud).

A scuba diver ascends Devil's Hole off Cayo Largo.

Cayo Largo
225 D1 & D2

This 15-mile-long (24 km) sliver of coral and powder beaches, 125 miles (200 km) southeast of Havana and 70 miles (112 km) east of Isla de la Juventud, is the easternmost of the low-lying coral cays of Archipiélago de los Canarreos. The island hosts international package vacationers, flying in from Havana or directly from abroad. You are greeted with limpid, warm waters of impossible blues lapping at dazzling white beaches. **Playa Sirena**, the westernmost and most spectacular beach, is reached by ferry from Marina Cayo Largo del Sur *(tel 45/24-8214)*. Dolphins perform in a shallow, netted **Delfinario**. Most of the hotel development concentrates along **Playa Lindamar** and **Playa Blanca**. Farther east, **Playa los Cocos** appeals to divers for its shallow corals and offshore shipwreck. The easternmost beach, **Playa Tortuga**, derives its name from scores of marine turtles that waddle ashore to nest in the warm sands. Turtle eggs are incubated at a turtle farm—**Granja de las Tortuga** *($)*—in the workers' dormitory hamlet of **El Pueblo**, north of the airport. Together these beaches span some 17 miles (27 km) running the length of the seaward side (the leeward side comprises mangrove lagoons). In all, Cayo Largo's waters shelter more than 30 dive sites, served from a dive center at Marina Puerto Sol. Other activities include sportfishing, snorkeling, and trips to deserted cays.

Birding is especially rewarding, with frigate birds, Caspian terns, and parakeets among those to list. All hotels have tour desks. ■

TRAVELWISE

Old Yankee *cacharros*

TRAVELWISE

PLANNING YOUR TRIP

When to Go

Cuba has a warm and humid tropical climate year-round. In general, dry season is November–April, when temperatures average a balmy 72–77°F (22–25°C). Cold fronts occasionally sweep down from the north during this period, bringing cool, sometimes stormy weather. The hottest months are May–October, when temperatures in Havana average 75–79°F (24–26°C), and humidity can make life uncomfortable. This is also the wet season, with near-daily showers and downpours often causing flooding. To avoid the risks of a hurricane, visitors are advised to keep up to date on weather conditions at the following website: nhc.noaa.gov.

Regional variations are pronounced. Temperatures increase eastward–Santiago de Cuba in the Oriente region is significantly warmer than Havana, especially in summer. Then, Oriente sizzles in heat, with Santiago de Cuba baking in a stifling basin, while Havana is caressed by cooling, near-constant breezes. Higher elevations are cooler–notably so in the Sierra del Escambray and Sierra Maestra. These heights also receive more moisture than lowland areas; those of far northeast Cuba are comparatively drenched and, hence, blessed with lush rain forests. The predominant winds are from the east, so that the lee of the mountains lies in relatively dry rain shadows. The southeast coast is fringed by semidesert.

Most tourists visit in winter, when many popular hotels in Havana are booked solid–elsewhere rooms are generally available year-round. Almost all hotels have low- and high-season rate fluctuations. Festivals occur year-round.

What to Take

Cuba has a tropical climate, so dress accordingly. Lightweight, loose-fitting cotton and synthetic clothes are best. Shorts and T-shirts prove comfortable and are acceptable everywhere, including Havana, although you'll want some more elegant wear for nighttime, especially for ritzier restaurants and nightclubs such as the Tropicana. Avoid tight-fitting clothes, which are uncomfortable and promote fungal growth in the hot, humid climate. A sweater and/or lightweight jacket are useful for the heavily air-conditioned restaurants and during November–April, when cold fronts moving south from North America may bring cool, rainy weather. A raincoat works well in warm-season downpours, and a fold-up umbrella is always useful.

Pack a comfortable pair of walking shoes or sneakers for exploring Havana and other cities. Hiking shoes will prove useful if you plan on exploring often muddy mountain trails or wilderness areas. And dress shoes are not out of place for restaurants and nightclubs.

You'll need insect repellent, particularly for coastal areas and during the wet season, even in cities. Mosquitoes can be ferocious (notably around mangrove ecosystems), but they are rare in upland or breeze-swept areas. Although dengue and malaria have been known on Caribbean islands, the risks in Cuba are minimal. For a full list of the recommended vaccines for visitors to Cuba, see the Centers for Disease Control and Prevention Website (cdc.gov).

Sunglasses are a necessity, as the tropical light is intense. And a sun hat or cap and sunscreen are mandatory, even for brief periods outdoors. It is never a wise move to underestimate the strength of the tropical sun.

If you are traveling within Cuba or staying in casas particulares (private room rentals), it's always a good idea to bring some extra toilet paper.

Medicines are in short supply, so bring a basic first-aid kit that includes aspirins, antidiarrheal medication, antiseptic lotions, Band-Aids, and other essentials. Bring a spare pair of glasses or contact lenses rather than a prescription, as replacements are virtually unobtainable. Similarly, bring all the photographic supplies and equipment you'll need, as these are in short supply and extremely expensive. Birders should also bring binoculars.

Insurance

Starting in May 2010, the government of Cuba requires that all travelers visiting from abroad purchase travel health insurance before entering the country. **Assistcard** (tel 888-854-9911, assistcard.com), based in Florida, has a regional assistance center in Cuba and offers a wide range of coverage, from trip cancellation to medical treatment and repatriation.

Entry Formalities

Foreign visitors require a valid passport to enter Cuba (U.S. citizens of Cuban origin need a Cuban passport, issued by the **Cuban Embassy**, 2630 16th St. N.W., Washington, D.C. 20009, tel 202/797-8518). No visas are necessary for tourists. Tourist cards for entry into the country are issued by approved travel agencies, or upon check-in for flights to Cuba; immigration officials stamp the tourist card rather than your passport. Foreigners are limited to a 30-day stay, plus an additional 30 days (prórroga) upon request ($25) from the **Inmigración y Extranjería** department (Calle 17 bet. J er K,

Vedado, Havana, tel 7/861-3462); Canadians are allowed a 90-day stay, plus a 90-day extension.

U.S. Regulations
U.S. law prohibits all financial transactions involving travel to Cuba except for 12 pre-authorized ("general license") categories, including journalists, professional research, family visits, support for the Cuban people etc., but "tourism" is still not allowed. All U.S. citizens may travel on organized "people-to-people" programs (see How to Get to Cuba, below), but not as individuals. Contact the **U.S. Treasury Dept.** *(1500 Pennsylvania Ave. N.W., Washington, D.C. 20200, tel 202/622-2480, treasury. gov/resource-center/sanctions/Programs/Pages/cuba.aspx)* for details. Cuba has no such restrictions and welcomes visitors arriving with or without official U.S. sanction.

HOW TO GET TO CUBA
By Airplane
The majority of flights arrive at José Martí International Airport *(tel 7/266-4644),* about 15 miles (25 km) southwest of downtown Havana. Other flights arrive at Antonio Maceo International Airport *(tel 22/69-8614),* 8 miles (12 km) south of Santiago de Cuba, and at international airports at Camagüey, Cayo Coco, Cayo Largo, Ciego de Ávila, Cienfuegos, Holguín, and Varadero.

Licensed charter flights operate to Cuba from Miami, New York, and other U.S. cities, and in 2016 scheduled flights were authorized to begin. U.S.-Cuba flights are restricted to licensed passengers. No such restrictions apply to carriers operating direct flights to Cuba from Canada, the Caribbean, and Central America, including:
  Air Canada *(aircanada.ca)*
  Cubana *(cubana.cu)*

  Avianca *(avianca.com)*
  Copa *(copaair.com)*
  Also, several airlines serve Cuba from the U.K. and mainland Europe.

By Sea
Private vessels berth at Marina Hemingway *(tel 7/204-5088),* 10 miles (16 km) west of Havana. U.S. skippers must be licensed by the **Treasury Department** (see Entry Formalities, p. 232) to legally pay berthing and other costs. Several foreign companies offer Cuba cruises and as of 2015 any U.S. cruise line is permitted to offer "people-to-people" cruises to Cuba (see Cruising to Cuba feature, pp. 54–55, and By Tour, below).

By Tour
Many Canadian and British companies offer a variety of tours. As of 2015 any U.S. organization is pre-authorized to offer group "people-to-people" cultural exchange programs ("tours"), which any U.S. citizen can join. **National Geographic Expeditions** *(tel 888/966-8687, nationalgeographicexpeditions. com)* offers such cultural trips, as does **Cuba Motorcycle Tours** *(tel 760-327-9879, cubamotorcycletours. com)*, of a more specialist bent.

GETTING AROUND
Taxis provide transport from the major international airports to the city centers. Public transport is restricted to overcrowded buses that are best avoided.

Public Transportation in Havana
By Bus
Guaguas (buses) serve most parts of the city, but many are overcrowded. Large Metro-buses—nicknamed *camellos* due to their characteristic "hump"—link outlying districts with Parque de la Fraternidad downtown, and run along major routes.

By Taxi
Havana's taxi service is fast and efficient. **Cubataxi** *(tel 7/855-5555)* operates radio-dispatched taxis. Tourist taxis also wait outside major hotels; rates are CUC 0.40–0.90 per kilometer. *Colectivos*—old Yankee jalopies—serve Cubans, charge in pesos, and follow fixed routes. *Cocotaxis* (motorized tricycles with three seats) can be hired outside major hotels, as can private classic convertibles *(from CUC 30 hourly).* Budget travelers can opt for the pedal-powered tricycles called *bicitaxis* that ply Habana Vieja and the Malecón *(CUC 3).*

By Train
Commuter trains depart Estación 19 de Noviembre *(Calles Tulipán & Hidalgo, Nuevo Vedado, tel 7/881-4431)* for Santiago de las Vegas.

Around Cuba
By Air
Major destinations are linked to each other, and to José Martí International Airport. Two domestic carriers serve regional airports:
  AeroGaviota *(tel 7/203-0668, aerogaviota.com)*
  Cubana *(tel 7/834-4446, cubana.cu)*
Typical fares between Havana and Santiago de Cuba are CUC 125 round-trip.

By Bus
Travel by bus is fast and efficient between major tourist destinations. **Víazul** *(Ave. 26 y Zoológico, Plaza de la Revolución, Havana, tel 7/883-6092, viazul.com)* provides express service using air-conditioned, modern buses *(CUC 10–51).* Travel by public bus is less reliable. Local demand far exceeds supply, and timetables are not strictly adhered to. Foreigners are not allowed to use domestic intercity buses. Guard against pickpockets and luggage theft. Travel light, as space is limited. Most Cubans travel by

camiones—trucks converted to crude buses.

By Car

To rent a car, you must be over 21 and hold a passport and a valid driver's license (a U.S. license is fine). A deposit *(usually CUC 200–500)* is required.

Rates vary from about CUC 42 daily for the smallest vehicles, and CUC 80 for midsize cars, to between CUC 110 and CUC 150 for top-of-the-line cars. Insurance costs CUC 12–25 extra daily. You should not need a 4WD vehicle. Thoroughly check your vehicle for damage and missing items before setting out. Don't accept a vehicle with a partially empty gas tank. Beware of additional charges that might appear on your bill when you return the car.

No international companies are represented. The following Cuban state entities rent cars:

Cubacar *(tel 7/835-0000, email: cubacar@transtur.cu),* **Havanautos** (tel 7/273-2277, havanautos@ transtur.cu), and **Rex** *(tel 7/835-6830, rex.cu)* are all divisions of **Transtur** *(tel 7/831-7333, transtur. com).* It is best to reserve through a private booking agency such as **Cuba Travel Network** *(tel 7/837-1602, cubatravelnetwork.com)* or **Vía Rent-a-Car** *(tel 7/206-9935, gaviota-grupo.com).*

These agencies ostensibly provide 24-hour breakdown assistance, but this can take hours when you're away from major cities. Gasoline is sold at Servi-Cupet and Oro Negro stations nationwide *(CUC 1.22 per liter).*

Roads everywhere are potholed and badly deteriorated in places. Drive slowly and be on your guard for wayward bicyclists, stray cattle, and wandering pedestrians.

By Ferry

Hydrofoils and a car ferry serve Isla de la Juventud from Suridero de Batabanó, in Havana Province: **Viajero** *(tel 46/32-4415, Nueva Gerona; in Havana, tel 7/878-1841).*

By Train

A central railway line links major cities to each other and to Havana. Interprovincial services operate on an ever-changing schedule. Havana's main railway station is closed for lengthy repairs. Trains now depart from Estación La Coubre *(Av. del Puerto, Habana Vieja, tel 7/860-3161)* or Estación 19 de Noviembre *(Tulipán at Hidalgo, Nuevo Vedado, tel 7/881-4431).* An overnight *especial* service runs between Havana and Santiago de Cuba *(13 hours, CUC 62.50),* stopping in two major cities en route; a *regular* train is slower, and makes more stops. Foreigners get reserved seats and can book through **Infotur** offices *(see Visitor Information, p. 236).*

PRACTICAL ADVICE
Communications

The Cuban state controls all media and keeps a tight rein on what may be published.

Email & Internet

Internet access has improved considerably in recent years, and Cubans now freely receive and send emails *(correos electrónicos)* and texts on their cellphones. Most tourist hotels have Internet, and many now have Wi-Fi; several public Wi-Fi zones were also opened in 2015; and every town has at least one cybercafé run by Etecsa. In all cases you need to purchase an access card (CUC 5 per hour; bring your passport.)

Newspapers

Granma, an 8-page daily newspaper, is the official mouthpiece of the party (Comité Central del Partido Comunista de Cuba). An English-language edition is published for tourists. *Juventud Rebelde,* the evening paper of the Communist Youth League, is a mirror image. Some special-interest magazines, such as *Bohemia* and *Prisma,* offer more in-depth reporting, covering the arts and general topics, respectively. Western-style newsstands do not exist and foreign publications are not sold.

Post Offices

It costs CUC 0.50 to mail a postcard to North America and CUC 0.80 for a letter. Never include politically sensitive comments, as mail is generally read by censors; and never mail anything of value, as theft is rampant within the postal service (Correos de Cuba). Allow two weeks for mail between Cuba and North America. Most towns have a post office, usually open Monday–Friday, 10 a.m.–5 p.m., and Saturday, 8 a.m.–noon. Many gift stores and hotels sell postage-paid letters and postcards.

Express Packages

DHL *(tel 7/204-1578, dhl.com)* has offices throughout Cuba and offers express international and domestic service.

Telephones

Etecsa *(www.etecsa.cu),* the Cuban state telephone company, has telephone bureaus—*centros telefónicos*—in major cities and also operates glass-enclosed telephone kiosks—*micropuntos*—on major streets throughout the island.

Most public phones utilize phone cards (which can be purchased at the kiosks or at most hotel tour desks), but not credit cards. Service is generally efficient, but public phones are slightly complicated to use.

Telephone numbers change frequently and the entire national territory is in the gradual process of changing to seven-digit numbers.

For direct-dial international calls, dial 119, then the country code and area code, then the number. Few hotels permit direct-dial international calls. For operator-assisted calls to the U.S., dial 66-1212.

For directory inquiries, call 113. Direct-dial calls to the U.S. are CUC 1 per minute from a residence; CUC 2.45 from a booth, with a card, or with a cellphone. Most U.S. cellphones will not work, but in 2015 Sprint and Verizon launched prepaid plans for Cuba. It is cheaper to buy a SIM card in Cuba.

Calling from the U.S., dial 011, plus Cuba's country code, 53, then the city code and number.

For calls between provinces, add a 0 before dialing the city code.

Television & Radio

Television reaches everyone (even the most remote rural community is linked to the national grid) and has been a key tool in spreading the revolution.

There are only two major national networks, Cubavision and TeleRebelde, which carry limited international programming on five channels (notably select news clips from CNN Español, and *telenovelas*—soap operas—from other Latin American countries). Most tourist hotels also offer some U.S. cable TV programs.

Cuba has only seven national radio stations. In addition, local radio stations serve regional areas. Reception is intermittent, and large areas of the country have no reception.

Conversions

Cuba uses the metric system for measurement. Useful conversions are:

1 mile = 1.61 kilometers
1 kilometer = 0.62 mile
1 meter = 39.37 inches
1 liter = 0.264 U.S. gallon

1 U.S. gallon = 3.78 liters
1 kilogram = 2.2 pounds
1 pound = 0.45 kilograms

Weather reports use Celsius. To convert quickly (but roughly) from Fahrenheit to Celsius, subtract 32 and divide by two. From Celsius to Fahrenheit, multiply by two and add 32.

0°C = 32°F
10°C = 50°F
20°C = 68°F
30°C = 86°F
100°C = 212°F

Electricity

Cuba operates on 110-volt AC (60 cycles) nationwide, although 220-volt is found in places. Most outlets use U.S. flat, two- or three-pin plugs.

Etiquette & Local Customs

Cuban society is extremely informal and egalitarian, especially compared to most other Latin nations. Cubans typically address each other by their first names, regardless of political or social standing. They often use the informal *tu* for "you," rather than the formal *usted,* even with strangers. Cubans are very open with their family and personal life and readily extend invitations into their homes.

Cubans of different colors intermingle with ease, and black visitors will experience little, if any, aloofness. Although institutional racism has been eradicated, subtle racism still exists.

Cubans are highly suspicious of tattletales, government agents, and police spies. They are loath to offer negative commentary regarding domestic politics in public or in the company of those they do not implicitly trust.

Both men and women can be flirtatious, and laxity in sexual relations is an accepted societal norm.

Outside the main tourist areas English may not be understood, so it is advisable to learn a few Spanish phrases. Most restaurants in tourist areas have menus in English.

Money Matters
Currency

The national currency is the peso. However, all tourist transactions are enacted in *pesos convertibles* (CUC), and very few items can be paid for in pesos. Foreigners must exchange foreign currency for *pesos convertibles* upon arrival: When possible, ask for small bills (1, 3, 5, 10, 20 CUC) to avoid problems with getting change. At press time, the exchange rate was CUC 1 to one dollar, but a 10 percent surcharge applies to U.S. dollars; Euros and Canadian dollars are exempt. A passport (or other ID) is required when presenting $50 and $100 bills. Excess notes can be exchanged for dollars at the airport when you are departing.

Banks in major towns usually offer currency exchange services, as do **Cadeca** currency exchange bureaus. Traveler's checks are rarely accepted and cannot be used as cash. Traveler's checks issued by non-U.S. banks can be cashed at a few specific banks.

Credit Cards

In 2015, President Obama legalized use of U.S. credit cards in Cuba, although there are few guarantees that your MasterCard or Visa will work. MasterCard and Visa issued elsewhere (e.g., Canada or Europe) are accepted at most tourist entities. Major banks will offer cash advances against non-U.S. credit cards. However, many credit cards issued outside the U.S. won't function in Cuba; check in advance to determine if the processing for your specific card is handled through a U.S. institution.

Tipping

Tipping is not a fact of life in Cuba, except in places frequented by tourists, where service workers are paid in *pesos* and rely on dollar tips to make ends meet. However, a tip is an acknowledgment of good service. If the service is not satisfactory, do not tip.

A 10–15 percent service charge is often added onto restaurant bills. Tour guides should be tipped about CUC 1 per person per day for group tours, and more for personalized services. Hotel porters should be given CUC 0.50 per bag, and room service staff CUC 1 per day. Taxi drivers do not expect tips, although a 10–15 percent tip is always appreciated.

National Holidays

Cuba observes the following national holidays:
January 1, Liberation Day
Good Friday
May 1, Labor Day
July 25–27, National Revolution Day
October 10, Anniversary of 1868 Céspedes's Declaration of Independence
December 25, Christmas Day

Most tourist sites and services stay open for these holidays, but banks and government offices close.

Opening Times

Most stores are open Monday–Sunday 10 a.m.–6:30 p.m. Most banks are open Monday–Friday 8:30 a.m.–3 p.m. Government offices are generally open Monday–Friday, 8:30 a.m.–4 p.m., usually with a one-hour lunch break.

Places of Worship

Most communities have at least one Roman Catholic church. Synagogues, Baptist, Pentecostal, Evangelical, and Anglican churches also exist in some communities, but are not as widespread. Many churches in Havana close from noon to 3 p.m. Check ahead for times.

Restrooms

Toilets often lack toilet seats and toilet paper. Many restaurants and hotels have attendants who distribute toilet paper and maintain the toilets for tips. Public street toilets are either nonexistent or best avoided.

Smoking

A large percentage of Cubans smoke, and smoking in public is neither frowned on nor forbidden. In 2005 a ban on smoking in restaurants was introduced, but it isn't enforced. Cigarettes, including popular U.S. brands, are sold at bars and gift stores. Cigars are sold at Casas de Tabaco and hotel gift stores, but not at bars.

Time Difference

Cuban time is the same as U.S. eastern standard time (EST), five hours behind Greenwich mean time (GMT). Cuba operates on daylight saving time March–October.

Travelers With Disabilities

Although paying lip service, Cuba does not display great sensitivity to the needs of disabled visitors. Few buildings have wheelchair access or provide special toilets. Buses aren't adapted for wheelchairs, and few curbs are sloped at corners. In fact, most sidewalks are major obstacle courses, with deep fissures, open gutters, etc. Some upscale hotels have wheelchair access and a few provide special suites. Older accommodations and restaurants usually present difficulties.

The following agencies provide information on traveling for visitors with disabilities: **Asociación Cubana de Limitados Físicos y Motores** *(Calle 6 #106, Miramar, Havana, tel 7/209-3099, www.aclifim.sld.cu)* and **Society for Accessible Travel & Hospitality** *(tel 212/447-7284, sath.org).*

Visitor Information

The Ministerio de Turismo de Cuba (Ministry of Tourism of Cuba) has a website: *mintur.gob.cu.* Cuba's tourist information offices abroad are represented by state tourism corporations.

In Canada, the **Cuban Tourist Board** has an office in Toronto *(1200 Bay St., Ste. 305, Toronto, ON M5R 2A5, tel 416/362-0700, www.gocuba.ca).* In the U.K., it has an office at 167 High Holborn, London WC1V 6PA *(tel 020/7240-6655, travel2cuba.co.uk).*

Infotur *(tel 7/204-7036, infotur. cu)* operates tourist information offices throughout Havana and in most major cities and tourist resorts, plus at most international airports. (See also sidebar p. 9.)

EMERGENCIES & HEALTH CARE
Crime & Police

Cuba is relatively free of violent crime. However, petty theft is rampant and far more prevalent than in most North American cities. Caution should be exercised at all times, especially if approached by *jineteros* or *jineteras*—hustlers and prostitutes. In towns, there is a danger of pickpockets and snatch-and-grab theft, so be especially wary in crowded areas, such as buses and markets. Scams are common, especially in private street transactions; never take your eyes off any items you purchase. And keep your possessions in a hotel safe or a locked suitcase.

Avoid leaving luggage or valuables in cars, and do not carry large quantities of cash or wear expensive jewelry. Keep passports and credit cards out of sight. If anything is stolen, report it immediately to the police and/or your hotel.

Report crimes to the **Policia Nacional Revolucionaria (PNR)**. If you are charged with a crime, request that your deposition be made in front of an independent witness (*testigo*). Visitors from the U.S. can request a representative of the U.S. Embassy be present.

Asistur *(Paseo del Prado #212, Havana, tel 7/866-8527 or 7/866-4499, www.asistur.cu)* exists to provide assistance to tourists in trouble.

Emergency Telephone Numbers

Ambulance, 104
Fire, 105 or 115
Police, 106 or 116

Embassies & Consulates

United States Embassy, Calzada & L/M, Vedado, Havana, tel 7/839-4100, cu.usembassy.gov

British Embassy, Calle 34 #702 at 7ma Ave., Miramar, Havana, tel 7/214-2200, gov. uk/world/organisations/british-embassy-havana

Canadian Embassy, Calle 30 #518 at 7ma Ave., Miramar, Havana, tel 7/204-2516, canadainternational.gc.ca/cuba

Health

Travel insurance is mandatory for visitors in Cuba; the Cuban government sells a travel insurance package to visitors arriving without such coverage. Travelers should ensure that insurance plans cover medical evacuation by air, medical emergencies, and repatriation of remains.

The hospital administration requires patients to pay in full for the care they've received before they will authorize their release. Sanitary and hygiene conditions

in hospital structures outside of Havana are precarious and medicines and medical supplies are often unavailable. Visitors are advised to travel with their own supply of essential medicines.

Medical services for foreigners are provided by **Clínica Internacional Cira García** *(Calles 20 & 41, Miramar, Havana, tel 7/204-2811, cirag.cu)*. Foreigners pay in CUC.

The following international pharmacies serve foreigners:

Farmácia Internacional *(Calles 41 & 20, Miramar, Havana, tel 7/204-2880)*

Farmácia Internacional *(Miramar Trade Center, Ave. 3ra, Calle 76/70, Miramar, Havana, tel 7/204-4515)*

Farmácia Internacional Camilo Cienfuegos *(Calles 13 & L, Vedado, Havana, tel 7/832-5555)*

Ópticas Miramar *(Ave. 7ma at Calle 24, Havana, tel 7/204-3618)* provides optician services. It also has branches in cities nationwide.

Most tourist centers also have Clínica Internacional and Óptica Miramar outlets. International *farmacies* can also be found in the Hotel Habana Libre, Hotel Sevilla, and Hotel Comodoro in Havana.

No vaccination is required. Visitors must follow the usual health and hygiene precautions taken in countries with a hot, humid climate: Drink bottled water and don't use ice that hasn't been made with *agua purificada*, purified water.

What to Do in Case of a Car Accident

In the event of an accident, do not move the vehicle or permit the other vehicle to be moved. Take down the license plate number and the name, address, and ID number from the *carnet de identidad* (legal identification) of any witnesses. Call the transit police at 106 or 116. If someone is seriously injured or killed, contact your embassy.

USEFUL WORDS & PHRASES

Excuse me *Perdón*
Hello *Hola*
Good-bye *Adiós*
Please *Por favor*
Thank you *Gracias*
You're welcome *De nada*
Good morning *Buenos días*
Good afternoon *Buenas tardes*
Good night *Buenas noches*
today *hoy*
yesterday *ayer*
tomorrow *mañana*
now *ahora*
later *más tarde*
this morning *esta mañana*
this afternoon/this evening *esta tarde*
Do you speak English? *¿Habla inglés?*
I am American *Yo soy amerícano/amerícana*
I don't understand *No entiendo*
Where is ... ? *¿Dónde esta ... ?*
I don't know *No lo sé*
At what time? *¿A que hora?*
Do you have ... ? *¿Tienes un ... ?*
a single room *una habitación sencilla*
a double room (double bed) *una habitación matrimonio*
a double room (twin beds) *una habitación con dos camas*
for one night *para una noche*
I need a doctor/dentist *Necesito un médico/dentista*
Can you help me out? *¿Me puede ayudar?*
hospital *hospital*
police station *comisaría de policia*
I'd like *Me gustaría*
How much is it? *¿Cuánto es?*
Do you accept credit cards? *¿Puedo pagar con tarjeta de crédito?*
cheap *barato*
expensive *caro*
post office *el correo*
visitor information center *la oficina de turismo*
open *abierto*
closed *cerrado*
every day *todos los días*

HOTELS & RESTAURANTS

Accommodations in Cuba run the spectrum, although standards vary widely and most hotels are overpriced. The types of facilities also vary, and it helps to understand the range when deciding where to stay. Tourism has boomed in recent years and hotels are often sold out well in advance, especially at Christmas and New Year's.

Havana offers a wide range of eating possibilities, and an ever-expanding range of places is enticing. Elsewhere menus can be repetitive and unimaginative, and usually restricted to fried chicken and perhaps a pork or fish dish, and rice and beans. Tourist hotels usually fare better, with more cosmopolitan options. State-run restaurants are often overpriced.

Making Reservations

Check details before reserving—particularly the availability of facilities for disabled guests or nonsmoking rooms, acceptance of credit cards (especially U.S. cards), and rates. Do not rely on booking by mail; email your reservation, and take your written confirmation with you.

Accommodations

The Cuban state owns all hotels and applies an overly-generous star-rating system.

Havana is blessed with charming historic properties, and most other major tourist destinations now boast at least one restored historic hotel. Most resort hotels (and top-of-the-line hotels in Havana) offer international standards, although large sections of the country are still served only by drab hotels dating back to the Soviet era.

Mid-range hotels are the norm, offering minimal service and often dowdy furniture. Recently built and/or renovated hotels usually feature state-of-the-art air-conditioning, safes, cable TV, and modern furniture. Most hotels now have Internet in the lobby; a few deluxe hotels have in-room Wi-Fi.

A handful of hotels target the eco-sensitive market, but few live up to their billing, and there are few wilderness or mountain lodges. Spa facilities also remain basic. Most resort hotels operate as all-inclusive centers under foreign management.

Private room rentals—*casas particulares*—offer good bargains, although standards vary markedly. Most offer the intimacy of a family environment and the option of home-cooked meals. Showers are often cold; warm (tepid) water may be provided by an electric element above the shower head. Cuban guests are permitted. Look for postings on home doors.

In all low-end hotels, sink plugs and toilet seats may be missing. Only top-end hotels provide toiletries.

Avoid "motels" and *posadas*, usually used for short-term sexual trysts. Since 2008, Cubans and foreigners may room together in hotels.

Unless otherwise stated, all hotels have dining rooms and private bathrooms, and are open year-round.

The following competing state entities operate hotels:
Cubanacán (*tel 7/833-4090, cubanacan.cu*)
Gaviota (*tel 7/866-8872, gaviota-grupo.com*)
Gran Caribe (*tel 7/204-0575, gran-caribe.cu*)
Habaguanex (*tel 7/867-1039, gaviotahotels.com*)
Islazul (*tel 7/842-7500, islazul.cu*)

It is generally more reliable to make reservations through a reputable travel agent specializing in Cuba, such as **Cuba Travel Network** (*cubatravelnetwork.com*).

Restaurants

Cuba is undergoing somewhat of a culinary revolution, and the entire restaurant scene is in flux. In 2013 the government initiated plans to turn all state restaurants into self-managing workers' cooperatives. Restrictions on private restaurants (*paladares*) have also been lifted, resulting in an explosion of *paladares*. Entrepreneurial Cubans experiment with newly available ingredients and international influences, often in partnership with foreign investors and/or chefs. In Havana, dozens of excellent *paladares* offer a wide variety of menu choices. Most other cities now boast a number of *paladares*, although menus tend to be more traditional *comida criolla*, while the ingredients are usually fresh and servings always filling.

State restaurants have also been forced to improve, assisted by a more regular availability of produce than in prior years (assisted by legalization of private markets). Menus vary little, but no longer is *"No hay!"* (There is none!) a ubiquitous mantra, although in some provincial restaurants *bocadillos* (sandwiches) of ham and cheese are often all that's available.

Most tourist hotels and restaurants are cocooned from the worst privations, though even there, most meals—usually continental fare—are bland by international standards. Away from major tourist resorts, service is usually slow and sometimes surly.

A selection of the best restaurants is given below. These include traditional *criollo* and more continental cuisine, with noted local associations wherever possible.

Organization & Abbreviations

Hotels and restaurants are listed by price, then in alphabetical order. The key at the bottom of each page explains the icons found after each listing.

B = Breakfast
L = Lunch
D = Dinner

MC = MasterCard
V = Visa

▶ HAVANA

HOTELS

GRAND HOTEL MANZANA KEMPINSKI
$$$$$
CALLE SAN RAFAEL,
BET. MONSERRATE & ZULUETA,
HABANA VIEJA
TEL 7/869-9100
kempinski.com

With your feet dangling in the covered pool, you can admire the spires of the Gran Teatro, the cupola of the Capitolio, and the roofs of the city. Hospitality is luxurious in these unique, contemporary rooms and suites. There is a wide choice of bars and restaurants.
196 rooms, 50 suites MC, V

HOTEL SANTA ISABEL
$$$$$
CALLE BARATILLO #9,
PLAZA DE ARMAS, HABANA
VIEJA
TEL 7/860-8201
gaviotahotels.com

Stately elegance and refinement define this gracious three-story hotel, once the palace of the Count of Santovenia. Offering an unrivaled location in the heart of Old Havana, it also boasts modern appointments. Antiques and works of art abound, as do

regal colonial touches. Some of the suites have canopied wrought-iron beds.
27 rooms, 10 suites MC, V

SOMETHING SPECIAL

HOTEL SARATOGA
$$$$$
PASEO DEL PRADO #603 &
DRAGONES, HABANA VIEJA
TEL 7/868-1000
EMAIL reservas@saratoga.co.cu
hotel-saratoga.com

Opened in 2005 as Havana's most resplendent hotel, this is the first hotel in Cuba to attain European levels of sophistication. The 19th-century facade is misleading: The interior is entirely new. Within, a gorgeous contemporary aesthetic, quality service, a great restaurant, and a hip bar make this the deluxe hotel of choice.
80 rooms, 7 suites Free MC, V

IBEROSTAR GRAND HOTEL PACKARD
$$$$$
CALLE PRADO N. 51, BET. CÁRCEL
& GENIOS, CENTRO HABANA
TEL 7/823-2100
www.iberostargrand
packard.com

The very recent construction at the intersection of Paseo and Malecòn has futuristic lines. The complex offers three restaurants, three bars, a cigar lounge, a wellness center, a gym, and even a pillow menu.
321 luxury rooms and suites In the lobby MC, V

MELIÁ COHIBA
$$$$$
PASEO, 1RA/3RA, VEDADO
TEL 7/833-3636
EMAIL jefe.ventas.
mco@meliacuba.com

A modern European-style high-rise at the foot of Paseo, this 22-story hotel is known

---

PRICES

HOTELS
An indication of the cost of a double room in the high season is given by **$** signs.

$$$$$	Over $200
$$$$	$150–$200
$$$	$100–$150
$$	$50–$100
$	Under $50

RESTAURANTS
An indication of the cost of a three-course meal without drinks is given by **$** signs.

$$$$$	Over $50
$$$$	$35–$50
$$$	$20–$35
$$	$10–$20
$	Under $10

---

for its gracious contemporary appointments. Spacious bathrooms gleam. A choice of fine restaurants includes Italian. An upscale shopping arcade and cabaret are highlights.
462 MC, V

MEMORIES MIRAMAR
$$$$$
AVE. 5TA, BET. 72 & 76, MIRAMAR
TEL 7/204-3584
memoriesresorts.com

Swank contemporary design sets this deluxe hotel apart. Spacious rooms boast lively decor. Three restaurants offer international cuisine, and facilities include tennis, squash, and volleyball.
427 MC, V

HOTEL IBEROSTAR PARQUE CENTRAL
$$$$
NEPTUNO & PASEO DEL
PRADO (ZULUETA), HABANA
VIEJA
TEL 7/860-6627
hotelparquecentral-cuba.com

A gracious conversion of a 19th-century mansion retains colonial hints in this modern hotel overlooking Parque Central. Foreign managed; efficient service. Choice of elegant eateries. Upscale boutiques. Cigar lounge.
🛈 281 🅿 🔁 🚹 🍴 ▨ 🏊
🍸 ▨ MC, V

🏨 HOTEL NACIONAL
$$$$
CALLES O & 21, VEDADO
TEL 7/836-3564
EMAIL reserva@gcnacio.gca. tur.cu
hotelnacionaldecuba.com
Havana's flagship hotel commands a headland overlooking the Malecón. Inaugurated on December 30, 1930, it has been declared a national monument. It has modern amenities and complete services, including a business center, cabaret, and atmospheric bars.
🛈 426 🅿 🔁 🚹 🍴 🏊 ▨
🍸 ▨ MC, V

🏨 HOTEL NH CAPRI
$$$$
CALLES 21 AND N, VEDADO
TEL 7/839-7207
www.nhcaprilahabana.com
Reopened in 2014, this landmark 1950s-Mafia-linked hotel has risen like a Phoenix from a decade-long hiatus. Stylishly contemporary, it has a rooftop pool and two casually elegant restaurants, and one of the city's top nightclubs occupies the former casino.
🛈 220 🅿 🚹 🍴 🏊 🍸
▨ MC, V

🏨 HOTEL RAQUEL
$$$$
CALLE SAN IGNACIO #103 & AMARGURA, HABANA VIEJA
TEL 7/860-8280
gaviotahotels.com
A gracious remodeling makes for a unique Havana hotel stay. This boutique hotel offers effusive art deco and beaux

arts period details and is designed in homage to Cuba's Jewish community. Guest rooms are appealing and well equipped, and proximity to Plaza Vieja is a plus (although streets just behind the hotel require caution).
🛈 25 🔁 🚹 🍴 🍸
▨ MC, V

🏨 HOTEL ROC PRESIDENTE
$$$$
CALZADA #110 AT AVE. DE LOS PRESIDENTES, VEDADO
TEL 7/838-1801
en.roc-hotels.com
Recently reopened after a complete restoration, this art deco high-rise near the Malecón boasts sumptuous classical French decor with modern furnishings and amenities. However, its location offers few advantages.
🛈 158 🅿 🔁 🚹 🏊
▨ MC, V

🏨 HOSTAL VALENCIA
$$$
CALLE OFICIOS #53 AT OBRAPÍA, HABANA VIEJA
TEL 7/801-1423
gaviotahotels.com
A gracious, if overpriced, property in the heart of the old town, this 18th-century town house recalls a Spanish posada, with wrought-iron balconies and period details. The ambience of the restaurant is pleasant. The bar and cigar shop are enjoyable as well.
🛈 12 🍴 ▨ MC, V

🏨 HOTEL BELTRÁN DE SANTA CRUZ
$$$
SAN IGNACIO #411 BET. E/ MURALLA & SOL, HABANA VIEJA
TEL 7/860-8330
gaviotahotels.com
Charm pervades this small historic hotel, housed in a restored mansion steps away from Plaza Vieja. Quintessential early colonial architecture

includes an ancient well.
🛈 11 🚹 ▨ MC, V

🏨 HOTEL CONDE DE VILLANUEVA
$$$
CALLE MERCADERES #202 AT LAMPARILLA, HABANA VIEJA
TEL 7/801-2293
EMAIL comercial.villanueva@ habaguanex.gaviota.cu
gaviotahotels.com
The former home of Count Claudio Martínez Pinillo (1789–1853) has metamorphosed into a delightful small inn with mezzanine humidor and sumptuous cigar lounge. Rooms on two levels surround a peaceful courtyard with rockers and feature beamed ceilings, terra-cotta tile floors, and tasteful modern appointments. One suite has a Jacuzzi.
🛈 9 🍴 ▨ MC, V

🏨 HOTEL FLORIDA
$$$
CALLES OBISPO & CUBA, HABANA VIEJA
TEL 7/801-3121
gaviotahotels.com
Stately 18th-century mansion tucked into Old Havana's liveliest thoroughfare, a short distance from the main plazas. Elegant appointments evoke a yesteryear graciousness. Bedrooms feature modern appointments and period decor. Chic restaurant and piano bar.
🛈 25 🅿 🍴 🚹 ▨ MC, V

🏨 HOTEL HABANA RIVIERA
$$$
PASEO & MALECÓN, VEDADO
TEL 7/836-4051
EMAIL reserva@gcrivie.gca.tur.cu
iberostar.com
Mafia associations lend a noir glamor to this high-rise 1950s grande dame which boasts a handsome lobby bar and top-class cabaret, plus a cigar store. A long-term refurbishment was

begun in 2014. Those rooms awaiting upgrade are dowdy and to be avoided, and dining options fail to inspire. The huge swimming pool is a highlight.

ⓘ 352 🅿 🔁 Ⓢ Ⓢ 🕿 🛥 🎽 🔗 MC, V

🏨 HOTEL LOS FRAILES
$$$

CALLE TENIENTE REY,
BET. OFICIOS & MERCADERES,
HABANA VIEJA
TEL 7/801-1796
gaviotahotels.com
An intimate option conjured from a colonial mansion and playing on a monastic theme. Staff dress in monks' habits *(habitos)* and decor includes life-size bronze monks. Wrought-iron and earth tones abound in small, dark but tastefully appointed rooms.

ⓘ 22 Ⓢ 🔗 MC, V

🏨 HOTEL MARQUÉS DE SAN FELIPE Y SANTIAGO DE BEJUCAL
$$$

CALLES OFICIOS #152 CORNER
AMARGURA, PLAZA DE SAN
FRANCISCO, HABANA VIEJA
TEL 7/801-2196
gaviotahotels.com
This restored colonial mansion is steps from major sites. Chic, contemporary stylings and furnishings, plus flat-screen TVs, contrast with aged coral stone walls. It has a small restaurant and an open-air atrium bar, but its principal draw is its superb location.

ⓘ 27 Ⓢ 🔗 Ⓢ 🔗 MC, V

🏨 HOTEL PALACIO O'FARRILL
$$$

CALLE CUBA #102 CORNER
CHACÓN
TEL 7/860-5080
gaviotahotels.com
Named for Ricardo O'Farrill, a Cuban slave and sugar trader of Cuban-Irish descent, this gracious boutique hotel

occupies a grand 18th-century manse in the heart of Habana Vieja. Rooms, on three levels, surround a soaring atrium lobby and are furnished with decor of the 18th, 19th, and 20th centuries. The mahogany-paneled bar—a soothing retreat—is renowned for live jazz.

ⓘ 35 🔗 🔗 MC, V

🏨 HOTEL TERRAL
$$$

MALECÓN AT CALLE LEALTAD,
CENTRO HABANA
TEL 7/860-2100
EMAIL jalojamiento.terral@
habaguanex.gaviota.cu
gaviotahotels.com
This small, newly minted boutique hotel has a sensational location on the Atlantic shorefront. A striking contemporary design extends to the decor in spacious well-lit rooms with modern conveniences. It has a bar, and superb restaurants are a short walk away.

ⓘ 14 🔗 Ⓢ 🔗 MC, V

🏨 MERCURE SEVILLA
$$$

AVE. TROCADERO #55 AT PRADO,
HABANA VIEJA
TEL 7/860-8560
EMAIL reserva@sevilla.gca.tur.cu
accorhotels.com
Built in 1980, this French-managed hotel has a Moorish motif. Newly renovated rooms boast gracious appointments, yet others remain drab and overpriced. Also offered are Internet access, a rooftop restaurant, and a pool.

ⓘ 178 🅿 🔁 🛥 🔗 🎽 🔗 MC, V

🏨 TRYP HABANA LIBRE
$$$

CALLES L & 23, VEDADO
TEL 7/834-6100
EMAIL tryp.habana.libre@
meliacuba.com
tryp-habanalibre.com
Landmark high-rise dating from the 1950s. Recently renovated

rooms offer stylish contemporary furnishings. Complete services include a bank, business center, shops, tour services, cabaret, and restaurants. Superb Vedado location.

ⓘ 532 🅿 🔁 Ⓢ Ⓢ 🕿 🎽 🔗 MC, V

🏨 CASA CONCORDIA
$$

CALLE CONCORDIA #151 APT B,
CORNER SAN NICOLÁS,
CENTRO HABANA
TEL 7/5254-5240
casaconcordia.net
Owned and operated by a British-Cuban couple, this charming apartment has been adorably restored and combines great ambience and comfort. Daily maid service included. Marvelous cityscapes through the fold-back balcony doors.

ⓘ 3 🔗 🔗 None

🏨 HOTEL AMBOS MUNDOS
$$

CALLE OBISPO #153
AT MERCADERES, HABANA VIEJA
TEL 7/860-9530
gaviotahotels.com
A 1920s eye-catcher favored by Ernest Hemingway (his Room 511 is now a museum). Rooms are small and modestly furnished, but offer the essentials. Lively piano bar. Rickety antique elevator. Superb location.

ⓘ 52 🅿 🔁 Ⓢ Ⓢ 🔗 MC, V

🏨 HOTEL DEL TEJADILLO
$$

CALLE TEJADILLO #12 AT
SAN IGNACIO, HABANA VIEJA
TEL 7/863-7283
gaviotahotels.com
Three converted colonial buildings form this gracious hotel. An elegant lobby opens to courtyards with fountains. Modern rooms offer space, safes, and period touches.

ⓘ 32 Ⓢ 🔗 MC, V

🏨 CASA MARYMAR

$

CALLE 173 #459 BET. E & F,
VEDADO
TEL 7/835-5056
EMAIL **marymar@nauta.cu**

Marzita and Margarita welcome you into their home with great care and discretion. The two colonial-style rooms have safes, private bathrooms with hot water, air-conditioning, and an entry that is separate from the rest of the house. Fresh fruit and an exquisite breakfast are served in the kitchen.

ⅈ 2 🍴 🌐 MC, V

SOMETHING SPECIAL

🏨 CASA PARTICULAR JORGE COALLA POTTS

$

CALLE I #456, BET. 21 & 23,
VEDADO
TEL 7/832-9032
EMAIL **jorgepotts@yahoo.co.uk**
havanaroomrental.com

This private room rental—one of Havana's finest—enjoys a splendid location in the heart of Vedado, close to the major hotels, shops, and entertainment centers. The impeccably clean bedroom is spacious, well lit, and airy, with fans, air-conditioning, and roomy bathroom.

ⅈ 1 🍴 🌐 None

🏨 HOSTAL DEL ÁNGEL

$

CALLE CUARTELES #118,
HABANA VIEJA
TEL 7/863-6738
pradocolonial.com

A lovely B&B awaits atop the marble staircase of this colonial townhouse. Stuffed with antiques, it has three bedrooms—one a simple attic option. The hostess is a delight.

ⅈ 3 🍴 🌐 None

RESTAURANTS

🍴 DON CANGREJO

$$$$

AVE. 1RA, BET. CALLES 16 & 18,
MIRAMAR
TEL 7/204-4169

This seafront mansion restaurant operated by the Ministry of Fisheries specializes in seafood and draws Cuba's elite. Crab claws, garlic shrimp cocktail, and paella are on the menu, which is backed by a large wine list. Fair weather permits patio dining.

🅿 🍴 🕐 Closed B 🌐 MC, V

🍴 EL FLORIDITA

$$$$

CALLE OBISPO #557 AT
MONSERRATE, HABANA VIEJA
TEL 7/867-1299

This famous Hemingway haunt specializes in lobster and seafood, but offers frogs'-leg soufflé and other French fare. Overbearing classical decor includes a lively mural. A (pricey) sugarless double daiquiri—"Papa Special"—is de rigueur. Bring a sweater. Expensive but worth the *fin de siècle* experience.

🅿 🍴 🕐 Closed B 🌐 MC, V

SOMETHING SPECIAL

🍴 LA GUARIDA

$$$$

CALLE CONCORDIA #418, BET.
GERVASIO & ESCOBAR, CENTRO
HABANA
TEL 7/866-9047
laguarida.com

Havana's hip showcase *paladar* is patronized by models, diplomats, and the elite. The operatic setting of the decrepit three-story town house may be familiar from the movie *Fresa y chocolate,* which was filmed here. The inventive French-*criollo* menu changes frequently, but eggplant caviar with red pepper coulis and fillet of snapper in white wine sauce are typical. A large wine list

spans the globe. Reservations recommended. After dinner, retire to the new rooftop alfresco bar.

🅿 🕐 Closed B 🌐 None

🍴 LA TORRE

$$$$

EDIFICIO FOCSA AT CALLES 17
& CALLE M, VEDADO
TEL 7/838-3088

Visit this restaurant atop the Focsa Building for the view from the 36th floor, though the fare is also among Havana's finest. The creative continental-*criollo* menu features foie gras, shrimp in honey, and poached fish in white wine with mashed potatoes and crisp vegetables, plus profiteroles. Also has a large wine list.

🅿 🍴 🕐 Closed B
🌐 MC, V

🍴 LA TORRE DEL ORO RESTAURANT

$$$$

SOFITEL SEVILLA, AVE. TRO-
CADERO #55, HABANA VIEJA
TEL 7/860-8560

Enjoy neoclassical decor and elegant place settings in this regal rooftop eatery with views over the city. Inspired French cuisine with savory sauces from a French chef. Note the Florentine-paneled ceiling.

🅿 🍴 🕐 Closed B & L
🌐 MC, V

🍴 RESTAURANTE ANACAONA

$$$$

HOTEL SARATOGA,
PASEO DEL PRADO #603
CORNER DRAGONES
TEL 7/868-1000

One of the city's chicest eateries, this Moorish-themed hotel restaurant has terrific ambience. Creative fusion cuisine can be overambitious, but most dishes—such as the saffron sea bass—are superb.

🍴 🌐 MC, V

🍴 TOCORORO
$$$$
CALLE 18 #302 AT AVE. 3RA,
MIRAMAR
TEL 7/204-2209
Elitist *criollo* cum continental
restaurant with fabulous
decor. The menu features
seafood brochette, grilled lamb
chops, and sushi (served in a
Japanese-themed room; open
seasonally). Live jazz musicians
often perform.
🅿 🅰 🕒 Closed B 🔲 MC, V

🍴 ATELIER
$$$
CALLE 5 #511 BET. PASEO & 2,
VEDADO
TEL 7/836-2025
One of Havana's top *pa-
ladares* draws local expats
and tour groups. Adorned
with contemporary art, this
late 19th-century mansion
has indoor and outdoor
space. Creative nouvelle
criollo dishes.
🕒 Closed B 🔲 None

🍴 CASA MIGLIS
$$$
CALLE LEALTAD #120
BET. ANIMAR & LAGUNAS,
CENTRO HABANA
TEL 7/864-1486
casamiglis.com
A remarkable ambience and
fine dining combine in this
converted townhouse. The
Swedish owner mixes Cuban
and globe-spanning flavors
and ingredients to produce
such mouthwatering dishes as
pork with herb-fried potatoes
in bean sauce. Live theme
nights on weekends.
🕒 Closed B 🔲 None

🍴 CORTE DI PRINCIPE
$$$
CALLE 9NA AT 74, MIRAMAR
TEL 5/255-9091
Run by an ebullient Italian
owner, this quintessential Ital-
ian restaurant offers a down-
home alfresco ambience and

superb cuisine, from pizzas
to gnocchi.
🅿 🕒 Closed B 🔲 None

🍴 EL ALJIBE
$$$
AVE. 7MA, BET. 24 & 26, MIRAMAR
TEL 7/204-1583
Open-air dining in an expansive
thatched eatery popular with
monied Cubans, tour groups,
and businessfolk. The house
dish—a consistently flavorful
and succulent roast chicken
in orange sauce—comes with
all-you-can-eat rice and beans,
fried plantains, French fries, and
salad. The menu is *criollo* and
includes coconut pie. Service is
surprisingly swift and efficient
for a state-run restaurant.
🅿 🕒 Closed B 🔲 MC, V

🍴 EL COCINERO
$$$
CALLE 26 BET. 11 & 13, VEDADO
TEL 7/832-2355
EMAIL elcocinerohabana@
yahoo.es
A converted former cooking
oil factory is the jaw-drawing
venue of this private restaurant,
accessed via a staircase spiral-
ing up the red-brick chimney.
Upscale restaurant offers
nouvelle Cuban dishes, and
the rooftop terrace lounge has
live music.
🅿 🕒 Closed B 🔲 None

🍴 LA CASA
$$$
CALLE 30 #865, BET. 26 & 41,
NUEVO VEDADO
TEL 7/881-7000
One of the city's best private
restaurants, this *paladar* is in a
1950s modernist home where
service is professional and the
multi-generational family fusses
over guests, who have included
everyone from Panamanian
presidents to Maradona. The
creative menu includes delights
such as octopus and onions,
and tasty caramel flan.
🅿 🅰 🕒 Closed B 🔲 None

🍴 LA COCINA DE LILLIAM
$$$
CALLE 48 #1311, BET. 13 & 15,
MIRAMAR
TEL 7/209-6514
This *paladar* combines a splen-
did aesthetic with a creative
continental-inspired *criollo*
menu featuring chicken breast
with pineapple, and a delicious
stew of lamb simmered with
onions and peppers. You dine
on comfy wrought-iron chairs
on the romantic garden patio,
or inside if inclement. Popular
with expatriates. Go early.
🅰 🕒 Closed B, Sat., & Dec.
🔲 None

🍴 LA MORALEJA
$$$
CALLE 25 #454, BET. I & J,
VEDADO
TEL 7/832-0963
This *paladar* restaurant is run by
a husband-and-wife team. The
courtyard exudes elegance and
often has live music, while an
air-conditioned section offers
relief from the heat. Try the
house special ceviche followed
by anise-and-garlic-flavored
shrimp in earthenware bowls.
🅿 🔲 None

🍴 LAS RUINAS
$$$
PARQUE LENIN, CALLE 100 &
CORTINA DE LA PRESA, BOYEROS
TEL 7/643-8286
A unique outskirts-of-Havana
blend of colonial ruins with
a modern concrete structure
featuring stained glass. The
expansive *criollo*-continental
menu includes lobster Bellevue
and shrimp enchilada.
🅿 🅰 🕒 Closed B & Mon.
🔲 MC, V

🍴 LE CHANSONNIER
$$$
CALLE J #257 BET. 15 & LINEA,
VEDADO
TEL 7/832-1576
lechansonnierhabana.com
One of the oldest *paladares* in

town, it offers steadfast service and recherché nouvelle Cuban dishes, enjoyed in a restored town house with soaring ceilings and avant-garde decor.

🕐 Closed L 🚫 None

🍴 EL TEMPLETE
$$

AVE. DEL PUERTO & NARCISO LÓPEZ, HABANA VIEJA
TEL 7/866-8807

An open-air restaurant facing the harbor, this breeze-swept state eatery specializes in seafood. Hits off the menu include oyster cocktail and a chocolate brownie.

🕐 Closed B 🚫 MC, V

SOMETHING SPECIAL

🍴 LA BODEGUITA DEL MEDIO
$$

CALLE EMPREDADO #207, BET. SAN IGNACIO & CUBA, HABANA VIEJA
TEL 7/867-1374

A Havana treat, this venerable *taberna* offers mouthwatering *criollo* dishes such as *ajiaco* (meat-and-vegetable stew) and roast pork with garlic yucca and fried plantain steeped in rum. The intimate bohemian setting is enhanced by troubadours and graffiti-covered walls. The *mojitos* can be insipid, and service can be slow.

🟦 🕐 Closed B 🚫 MC, V

🍴 LA TERRAZA
$$

CALLE REAL #161, COJÍMAR
TEL 7/766-5151

Famous seafood restaurant with Ernest Hemingway associations. Try the paella, washed down by the house cocktail, named in honor of the late patron Gregorio Fuentes. Fish soups, shrimp cocktails, and lobster dishes are offered.

🅿 🟦 🕐 Closed B 🚫 MC, V

🍴 LOS NARDOS
$$

PASEO DE MARTÍ #563, BET. TENIENT REY & DRAGONES, HABANA VIEJA
TEL 7/863-2985

In a decrepit building opposite the Capitolio, this upstairs eatery exudes ambience. Cuban staples include *ropa vieja* and shrimp in tomato sauce. Expect a long line. Avoid the sterile upper-floor restaurant.

🚫 MC, V

🍴 MAMA INÉS
$$

CALLE DE LA OBRAPÍA #60, HABANA VIEJA
TEL 7/862-2669

One of Fidel's former private chefs, Erasmo Hernández, owns and operates this charming little restaurant just off Plaza San Francisco. Erasmo infuses mouthwatering flavors in his nouvelle Cuban *criollo* dishes.

🕐 Closed B 🚫 None

🍴 MONEDA CUBANA
$$

CALLE EMPEDRADO #152, PLAZA DE LA CATEDRAL, HABANA VIEJA
TEL 7/861-5304

Just off Plaza de la Catedral, this *paladar* has heaps of ambience and serves excellent *criollo* fare. Choose an antique-filled room or the rooftop terrace, accessed by a tight staircase.

🕐 Closed B 🚫 None

🍴 EL DANDY
$

PLAZA DEL CRISTO, BET. VILLEGAS & BRASIL, HABANA VIEJA
TEL 7/867-6463
bareldandy.com

Good for a refreshment break. Quick, tasty dishes that won't be found on a typical menu. The atmosphere is relaxed and informal in a square that's absolutely vibrant. Take a good look around you: The photos and objects displayed are works

by Cuban artists and they're for sale.

🕐 Closed Mon. 🚫 None

🍴 LA CHUCHERÍA
$

CALLE 1RA BET. C & D, VEDADO
TEL 7/830-0708

Resembling a piece of Miami's South Beach transplanted, this popular *paladar* is *the* place to enjoy thin-crust pizza followed by a fruit milkshake.

🅿 🚫 None

▶ **FAR WEST**

CAYO LEVISA

🏨 VILLA CAYO LEVISA
$$

CAYO LEVISA, PINAR DEL RÍO
TEL 48/75-6501
hotelescubanacan.com

Known as a dive resort, this tranquil facility makes for a good beach break. Simple thatched cabins sprawl along a superb beach. Newer rooms in two-story units are plusher.

Water sports are offered.

[i] 40 [S] [C] MC, V

PINAR DEL RÍO

HOTEL VUELTABAJO
$$
CALLE MARTÍ #103
TEL/FAX 48/75-9381
islazul.cu
Lovingly restored, this historic property is graciously appointed and furnished with antiques and reproductions. It has the best restaurant in town, a pharmacy, plus Internet café, and is perfectly positioned for exploring.

[i] 39 [S] [C] MC, V

SAN DIEGO DE LOS BAÑOS

HOTEL MIRADOR DE SAN DIEGO
$
CALLE 23 FINAL
TEL 48/77-8338
islazul.cu
Handsome neocolonial property a stone's throw from the mineral spa. Recent refurbishment has blessed rooms with lively modern decor. An elegant restaurant serves *criollo* and continental fare.

[i] 30 [P] [S] [C] [C] MC, V

SOROA

VILLA HORIZONTES SOROA
$$
CARRETERA DE SOROA KM 8,
CANDELARIA
TEL 48/52-3534
EMAIL reserva@hvs.tur.cu
Mountain hotel. Simple cabins with modern appointments set around a landscaped pool, with a forest at hand for hikes and horseback rides. The restaurant serves *criollo* dishes.

[i] 49 [P] [S] [C]
[C] MC, V

CASA-ESTUDIO DE ARTE
$
CARRETERA SOROA, 5 MILES/
8.5 KM N OF CANDELARIA
TEL 48/59-8116
A delightful couple—Alyshka and Jesús—run this charming B&B, infused with their art. You'll sleep in a simple thatched cottage with a modern bathroom. Filling meals are served. Spanish-language tuition offered.

[i] 2 [P] [C] None

LAS TERRAZAS

HOTEL MOKA
$$
AUTOPISTA NACIONAL KM 52,
CANDELARIA
TEL 48/57-8555
hotelescubanacan.com
This charming eco-resort boasts neocolonial architecture in a woodsy hilltop location overlooking a lake and Las Terrazas village. Spanish tile, terracotta floors, and wood beams grace guest rooms.

[i] 26 [P] [S] [S] [C] [C] MC, V

LA FONDA DE MERCEDES
$$
UNIT 9, LAS TERRAZAS
TEL 48/57-8647
What a treat! The family of Mercedes Dache prepare delicious traditional *criollo* three-course meals served on an airy veranda overlooking the village. Reservations required.

[P] [C] Closed B [C] None

VIÑALES

HOTEL LOS JAZMINES
$$$
CARRETERA DE VIÑALES KM 23
TEL 48/79-6205
EMAIL reserva@vinales.tur.cu
Awesome views over the valley from this historic hilltop hotel with a choice of three types of accommodation. The *cabinas*

appeal more than the rooms in the main building.

[i] 78 [P] [S] [C]

HOTEL LA ERMITA
$$
CARRETERA A LA ERMITA KM 1.5
TEL 48/79-6071
EMAIL carpeta@ermita.tur.cu
hotelescubanacan.com
A spectacular setting overlooking Viñales Valley is the main draw for this open-plan property with pool set amid lawns. Rooms offer simple decor and columned balconies, but the restaurant is lackluster.

[i] 62 [P] [S] [C] [C] [C] MC, V

CASA DE DON TOMÁS
$$
CALLE SALVADOR CISNERO #140
TEL 48/79-6300
Hearty *criollo* fare in a mellowed 1822 wooden mansion with balcony dining. Troubadours entertain.

[P] [C] None

RESTAURANTE EL OLIVO
$$
CALLE CISNEROS #89
TEL 48/69-6654
The best of several newly opened *paladares,* this small restaurant offers a relatively sophisticated ambience. Mediterranean-inspired dishes include lasagna and Galician-style octopus.

[P] [C] Closed B [C] None

▶ ## WESTERN CUBA–NORTH

CAYO SANTA MARIA

SOL CAYO SANTA MARÍA
$$$
TEL 42/35-0200
sol-cayosantamaria.com
This Spanish-run resort caters to a predominantly European

[S] Nonsmoking [S] Air-conditioning [S] Indoor Pool [S] Outdoor Pool [S] Health Club [S] Wi-Fi [S] Credit Cards

crowd. Lively contemporary decor. Three restaurants, plus a bevy of bars, tennis courts, water sports, and entertainment.

🏨 300 🅿 🚫 🛗 🏊
🚫 MC, V

🏨 VILLAS LAS BRUJAS
$$
CAYO LAS BRUJAS, CAIBARIÉN
TEL 42/35-0023
EMAIL **reservas@villa.lasbrujas. co.cu**
The only budget option in the cays, this rustic enclave of wood-and-stone cabins sits atop craggy Punta Periquillo. A thatched restaurant offers views over a spectacular beach and cove. Remote setting good for birders and anglers.

🏨 24 🅿 🛗 🚫 MC, V

MATANZAS

🏨 HOTEL E VELASCO
$$$
CALLE CONTRERAS BET. SANTA TERESA & AYUNTAMIENTO
TEL 45/25-3880
EMAIL **recepcion3@velasco. mtz.tur.cu**
hotelescubanacan.com
A relative newcomer, this lovely boutique hotel overlooks the main square. Gracious furnishings and modern bathrooms. Some rooms lack windows. Suites overlook the plaza.

🏨 17 🚫 🛗 🚫 MC, V

🍽 PALADAR MALLORCA
$$
CALLE 334 #7705 BET. 77 & 79
TEL 45/28-3282
This excellent *paladar* is tucked out of sight atop the hill west of town. A globe-spanning menu ranges from fish fillet in white wine sauce with spinach to shrimp chop suey. Airy outdoor, plus air-conditioned, options.

🅿 🕐 Closed B 🚫 None

REMEDIOS

🏨 HOTEL E BARCELONA
$$$
CALLE JOSÉ PEÑA #67
TEL 42/39-5144
hotelescubanacan.com
A superb restoration of a derelict 19th-century mansion, this gracious hotel opened in 2013. Lovely decor and ambience, modern amenities, and a delightful lobby.

🏨 24 🅿 🚫 🛗 🚫 MC, V

🏨 HOTEL E MASCOTTE
$$
CALLE MÁXIMO GÓMEZ #114
TEL 42/39-5144
EMAIL **reservas@mascotte. vcl.tur.cu**
hotelescubanacan.com
Charming, recently restored small historic hotel. Modest yet gracious furnishings and modern appliances. On the main plaza.

🏨 10 🛗 🚫 MC, V

SANTA CLARA

🏨 HOSTAL LA CARIDAD
$
CALLE SAN PABLO #19, BET. ESTEVES & MÁXIMO GÓMEZ
TEL 42/22-7704
EMAIL **lacaridad8@gmail.com**
Splendid, quiet location on Plaza del Carmen, a short walk from downtown. Spacious, simply appointed rooms and clean, modern bathrooms. Filling meals are served upon request. Gracious hosts.

🏨 2 🅿 🛗 🚫 None

🍽 RESTAURANTE FLORIDA CENTER
$$
CALLE MAESTRA NICOLASA #56 BET. COLÓN & MACEO
TEL 42/20-8161
EMAIL **angel.floridacenter@ yahoo.com**
This restaurant is part of an antique-filled B&B, whose

owners offer delicious *criollo* dishes, such as shrimp enchilada and a huge seafood platter, served on a candlelit patio.

🕐 Closed B 🚫 None

VARADERO

HOTELS

🏨 BLAU VARADERO HOTEL
$$$$$
CARRETERA LAS MORLAS KM 15
TEL 45/66-7545
www.blau-varadero.com
Impressive all-inclusive resort with dramatic architecture featuring a skylit atrium lobby-lounge and sophisticated contemporary furnishings. Vast pool complex, state-of-the-art gym and theater, plus excellent choice of eateries.

🏨 395 🅿 🛗 � 🚊 🍴
🚫 MC, V

🏨 FIESTA AMERICANA PUNTA VARADERO
$$$$$
PUNTA HICACOS FINAL
TEL 45/66-9966
fiestamericana.com
Varadero's finest all-inclusive hotel—this one all-suite—enjoys a reclusive setting behind sand dunes at the tip of the peninsula. Gorgeous and calming contemporary aesthetic, a full complement of services, and well-trained staff.

🏨 633 🅿 🛗 🔄 🚊 🍴
🚫 MC, V

SOMETHING SPECIAL

🏨 MELIÁ MARINA VARADERO
$$$$$
AUTOPISTA DEL SUR & FINAL
TEL 45/66-7330
melia-marinavaradero.com
Setting a new standard in Varadero when it opened in 2013, this Spanish-run property anchors the new marina. A boldly contemporary resort

hotel, it offers a gorgeous aesthetic and Meliá's management know-how, plus a bevy of services, including ten fine-dining restaurants, and full-service spa. Accommodations include luxury apartments. A short distance from the beach, it's located bay side at the tip of the peninsula.

🏨 423 P 🚫 🛠 🏊 🏋
🗝 Most major cards

SOMETHING SPECIAL

🏨 MANSION XANADU
$$$$
AUTOPISTA SUR KM 8.5
TEL 45/66-8482 OR 66-7388
varaderogolfclub.com
Varadero's most exclusive address. Exquisite 1930s period decor recalls the days when Irénée du Pont lived here. Marble floors, wrought-iron beds, and throw rugs are mixed with modern accoutrements such as minibars and cable TV. Marble bathrooms boast walk-in showers. A superb restaurant and bar, plus unrivaled coastal views. Guests get privileges at Meliá Las Américas hotel. The mansion doubles as the clubhouse for Varadero Golf Club.

🏨 6 P 🚫 🛠 🗝 MC, V

🏨 VILLA PUNTA BLANCA
$$$$
AVE. KAWAMA FINAL
TEL 45/66-2411
EMAIL director@pblanca.mtz.tur.cu
A unique option, this intimate hotel at the western end of the peninsula combines three 1950s modernist villas. Spacious rooms have functional furnishings. It also has a restaurant and a bar.

🏨 21 P 🛠 🗝 MC, V

🏨 STARFISH CUATRO PALMAS
$$$
AVE. 1RA, BET. CALLES 60 & 64
TEL 45/66-7040
bluediamondresorts.com
A mid-range favorite of tour groups. Renovations have added modern decor and livelier ambience while retaining a Spanish colonial feel. Central location.

🏨 160 P 🚫 🛠 🏊 🏋
🗝 MC, V

🏨 CASA BENY
$
CALLE 55 #124 BET. 1RA & 2DA
TEL 45/61-1700
One of the best private room rental options in Varadero. The nicely furnished 1950s villa sits in a landscaped garden in the heart of the beach resort. Each bedroom has an en-suite bathroom. Secure parking. Breakfast (included in rates) is served on the garden patio.

🏨 3 P 🚫 🛠 🗝 None

RESTAURANTS

🍴 RESTAURANTE KIKE-KCHO
$$$
AUTOPISTA DEL SUR & FINAL
TEL 45/66-4115
melia-marinavaradero.com
On a pier over the bay at the Meliá Marina Varadero, this seafood restaurant is named for world-renowned Cuban artist Kcho, whose artwork is featured as decor. Grilled lobster is a specialty.

P 🛠 Closed B 🗝 None

🍴 RESTAURANTE LA FONDUE
$$$
AVE. 1RA, CORNER 62
TEL 45/66-7747
A one-of-a-kind restaurant serving a variety of fondues,

including specialty cheeses such as Gouda and Sbrinz. Elegant place settings, a large wine list, and soothing music.

🚫 🛠 Closed B 🗝 MC, V

🍴 PALADAR VARADERO 60
$$
CALLE 60 CORNER 3RA
TEL 45/61-3986
A popular *paladar* known for its wood-fired barbecue grill, and retro 1960s decor. The menu ranges from traditional *criollo* fare to more inventive continental creations, such as shrimp with brandy to crêpe desserts with fruit sauce.

P 🛠 Closed B 🗝 None

SOMETHING SPECIAL

🍴 SALSA SUÁREZ
$$
CALLE 31 #103
TEL 45/61-4194
A superb *paladar* with a chic ambience and both air-conditioned and alfresco dining. The bargain-priced gourmet dishes here truly impress. The weekly menu might include such mouthwatering treats as beef carpaccio with capers and olive oil, spiced octopus with mussels, and the house special: chicken and pork with Roquefort cheese, plus peppers and onions. Excellent service.

P 🛠 Closed B & Tues.
🗝 None

▶ WESTERN CUBA— SOUTH

CIENFUEGOS

🏨 HOTEL JAGUA
$$
CALLE 37, BET. 0 & 2
TEL 43/55-1003
EMAIL jefe.ventas.ija@meliacuba.com
Recent restorations have

bestowed modern decor and amenities on this high-rise, although it suffers quirks such as power outages and sudden loss of hot water. Rooms offer fine views. Has nightly music, plus shops and touristic services.

 149 🅿 🚫 🅂
🏊 🛗 🚭 MC, V

🏨 HOTEL LA UNIÓN
$$
AVE. 54 AT CALLE 31
TEL 43/55-1020
EMAIL hotel.launion@meliacuba.com
A restored colonial-era hotel one block from the main plaza. This charmer combines traditional ambience with modern amenities, including a gym and sauna. Bedrooms are appointed with antique reproductions.

🛏 49 🅿 🚫 🅂
🏊 🛗 🚭 MC, V

🏨 FINCA LOS COLORADOS
$
CARRETERA DE PASACABALLO KM 18, PLAYA RANCHO LUNA
TEL 43/54-8044
This casa particular has pleasant guest rooms combining antiques and modern fittings. Better-than-average meals can be enjoyed beneath an arbor. Gracious host and a dramatic albeit lonesome setting.

🛏 2 🅿 🚫 🚭 None

SOMETHING SPECIAL

🍴 FINCA DEL MAR
$$
CALLE 35 BET. AVE. 18 & 20, PUNTA GORDA
TEL 52/82-4133
A stellar restaurant by any standard, this paladar is overseen by a savvy owner. Choose alfresco or air-conditioned sections. Service is prompt and friendly, but it's the dishes that most impress. The globe-spanning menu includes curried chicken, lamb with herbs and olive oil, and grilled lobster—all prepared to perfection.

🅿 🕘 Closed B 🚭 None

🍴 VILLA LAGARTO
$$
CALLE 35 #4B, PUNTA GORDA
TEL 43/51-9966
villalagarto.com
This popular open-air paladar at the very tip of the Punta Gorda peninsula has a lovely bayfront setting. It specializes in all-you-can-eat set criollo meals, including roast pork, seafood, and often rabbit.

🕘 Closed B 🚭 None

🍴 HOSTAL BAHÍA
$
AVE. 20 CORNER CALLE 35, PUNTA GORDA
TEL 43/52-6598
One of the nicest casas particulares in town, this well-run option offers cozy comfort and modern facilities. Bay views from shaded balconies. Breezes ease through the cross-ventilated upstairs lounge, and the Finca del Mar paladar adjoins.

🛏 4 🅿 🚭 None

PLAYA GIRÓN

🍴 RESTAURANTE EL COCODRILO
$$
CARRETERA DE LA CIENAGA
TEL 52/82-9686
Crocodile features on the menu of this African-style thatched restaurant and bar overhanging the lagoon at La Boca de Guamá. The menu is wholeheartedly criollo. Splendid ambience.

🅿 🚫 🕘 L only 🚭 None

PLAYA LARGA

🏨 HOSTAL ENRIQUE
🍴 $$
CALLE CALETÓN
TEL 45/98-7425
The choice B&B in Playa Larga also doubles as a restaurant popular with tour groups. This solid coral-stone home is steps from the beach. All rooms are pleasantly furnished and have private bathrooms. Breeze-swept rooftop solarium with bay views. Enrique arranges fishing and nature activities. Filling and delicious seafood meals are served to nonguests by request.

🛏 5 🅿 🕘 Closed B 🚭 None

SANCTI SPÍRITUS

🏨 HOTEL E RIJO
$$
CALLE MÁXIMO GÓMEZ, PLAZA HONORATO DEL CASTILLO
TEL 41/32-8588
islazul.cu
This restored colonial mansion turned hostelry is entered via grand carriage doors. Terracotta tiles, wrought-iron lamps, and beamed ceilings hark back in time. Amenities include cable TV and period-themed art.

🛏 16 🅂 🚭 None

🏨 HOSTAL LAS AMÉRICAS
$
CARRETERA CENTRAL #157 SUR
TEL 41/32-3984
An excellent B&B a short distance from the town center and close to the bus station. This pleasantly furnished 1950s home has a lovely garden where meals are served.

🛏 2 🅿 🚭 None

🍴 MESÓN DE LA PLAZA
$
CALLE MÁXIMO GÓMEZ #34
TEL 41/32-8546
A Spanish bodega serving classic Cuban-Iberian fare such as pollo asado and garbanzos with pork and sausage washed down by sangria. The menu and the surroundings offer a charming, rough-hewn ambience.

🕘 Closed B 🅂 🚭 MC, V

TRINIDAD

SOMETHING SPECIAL

🏨 GRAN IBEROSTAR TRINIDAD
$$$$
CALLE MARTÍ #262 CORNER LINO PÉREZ
TEL 41/99-6070
EMAIL comercial@iberostar.trinidad.co.cu
iberostar.com
Supremely elegant, this hotel is Cuba's most upscale city hotel outside Havana. A three-story colonial structure with 21st-century facilities and amenities, the Iberostar exudes sophistication with its gleaming marble floors and wrought-iron chandeliers. Deluxe rooms are furnished in colonial style. It also has a billiards room and Internet café, a snazzy cigar lounge, and a gourmet restaurant that serves a prix-fixe dinner. No children.

🛏 40 🚭 ⬆ 🛜 Café 🏧 MC, V

🏨 CASA PARTICULAR CARLOS SOTOLONGO
$
CALLES SIMÓN BOLÍVAR & FRANCISCO JAVIER
TEL 41/99-4169
Located directly overlooking Plaza Mayor, this exquisite colonial home is filled with antiques and fine art. The two rooms vary: One is modern and air-conditioned, whereas the second is colonial and features a metal-frame bed.

🛏 2 🏧 None

SOMETHING SPECIAL

🏨 HOSTAL CASA MUNOZ
$
CALLE MARTÍ #401 CORNER SANTIAGO ESCOBAR
TEL/FAX 41/99-3673
trinidadphoto.com
Dating back to 1800, this private *casa particular* is a treasure, replete with antiques that draw tour groups.

Modern bathrooms dispense piping-hot water, and a patio provides a calm spot for reading and sun. The owner—an accomplished photographer—offers guided horseback excursions. Good for families.

🛏 2 🅿 🚭 🛜 🛜 MC, V

🍴 VISTA GOURMET
$$
CALLEJÓN DE GALDÓS
TEL 41/99-6700
The best views in town from this hilltop *paladar* with breeze-swept, shaded rooftop dining. An excellent dinner buffet is offered, and à la carte lunches include lamb in Pernod and other flavorful *criollo* dishes. Up a cobbled sloping alley off Plaza Seguarte.

🕐 Closed B 🏧 None

🍴 GUITARRA MÍA
$
JESÚS MENÉNDEZ #19
TEL 41/99-3452
This small and cozy *paladar* is lent atmosphere by live musicians. The chef works magic with local ingredients to create unusual interpretations of *criollo* fare.

🅿 🕐 Closed B 🏧 None

▶ CENTRAL CUBA

CAMAGÜEY

🏨 COLÓN HOTEL MELIÁ
$$$
CALLE REPÚBLICA #472
BET. SAN JOSÉ & SAN MARTÍN
TEL 32/25-1520
meliacuba.es
This exquisite conversion of a colonial-era hotel offers comfortable rooms with modern amenities. A good restaurant, plus an atmospheric bar, an Internet café, and a tour desk.

🛏 48 🚭 🛜 Café 🏧 MC, V

🏨 HOTEL E CAMINO DE HIERRO
$$$
PLAZA DE LA SOLIDARIDAD #76
TEL 32/28-4264
Opened in 2013 as a fine restoration of a grand mansion, it has charming accommodations combining antique reproductions and LCD TVs, plus Wi-Fi. An excellent restaurant and fine location.

🛏 10 🚭 🛜 Free 🏧 MC, V

🏨 GRAN HOTEL MELIÁ
$$
CALLE MACEO #67, BET. IGNACIO AGRAMONTE & GENERAL GÓMEZ
TEL 32/29-2093
meliacuba.es
Caringly restored 18th-century hotel in the heart of the historic city. Antiques and a period aesthetic abound. Piano bar. The rooftop restaurant serves continental buffets, plus a creative *criollo* menu featuring lobster enchiladas. Caters to both Cubans and foreigners.

🛏 72 🅿 🚭 🚭 🏊 🏧 MC, V

🍴 RESTAURANT 1800
$$
PLAZA SAN JUAN DE DÍOS
TEL 32/28-3619
1800restaurante.com
An exceptional and romantic candlelit private restaurant right on a cobbled plaza, it is antique filled and serves an excellent buffet, plus à la carte dishes.

🕐 Closed B 🏧 None

CAYO COCO & CAYO GUILLERMO

🏨 MELÍA CAYO COCO
$$$$$
CAYO COCO
TEL 33/30-1180
melia-cayococo.com
Sprawling, all-inclusive resort under Spanish management. Exquisite landscaping

makes good use of the lagoon-and-beach setting. Full range of services and sports facilities includes water sports, boutiques, and nightly entertainment.

[i] 250 P ⊙ ⊕ 🏊 🍸 ⊗ MC, V

IBEROSTAR DAIQUIRÍ
$$$$
CAYO GUILLERMO
TEL 33/30-1650
EMAIL ventas@ibsdaiq.gca.tur.cu
iberostar.com

The Iberostar Daiquirí is a fine foreign-managed, all-inclusive hotel on a scintillating beach. Contemporary Spanish-style public areas feature marble. Lively furnishings blend with modern appointments, including bathrooms with colonial tiles. A full range of activities includes water sports.

[i] 312 P ⊙ ⊕ 🏊 🍸 ⊗ MC, V

🏨 SOL CAYO GUILLERMO
$$$$
CAYO GUILLERMO
TEL 33/30-1760
meliacuba.com

Lively tropical colors abound at this mid-range all-inclusive resort. King-size beds and elegant furnishings. Choice of restaurants and complete range of water sports. Activities include theme parties.

[i] 268 P ⊙ ⊕ 🏊 🍸 ⊗ MC, V

SANTA LUCÍA

🏨 GRAN CLUB SANTA LUCÍA
$$$
PLAYA SANTA LUCÍA
TEL 32/33-6109
hotelescubanacan.com

The best of a motley bunch of hotels in Santa Lucia, this three-star resort is popular with Italian package groups. Safes, minibars, and TVs are

standard. Beach volleyball, water sports, car rental, and excursions are offered.

[i] 252 P ⊙ ⊕ 🏊 🍸 ⊗ MC, V

▶ WESTERN ORIENTE

BARTOLOMÉ MASÓ

🏨 VILLA SANTO DOMINGO
$
CARRETERA LA PLATA, KM 16
SANTO DOMINGO
TEL 23/56-5635

Sitting over the Río Yara at the base of Pico Turquino, this rustic complex is a good base for hikers. Simple rooms have safes and refrigerators. A video room, game room, and bar are on hand. It also has roomy safari-style tents.

[i] 20 P ⊕ ⊗ None

BAYAMO

🏨 HOTEL E ROYALTON
$
CALLE MACEO #53,
PLAZA CÉSPEDES
TEL 23/42-2290
islazul.cu

A recently restored historic hotel. A marble staircase leads to the small, modestly furnished rooms (one room is handicapped accessible). Cable TV and telephones are standard. A small nightclub is popular with locals.

[i] 33 P ⊕ ⊗ None

CAYO SAETÍA

🏨 VILLA CAYO SAETÍA
$$
CAYO SAETÍA, MAYARÍ
TEL 24/51-6900
EMAIL ejecutivo.comercial@cayosaetia.co.cu
gaviota-grupo.com

Small, secluded resort on an island sheltering African

PRICES

HOTELS
An indication of the cost of a double room in the high season is given by **$** signs.

$$$$$	Over $200
$$$$	$150–$200
$$$	$100–$150
$$	$50–$100
$	Under $50

RESTAURANTS
An indication of the cost of a three-course meal without drinks is given by **$** signs.

$$$$$	Over $50
$$$$	$35–$50
$$$	$20–$35
$$	$10–$20
$	Under $10

game. Rustic accommodations feature TVs, refrigerators, and telephones. Jeep and horseback excursions are offered. Beaches lie at hand. Animals shot on "safari" stare down in the restaurant, where antelope is on the menu.

[i] 12 P ⊕ 🏊 ⊗ MC, V

GIBARA

🏨 IBEROSTAR GIBARA ORDOÑO
$$
CALLE J. PERALTA BET. DONATO
MARMÓL & INDEPENDENCIA
TEL 24/84-4448
iberostar.com

Occupying a beautiful and recently restored centenary mansion, this hotel is pleasantly furnished and has the best restaurant in town. Stunning murals in the master suite.

[i] 21 ⊙ ⊕ ⊗ MC, V

🏨 LA CASA DE LOS AMIGOS
$
CALLE CÉSPEDES #15 BET. LUZ
CABALLEROS & PERALTA

TEL 24/84-4115
EMAIL lacasadelosamigos@
yahoo.fr
A French-Cuban couple have
adorned this superb B&B with
avant-garde art and delightful
modern bathrooms and lovely,
if quirky, furnishings. Meals
served on a garden patio with
thatched bar.

🈁 3 🚭 ❄ 🛇 None

GUARDALAVACA

🏨 PARADISUS RÍO DE ORO
$$$$$
PLAYA ESMERALDA, CARRETERA
GUARDALAVACA
TEL 24/43-0090
paradisus-riodeoro.com
Colorful contemporary decor
and a full roster of amenities in
this modern, upscale all-inclusive. Accommodation is
in junior suites, some with
king-size beds. Cable TV, safes,
and minibars are standard.
Beach volleyball and scuba diving. Car rental and excursions.
Internet access.

🈁 354 P 🚭 ❄ 🏊 🛗
🛜 Free 🛇 MC, V

🏨 BRISAS GUARDALAVACA
$$$$
GUARDALAVACA
TEL 24/43-0218
hotelescubanacan.com
Well-run all-inclusive serving
a predominantly Canadian
clientele. Choice of accommodations, including suites
and villas, all in a neoclassical
theme. Beauty salon, shops,
tennis, water sports center,
and a choice of restaurants.

🈁 437 P 🚭 ❄ 🏊 🛗 🛇 MC, V

🍴 RESTAURANT LA MAISON
$$
UPHILL, 100 YARDS/91 M
W OF PLAYA MAYOR
TEL 55/32-1066
Although the only *paladar*
competing with the state-run
resort restaurants, it outshines
them all. Tremendous hilltop
views and filling *criollo* meals.
Also paella. Patio dining
shaded by an arbor.

P 🕐 Closed B 🛇 None

HOLGUÍN

🏨 HOSPEDAJE LA PALMA
$
CALLE MACEO #52, BET. 16 & 18
TEL 24/42-4683
Once elegant 1950s home
with a lounge and dining
room graced by period furnishings and the gracious
host family's own accom-
plished works of art.
Delightfully appointed
bedrooms, and a huge rear
garden. Quiet neighborhood,
within walking distance of the
historic center.

🈁 2 P ❄ 🛇 None

🏨 VILLA LIBA
$
CALLE MACEO #46
TEL 53/42-3823
EMAIL marielayoga@cristal.hlg.
sld.cu
This *casa particular* retains its
original (if slightly jaded) 1950s
decor and furnishings. The middle-class home is one of Cuba's
finest private room rentals.
Rooms share bathrooms. A
vine arbor graces the patio.
Jorge, the host, is a fascinating
conversationalist.

🈁 2 P ❄ 🛇 None

LAS TUNAS

🏨 EL CABALLO BLANCO
🍴 $
CALLE FRANK PAÍS #85 CORNER
GONZALO DE QUESADA
TEL 31/37-3658
This impressive *casa particular*
rents two nicely appointed
rooms with modern bath-
rooms. Its entrepreneurial
owner also runs the best
paladar in town, with patio
dining and delicious *criollo*
dishes such as *ropa vieja* and
garlic shrimp. Open for
breakfast.

🈁 2 🚭 ❄ 🛇 None

🏨 HOTEL LAS TUNAS
$
AVE. 2 DE DICIEMBRE
TEL 31/34-5014
This soulless five-story hotel
serves mostly Cubans, but
is one of only two hotels in
town. Its many amenities
include car rental and bar.

🈁 142 P 🚭 ❄ 🛇 MC, V

MANZANILLO

🏨 CASA DE ADRIAN Y TONIA
$
CALLE MÁRTIRES DE VIETNAM
#49 CORNER CARIDAD
TEL 23/57-3028
An excellent location overlooking the city is a highlight
at this beautifully furnished
and kept B&B run by a charming couple. The independent
apartment has a rooftop
terrace and overlooks Monumento Celia Sánchez.

🈁 1 🚭 ❄ 🛇 None

MAREA DEL PORTILLO

🏨 CLUB AMIGO MAREA DEL PORTILLO
$$
CARRETERA GRANMA KM 12.5,
PILÓN
TEL 23/59-7102
hotelescubanacan.com
Most upscale of four local
hotels; refurbished in 2014,
this hilltop all-inclusive
offers modern decor and
amenities. Expansive pool
terrace with swim-up bar.
Boutiques, car rental,
excursions, and cabaret.

🈁 283 P 🚭 ❄ 🏊 🛗 🛇 MC, V

🚭 Nonsmoking ❄ Air-conditioning 🏊 Indoor Pool 🏊 Outdoor Pool 🛗 Health Club 🛜 Wi-Fi 🛇 Credit Cards

PINARES DE MAYARÍ

🏨 VILLA PINARES DE MAYARÍ

$

LOMA LA MENSURA, MAYARÍ
TEL 24/52-1412
EMAIL **comercial@vpinares.co.cu**
gaviota-grupo.com

No-frills mountain lodge with rustic wooden cottages and rooms, fitted with hot showers. Operates as an eco-resort offering hiking, horseback rides, and spa treatments. Communal meals.

ℹ️ 29 🅿️ 🔆 🏊 📺
🆖 MC, V

▶ EASTERN ORIENTE

SANTIAGO DE CUBA

HOTELS

🏨 IBEROSTAR HERITAGE 🍴 CASA GRANDA

$$$$

CALLE HEREDIA #201,
BET. SAN FÉLIX & SAN PEDRO
TEL 22/65-3021
iberostar.com

Superb location overlooking Parque Céspedes. Newly restored, this grande dame offers modern conveniences. Suites boast antiques. Parisian-style patio lobby bar good for watching events in the plaza; it also serves inexpensive, filling meals. The **Restaurante Casa Grande** offers a touch of class, plus continental and *criollo* dishes and value breakfasts.

ℹ️ 58 🅿️ 🔆 📺 🆖 MC, V

🏨 MELÍA SANTIAGO DE CUBA

$$$$

AVE. LAS AMÉRICAS & CALLE M,
REPARTO SUEÑO
TEL 22/68-7070
melia-santiagodecuba.com

Santiago's showcase hotel,

this modern high-rise offers spacious rooms with a contemporary aesthetic and oversize bathrooms. Amenities include a cigar store, beauty parlor, business center, sauna, and rooftop bar with cabaret. Choice of four restaurants. Spanish managed.

ℹ️ 302 🅿️ 🔆 🏊 📺
🆖 MC, V

🏨 HOTEL SAN JUAN

$$

CARRETERA SIBONEY KM 1.5,
LOMA SAN JUAN
TEL 22/68-7200
islazul.cu

Suburban hotel adjacent to San Juan Hill. Modestly furnished in contemporary decor. Upper-level rooms are preferred for their lofty ceilings. Tour desk and car rental. A cabaret is hosted.

ℹ️ 110 🅿️ 🔆 🏊 📺
🆖 MC, V

🏨 CASA PARTICULAR ESMERALDA GONZÁLEZ

$

AVE. PUJOL #107 & 5TA, REPARTO
VISTA ALEGRE
TEL 22/64-6341
EMAIL **rachelbarreriro@yahoo.es**

Pleasant middle-class 1950s home with a well-lit guest room with period furnishings and a gleaming bathroom. Separate entrance. Leafy suburban location.

ℹ️ 1 🅿️ 🔆 🆖 None

🏨 CASA PARTICULAR FLORINDA CHAVIANO

$

CALLE I #58, 2DA/3RA, REPARTO
SUEÑO
TEL 22/65-3660

Modern, nicely furnished home with a TV lounge, and rear patio with arbor good for enjoying home-cooked meals. Well-lit guest room features a clean, modern bathroom. Quiet neighborhood, close to Moncada.

ℹ️ 1 🅿️ 🔆 🆖 None

🏨 HOSTAL AMANECER

$

CALLE SANTA RITA #465
BET. RELOJ & CALVARIO
TEL 22/62-2886
it.hotels.com

This recently opened B&B inside a city home is just a few blocks away from the Parque Céspedes. Its simply furnished rooms share a large living room and terrace. On request, delicious meals and tours of the area are available.

ℹ️ 2 🔆 🔆 🆖 None

🏨 HOTEL E SAN BASILIO

$

CALLE SAN BASILIO #403 BET.
CALVARIO & CARNICERÍA
TEL 22/65-1702
hotelescubanacan.com

A delightful conversion of a colonial mansion, retaining period decor. Modern amenities include satellite TVs and modern bathrooms. In the heart of downtown, steps from Parque Céspedes.

ℹ️ 8 🔆 🆖 None

RESTAURANTS

🍴 RESTAURANTE LA FONTANA

$$$

HOTEL MELIÁ SANTIAGO,
AVE. DE LAS AMÉRICAS
TEL 22/68-7070

This alfresco eatery is one of the best in town and serves Italian and European dishes, such as fish fillet with capers in white wine sauce. Popular with monied locals.

🅿️ 🆖 MC, V

🍴 PALADAR SALÓN TROPICAL

$

CALLE FERNÁNDEZ MARCANÉ
#310, BET. 9 & 10,
REPARTO SANTA BARBARA
TEL 53/64-1161

One of the few *paladares* in town providing both ambience and value. You dine beneath an arbor on a rooftop patio. The *criollo* menu includes garbanzo stew and a barbecue chicken special.

P ⊕ Closed B, Mon.–Fri. None

🍴 RUMBA CAFÉ
$
CALLE SAN FÉLIX #455 BET. SAN FRANCISCO & SAN GERÓNIMO
The perfect place to break an exploration of Reparto Los Hoyos, this tapas bar and café has a European savoir faire, thanks to an Italian owner, Fabio. Great pastries and desserts.

⊕ Closed Sun None

BARACOA

🏨 HOSTAL LA HABANERA
$$
CALLE MACEO #126 CORNER FRANK PAÍS
TEL 21/64-1565
gaviota-grupo.com
This is the nicest place in town, with a pleasing colonial ambience and modern accoutrements, including snazzy bathrooms. Above-average restaurant and bar.

🚪 10 🚭 MC, V

🏨 HOTEL EL CASTILLO
$$
CALLE GALIXTO GARCÍA, LOMA EL PARAÍSO
TEL 21/64-5165
gaviota-grupo.com
A handsome and respectful conversion of an ancient castle, with grand views over town and toward El Yunque. Terracotta tiles, plentiful hardwoods, and modern appointments in guest rooms. A small swimming pool studs the forecourt. Car rental and tour desk. A bodega-style restaurant serves regional *criollo* meals.

🚪 62
P 🚭 🏊 MC, V

🏨 HOSTAL RÍO MIEL
$
AVENIDA MALECÓN CORNER CIRO FRIAS
TEL 21/64-1207
www.gaviotahotels.com
Near Malecón, the hostal has twelve rooms distributed on three floors and a shared dining room where guests can socialize. The furnishings are simple and the bathrooms are modern and have hot water.

🚪 12 🚭 None

🏨 CASA PARTICULAR EL MIRADOR
$
CALLE MACEO #86, 24 DE FEBRERO/10 DE OCTUBRE
TEL 21/64-2647
EMAIL ilianacu09@gmail.com
Colonial mansion with breeze-swept rooms upstairs. A balcony has rockers, and a rear veranda offers views of El Yunque. Shared bathroom. Gracious hostess.

🚪 2 🚭 None

SOMETHING SPECIAL

🍴 EL POETA
$$
CALLE MACEO #159 BET. CIRO FRIAS & CÉSPEDES
TEL 21/64-3017
Dining at this one-of-a-kind *paladar* is memorable, not simply for the rusticity of the venue, nor the excellent cuisine typical of the region, such as spicy shrimp with coconut-flavored rice, and crab-stuffed tamales. The main draw is Pablo Leyva, the eccentric owner, who, dressed in his *campesino* gear, sings impromptu *décima* verses in praise of female patrons. One block east of Plaza Independencia.

P ⊕ Closed B 🚭 None

🍴 PALADAR LA COLONIAL
$
CALLE MARTÍ #123,

BET. MARTÍ & FRANK PAÍS
TEL 52/71-8558
Exquisite colonial decor in this historic home turned private restaurant, today the only *paladar* in town. Filling portions and efficient service. The menu is heavy on seafood, including swordfish. Dine early, as many items sell out quickly.

🚭 ⊕ Closed B None

CHIVIRICO

🏨 BRISAS SIERRA MAR
$$$
CARRETERA DE CHIVIRICO KM 60
TEL 22/32-9110
hotelescubanacan.com
All-inclusive hilltop property overlooking Playa Sevilla Guamá. Expansive views from the lively pool terrace with waterslide. Complete amenities include entertainment, water sports, choice of bars, and excursions. Popular with Canadians.

🚪 200 P 🚭 🏊 🏋
🚭 MC, V

GUANTÁNAMO

🏨 CASA SEÑOR CAMPOS
$
CALLE CALIXTO GARCÍA #718 BET. NARSICO LÓPEZ & JESÚS DEL SOL
TEL 21/35-1759
EMAIL mcamposcreme@gmail.com
Simple yet spacious accommodations with modern bathrooms in this family home with yesteryear decor. Filling breakfasts are served.

🚪 3 🚭 None

🏨 HOTEL MARTÍ
$
CALLE CALIXTO GARCÍA AT AGUILERA
TEL 21/32-9500
islazul.cu
A newcomer adjoining the main plaza, this modest option provides comfy rooms with modern bathrooms. Restaurant, plus rooftop bar with

Wi-Fi. A delightful café and chocolate shop adjoins.

(i) 21 **P** **(S)**
(WiFi) Free in bar **(S)** None

🍴 **MIRADOR LA GOBERNADORA**
$
GLORIETA, 14 MILES (20 KM) E OF GUANTÁNAMO
TEL 21/57-8908
A simple menu with ham and cheese sandwiches, pizza, and grilled chicken plays second fiddle to the superb hilltop location of this breeze-swept open-air restaurant overlooking the bay and U.S. naval base. Soviet-made tanks can often be viewed on maneuver below.

P **(S)** None

PARQUE NACIONAL ALEJANDRO DE HUMBOLDT

🏨 **VILLA MAGUANA**
$$
CARRETERA DE MOA BAHÍA DE TACO, KM 22
TEL 21/64-1204
www.gaviotahotels.com
A reclusive historic villa-hotel nestled on golden sands backed by forested mountains. Charming albeit simple furnishings plus satellite TVs. A recent upgrade includes newer rooms in fourplex wooden two-story cabins.

(i) 16 **P** **(S)** **(S)** None

▶ ## ARCHIPIÉLAGO DE LOS CANARREOS

CAYO LARGO

🏨 **SOL PELICANO**
$$$$
PLAYA LINDAMAR, 3 MILES (5 KM) FROM AIRPORT
TEL 45/24-8333
sol-pelicano.com
Low-rise, sprawling resort in colonial style. Guest rooms face the ocean: Deluxe rooms feature TVs and minibars. Water sports are offered. A piano bar, nightclub, and cabaret draw guests from other hotels. Though relatively new, this hotel looks worn and tired.

(i) 307 **P** **(S)** **(S)**
(S) **(S)** MC, V

🏨 **SOL CAYO LARGO**
$$$
PLAYA LINDAMAR, 3 MILES (5 KM) FROM AIRPORT
TEL 45/24-8260
sol-cayolargo.com
Opened in 2001 and still looking fresh, this beautiful, all-inclusive property offers Cayo Largo's only truly quality hotel that lives up to its star rating. Sponge-washed walls and tropical color schemes add vitality. Guest rooms feature contemporary vogue. Full resort services, including shops. Tennis courts. This hotel represents a better bargain than the sibling Sol Pelicano.

(i) 296 (including 7 junior suites and 52 with sea views) **P** **(S)**
(S) **(S)** **(S)** MC, V

ISLA DE LA JUVENTUD

🏨 **HOTEL EL COLONY**
$$
CARRETERA SIGUANEA KM 42
TEL 46/39-8181
EMAIL reservas@colony.co.cu
gran-caribe.cu
This former 1950s mobster hotel now caters mainly to scuba divers and package vacationers. Modestly decorated rooms feature TVs. Water sports, scooter rental, and excursions are offered. Its remote location near a prime wildlife reserve is attractive to birders and hikers. It's also a passable option for divers and sportfishermen; otherwise, you'd be best advised to give it a miss.

(i) 80 (including 24 bungalows) **P** **(S)** **(S)** **(S)** MC, V

🏨 **CASA DE LA ALEGRÍA**
$
CALLE 43 #3602, BET. 36 & 38
TEL 46/32-3664
One of the better private room rentals in town. Rooms are modestly furnished; each has its own clean bathroom. The house has a comfortable TV lounge. The congenial hosts will rent out the entire house long term.

(i) 2 **P** **(S)** **(S)** None

SHOPPING IN CUBA

The tourist boom has spawned a great deal of kitsch but also an outpouring of quality crafts, from wooden carvings, papier-mâché figurines, and knitted lace to jewelry, leatherwork, and vibrant paintings of landscapes, sensual *mulattas,* and street scenes that capture the surrealism of Cuban life. Havana has numerous crafts markets and state-run art galleries, the latter reflecting the tremendous vitality and often explicitly erotic experimentalism of Cuban art.

Model classic cars are a favorite subject, crafted from copper wire, papier-mâché, or recycled soda cans. Typically, jewelry sold at crafts markets makes use of recycled silverware. Unfortunately, much jewelry uses endangered black coral—refrain from buying. Bargaining is the norm at markets, but prices are usually already discounted substantially.

Cuban cigars, unavailable in the United States, are of renowned quality and a great bargain. Buy at state-run **Casas del Habano,** and avoid *jineteros*—street hustlers—passing off fake or inferior stogies as the real McCoy. Street scams are common. Buy premium export-grade coffee, sold prepackaged; domestic coffee is inferior. When buying rums, stick with the quality—albeit more expensive—brands, such as Havana Club and Matusalem. Music CDs and cassettes are no bargains, but the choice is wide and includes rare sounds of *danzón,* cha-cha, and *son.*

Most upscale tourist hotels have gift stores selling cigars, coffee, CDs, and arts and crafts. The **Fondo Cubano de Bienes Culturales** (*Calle 17 #157 e/ K y L, Vedado, Havana, tel 7/833-0834, fcbc.cu*) is another good source and has outlets nationwide. The **Feria Internacional de Artesanía,** held at Pabexpo in January and February, is Cuba's annual international handicrafts fair. Cuba suffers from a dearth of shops or markets outside the main tourist centers.

Since 2015, U.S. citizens or other travelers subject to U.S. law, traveling to Cuba with a license,

may bring back up to $400 of Cuban goods, including $100 of cigars and/or rum, except for an unlimited quantity of "educational" items that include but are not limited to art and books.

■ HAVANA

The capital city is blessed with shopping opportunities. Most arts and crafts outlets are in Habana Vieja; Calle Obispo is lined with *expoventas*—private art galleries. The **Almacenes de San José,** Ave. del Puerto, Habana Vieja, is the nation's largest arts and crafts fair. Crocheted clothing can be found in the main plazas; skirts, shawls, blouses, and crocheted bikinis and *tangas* are popular items.

Arts & Antiques

No antiques may be exported from Cuba, including antiquarian books. Quality art requires an export permit. State galleries issue permits with your purchase; otherwise contact the **Registro Nacional de Bienes Culturales** (*Calle 17 #1009, bet. 10 & 12, Vedado, tel 7/831-3362, cnpc. cult.cu*).

Dozens of private art galleries and studios line the streets of Habana Vieja, and several world-renowned artists maintain galleries in their own homes.

Asociación Cubana de Artesana Artistas (*Obispo #411, Habana Vieja, tel 7/860-8577, acaa.cult.cu*) represents various artists.

Galería Haydeé Santamaría (*Calle G, 3ra & 5ta, Vedado, tel 7/55-2706*). This prime gallery sells art of the Americas, featuring premier Cuban artists.

Taller Experimental de Gráfica (*Callejón de Chorro, Plaza de La Catedral, Habana Vieja, tel 7/867-7622*). Lithographic workshop selling original lithos.

Books & Maps

Cuba lacks a bookstore worthy of so literate a nation. The annual **Feria Internacional del Libros** (*tel 7/832-9526, www.filcuba.cult.cu*) is hosted each February in the Fortaleza San Carlos de la Cabaña (see p. 83).

Librería Fernando Ortíz (*Calles L & 27, Vedado, tel 7/832-9653*). Mostly Spanish titles, but some works in English.

Librería La Internacional (*Calle Obispo & Bernaza, Habana Vieja, tel 7/861-3238*). Modest offering of English-language titles spanning literature to natural history.

Mercado de Libros (*Plaza de Armas, Habana Vieja*). Secondhand book market selling politically correct tomes by and of Fidel and Che, plus atlases, 19th-century illustrated books, and novels.

Cigars

Casa del Habano (*Fábrica Partagás, Calle Industria #520, Barcelona & Dragones, Habana Vieja, tel 7/862-8060*). Large walk-in humidor with knowledgeable staff. With a private smoking lounge and bar to the rear.

Casa del Habano (*Hostal Conde de Villanueva, Calle Mercaderes & Lamparilla, tel 7/866-9682*). Huge range of quality cigars and a sumptuous smokers' lounge.

Casa del Habano (*Hotel Nacional, Calles O & 21, Vedado, tel 7/873-3564*). Large humidor with complete range of quality cigars.

Casa del Habano (Ave. 5ta e 16, Miramar, tel 7/204-7975). Huge, well-stocked humidor and professional staff. Bar and smoking lounge.

Casa del Tabaco Parque Central (Hotel NH Parque Central, Calle Neptuno, Prado e Zulueta, Habana Vieja, tel 7/866-6627). Modern smoking lounge with expert staff.

Club Havana (Ave. 5ta, 188 e 190, Miramar, tel 7/204-0366). Complete cigar range. Expert staff.

El Corojo (Hotel Meliá Cohiba, Paseo, 1ra e 3ra, Vedado, tel 7/833-3636). Large stock and personable, professional staff.

Palacio del Tabaco (Fábrica la Corona, Agramonte #106, Colón e Refugio, Habana Vieja, tel 7/833-8389). Large selection includes some rarer smokes.

Clothes e Accessories

Clandestina (Villegas n. 403, bet. Teniente Rey e Muralla, Habana Vieja, tel 7/860-0997, clandestina. co). A Cuban clothing brand, this original artisanal workshop also sells its clothes online.

Jacqueline Fumero Café Boutique (Calle Compostela #1, Habana Vieja, tel 7/862-6562). Avant-garde Cuban-themed fashion-wear for women by one of Cuba's leading designers.

La Maison (Calle 16 e Ave. 7ma, Miramar, tel 7/204-1543). Series of upscale boutiques, plus jewelry and cosmetics stores. Fashion shows are held nightly.

Paul e Shark (Calle Muralla #105, Plaza Vieja, tel 7/866-4326). Italian imported men's and women's designer wear, including fine jackets.

PiscoLabis (Calle San Ignacio #75, Habana Vieja, tel 5843-3219, piscolabishabana.com). Private home decor and clothing gallery with designer guayaberas, blouses, bags, and accessories.

El Quitrín (Calle Obispo #163, bet. San Ignacio e Mercaderes, Habana Vieja, tel 7/862-0810). Handmade guayaberas for men. Also skirts, dresses, and blouses, plus embroideries. Items made to order.

Art, Crafts, e Jewelry

Bazar Estaciones (Calle 23 n. 10, tra J e I, Vedado, tel 7/832-9965). Local crafts souvenirs that are unusual and original.

Casa del Abanico (Calle Obrapía #107, bet. Oficios e Mercaderes, Habana Vieja, tel 7/863-4452). Traditional decorated Spanish fans made and hand-painted on-site.

Galería Victor Manuel (Plaza de La Catedral, Habana Vieja, tel 7/861-2955). Splendid handmade silver jewelry, creative wood carvings, and quality paintings.

Tienda Museo El Reloj (Calle Oficios corner Muralla, Habana Vieja, tel 7/864-9515). Deluxe Swiss-made watches and jewelry specific to this store under the Cuban brand name Cuevos y Sobrinos.

Gifts

Farmácia Taquechel (Calle Obispo #155, Mercaderes e San Ignacio, Habana Vieja, tel 7/862-9286). Natural products, including face creams, fortifiers, oils, potions, and sponges.

Habana 1791 (Calle Mercaderes #156 at Obrapía, Habana Vieja, tel 7/861-3525). Quality Cuban and imported perfumes, soaps, lotions, colognes, and toiletries.

El Soldadito de Plomo (Calle Muralla #164, bet. San Ignacio e Cuba, tel 7/866-0232). Miniature lead soldiers, with figurines from Cuba's wars of independence.

Markets

Almacenes de San José (Ave. del Puerto corner Desamparados, Habana Vieja, tel 7/864-7793). Offers the largest collection of arts and crafts in Cuba. Paintings, wood carvings, cow-horn sculptures, straw hats, musical instruments, dolls, berets, and other Che memorabilia, plus crocheted bikinis, dresses, and sexy wraps.

Miscellaneous

La Carolina Pastelería y Dulcería (Calle 19 n. 1356, tra 24 e 26, Vedado, tel 7/830-6466). Cakes, tarts and pastries: artisanal pastry making at its best with the puff-pastry dessert that gives it its name.

Casa del Chocolate (Calle Mercaderes #255, corner Amargura, tel 7/866-4431). Delicious Cuban chocolates, including figurines, all made on-site.

Centro Cultural Cinematográfico (Calle 23 #1155, bet. Calles 10 e 12, Vedado, tel 7/831-1101). The Cuban Film Institute sells Cuban films on video. Also silk-screen prints.

Jardín Wagner (Mercaderes #113, bet. Obrapía e Obispo, tel 7/866-9017). Fresh-cut flowers, floral displays, and potted plants, including home delivery.

Music

Casa de la Música Egrem (Calle 20 #3308, bet. Calles 33 e 35, Miramar, tel 7/204-0447). A vast collection of CDs and cassettes spanning the Cuban musical spectrum. Also musical instruments.

Industria de Instrumentos Musicales Fernando Ortíz (Calle Pedroso #102 at Calle Nueva, Cerro, tel 7/879-3161, sonoc@cubarte.cult.cu). Workshop making guitars, drums, claves, and other musical instruments.

Longina Música (Calle Obispo #360, Habana Vieja, tel 7/862-8371). Large CD collection, plus bata drums and other instruments.

Rum

Fábrica de Ron Bocoy (Calzada de Cerro, Patria e Auditor, Cerro, tel 7/877-5781). Rare Bocoy and other rums produced here. Sample the goods in the tasting room, upstairs, as some rums are disappointing.

Fundación Havana Club *(Museo del Ron, Ave. San Pedro #262 & Sol, tel 7/861 8051).* Well-stocked rum store selling Havana Club brand, gift sets, T-shirts, and other souvenirs.

Taberna del Galeón *(Calle Baratillo & Obispo, Habana Vieja, tel 7/866-8476).* Colonial mansion housing a rum store that sells a wide range of brands. Be sure to avail of the rum-tasting in the upstairs bar.

The stores in the departure lounge at Havana airport also sell an excellent selection.

▨ FAR WEST

The region is not blessed with shopping opportunities. The town of Pinar del Río is an exception.

Gifts

Fábrica de Bebidas Guayabita *(Calle Isabel Rubio #189, Pinar del Río, tel 82/75-2966).* The region's famed brandylike *guayabita* is made here from rum and wild guava. You can take a group tour and have a sample.

Fábrica de Tabacos Francisco Donatien *(Calle Maceo Oeste #157, Pinar del Río, tel 82/77-3069).* This small cigar factory produces for domestic consumption, but the store sells export-brand cigars, including Vequeros, produced on-site.

▨ WESTERN CUBA— NORTH

Buying opportunities are mainly in Varadero, where most upscale hotels have gift stores. Some boast their own Casa del Habanos, with well-stocked humidors. In Santa Clara, "El Bulevar" *(Calle Independencia, bet. Maceo & Zayas)* is lined with boutiques and stores.

Cigars

Casa del Habano *(Calle 63, Aves. 1ra & 3ra, Varadero, tel 45/66-7843).* A large humidor offers premium cigars. Enjoy your stogie in the smoking lounge, upstairs.

Art, Crafts, & Jewelry

Casa de las Artesanías Latinoamericanas *(Ave. 1ra & Calle 63, Varadero).* Quality Latin American craft products and textiles.

Galería de Arte *(Ave. 1ra & Calle 59, Varadero, tel 45/66-8260).* Quality artwork, including erotic hardwood and marble carvings, as well as paintings and prints by top Cuban artists.

Taller de Cerámica Artística *(Ave. 1ra & Calle 59, Varadero, tel 45/66-7554).* Magnificent kitchen sets and other hand-painted ceramics produced by leading Cuban artists such as Alfredo Sosabravo and Sergio Roque.

Market

Fería de Artesanía *(Ave. 1ra, bet. Calles 44 & 46, Varadero).* A large crafts market with dozens of stalls selling arts and crafts, from kitschy berets with Che's image to cow-horn sculptures, crocheted bikinis, straw hats, and Santería dolls.

Miscellaneous

Ediciones Vigía *(Calle 272, Calles 85 & 91, Matanzas, tel 45/24-4845).* This unique institution produces hand-bound, limited-edition books. You can tour the facility before buying a first edition.

Music

Casa de la Musica *(Ave. de la Playa e Calle 42, Varadero).* A popular place which offers quality performances. Here, you can drink, dance and buy music.

Rum

La Casa del Ron *(Ave. 1ra corner Calle 63, Varadero, tel 45/66-8393).* Vast selection of rums totaling more than 100 labels. Samples are offered.

▨ WESTERN CUBA— SOUTH

Trinidad is a trove of crafts, with Plazuelita Las Tres Palmitas and the streets east and south of Plaza Mayor the major centers. Cienfuegos has several boutiques and stores concentrated along Ave. 54, a pedestrian precinct colloquially called "El Bulevar."

Cigars

Casa del Habano *(Calle Maceo corner Zerquera, tel 41/99-6256).* Large stock of premium Cuban smokes as well as rum.

Art, Crafts, & Jewelry

El Alfarero Casa Chichí *(Calle Andrés Berro Macias #51, Pepito Tey & Abel Santamaría, Trinidad, tel 41/99-3146).* Family-run cooperative producing ceramics.

Casa-Estudio Carlos Mata Pich *(Calle Piro Guinart #367, Trinidad, tel 41/99-4380).* Watch the "artist of the night" paint his magnificent art, then buy from the artist himself.

Estudio-Galería Lázaro Neibla *(Calle Rasio #452, Trinidad, tel 5294-0210, lazaroneibla@yahoor.es).* Astonishing bas-relief wood carvings.

Galería de Arte Benito Ortíz *(Calle Rubén Martínez Villena #357, Plaza Mayor, Trinidad, tel 41/99-4432).* Two-story art gallery displaying contemporary art and classical pieces.

Galería Maroya *(Ave. 54 #2506, Parque Martí, Cienfuegos, tel 43/55-1208).* Diverse array of arts and crafts that includes batiks, carvings, leatherwork, paintings, and artisan Fidel López's incredible handmade model galleons.

Market

Many of the cobbled streets of Trinidad host street markets selling all manner of crafts.

Fería de Artesanía *(Calle Jesús Menéndez & Fernández Hernández, Trinidad).* The largest of several arts and crafts street fairs.

Music

Artex El Topacio *(Ave. 54 #3510, bet. Calles 35 & 37, Cienfuegos, tel 43/55-1126).* A broad selection of music CDs and cassettes, plus musical instruments.

    Casa de la Música *(Calle Juan Manuel Márquez, bet. Simón Bolívar & J. Menéndez, Trinidad, tel 41/99-3414).* One of the country's best-stocked music stores.

■ CENTRAL CUBA

Art, Crafts, & Jewelry

Estudio-Galería Martha Jiménez *(Plaza del Carmen, tel 32/25-7559, martha-jimenez.es).* Wonderful art, much of it erotic, produced and sold on-site by the eponymous artist.

    Fondo Cubano de Bienes Culturales *(Ave. de la Libertad #112, Camagüey, tel 32/228-5382).* A small yet well-stocked shop selling arts, crafts, T-shirts, etc. Look for miniature ceramic *tinajónes*.

Gifts

Fábrica de Instrumentos Musicales *(Calle Camilo Cienfuegos, Minas, tel 32/69-6232, closed Mon.).* This cooperative produces guitars, violas, cellos, and other musical instruments. The items offered for sale to tourists are of inferior quality; make sure you ask to see the real McCoy.

■ WESTERN ORIENTE

Art, Crafts, & Jewelry

Fondo Cubana de Bienes Culturales *(Calle Frexes #196, Parque Calixto García, Holguín, tel 24/42-3783).* Beautiful artwork, including impressive ceramics, hardwood lamp shades, and Daliésque paintings.

    Fondo Cubana de Bienes Culturales *(Calle Francisco Varona #171, Plaza Martí, Las Tunas, tel 32/28-5382).* Offers an impressive selection of straw baskets,

leather saddles, paintings and prints, plus bas-relief ceramics.

■ EASTERN ORIENTE

In Santiago de Cuba, most hotels have souvenir stores selling *muñecitas* (dolls) of the orishas, and music CDs—notably of *son*, cha-cha, and other local sounds.

Art, Crafts, & Jewelry

Comunidad Artística El Oasis *(Carretera de Baconao, Baconao).* This community of artists produces quality work—paintings, ceramics, sculptures—sold in open studios.

    Comunidad Artística Los Mamoncillos *(Playa Verraco, Carretera de Baconao, Baconao).* Another dedicated artists community with individual studios selling experimental paintings, sculptures, and pottery.

    Galería de Arte UNEAC *(Calle Heredia #266, Hartmann & Pío Rosada, Santiago de Cuba, tel 22/65-3465 ext. 106).* A large collection of dynamic art.

    Galería las Musas *(Calle Maceo, bet. Maraví & Frank País, Baracoa).* Studio of artists Roel Caboverde and Orlando Piedra.

    Taller Aguilera *(Calle 6 #211, Rpto. Vista Alegre, Santiago de Cuba, tel 22/64-1817, carlosreneaguilera.jimdo.com).* Art studio and gallery where several Aguilera family members work.

Gifts

Casa de Habano *(Ave. Aguilera & Jesús Menéndez, Santiago de Cuba, tel 22/65-4207).* The well-stocked humidor sells most well-known cigar brands.

    Fábrica de Ron Caney *(Ave. Peralejo #103, Santiago de Cuba, tel 22/62-5575).* Famous rum factory with sampling room sells locally produced rums, including Ron Paticruzados ("cross-legged rum").

    Librería Internacional *(Calle*

Heredia, tra General Lacret e Félix Peña, Santiago de Cuba). Books in Spanish and English, non-fiction and postcards.

Music

Artex *(Calle Heredia #304, bet. Calvario & Carnicería, Santiago de Cuba, tel 22/62-7037).* Cultural center with live music daily. Large selection of cassettes and CDs.

    Discoteca Egrem *(Calle José A Saco n. 309).* The record company, Egrem Studios' retail store.

    Fábrica de Instrumentos Musicales Sindo Garay *(Calle Patricio Lumumba #55, Santiago de Cuba, tel 22/62-5256).* This workshop makes and sells guitars, drums, and a range of other musical instruments.

■ ARCHIPIÉLAGO DE CANARREOS

Art, Crafts, & Jewelry

Centro Experimental de Artes Aplicadas *(Calle 40, Calles 37 & 39, Isla de la Juventud, tel 46/32-4860).* This experimental workshop has a store selling ceramics.

    Fondo Cubano de Bienes Culturales *(Calle 39, Calles 24 & 26, Nueva Gerona, Isla de la Juventud, tel 46/32-4574).* An attractive array of locally made bas-relief ceramics and wooden reliefs.

    Taller de Cerámica Artística *(Calles 26 & 37, Nueva Gerona, Isla de la Juventud, tel 46/32-2634).* Potters produce plates, tea sets, and surrealistic figurines.

Gifts

Caracol, Playa Larga *(Cayo Largo, tel 45/24-8132).* Catering mostly to beachgoing vacationers, this store stocks swimwear, T-shirts, and sandals, but also has crafts and souvenirs. To help preserve the island's wildlife, avoid to buy the inflated toads, stuffed turtles, and black coral items.

ENTERTAINMENT & ACTIVITIES

Havana befits its role as capital city with entertainments from classical concerts to hip discos. Events are listed in *Cartelera* and *Guía Cultural de la Habana*, available at hotels, and *Granma*. The website lahabana.com posts entertainment updates.

Most Cubans are inventive in their entertainment. *Cumbanchas*—street parties—and *pesas* (musical gigs) are popular. Most towns have a communal street party on Saturday nights; you'll need your own cup to buy the cheap rum sold at street stalls. Provincial cities each have their own cultural life, usually centered on the local Casa de la Cultura (House of Culture)—relaxed community venues hosting state-sponsored bolero, Afro-Cuban rumba, and folkloric performances, art classes, and exhibitions. Times and performances vary daily. Local communities are also served by a Casa de la Trova, where traditional *trova* music is regularly performed.

The casinos are long gone, but Vegas-style *cabarets espectáculos*, with befeathered, G-stringed *mulattas* (no longer topless), remain immensely popular with Cubans.

Most regions have their own festivals and musical traditions.

Activities

The nation has not yet made the most of its potential for activities, especially regarding nature, although things are changing.

Water sports are well developed; most upscale resorts offer a selection of watercraft, plus scuba diving and snorkeling. **Marlin S.A.** *(Calle 184 #123, bet. 1ra & 5ta, Rpto. Flores, Havana, tel 7/273-7912, nauticamarlin.com)* organizes most water sports.

In most other areas, Cuba is virtually starting from scratch, including ecotourism, which is the bailiwick of **Ecotur** *(Ave. Independencia #116, corner Santa Catalina,* *Rpto. Cerro, Havana, tel 7/41-0306, ecoturcuba.tur.cu).*

Cubadeportes *(Calle 20 #710, bet. 7ma & 9na, Miramar, Havana, tel 7/204-0348, www.cubadeportes. cu)* handles sports tourism.

Bicycling

Cycling is an increasingly popular way to experience Cuba. If on your own, bring spare parts. Bicycles can be rented from **Cubalinda** *(Calle E #158, Piso 4-A, corner 9na, Havana, tel 7/264-9034, cubalinda.com)*

The following offer organized tours:

Cubania Travel *(Edif. Santiago, Miramar Trade Center, Av. 5ta, bet. 76 & 80, Miramar, Havana, tel 7/207-9888, cubaniatravel.com).*

WowCuba *(430 Queen St., Charlottetown, PEI, C1A 4E8, Canada, tel 902/368-2453, in Cuba, tel 7/796-7655, wowcuba.com)*

Birding

Good books for birding and hiking are *Field Guide to the Birds of Cuba* by Orlando H. Garrido and Arturo Kirkconnell, and *Natural Cuba* by Alfonso Silva Lee.

Quest Nature Tours *(491 King St., Toronto, ON M5A 1L9, Canada, tel 416/633-5666, questnaturetours. com)* organizes birding trips.

Real Cuba *(Box 2345, Swan River, MB R01 1Z0, Canada, realcubaonline.com)* provides tours throughout the island.

Cubanacan *(tel 7/208-9920, cubanacanviajes.com)* runs a ten-day birding trip.

Fishing

The Gulf Stream—Hemingway's "great blue river"—is flush with feisty billfish and tuna. Sportfishing is available in Havana and major resorts. Boat charters cost CUC 140–350 a half day (as many as four people).

Sportfishing excursions are operated by **Marlin S.A.** *(Marina Hemingway, tel 7/273-7912, nauticamarlin.com).* Sportfishing is also offered from eight other marinas.

The lagoons of Zapata and the shallow waters of the Jardines de la Reina and Jardines del Rey offer prime fishing for tarpon, bonefish, and other hard-fighting species. Lake Zaza and Lake Habanilla are among the more popular of several inland lakes containing prize-size bass. The following offer freshwater fishing:

CubaWelcome *(cubawelcome. com),* in the U.K.

Avalon *(cubanfishingcenters. com)* offers fishing in the Jardines de la Reina.

Golfing

Golf courses are found only in Varadero and Havana (see regional entries). More are planned for Cayo Coco and Holguín Province.

Music & Dance

Immerse yourself in Cuba's vibrant music and dance scene and learn hip-swiveling moves. The following offer music and dance tours:

Classic Journeys *(tel 1-800-200-3887, classicjourneys.com).*

PlazaCUBA *(tel 510/872-9505, plazacuba.com).*

Scuba Diving

Coral reefs surround Cuba, enchanting divers. Whale sharks

are often seen in Bahía de Corrientes. Spanish galleons and coral formations highlight diving off Isla de la Juventud, Cayo Largo, and Jardines de la Reina. Visibility is excellent. Temperatures average 81–84°F (27–29°C) year-round. Dive centers are found throughout the island. See regional entries.

■ HAVANA

The Arts

Gran Teatro Alicia Alonso *(Paseo de Martí #458, bet. San Rafael & San Martín, Habana Vieja, tel 7/861-3079).* Classical and ballet performances; $10 best orchestra seats. Dress code (no shorts).

Basilica de San Francisco de Asís *(Plaza San Francisco, Habana Vieja, tel 7/862-9683).* Classical, baroque, and chamber concerts, including on Saturday evenings.

Teatro Karl Marx *(Ave. 1ra & 8, Vedado, tel 7/203-0801).* Big-name bands such as Los Van Van.

Teatro Mella *(Calles 7 & A, Vedado, tel 7/833-5651).* Contemporary dance, avant-garde theater.

Teatro Nacional *(Paseo & 39, Plaza de la Revolución, tel 7/879-5590, email: tnc@cubarte.cult.cu).* Theater, exhibitions, dance and music performances.

Cultural Centers

Asociación Cultural Yoruba de Cuba *(Prado #615, bet. Dragones & Monte, tel 7/863-5953).* Traditional Afro-Cuban music and dance on Sunday evenings.

Casa de la Amistad *(Paseo #406, 17 & 19, Vedado, tel 7/830-3114).* Live performances of *son*, and boleros, Tuesday and Saturday.

Casa de las Américas *(Calle 3ra & Presidentes, Vedado, tel 7/55-2706, casadelasamericas.org).* Movies, lectures, and art exhibits.

La Colmenita *(Teatro de la Orden Tres, Calle Obispo at Churrusco, Habana Vieja, tel 7/860-7699, colmenitadecuba.blogspot.com).* Astounding children's community musical theater group.

Conjunto Folklórico Nacional *(Calle 4 #103, bet. Calzada & 5ta, Vedado, tel 7/830-3060)* hosts an Afro-Cuban rumba on Saturday afternoons.

Hurón Azul *(UNEAC, Calle 17 #351, corner H, Vedado, tel 7/832-4551, uneac.org.cu).* The Writers and Artists Union hosts regular cultural events, from literary gatherings to music and dance.

Festivals

FEBRUARY/MARCH

Festival Internacional de Jazz *(tel 7/862-4938, decubajazz.cult.cu).* Various venues.

APRIL

Habanos Festival *(tel 7/204-0510, habanos.com).* Annual cigar festival draws VIPs.

MAY

International Guitar Festival & Contest *(biennial, tel 7/832-3503)*

May Day Parade *(May 1, Plaza de la Revolución).* Political parade; more than a million Cubans show their solidarity.

Havana Biennale *(various venues, tel 7/861-2096).* International artists exhibit.

JULY/AUGUST

Carnaval de La Habana *(Paseo de Martí & Malecón, tel 7/832-3742).* Processions, floats, music, dance.

OCTOBER

International Ballet Festival *(biennial, Gran Teatro Alicia Alonso and other venues, tel 7/832-4625, balletcuba.cult.cu).* Cuba's National Ballet highlights this festival.

DECEMBER

New International Latin-American Film Festival *(Hotel Nacional & other venues, tel 7/838-2354, habanafilmfestival.com)*

Procession of the Miracles *(December 17, Santuario de San Lázaro, Rincón).* Annual religious procession to request or give thanks for miracles.

Music & Dance

Café Taberna *(Calle Mercaderes #531, corner Brasil, Habana Vieja, tel 7/861-1637).* Nightly performance by old crooners à la *Buena Vista Social Club.*

Casa de la Trova *(Calle San Lázaro #661, Centro Habana, tel 7/879-3373).* Traditional music and poetry. Thursday–Sunday 7–10 p.m.

Caserón del Tango *(Calle Justíz #21, Habana Vieja, tel 7/861-0822).* Informal tango *peñas*, Wednesday and Friday; shows on Saturday evenings.

Rumba del Cayo *(Callejon de Hamel & Hospital, Centro Habana, tel 7/878-1661).* Afro-Cuban rumba and celebration of Santería. Sunday noon, every third Saturday for kids.

Nightlife

Most nightclubs draw expatriates and tourists. *Jineteras* often try to hang on patrons' coattails to gain entry. Drinks in touristy discos are often exorbitant; follow the Cuban example and buy a bottle of rum to share around. Many bars and upscale restaurants feature live musicians.

La Bodeguita del Medio *(Calle Empedrado #207, Habana Vieja, tel 7/867-1374).* Rustic bar with Hemingway associations.

Cabaret Copa Room *(Hotel Riviera, Paseo & Malecón, tel 7/834-4228).* Cabaret followed by dancing, Monday–Saturday.

Cabaret Parisién *(Hotel*

Nacional, Calles O & 21, tel 7/873-3564). Spectacular cabaret second only to the Tropicana, .

Cabaret Tropicana *(Calle 72 #4504, Marianao, tel 7/267-1717, cabaret-tropicana.com).* Full-on cabaret extravaganza, nightly under the stars. Pricey, but a "must visit."

Café Concert Gato Tuerto *(Calle O, 17 & 19, Vedado, tel 7/838-2696).* Bolero, rap, and "feeling music" draw Cubans and foreigners alike to this tight-packed, smoke-filled club.

Jazz Café *(Galerías de Paseo, Paseo & 1ra, Vedado, tel 7/838-3302).* Top jazz bands, nightly.

Salón Rojo *(La Giraldilla, Calle 21, bet. N & O, Vedado, tel 7/833-3747).* Havana's hottest salsa nightclub with big-name bands.

Salón Turquino *(Hotel Habana Libre, Calle L, Vedado, tel 7/834-6100).* Varying entertainment plus dancing; cabarets.

Sangri La *(Calle 42 corner 21, Playa, tel 5264-8343).* Dance-until-dawn private nightclub. As close to Miami's South Beach as it gets in Havana.

Sarao's Bar *(Calle 17 corner E, Vedado, tel 5263-8037).* Chic private nightclub with dancing.

La Zorra y el Cuervo *(Calle 23 at O, Vedado, tel 7/833-2402).* Jazz greats such as Chucho Valdéz play this subterranean club.

Special Events

Ceremonia del Cañonazo, Fortaleza de San Carlos de la Cabaña *(tel 7/862-0671 or 862-4095).* Lighting of the cannon by soldiers in period uniform, nightly at 8:30 p.m.

Noche en la Plaza de La Catedral *(Plaza de La Catedral, Habana Vieja).* Cocktails, dinner, and folkloric *espectáculo* in the cathedral square, third Saturday monthly. Also at **Plaza de San Francisco.** Reservations c/o Habaguanex *(tel 7/867-1039).*

Other Activities

Baseball
Estadio Lationamericano *(Calle Zequeira #312, Cerro, tel 7/870-6526).* Cuba's main stadium.

Boxing
Gimnasio de Boxeo Rafael Trejo *(Calle Cuba #815, Habana Vieja, tel 7/862-0266)*

Sala Polivalente Kid Chocolate *(Prado at Teniente Rey, Habana Vieja, tel 7/862-8634)*

Dance Lessons
Cátedra de Danza *(Calle 5ta #253, D & E, Vedado, tel 7/832-4625, balletcuba.cult.cu).* Ballet and modern dance.

Club Salseando Chévere *(Calle 49 & Av. 28, Kohly, tel 7/204-4990, club-salseando-chevere. com).* Salsa tuition by a professional dance company.

Folkcuba *(Calle 4 #103, Calzada/5ta, Vedado, tel/fax 7/830-3939, folkcuba.cult.cu).* Cuban dance.

Golf
Club de Golf Habana *(Calzada de Vento Km 8, Capdevila, tel 7/649-8918).* 18-hole course.

Horseback Riding
Centro Ecuestre *(Parque Lenin, tel 7/647-2436).* CUC 15 per hour for lessons, CUC 10 for riding.

Scuba Diving
Centro de Buceo La Aguja *(Marina Hemingway, Ave. 5ta & Calle 248, Santa Fe, tel 7/204-5088)*

Sportfishing
Marlin S.A. *(Marina Hemingway, Ave. 5ta & Calle 248, Miramar, tel 7/204-1150 ext 735)*

■ FAR WEST
The Arts
Teatro José Jacinto Milanés, Pinar del Río *(tel 48/75-3871).* One of Cuba's oldest venues, the wooden, 540-seat Teatro José Jacinto Milanés dates from the mid-1800s. Hosts theater, dance,

and both national and international music concerts.

Cultural Center
Casa de Cultura, Pinar del Río *(Máximo Gómez #108, tel 48/75-2324).* Known for *punta campesina* folkloric dances.

Festival
Humor Bienal Internacional, San Antonio de los Baños *(tel 47/38-2817).* Biennial comedy festival, March—April.

Nightlife
Cabaret Rumayor, Pinar del Río *(tel 48/76-3007).* Small *espectáculo* Tuesday—Sunday evenings.

Other Activities
Baseball
Estadio Capitán San Luís, Pinar del Río *(tel 48/75-3895)*

Birding
Centro Ecológico Las Terrazas *(tel 48/57-8700, lasterrazas.cu)*
Villas Turística Soroa *(tel 48/52-3534)*

Guided Hikes
Centro Ecológico Península de Guanahacabibes *(tel 48/75-0366)*
Centro de Visitantes, Viñales *(tel 48/79-6144)*
Villas Turística Soroa *(tel 48/52-3534)*

Scuba Diving
Cayo Levisa *(tel 48/75-6501)*
María la Gorda International Dive Center *(tel 48/77-8131)*

Train Rides
Hershey Train *(tel 7/862-4888).* Casablanca to Matanzas, daily.

■ WESTERN CUBA– NORTH
The Arts
Teatro Sauto, Matanzas *(tel 45/24-2721).* Classical concerts, Friday—Sunday.

Cultural Centers

Casa de la Cultura, Matanzas *(tel 45/29-2709)*

Casa de la Cultura, Remedios *(tel 42/39-5581)*

Casa de la Cultura, Santa Clara *(tel 422/20-7181)*

Casa de Danzón *(tel 45/28-7061)*. *Danzón* performances.

Festivals

Brutal Fest, Santa Clara *(August)*. The best of Cuban rock and heavy metal bands.

Festival of the Cuban Danzón, Matanzas *(November, biennial, tel 45/24-3512)*. Workshops and competitions of *danzón* and other folk dances.

Parranda Remedianas, Remedios and neighboring villages *(December)*. Ferocious fireworks battles and floats.

Nightlife

Bar Club Bulevár, Santa Clara *(tel 42/21-6236)*. Cabaret acts, live music, and disco.

Cabaret Continental *(Hotel Varadero Internacional, Varadero, tel 45/66-7038)*. Cabaret, Tuesday–Sunday evenings.

Cabaret Los Laureles, Sancti Spíritus *(tel 41/32-7016)*. Cabaret and disco, Friday–Saturday.

Club Nocturno Havana Club, Varadero *(tel 45/66-7500)*. Disco.

La Comparsita, Varadero *(tel 45/66-7415)*. Live music, cabaret, followed by disco. Open air.

Cueva del Pirata, Varadero *(tel 45/66-7751)*. *Cabaret espectáculo* in a cave. Closed Sunday and Tuesday.

Mambo Club *(Gran Hotel, Km 14 Carretera Las Morlas, Varadero, tel 45/66-8565)*. Live music.

Palacio de la Rumba *(Km 4.5 Ave. de las Américas, Varadero, tel 45/66-8210)*. Video discoteque and Latin music.

Tropicana Matanzas, Matanzas *(tel 45/26-5555, email: reservas@trpivar.co.cu)*. Sensual,

outdoor *cabaret espectáculo*. Closed Monday.

Special Events

Festival de Verano, Varadero *(June, July, August)*. International music, performances and beach parties.

Encuentro Harlistas Cubanos, Varadero *(December, tel 7/866-2559, harlistascubanosrally.com)*. Annual rally of Cuba's Harley-Davidson owners.

Other Activities

Fishing

Cayo Santa María (see p. 130)

Golf

Varadero Golf Club, Varadero *(tel 45/66-7788, varaderogolfclub.com)*. Cuba's only 18-hole championship course.

Guided Hikes

Reserva Ecológico Varahicacos, Varadero (see p. 123)

Scuba Diving

Barracuda Marlin, Varadero *(Calle 3a, Rpto. Kawama, tel 45/61-3481, comercial@marlin.mtz.tur.cu)*

Club Octopus International Dive Center, Playa Larga *(tel 45/91-7294)*

Diving Center Acua, Varadero *(tel 45/66-8063)*

Gaviota Diving Center *(Marina Gaviota, Autopista Sur Km 21, tel 45/66-7755)*

Skydiving

Skydive Varadero, Varadero *(tel 45/61-1220, skydivingvaradero.com)*

Sportfishing

Marina Chapelín, Varadero *(tel 45/66-8727)*

■ WESTERN CUBA– SOUTH

The Arts

Cantores de Cienfuegos, Cienfuegos *(tel 5343-6214, cantoresdecienfuegos@yahoo.es)*. Superb a capella group plays at various venues.

Teatro Tomás Terry, Cienfuegos

(tel 43/51-3361). Dating from 1889, the 950-seat auditorium features Carrara marble, hand-carved Cuban hardwoods, and whimsical ceiling frescoes.

Cultural Centers

Casa de la Cultura, Cienfuegos *(tel 43/51-6584)*

Casa de la Cultura, Sancti Spíritus *(tel 41/32-3772)*

Casa de la Cultura, Trinidad *(tel 41/99-4308)*

Festivals

El Recorrido de la Vía Cruz, Trinidad *(April)*. Easter procession.

International Popular Music Festival Benny Moré, Cienfuegos *(September, biennnial)*. Celebrating singer and songwriter Moré.

Music & Dance

Casa de la Trova, Sancti Spíritus *(tel 41/32-8048)*. Traditional music, Thursday–Sunday.

Casa de la Trova, Trinidad *(tel 41/99-6445)*. Traditional music.

Nightlife

Centro Cultural El Cubanismo, Cienfuegos *(Calle 25, bet. 16 & 18, tel 43/55-1255)*. Themed shows followed by dancing.

Centro Nocturno Tropisur, Cienfuegos *(Calle 37 at 48)*. Cabaret.

Club Beny Moré, Cienfuegos *(tel 43/55-1105)*. Cabaret theater.

Other Activities

Birding

Parque Nacional Ciénaga de Zapata, Playa Larga *(tel 45/98-7249)*. Fantastic birding.

Fishing

Fishing is spectacular in the Laguna de las Salinas, Ciénaga de Zapata. Freshwater fishing in Embalse Habanilla and Presa Zaza (see p. 152).

Guided Hikes

The Sierra del Escambray offer mountain forests and rich bird-life (see p. 140).

Complejo Turístico Topes de Collantes, Sierra Escambray (tel 42/54-0330, gaviota-grupo.com)

Scuba Diving

Club Amigo Ancón, Playa Ancón (tel 41/99-6120)

Club Amigo, Rancho Luna (tel 43/54-8087)

Marina Marlin, Cienfuegos (tel 43/55-1699)

Marina Trinidad (tel 41/99-6205, nauticamarlin.com)

■ CENTRAL CUBA

The Arts

Teatro Principal, Camagüey (tel 32/29-3048). Performances by world-class Camagüey Ballet.

Cultural Centers

Casa de la Cultura, Camagüey (tel 32/29-3366)

Casa de la Cultura, Ciego de Ávila (tel 32/22-9374)

Casa de la Cultura, Morón (Calle Martí #224, tel 33/50-4309)

Festival

Theater Festival of Camagüey (September, every other year; tel 32/29-3048)

Music & Dance

Casa de la Trova, Camagüey (tel 32/29-1357). Traditional music.

Casa de la Trova, Ciego de Ávila (Calle Ibertad #130). Traditional music.

Casa de la Trova, Morón (tel 33/50-4158). Traditional music. Closed Tuesday.

Nightlife

Tourist hotels on Cayos Coco and Guillermo have bars and offer in-house entertainment.

Centro Nocturno El Colonial,
Camagüey (tel 32/78-5239). Small cabaret and popular disco, Friday–Sunday.

Gran Hotel, Camagüey (tel 32/29-8935). Lively piano bar.

Other Activities

Birding

Flamingos parade through the lagoons of Cayos Coco, Guillermo, and Sabinal.

Fishing

Centro Turístico la Redonda, Morón (tel 33/30-2489). Fantastic bass fishing.

Horseback Riding

King Ranch, Playa Santa Lucía (tel 5219-4139), c/o hotels in Playa Santa Lucía.

Sitio la Güira, Cayo Coco (tel 33/30-1208)

Scuba Diving

Coral reefs at Jardines del Rey and Jardines de la Reina. Most hotels on Cayos Coco and Guillermo offer scuba diving.

Avalon Dive Center, Parque Nacional Jardines de la Reina (cubandivingcenters.com)

Blue Diving, Cayo Coco (tel 33/30-8179)

Sportfishing

Avalon Dive Center, Parque Nacional Jardines de la Reina (cubanfishingcenters.com)

Marina Marlin Aguas Tranquilas, Cayo Coco (tel 33/40-1328)

Marina Marlin Cayo Guillermo, Cayo Guillermo (tel 33/30-1718)

■ WESTERN ORIENTE

The Arts

Teatro Comandante Eddy Suñol, Holguín (tel 24/46-3161)

Cultural Centers

Casa de la Cultura, Bayamo (tel 23/42-5917)

Casa de la Cultura, Holguín (tel 24/42-7492)

Festivals

El Cucalambé Festival, Las Tunas, (June, biennial; tel 31/34-7770). Renditions of decimas, musical compositions in ten verses.

Festival Cubain Bayamo Bayamo (July). Celebrates the roots of the national identity.

Festival of Iberian-American Culture, Holguín (October; tel 24/42-4964). Honors the Spanish heritage in Cuban culture.

Nightlife

Tourist hotels in Guardalavaca, Playas Esmeralda and Pesquero have bars and entertainment.

Cabaret Bayamo, Bayamo (tel 23/48-1698), Saturday–Sunday evenings.

Cabaret Nocturno, Holguín (tel 24/42-5185). Cabaret espectáculo.

Cabaret Salón Benny Moré, Holguín (Maceo corner Luz Cablilero). Open-air live music and events.

Cabaret Taíno, Las Tunas (tel 31/34-3823). Cabaret espectáculo, Friday–Sunday evenings.

Casa de la Trova, Bayamo (tel 23/42-5673)

Casa de la Trova, Manzanillo (tel 23/57-5423)

Casa de la Trova "El Guayabero," Holguín (tel 24/45-1304)

La Caverna The Beatles, Calle Maceo, Holguín (tel 24/45-3440). Beatles-themed bar.

Centro Nocturno Costa Azul, Manzanillo (tel 23/57-3158). Cabaret and disco.

Cine Disco Luanda, Las Tunas (tel 31/34-8671). Disco and nightclub.

Jazz Club, Holguín (tel 24/47-4312).

Piano Bar, Holguín (tel 24/42-4322). Pianist and elegant bar.

Other Activities

Baseball

Estadio Calixto García, Holguín (tel 24/46-2606)

Guided Hikes
Parque Nacional Desembarco del Granma (see p. 194)
Parque Nacional La Mensura (see p. 186)
Parque Nacional Pico Turquino (see p. 191)
Reserva Ecológica Las Guanas, Playa Esmeralda (see pp. 182–183)

Scuba Diving
Hotels at Playa Esmeralda have on-site dive facilities.
Eagle Ray Dive Center, Guardalavaca *(tel 24/43-0316)*
Nautica Base Marlin, Guardalavaca *(tel 24/43-0774)*

■ EASTERN ORIENTE

The Arts
Teatro Heredia, Santiago *(tel 22/64-3190)*. Classical and other musical concerts.

Cultural Centers
Casa de la Cultura, Baracoa *(tel 21/64-2364)*
Casa de la Cultura, Guantánamo *(tel 21/32-6391)*
Casa de la Cultura, Santiago *(tel 22/62-5710)*

Festivals
Festival Boleros de Oro, Santiago de Cuba *(July)*
Festival of the Caribbean, Santiago de Cuba *(July; tel 22/62-3569)*. Carnival celebrating Caribbean folk cultures.
International Chorus Festival, Santiago de Cuba *(November–December)*. Weeklong biennial with Cuban and foreign choral singers.
Festival Nacional de Changüí, Guantánamo *(December; tel 21/32-2296)*. Folkloristic dances and changüí music concerts, typical of this area.

Music & Dance
Watch for traditional performances by Ballet Folklórica

Cutumba (see sidebar p. 203); and Conjunto Folklórico de Oriente.
Alianza Francesca, Santiago *(tel 22/64-1503)*. *Tumba francesa.*
Bello Bar, Santiago de Cuba *(tel 22/68-7070)*. Upscale bar with live music and dancing atop the Meliá Santiago Hotel.
Casa de la Música, Guantánamo *(tel 21/32-7266)*. The place for salsa, plus jazz.
Casa de la Trova, Baracoa *(Maceo #149, Plaza Independencia)*
Casa de la Trova, Santiago (see p. 205)
Casa de los Tradiciones, Santiago *(Calle Rabí #154, bet. Princesa & San Fernando, tel 22-65-3892)*. Afro-Cuban rumba.
Club Nevada, Guantánamo *(tel 21/35-5447)*. Lively rooftop bar with music videos.
Museo del Carnaval (see p. 205). Afro-Cuban rumba, Sunday evenings.
Patio de Artex, Santiago de Cuba *(tel 22/65-4814)*. Traditional music and salsa.

Nightlife
Cabaret San Pedro del Mar, Santiago *(tel 22/69-4037)*. Small *cabaret espectáculo,* Friday–Sunday evenings. Draws mainly a gay clientele.
La Maison, Santiago *(tel 22/64-0108)*. Fashion show, disco, nightly.
Pico Real Bar *(Hotel Meliá Santiago, Santiago, tel 22/68-7070)*. *Cabaret espectáculo,* disco.
Tropicana Santiago, Santiago de Cuba *(tel 22/68-7020)*. Sensational *cabaret espectáculo,* Monday to Saturday high season; Saturday only low season.

Other Activities
Baseball
Estadio Guillermón Moncada, Santiago de Cuba *(Ave. de las Américas, tel 22/64-2655)*. Baseball championship games:

Tuesday through Thursday, Saturday evening and Sunday morning from October to April.

Birding
Cuchillas del Toa Biosphere Reserve (see p. 221)
Real Cuba, Santiago de Cuba *(realcubaonline.com)*

Guided Hikes
Ecotur, Baracoa *(tel 21/64-3665)*
Gaviotatours, Baracoa *(tel 21/64-4115)*

■ ARCHIPIÉLAGO DE LOS CANARREOS

Cultural Center
Casa de la Cultura, Nueva Gerona *(tel 46/32-3591)*

Festival
Grapefruit Festival, Nueva Gerona *(March)*. Carnival celebrating the *toronja* harvest.

Nightlife
Cabaret e La Cubana, Nueva Gerona *(tel 46/32-3740)*. Small *cabaret espectáculo* followed by dancing. Friday–Sunday evenings.

Other Activities
Baseball
Estadio Cristóbal Labra, Nueva Gerona *(tel 46/32-1044)*
Birding
Ecotur, Nueva Gerona *(tel/fax 46/32-7101)*
Scuba Diving
"Colony" International Scuba Diving Center, Siguanea *(tel 46/39-8181)*
Marina Cayo Largo del Sur, Cayo Largo *(tel 45/24-8214, email: buceo.marina@repgc.cls.tur.cu)*
Sportfishing
Avalon Fishing Club, Cayo Largo *(tel 5282-7715, cubanfishingcenters.com)*

INDEX

ILLUSTRATIONS CREDITS

Primary photography:

Pablo Corral Vega

4, 13, 14-15, 24, 28-29, 48-49, 56-57, 58-59, 61, 66, 69, 70, 72, 74, 77, 84, 94, 95, 99, 143, 144, 148, 152, 153, 157, 158, 169, 172, 195, 197, 209, 217, 231.

Cristobal Corral Vega

16, 18-19, 42, 44, 82, 93, 101, 102, 106-107, 108, 110, 111, 112, 114, 116, 117, 120, 123, 127, 128, 130, 131, 134, 136, 138, 142, 166, 168, 171, 179, 180, 182, 184, 189, 190, 192, 194, 196, 202, 207, 214, 220, 221, 223, 226, 227, 229.

Additional images:

Christopher P. Baker: 2-3, 73, 90, 100, 105, 176, 211, 212; Walter Callens: 8; National Geographic Creative: 12 (Kike Calvo), 40-1 (Alex Saberi), 97 (Ira Block); Getty Images: 21 (Yamil Lage/AFP), 35 (Sven Creutzmann/Mambo photo), 37 (Keystone/Hulton Archive), 39 (Chip Somodevilla), 146 (Education Images), 186 (Philip Friskorn/Foto Natura/Minden Pictures); Alamy: 27 (North Wind Picture Archives), 47 (Lee Dalton), 80 (José Fuste Raga), 124 (George Brice), 150 (Riccardo Lombardo/CuboImagessrl), 210 (George Brice); Chicago Historical Society: 32-33; age fotostock: 50 (Martin Moxter/imageBROKER), 55 (Angelo Cavalli), 204 (Jorge Fernández), 206 (Patrick Frilet/Marka); Redux Pictures: 53 (Bernd Jonkmanns/laif), 86 (Lucas Vallecillos/VWPics), 200 (Christian Franz Tragni); eStock Photography: 54 (Huber/Sime); Shutterstock: 63 (Kamira), 121 (Tupungato); Corbis: 75 (Jeremy Horner); Dreamstime.com: 89 (Icara), 141 (Roxana González); Kike Calvo: 104; David Alan Harvey: 154, 219; AP Photo: 174 (Andres Leighton); National Geographic My Shot: 225 (Carlos Suarez); David Doubilet: 230; Chiara Schiavano: 11; Irena Sommerová/123RF: 39; Felix Lipov/123RF: 162, 164, Pablo Hidalgo/123RF; Elisa Bonomini/123RF, 219

Cutaway illustrations on on pp. 78–79 and 160–161 by Maltings Partnership, Derby, England.